GERMAN

FOR ADVANCED STUDENTS

E. P. DICKINS

DEPARTMENT OF GERMAN
UNIVERSITY OF KEELE

OXFORD UNIVERSITY PRESS

Oxford University Press, Walton Street, Oxford OX2 6DP

OXFORD LONDON GLASGOW
NEW YORK TORONTO MELBOURNE WELLINGTON
KUALA LUMPUR SINGAPORE JAKARTA HONG KONG TOKYO
DELHI BOMBAY CALCUTTA MADRAS KARACHI
IBADAN NAIROBI DAR ES SALAAM CAPE TOWN

© *Oxford University Press 1963*

First published 1963
Reprinted 1964, 1965, 1967 (with corrections)
Second edition 1973
Reprinted 1975, 1977, 1978, (with appendix on
Strong and Anomalous Verbs)

Printed in Great Britain
at the University Press, Oxford
by Vivian Ridler
Printer to the University

PREFACE

THIS book offers graded material for a three-year course in advanced German. It is directed primarily to the needs of those preparing for Advanced Level and university entrance and scholarship examinations, but the scope and arrangement of the material are such that the book may also be used for German language courses at universities and evening institutes.

It is a common complaint that advanced students are often not sufficiently well acquainted with the basic syntax of German and that they lack feeling for the morphology of the language. Another criticism is that knowledge of common vocabulary is often sketchy. I have attempted in this book to provide a scheme of study, including a wide range of vocabulary, which shall lead from revision of perennial O Level difficulties through more advanced problems of syntax and word-formation towards questions of style.

The first year work (PART I) is arranged in 20 'Topics' designed to enable the student to build up his knowledge of grammar and vocabulary and to increase his feeling for the language in a methodical way. Two 'Revision Topics' are included, in which no grammar is presented but which in other respects follow the usual pattern of the Topics. Each Topic is self-contained in that it deals with an important aspect of grammar and emphasizes a particular *Wortfeld*. The two themes are stressed throughout the Topic—in the German–English translation passages, the prose composition passages and sentences (which both introduce a number of the words, phrases, and usages already met in the 'translation' material of the Topic), the essay and discussion subjects, and in the suggestions for further vocabulary and grammar work. References to the separate Grammar Section (see below) have been kept to a minimum in Part I.

I have assumed that most teachers devote a good deal of time in the first year of Sixth-Form work to the detailed study of the vocabulary and grammar met in language exercises, and have accordingly arranged Part I to meet this need. PART II is intended primarily to help the student to reach A Level standard in language work through practice in translations and proses of A Level type. In order to encourage the student to continue building up his knowledge of vocabulary and usage in a co-ordinated way, groups of ten sentences for translation into

German, based on the last two German–English translation passages in each case, occur throughout the (prose) translation section; and the first ten translation passages are related in theme to the first ten of the prose composition passages. Thereafter the passages of German and English are not deliberately chosen for similarity of content but rather for their intrinsic merit, whether in a literary sense or for the vocabulary they offer and the grammar points in which they afford practice. A number of poems are included for translation into English and prose composition passages set in A Level examinations in recent years by the Oxford and Cambridge Schools Examination Board and by London University are given—without footnotes, for practice purposes—at regular intervals. A selection of essay subjects of A Level type is also given at the end of Part II. Footnote references are made to the Grammar of the Topics in Part I and to the articles of the Grammar Section.

The *Grammar Section* seeks to provide: (*a*) a reference and revision grammar for problems which commonly arise in the Sixth-Form study of German and which have not been covered (or have only been partially covered) in the grammar of Topics in Part I; and (*b*) a reference grammar for difficulties arising in the translation and prose composition material of Parts II and III. Examples are drawn to a certain extent from Parts I and II (occasionally from Part III) and their source indicated by a page reference in square brackets. Much of the material is based on or drawn from *Duden — Grammatik* (1959 edition).

PART III ('scholarship' work) consists of passages for translation into English and German, followed by a graded selection of prose passages and poems for literary appreciation and commentary, of the type set by the various examination boards in S Level examinations. I have made no deliberate attempt to relate translation to prose passages, but it will be found that a number of the pieces may usefully be compared and *Wortfelder* built around them. Reference is again made to the Grammar Section and occasionally to the Topic grammar given in Part I. The last fifteen prose composition passages are given without footnotes in order that they may be used for examination practice.

Extracts for translation into English are taken throughout almost exclusively from modern German authors. No word-list is provided, but guidance is given in the footnotes to exercises on vocabulary and on difficulties of idiom and grammar. The use of a dictionary is one of the skills which a modern linguist must acquire, and thoughtless reference to a ready-made word-list is perhaps likely to do the student far less good in the long run than the searching out of words and phrases in a dictionary, even though this may sometimes lead to bad errors. Moreover, it is precisely self-reliance in observing words and usages and in building vocabulary patterns which I hope this book may stimulate.

I have to thank most particularly Studienrat Dr. Günther Bohling, of the Collegium Josephinum, Bonn, for the detailed checking of the grammatical material and footnotes, and for constant encouragement and guidance; Trevor Jones, Esq., M.A., of Jesus College, Cambridge, for many helpful suggestions in Part I; Philip Davies, Esq., M.A., of the Lower School of John Lyon, Harrow, for scrutinizing the manuscript; Herr G.-D. Politz for guidance on a number of points of idiom; and M. P. Savage, Esq., for assistance with the Grammar Index.

E. P. D.

August 1962

PREFACE TO THE SECOND EDITION

THIS new edition provides substantial emendations to the earlier version, including:

(1) further clarification of idioms and grammatical points;
(2) modifications to some translation and composition passages, or substitution of entirely new passages where needed, and changes in the accompanying footnotes;
(3) variation of titles set for essay work.

Much of this revision was needed in order to reflect changes in the contemporary scene. The passage on *The Times* needed to be revised to correspond with the paper's new format, for instance; some reference to moonshots seemed desirable; the names of certain statesmen and institutions required replacing by other, more contemporary, references; and the details about German radio stations had to be brought up to date.

The translation of poems is not usually an examination exercise nowadays. Nevertheless, it seemed to me right to keep the poems in Part I and II, in addition to those in Part III. They offer some insight into the rich poetic tradition of Germany; they should help to stimulate interest in the character and possibilities of the language, and they can profitably be used in class for discussion, verse-speaking, style analysis, and for translation—which is surely one approach to foreign poetry that every linguist needs to make from time to time.

The intentions of the book are described in the original preface. It may be as well to draw attention to the fact that the material, especially in Part I, is designed to be worked through methodically; for the graded presentation of material helps one to focus attention on aspects of the language which must be mastered if one is to make worthwhile progress as an advanced student. The revised edition is appearing at a time when the future of advanced studies in German appears to be uncertain. I hope that the book will be of service to teachers and students who believe that in spite of changing emphases, and in common with all other disciplines, the study of German calls for patient and detailed observation, creative interest, and enthusiastic commitment.

E. P. D.

Keele
January 1973

ACKNOWLEDGEMENTS

THE author and publishers acknowledge with thanks permission received from the following firms and individuals to reproduce extracts from copyright works.

George Allen & Unwin Ltd.: Thor Heyerdahl, *The Kon-Tiki Expedition*, and Bertrand Russell, *Portraits from Memory*.

Verlag der Arche, Zürich: Werner Bergengruen, 'Totenspruch auf einen Vogel' from *Figur und Schatten*, and *Sternenstand*; Gertrud von le Fort, *Das Kleine Weihnachtsbuch*.

Edward Arnold Ltd.: E. M. Forster, *Abinger Harvest*.

Herr Professor Helmut Arntz and the Presse-und Informationsamt der Bundesregierung, Bonn: *Germany in a Nutshell*.

Atlantis, Zürich: Bettina Hürlimann, 'Kreuz und quer durch den Peloponnes', and K. G. Kachler, 'Heutige und antike Theaterprobleme'.

Aufbau-Verlag, Berlin: Heinrich Mann, *Der Untertan*.

August Bagel Verlag, Düsseldorf: Benno von Wiese, *Die deutsche Novelle*.

Johann Ambrosius Barth Verlag, München, and Dr. N. Planck: Max Planck, *Vorträge und Erinnerungen*.

B. T. Batsford Ltd.: Monk Gibbon, *Western Germany*.

Verlangsanstalt Benziger & Co. AG., Zürich: Friedrich Dürrenmatt, *Der Richter und sein Henker*.

Bibliographisches Institut AG., Mannheim: Ludwig Reiners, *Duden—Stilwörterbuch*.

Blandford Press Ltd.: C. H. Falcon, 'How Girls Camp in the U.S.A.' from *The Second Rucksack Book*.

The Bodley Head Ltd.: Henry Williamson, *Tarka the Otter*.

Herr Heinrich Böll: *Die blasse Anna*.

Herr Heinrich Böll and Friedrich Middelhauve Verlag, Opladen: *Wanderer, kommst du nach Spa. . . .* Copyright 1950 by Friedrich Middelhauve Verlag.

F. A. Brockhaus, Wiesbaden: Henry Hoek, *Wetter, Wolken, Wind*.

Curtis Brown Ltd.: Eric Linklater, *Poet's Pub*.

Cambridge University Press: Alfred North Whitehead, *Science and the Modern World*.

Jonathan Cape Ltd.: Ernest Hemingway, *A Farewell to Arms* (and Charles Scribner's Sons); William Plomer, *Four Countries*; Sherwood Anderson, *Winesburg, Ohio* (and the Viking Press, Inc. © 1919 by B. W. Huebsch, Inc., renewed 1947 by E. C. Anderson).

Cassell & Co. Ltd.: J. S. Davies, *From Charlemagne to Hitler*.

The Caxton Press, Christchurch, N.Z.: A. P. Gaskell, *The Big Game*.

Chatto & Windus Ltd. and Mrs. Laura Huxley: Aldous Huxley, *Those Barren Leaves* and *Grey Eminence*.

Werner Classen Verlag, Zürich: Hermann Hesse, *Eine Bibliothek der Weltliteratur* and *Dank an Goethe*.

Miss D. E. Collins and A. P. Watt & Son: G. K. Chesterton, *The Club of Queer Trades*.

Peter Cotes and R. Niklaus: Peter Cotes and Thelma Niklaus, *The Little Fellow*.

viii   ACKNOWLEDGEMENTS

J. G. Cotta'sche Buchhandlung Nachf. GmbH, Stuttgart: Wilhelm Schäfer, *Anekdoten*.
Allert de Lange, Amsterdam: Joseph Roth, *Panoptikum*.
Verlag Kurt Desch, München: Ernst Wiechert, *Das einfache Leben*.
Deutsche Verlags-Anstalt GmbH, Stuttgart: Ina Seidel, *Lennacker*.
Deutsche Verlags-Anstalt and Herr Heini Waser: Maria Waser, *Der heilige Weg*.
Eugen Diederichs Verlag, Düsseldorf: Ricarda Huch, *Aus der Triumphgasse*, and Agnes Miegel, 'Ich' from *Gesammelte Gedichte*.
The English Universities Press Ltd.: Margaret Mann-Phillips, *Erasmus and the Northern Renaissance*.
S. Fischer Verlag, Frankfurt: Franz Kafka, *Das Schloß* and *Der Prozeß*; Max Brod, *Franz Kafka: Eine Biographie*; Thomas Mann, *Der kleine Herr Friedemann*, *Tonio Kröger*, *Enttäuschung*, *Herr und Hund*, *Der Zauberberg*, *John Galsworthy zum sechzigsten Geburtstag*; Carl Zuckmayer, *Der Seelenbräu* and *Elegie von Abschied und Wiederkehr*; Franz Werfel, *Der veruntreute Himmel* and *Auf den alten Stationen*; Albrecht Goes, *Gedichte*; Stefan Zweig, *Sternstunden der Menschheit*, *Die Welt von Gestern* and *Phantastische Nacht*; Helmut Gollwitzer, 'Begegnung mit Luther' from *Luther*, ed. K. G. Steck.
Francke Verlag, Bern: Hans Eichner, *Thomas Mann*; Emil Franzel, *Von Bismarck zu Adenauer*; Fritz Strich, *Deutsche Klassik und Romantik*.
Paul Franke Verlag, Berlin: Anton Mayer, *1000 Jahre Seefahrt*.
Frankfurter Allgemeine Zeitung: Wilhelm Seuss, 'Nachtflug über den Atlantik'.
Verlag der Freizeit-Bibliothek, Hamburg: Rudolf Binding, *Unruhige Nacht*.
Fretz & Wasmuth Verlag AG., Zürich: Hermann Hesse, *Gewitter im Urwald*.
German Tourist Information Bureau: *Berlin* and *Nürnberg*.
The Executors of the late Sir W. H. Hadow and Oxford University Press: *Richard Wagner*.
Sir Rupert Hart-Davis: Sir Hugh Walpole, *Mr. Perrin and Mr. Traill* and *The Green Mirror*.
Rupert Hart-Davis Ltd.: Alistair Cooke, *Letters from America*.
Dr. G. F. Hartlaub: Felix Hartlaub, *Im Sperrkreis*.
A. M. Heath: George Orwell, *Animal Farm*.
Jakob Hegner Verlag, Köln: Edzard Schaper, *Der Gouverneur* and *Das Christkind aus den großen Wäldern*; Sigismund von Radecki, *Was ich sagen wollte*.
Ernst Heimeran Verlag, München: Ernst Heimeran, *Es hat alles sein Gutes*.
William Heinemann Ltd.: Frances Hodgson Burnett, *The Secret Garden*, and John Galsworthy, *The Man of Property* (and Charles Scribner's Sons).
Heliopolis-Verlag, Tübingen: Ernst Jünger, *Heliopolis*.
Verlag Herder KG, Freiburg: *Wunderbare Welt*.
Frau Dolly E. Hey: Hans Fallada, *Damals bei uns daheim*.
David Higham Associates Ltd.: Elizabeth Goudge, *The Heart of the Family* (Hodder & Stoughton); Dorothy L. Sayers, *A Treasury of Sayers Stories* (Gollancz); Frank Howes, *Full Orchestra* (Secker & Warburg).
The Trustees of the late James Hilton and John Farquharson Ltd.: *Lost Horizon* (Macmillan).
The Hutchinson Publishing Group: P. H. Fawcett, *Exploration Fawcett*; David Grayson, *Adventures in Contentment*; J. D. Mabbott, *The State and the Citizen*.
Insel-Verlag, Frankfurt: Ricarda Huch, *Gottfried Keller*; Hans Carossa, *Das Jahr der schönen Täuschungen*; Rainer Maria Rilke, 'Das Karussell' from *Ausgewählte Gedichte*.
Herbert Jenkins Ltd.: Bernard Newman, *Visa to Russia*.
Dr. Erich Kastner and Atrium Verlag: 'Der Mai' from *Die dreizehn Monate*.

Kösel-Verlag, München: Peter Bamm, *Die unsichtbare Flagge*.

Alfred Kröner Verlag, Stuttgart: note on Nietzsche's life in Kröner edition of *Also sprach Zarathustra*.

The Longman Group: G. M. Trevelyan, *An Autobiography and other Essays*.

The Trustees of the late E. V. Lucas and Methuen & Co. Ltd.: *Mr. Ingleside*.

MacGibbon & Kee: Rex Warner, *Men and Gods*.

Macmillan, London and Basingstoke: C. P. Snow, *The Masters*.

Harry T. Madden and Laurence Pollinger Ltd.: *The Saturday Evening Post Stories* (Elek Books Ltd.).

Methuen & Co. Ltd. and the Bodleian Library: Kenneth Grahame, *The Wind in the Willows*.

Mitteldeutscher Verlag, Halle/Saale: Christa Wolf, *Der geteilte Himmel*.

Sigbert Mohn Verlag, Gütersloh: Jakob Wassermann, *Der Fall Maurizius*, and Paul Ernst, *Das zweite Gesicht*.

John Murray Ltd.: F. Anstey, *Vice Versa*, and A. C. Benson, *From a College Window*.

John Murray Ltd. and the Trustees of the Estate of the late Sir Arthur Conan Doyle: *The Memoirs of Sherlock Holmes*.

George Newnes Ltd.: *The Outline of Literature*, ed. John Drinkwater.

The Observer: Pierre d'Harcourt, 'Unspoilt Austria'.

Max Peacock and Curtis Brown Ltd.: *The House on the Cliff*.

A. D. Peters & Co.: Martin Armstrong, 'The Pipe-smoker' from *Selected Stories*; Evelyn Waugh, *Edmund Campion*; J. B. Priestley, *Delight* and *Angel Pavement*.

R. Piper & Co. Verlag, München: Carl Jaspers, *Über das Tragische*, and Christian Morgenstern, 'Die zwei Parallelen' from *Galgenlieder*.

Port Verlag, Esslingen/N.: Johannes Haller, *Die Epochen der deutschen Geschichte*.

Ernst Reinhardt Verlag, München, Basel: Helene V. Lerber, *Conrad Ferdinand Meyer*.

Rheinischer Merkur, Köln: *Funknotizen*; K.M., *Das Setzei des Kolumbus*; Stephan W. Pollack, *Fürst der Paradoxe*; Heinz Rein, *Fremd in Oberwiesenau*; Richard Gerlach, *Rotschwänzchen*; Karl Ritter von Frisch, *Die Bienen und ihr Himmelskompaß*; Magdalene Zimmermann, *Glück der Kinder*; Paul Hindemith, *Wilhelm Furtwängler*.

Herr Eugen Roth: *Der Falter*.

Rowohlt Verlag GmbH, Hamburg: Alfred Polgar, *Doppelgänger, du bleicher Geselle*; Wolfgang Borchert, *Die Hundeblume*; Sigismund von Radecki, *Das ABC des Lachens*; Ernst Kreuder, *Die Gesellschaft vom Dachboden*.

Eugen Salzer-Verlag, Heilbronn: Else Hueck-Dehio, *Ja damals*.

E. Schreiber, Graphische Kunstanstalten, Stuttgart: 'Der Bürger im Staat' from *Die Bundesrepublik Deutschland*.

Schweizerische Verkehrszentrale, Zürich: Peter Mayer, *Kunst in der Schweiz*.

Verlag Erich Seemann GmbH, Freiburg: Wilhelm Raabe, *Der Hungerpastor*.

Sidgwick & Jackson Ltd. and the Society of Authors: E. M. Forster, *The Collected Short Stories*.

The Society of Authors as the literary representative of the Estate of John Masefield, and The Macmillan Company, New York: *So Long to Learn*. © 1952 by John Masefield.

Adolf Sponholtz Verlag, Hannover: Hermann Löns, 'Der Geizhals' and 'Glitsch' from *Tiergeschichten*.

J. H. Stembridge and the Oxford University Press: *A Portrait of Canada*.

Süddeutsche Zeitung, München: Curt Geyer, article on *The Times* newspaper.

P. Suhrkamp Verlag, Berlin und Frankfurt: Hermann Hesse, *Peter Camenzind* and *Narziß und Goldmund*; Max Frisch, *Tagebuch*; Hermann Kasack, *Die Stadt hinter dem Strom*.

Frau Vera Tügel-Dehmel: Richard Dehmel, *Die stille Stadt*.

Unsere Zeitung, Bremen: 'Vergessene Natur'.

Carl Friedrich Freiherr von Weizsacker and Vandenhoeck & Ruprecht, Göttingen und Zürich: *Die Verantwortung der Wissenschaft im Atomzeitalter*.

A. P. Watt & Son: W. Somerset Maugham, *The Painted Veil* and *Cakes and Ale* (Heinemann).

The Executors of the late H. G. Wells and A. P. Watt & Son: *The Collected Short Stories of H. G. Wells* (Benn).

Rainer Wunderlich Verlag Hermann Leins, Tübingen: Ricarda Huch, *Die Romantik*.

Die Zeit, Hamburg and Gerd Löhrer: Gerd Löhrer, 'Die ungeliebten Spots'; and 'Der letzte Apollo'.

Oxford and Cambridge Schools Examination Board and University of London Publications Department: passages from G.C.E. A Level papers.

The author and publishers have made every effort to obtain permission from copyright owners of works still in copyright. If, however, any have been overlooked, they apologize for the omission and will make suitable acknowledgement in future reprints.

CONTENTS

PART I

PART II

[1] After every *two* passages a set of ten 'prose' sentences is included for revision. These sentences are based on the vocabulary of the preceding two passages.

[2] Each of the first ten prose composition passages is related in theme to the corresponding passage of the first ten 'translations'.

[3] The General Grammar Index relates both to the grammar of Topics in Part I and to the articles of the Grammar Section.

PART III

PART I

Topic 1

Inflexions of Adjectives and Pronouns: Revision Summary

1. Adjectives

The inflexions of adjectives (and of pronouns derived from adjectives) fall into three groups:

Groups:

1	2	3
der gute	*ein guter*	*guter Wein*
den guten	*einen guten*	*guten Wein*
des guten	*eines guten*	*guten Wein(e)s*
dem guten	*einem guten*	*gutem Wein(e)*
die frische	*eine frische*	*frische Milch*
die frische ‚	*eine frische*	*frische Milch*
der frischen	*einer frischen*	*frischer Milch*
der frischen	*einer frischen*	*frischer Milch*
das klare	*ein klares*	*klares Wasser*
das klare	*ein klares*	*klares Wasser*
des klaren	*eines klaren*	*klaren Wassers*
dem klaren	*einem klaren*	*klarem Wasser*

Plural

die jungen	——	*junge Männer, Frauen, Kinder*
die jungen	——	*junge Männer, Frauen, Kinder*
der jungen	——	*junger Männer, Frauen, Kinder*
den jungen	——	*jungen Männern, Frauen, Kindern*

Group 1: After the Definite Article and the following:
Singular and Plural: *dies-, jen-, welch-, all-, manch-, solch-*
Plural only: *kein-* and all possessive adjectives (*mein-, dein-, sein-/ihr-, unser-, eur-, ihr-/Ihr*); and *beid-*
Singular only: *jed-*

Group 2: After the Indefinite Article and the following:
kein(-) and all possessive adjectives in the singular.

Group 3 : Where there is no introductory article as attribute or where there is some other attributive adjective not mentioned above. Common attributive adjectives which should be known:

allerlei and *allerhand* (all kinds of), *andere, ein bißchen, ein paar, ein wenig, einige, einzelne* (individual), *etwas* (some—singular only), *gewisse* (certain), *manche, mehrere, sämtliche* (all, complete), *solche, sonstige* (other, further), *verschiedene* (various), *viel* and *viele, wenig* and *wenige.*

Also the cardinal numbers *zwei, drei, vier,* &c.

Notes on inflexions
all

(*a*) Compare:

all der Wein	all the wine
all das Geld	all the money
all die Freunde	all the friends, all friends[1]

and

aller Wein	all wine
alles Geld	all money
alle Freunde	all friends, all the friends[1]

(*b*) *alle* } *diese (jene, solche,* and *meine, deine, seine,* &c.)[2] *neuen*
      all } Bücher.

Der Preis *aller* } *dieser (jener, solcher, meiner,* &c.)[2] *neuen Bücher.*
          all }

(*c*) *Der Kaffee ist alle*[3]—the coffee is all used up.

[1] Generally speaking, the article is used in the plural as in English.   [2] i.e. *these* adjectives following *all(-)* are declined like *all-.*   [3] Invariable for all genders, singular and plural.

manch and solch

These are included in both group 1 and group 3 above, since both strong and weak inflexions of the following adjective are found in the plural:

manche alte Häuser and *manche alten Häuser*
die Farben mancher schöner Blumen and *die Farben mancher schönen Blumen*
solche alte Häuser and *solche alten Häuser*
die Dächer solcher alter Häuser and *die Dächer solcher alten Häuser*

manch sometimes occurs uninflected before another adjective, but this is less common nowadays, except in poetry:

manch schöner Schmetterling—many a beautiful butterfly
mancher schöne Schmetterling is normal in prose.

solch may be used, in the singular, in either of the following ways:

solch ein alter Mann or *ein solch alter Mann*

The first of these is the more common.

viel and mehr, wenig and weniger

viel is usually invariable in the singular, but normally inflects in the plural:

viel Mut; mit viel Freude; ohne viel Vergnügen
but: *mit vielen schönen Hoffnungen; ohne viele Worte*, &c.

However, when *viel* in the singular is preceded by the definite article, it is inflected:

Wo soll ich das viele Geld hernehmen? Where am I to get all the money from?

mehr, the comparative of *viel*, is invariable in both singular and plural:

mehr Zeit; mehr Licht; mehr Leute; ohne mehr Zeit; mit mehr Licht, &c.

wenig and *weniger* are treated in exactly the same way as *viel* and *mehr*:

wenig Mut; mit wenig Freude, &c.; *mit wenigen schönen Hoffnungen*, &c.
Was kann ich für die wenigen Bücher bekommen? What can I get for these few books?

Similarly:

weniger Zeit; weniger Licht; weniger Leute, &c.—less time; less light; less people, &c.

Invariable adjectives

The following adjectives of group 3 are invariable for all cases and genders:

allerlei, allerhand, ein bißchen, ein paar, ein wenig, etwas (a certain amount of, some).

Cardinal numbers

Cardinal numbers are invariable, but the genitive plurals *zweier* and *dreier* are used where there is no attributive word (article or adjective) to indicate the case:

> *Die Namen zweier Staatsmänner dieses Jahrhunderts sind allge-mein bekannt.* The names of two statesmen of that century are generally known.

2. Pronouns derived from adjectives

These follow the pattern of adjective inflexions described above. Wherever possible, these pronouns must show the gender, case, and number of the nouns for which they stand.

N.B. All German pronouns are written with a small letter, with the exception of *Sie* (nom. and acc.) and *Ihnen* (polite address). In direct address—notably in letters—*du, dich, dir, dein, dein-,* and *ihr, euch, euer, eur-* are written *Du, Dich, Dir, Dein, Dein-,* and *Ihr, Euch, Euer, Eur-.*

Examples of pronoun inflexions:

> *Dieser Stuhl ist neu, aber jener ist alt.*
> *Welches von den Büchern hast du genommen?—Keines von beiden.*
> *Alle wollten reden, aber nur einer hat etwas gesagt.*
> *Für manche hat der neue Arzt Wunder gewirkt.*
> *Ihr Freund spricht ein besseres Deutsch als meiner.*
> *Unser Briefträger muß heute krank sein, denn ein anderer ist gekommen.*
> *Manchem fällt das Studium schwer.* For many (a one) study comes hard.
> *Mit jeder der Krankenschwestern hat die Königin ein paar Worte gewechselt.* The queen exchanged a few words with each of the nurses.
> *Ich habe allerlei gelesen.*
> *Kannst du mir ein bißchen leihen?* Can you lend me a little?

N.B. *Trotz allem* (dat., not gen.) *wollen wir hier bleiben.*

Topic 1. Domestic Vocabulary

REVISION OF ADJECTIVE AND PRONOUN INFLEXIONS

A Home in an Old Hanseatic City

Das graue Giebelhaus, in dem Johannes Friedemann aufwuchs, lag am nördlichen Tore der alten, kaum mittelgroßen Handels-stadt. Durch die Haustür betrat man eine geräumige, mit Stein-fliesen versehene Diele, von der eine Treppe mit weißgemaltem

Holzgeländer in die Etagen hinaufführte. Die Tapeten des Wohnzimmers im ersten Stock zeigten verblichene Landschaften, und um den schweren Mahagonitisch mit der dunkelroten Plüschdecke standen steiflehnige Möbel.

Hinter dem Haus war ein kleiner Garten, in dem man während des Sommers einen guten Teil des Tages zuzubringen pflegte, trotz des süßlichen Dunstes, der von einer nahen Zuckerbrennerei fast immer herüberwehte. Ein alter, knorriger Walnußbaum stand dort, und in seinem Schatten saß der kleine Johannes oft auf einem niedrigen Holzsessel und knackte Nüsse, während Frau Friedemann und die drei nun schon erwachsenen Schwestern in einem Zelt aus grauem Segeltuch beisammen waren.

THOMAS MANN: *Der kleine Herr Friedemann*
(abridged extract)

Difficulties of Life in Austria after the First World War

... Wir fanden unser Heim in einem fast unbewohnbaren Zustand. Der Regen tropfte munter in die Zimmer, nach jedem Schnee schwammen die Gänge, und eine richtige Reparatur des Dachs war unmöglich, denn die Zimmerleute hatten kein Holz für die Sparren, die Spengler[1] kein Blei für die Rinnen; mühsam wurden mit Dachpappe die schlimmsten Lücken verklebt, und wenn neuer Schnee fiel, half nichts, als selbst auf das Dach zu klettern, um rechtzeitig die Last wegzuschaufeln. Das Telephon rebellierte, denn für den Leitungsdraht hatte man Eisen statt Kupfer genommen; jede Kleinigkeit mußte, da niemand lieferte, von uns selbst den Berg heraufgeschleppt werden. Aber das Schlimmste war die Kälte, denn Kohle gab es im weitesten Umkreis keine, das Holz aus dem Garten war zu frisch und zischte wie eine Schlange, statt zu heizen, und spuckte krachend, statt zu brennen. In der Not halfen wir uns mit Torf, der wenigstens einen Schein[2] von Wärme gab, aber drei Monate lang habe ich meine Arbeiten fast nur im Bett mit blaugefrorenen Fingern geschrieben, die ich nach jeder beendeten Seite zur Wärmung immer wieder unter die Decke zog.

STEFAN ZWEIG: *Die Welt von Gestern*

[1] der *Spengler* in S. Germany and Austria; der *Klempner* in N. Germany.
[2] der *Schein*—(here) semblance.

Buying a House[1]

The next day we went to see[2] the house which my neighbour had mentioned to me.[3] It was an old one, as he had said, but still apparently in good condition. An elderly man opened the door to us and led us through the hall, along a dark passage, and into a spacious lounge. I had the impression that there was too much furniture here, however.[4] In the centre of the room stood a grand piano and a stool; in one corner was an enormous cupboard and next to it a mahogany table. In front of the latter were several chairs, and on one of these a large black cat was sleeping on a cushion. All the furniture in the room was dusty and old-fashioned. On the floor was a dirty carpet; the faded green wallpaper was obviously damp, the ceiling almost black.

The old gentleman now took[5] us upstairs. We walked behind him,[6] wondering[7] what we should see here. It was just the same:[8] a series of untidy, overfurnished, and gloomy rooms. We thanked the owner and asked him[9] to show us the garden. This was so overgrown[10] with weeds that it was impossible to distinguish the flower-beds. We had both decided that we did not want to buy the house. We told the owner that we would ring him up later, and took our leave. We were glad to be gone.

[1] *Der Kauf eines Hauses.*   [2] See Gram. 24.   [3] *mir gegenüber erwähnen* —'to mention in conversation with me'.   [4] What is the best position for *aber?*   [5] Not *nehmen.*   [6] *Wir gingen hinter ihm her*—'we walked along behind him', 'followed on'.   [7] *Wir waren gespannt* (or *neugierig*), . . .—lit. we were tense (curious). Omit 'to know' in translation.   [8] *derselbe, dieselbe, dasselbe,* &c., are written as one word.   [9] *fragen* or *bitten?* Both govern the person 'asked' in the accusative.   [10] Inseparable verb: care with the past participle.   [11] *das Unkraut:* singular noun with collective meaning.

1. In both rooms on the first floor there were a few low chairs and two medium-sized tables.
2. Do all these uninhabitable houses in our town cost as much as that one?
3. Her grown-up brother used to spend a fair part of the day in the nearby village.
4. Which dark-red blankets did you want for the best room? The new ones?
5. Klaus and Willi! Bring your new tent on to the lawn, instead of playing in those hot rooms!
6. While Franz was shovelling away the newly fallen snow, Luise was looking for[1] dry wood in the garden.
7. The worst thing was that for two years we had little money for the necessary repairs.
8. Which of those wallpapers we saw did you like best? Not one of them had much colour.

[1] *suchen nach.*

ESSAY

Beschreibung eines alten Hauses.
Das moderne Heim.
Das Studierzimmer, das ich mir wünsche.
Ein Haus, in dem es spukt.

DISCUSSION

Mein ideales Heim.
Wie sieht es bei uns zu Hause aus?

Topic 2

Order of Sentence Units; Stress Position
Punctuation: Use of the Comma

1. Order of sentence units; stress position

It is essential, both when writing and speaking German, to learn to feel instinctively what is a Main Clause and what is Subordinate, to appreciate how the clauses should be composed and to develop a sense for stress—i.e. the correct (and in some instances the more effective) placing of words in order to draw attention to a particular thought or in order that the sentence may have a proper balance and rhythm.

These are aspects of the language which the student should bear constantly in mind, studying them in his reading (and listening) and practising them in his oral and written work.

General principles of Main Clause word-order

Basic rule:

Subject or direct object, indirect object, adverb, phrase, quoted speech, or subordinate clause as *first idea* of the sentence

is followed by

verb, auxiliary verb (note 1, p. 11), verbal part of a separable verb (note 2, p. 11) as *second idea*. See below for the order of participles and infinitives at the end of the clause.

If it does not begin the clause, the subject must generally follow the verb immediately. (But see notes on position of adverbs and object pronouns below.)

Order of direct and indirect objects:

Two pronouns:	direct before indirect.
Two nouns:	indirect before direct.
Noun and pronoun:	pronoun before noun.

e.g.
Kannst du es ihm leihen? (lend)
Kannst du meinem Bruder zwei Mark leihen?
Kannst du ihm zwei Mark leihen? Kannst du es meinem Bruder leihen?

Reflexive pronouns follow the same rule.

This aspect of word-order tends to cause particular difficulty and requires care.

Adverbs and adverbial phrases:

The general rule is to place the adverb or adverbial phrase as close as possible to the verb, auxiliary verb, past participle, infinitive or other part of speech to which it refers.

The following points should be specially noted:

(i) Pronoun objects precede the adverb in such sentences as:

Er lächelte mich freundlich an. Sie sah mir freudig ins Gesicht.

See Stress position, p. 11, 'lighter' units.

(ii) Adverbial phrases of Time, Manner, and Place should be introduced into the clause in that order unless a particular stress is required (see Stress Position, p. 11).

(iii) Two or more adverbs or adverbial phrases do not normally occur together at the beginning of the clause. The normal practice is to begin the clause with one of them and introduce the other after the verb:

Heute werde ich wahrscheinlich zu Hause bleiben.

Nach zehn Uhr gibt es auf dieser Straße wenig Verkehr. There is little traffic in this street after ten o'clock.

Of course, such phrases as *fast immer, noch jetzt*, &c., consisting of two adverbs, cannot be separated and may begin a sentence:

Fast immer sieht man auf dieser Straße viel Verkehr.

(iv) Where two main clauses are linked by a co-ordinating conjunction (*und, aber, sondern, oder, denn, allein*) and the second clause begins with an adverb, the subject of the second clause *must* be stated:

Sie gingen zusammen spazieren; und manchmal gingen **sie** *mit Freunden ins Theater.*

Participles and Infinitives:

All non-finite parts of the verb (i.e. participles or infinitives) normally stand at the end of their clause or phrase:

Eine große Rauchwolke ausstoßend, zog die Lokomotive an. Emitting a large cloud of smoke, the locomotive started off.

Von allen Freunden verlassen, wohnte er hier in diesem kleinen Zimmer.

Ich werde (will, möchte, &c.) eine Geschichte erzählen.

Ich habe (hatte) eine Geschichte erzählt.

Where there is more than one non-finite part to the verbal idea at the end of the clause, the word-order of the verbs is *the reverse of the English order*:

Er kann es nicht gesagt haben.

Warum hatte er nicht viel früher nach Berlin fahren wollen?

General principles of Subordinate Clause word-order

Basic rule:

The subordinate clause preserves the word-order of the main clause except for the position of the verb(s), which must occur *at the end of the clause*. Where the verbal idea consists of more than one verb, the word-order is *the reverse of the English order*. But: if the verbal idea contains a modal infinitive, this must stand at the end (see also pp. 53, 55):

Ich kann es gut glauben — obschon sie es nicht hätte sagen sollen!
I can well believe it—although she shouldn't have said it!

Da wir das Haus nicht werden kaufen können, müssen wir sofort anrufen.

Separable verbs:

See note 2.

Omission of *daß, wenn, ob*:

The word *daß* may be omitted in the subordinate noun clause representing a thought or opinion (indeed it is considered better style to omit *daß* in this context); the word-order is then the same as that of a main clause:

Ich glaubte, du wärest schon weggefahren.

Sie hatte gesagt, sie könne ihn jederzeit vom Bahnhof abholen.
She had said she could meet him at the station at any time.

The word *wenn* (if . . ., whenever . . .) is frequently omitted from its clause. Where this occurs, the verb or auxiliary verb is placed at the beginning of the clause:

Hätte ich das nur gewußt, so hätte ich sofort geschrieben.

Kann er mir nicht helfen, werde ich jemand anders suchen. If he cannot help me, I shall look for someone else.

The word *ob* is frequently omitted from the conjunction *als ob* (as though). See Topic 8, p. 53. Where this occurs, the verb or auxiliary verb follows *als* immediately:

Als wäre er ganz allein, begann er leise zu sprechen.

Es war mir, als hätte ich das schon irgendwo gelesen. It seemed to me as though I had read it somewhere before.

Stress position

The German sentence has two main stress positions: one at the beginning and the other at (or close to) the end. Of these, the end stress is the stronger. The middle of the sentence is the part which should bear least stress. The important ideas are built up towards the end, and sentence units which are 'lighter' in importance or in sound tend to be mentioned before those which are 'heavier'. But it is also important to know that almost any idea of the sentence may be singled out for emphasis by being placed at the beginning. Thus it is not uncommon to find sentences beginning with a direct or indirect object, or even with an infinitive or past participle, where the speaker or writer wishes to focus attention (perhaps only for the moment) on that particular idea:

Meinen Vater habe ich nie gekannt.
Mich kann keiner beschwindeln! No one can swindle me!
Schwimmen möchte ich heute nicht.
Ich habe ihn im Radio gehört; gesehen habe ich ihn aber nicht.

¹ Auxiliary verbs: *haben, sein* (in Perfect tenses); *werden* (for Future and Passive); *würd-* (for Conditional); and the modal verbs *dürfen, können, mögen, müssen, sollen, wollen*; and *lassen*.   ² The separable part of the separable verb is placed at the end of the clause in the Present, Imperfect, and Imperative in main clauses. In subordinate clauses, the separable verb is not separated.

2. Punctuation: Use of the comma

The use of the comma in German differs from its use in English in certain important respects. The following rules should be carefully noted. (The examples below are drawn mainly from the German–English passages of Topics 1 and 2.)
The comma is used:

(i) To separate the subordinate clause from the main clause:
   Ich fand niemanden mehr in der Stadt, den ich kannte.
   Jedesmal, wenn sie mir den Kaffee oder das Essen ins Zimmer brachte, blieb sie länger, als mir lieb war.
   „Sind Sie sicher, daß Sie ihn nicht gekannt haben?"

(ii) To mark off a participle phrase:
   Hier starb er, von der ganzen Gemeinde betrauert, im Jahre 1890. Here he died, mourned by the whole community, in 1890.
   Unser Dorf, tief unten liegend, sah von dieser Höhe winzig aus.
   Our village, lying far below, looked tiny from this height.

(iii) To introduce or conclude a dependent infinitive phrase:

Wenn neuer Schnee fiel, half nichts, als selbst auf das Dach zu klettern, um rechtzeitig die Last wegzuschaufeln.
Arbeiten zu gehen, hatte ich keine Lust.

(iv) In compound sentences where the subject is *changed or repeated* after the co-ordinating conjunction:

Erst im Frühjahr 1950 kehrte ich aus dem Kriege heim, und ich fand niemanden mehr in der Stadt, den ich kannte.
Ich gab meiner Wirtin Geld, und sie kaufte alles für mich und bereitete mir das Essen.

(v) To separate sentence units of the same kind occurring in a sequence (clauses, phrases, adjectives, adverbs, &c.):

Ein großes, neues Haus.
Ein alter, knorriger Walnußbaum stand dort.
Es war noch früh an der Zeit; ich schnürte sofort mein Bündel auf, nahm meinen etwas schäbigen Rock heraus, zog mich sauber in meine besten Kleider an, . . .

(vi) To mark out a phrase in apposition:

Ich mußte das Bild ihres Sohnes betrachten, ein Buntphoto, das über dem Sofa hing.

N.B. The comma is *not* used:

(i) To mark off the word *aber* with the meaning *however* from the rest of the sentence (although this is the case in English):

Ihr Sohn war aber nicht aus dem Krieg zurückgekehrt.

(ii) To introduce a quotation. The colon is used for this purpose:

Jedesmal drehte ich mich zur Wand und sagte: „Nein, wirklich nicht.“

(iii) In a sequence of adjectives before a noun when *und* is not implied:

ein lachender blonder Junge;
Ich ging in das nächste kleine Wirtshaus hinein . . .
die drei nun schon erwachsenen Schwestern.

Topic 2. Simple Actions

ORDER OF SENTENCE UNITS; STRESS POSITION;
USE OF THE COMMA

Arrival

Nach einer glücklichen, jedoch für mich sehr beschwerlichen Seefahrt erreichten wir endlich den Hafen. Sobald ich mit dem Boot
an Land kam, nahm ich meine paar Sachen in die Hand, drängte
mich durch die wimmelnde Menge auf dem Kai, und ging in das
nächste kleine Wirtshaus hinein. Ich bat um ein Zimmer. Der
Hausknecht maß mich mit einem Blick[1] und führte mich zu einem
engen Dachzimmer hinauf. Ich ließ mir frisches Wasser geben
und fragte nach, wo Herr Thomas John wohne. — „Vor dem
Nordertor, das erste Landhaus rechts von der Straße, ein großes,
neues Haus aus rotem und weißem Marmor, mit vielen Säulen."
Gut. — Es war noch früh an der Zeit; ich schnürte sofort mein
Bündel auf,[2] nahm meinen etwas schäbigen Rock heraus, zog
meine besten Kleider an, steckte das Empfehlungsschreiben ein,
und machte mich sogleich auf den Weg.

Nachdem ich die lange Norderstraße hinaufgestiegen war und
das Tor erreicht hatte, sah ich bald die Säulen durch die Bäume
schimmern. — „Also hier", dachte ich. Ich wischte den Staub
von meinen Stiefeln mit dem Taschentuch ab, zog die Krawatte
zurecht, und klingelte.

ADALBERT VON CHAMISSO (1781–1838): *Peter Schlemihl* (adapted).

[1] *jn. mit einem Blick messen*—to measure s.o. with a glance, look s.o. up and down.
[2] Care. Cf. meaning of *die Tür aufmachen*.

Idleness

Erst im Frühjahr 1950 kehrte ich aus dem Kriege heim, und ich
fand niemanden mehr in der Stadt, den ich kannte. Zum Glück
hatten meine Eltern mir Geld hinterlassen. Ich mietete ein Zimmer in der Stadt, dort lag ich auf dem Bett, rauchte und wartete
und wußte nicht, worauf ich wartete. Arbeiten zu gehen, hatte
ich keine Lust. Ich gab meiner Wirtin Geld, und sie kaufte alles
für mich und bereitete mir das Essen. Jedesmal, wenn sie mir
den Kaffee oder das Essen ins Zimmer brachte, blieb sie länger,
als mir lieb war. Ihr Sohn war in einem Ort gefallen, der Kalinowka[1] hieß, und wenn sie eingetreten war, setzte sie das Tablett
auf den Tisch und kam in die dämmrige Ecke, wo mein Bett

stand. Dort döste ich vor mich hin, drückte die Zigaretten an der Wand aus, und so war die Wand rings um mein Bett voller schwarzer Flecken. Meine Wirtin war blaß und mager, und wenn im Dämmer ihr Gesicht über meinem Bett stehenblieb, hatte ich Angst vor ihr. Zuerst dachte ich, sie sei verrückt, denn ihre Augen waren sehr hell und groß, und immer wieder fragte sie mich nach ihrem Sohn.

„Sind Sie sicher, daß Sie ihn nicht gekannt haben? Der Ort hieß Kalinowka — sind Sie nicht dort gewesen?"

Aber ich hatte nie von einem Ort gehört, der Kalinowka hieß, und jedesmal drehte ich mich zur Wand und sagte: „Nein, wirklich nicht, ich kann mich nicht entsinnen."

Meine Wirtin war nicht verrückt, sie war eine sehr ordentliche Frau, und es tat mir weh, wenn sie mich fragte. Sie fragte mich sehr oft, jeden Tag ein paarmal, und wenn ich zu ihr in die Küche ging, mußte ich das Bild ihres Sohnes betrachten, ein Buntphoto, das über dem Sofa hing. Er war ein lachender blonder Junge gewesen, und auf dem Buntphoto trug er eine Infanterie-Ausgehuniform.

HEINRICH BÖLL: Die blasse Anna

[1] Kalinowka. German, like other languages, has to transliterate the spelling of Russian words. Cf. also: *Wolga*; *Kiew*; *Tolstoj*; *Dostojewski*.

An Important Day

As soon as Richard heard the alarm-clock ringing he got out of bed. Not until he had washed, shaved, and dressed did it occur to him[1] to put the kettle on the gas to prepare his coffee. But it did not matter. It was still early, he would have half an hour to catch his train; but he wanted to avoid any haste[2] and keep[3] himself as calm as possible, for today's visit to Cologne[4] was important for him—perhaps more important than any[5] he had made before. Aunt Mary wanted to see him urgently, so she had said in her letter. Whenever Aunt Mary wanted to see someone urgently it was always to do with[6] her will—every member of the family knew that. And he knew that she had promised to leave him something.

At last the water was boiling and he could make the coffee.[7] He needed only ten minutes to drink it and get ready. He put Aunt Mary's letter in his pocket, arranged his tie, put on his overcoat and hat, and was about to[8] go downstairs. Something caused him still to hesitate, however. He paused on the landing and said aloud to himself, 'What am I waiting for? I've forgotten *something*. Now, what can it be?' At once he thought of the gas. Had he turned it out?[9] Yes, the gas was all right.[10] As he went downstairs, shut the door and set off for the station, he kept thinking, 'This is a bad beginning. I'm sure I shan't have any luck today.'

[1] it occurs to me (that I must do s.th.)—*es kommt mir in den Sinn.* [2] *jegliche Eile.* [3] *halten.* [4] Use the adjective *heutig.* to—*in.* [5] Use *irgendein-* [6] *es hatte mit . . . zu tun* or *es handelte sich um . . .* [7] *den Kaffee aufgießen.* [8] *wollte eben . . .* [9] Questions of this type (implying 'he wondered') are often introduced by *ob . . .* [10] Cf. that is all right—*das ist in Ordnung.*

1. Will you have to go to London by car every day?
2. After we have had breakfast I will give you the list and you can go shopping.
3. All day we steamed southwards and we reached port about four o'clock in the afternoon.
4. My landlady has only lent me the money; she did not *give* it to me!
5. Although I had grown up in Berlin, at least half the city[1] was always unknown to me.
6. Before the girls were allowed to go out the kitchen had to be cleaned.
7. Can you tell me why they wanted to use copper instead of iron here?
8. If the letter of introduction is ready, I shall be able to take it at once.

[1] *die halbe Stadt* or *die Hälfte der Stadt.*

ESSAY

Die Freuden der Faulheit.
Ankunft.
Beschreiben Sie, wie Sie einen Abend verbracht haben.
Setzen Sie die Erzählung von Chamisso oder Böll fort.

DISCUSSION

Was würden Sie tun, wenn Sie nicht zu arbeiten brauchten?
Erzählen Sie in Ihren eigenen Worten, was in den beiden Auszügen[1] geschieht.

[1] *Auszüge*—extracts.

VOCABULARY WORK

Make a list of all the expressions of time which have occurred so far, grouping them under
  (i) Expressions in the accusative case,
  (ii) Expressions in the genitive case,
  (iii) Expressions introduced by a preposition,
  (iv) Adverbs or adverb groups (*schon längst, immer noch, jederzeit,* &c.)

Topic 3

Revision of Prepositions. Notes on the position of Prepositions in their phrases. Use of Prepositions: notes on certain difficulties

1. Revision of prepositions

(i) Prepositions which *always* govern the Dative:

aus, außer (apart from), *bei, entgegen, gegenüber, mit, nach, seit, von, zu.*

For less common prepositions governing the dative, see Grammar Section, 137.

(ii) Prepositions which *always* govern the Accusative:

bis, durch, für, gegen, hindurch, ohne, um, wider. (*entlang* usually governs the accusative; but see 2 below).

For less common prepositions governing the accusative, see Grammar Section, 138.

(iii) Prepositions which govern the Dative *or* the Accusative according to context (Where? *or* To where?):

an, auf, außer (outside), *hinter, in, neben, über, unter, vor, zwischen.*

(iv) Prepositions which govern the Genitive:

außerhalb (outside), *diesseits* (on this side of), *inmitten, innerhalb* (within), *jenseits, statt, um . . . willen* (for the sake of), *während, wegen* (on account of, because of).

N.B. *wegen* is often found governing the dative in S. German. *trotz* (in spite of) usually governs the genitive, but is also found governing the dative.

binnen (within, referring to time) governs the genitive in choice language, but usually governs the dative.

For less common prepositions governing the genitive, see Grammar Section, 139.

2. Notes on the position of prepositions in their phrases

Most prepositions precede the noun. Note, however:

hindurch always follows the noun.

entgegen and *entlang* usually follow the noun. *entlang* may sometimes be found preceding the noun and governing the dative or the genitive: *Sie gingen entlang der Straße* (more usually: *Sie gingen die Straße entlang*).

gegenüber may follow or precede the noun, but always *follows* the pronoun: *dem Park gegenüber* or *gegenüber dem Park*; but only: *mir gegenüber*.

nach with the meaning 'according to' often follows the noun: *meiner Meinung nach*—in my opinion.

wegen is sometimes found following the noun. N.B. *meinetwegen*—on my account, *seinetwegen, ihretwegen*, &c. The expression *meinetwegen* is often used to mean 'for all I care', 'I don't mind'.

um . . . willen: the two words are placed around the noun: *um der Wahrheit willen*—for the sake of truth. N.B. *um meinetwillen, seinetwillen*, &c.—for my sake, his sake, &c.; and *um dessentwillen, um derentwillen* or *um deretwillen*—for whose sake.

The choice of position for such prepositions as *entgegen, entlang, gegenüber, nach* ('according to'), *wegen* is a question of usage and sentence rhythm.

entgegen and *entlang, gegenüber* and *hindurch* often become the separable parts of separable verbs, e.g. *entgegenlaufen*—run towards, *entlangwandern*—stroll along (a road, &c.), *gegenübertreten* —come to face (s.o. or s.th.), *hindurchgehen*—go through. See also Topic 13, pp. 87–89.

3. Use of prepositions: notes on certain difficulties

Group (i)

aus

Movement:
Er lief aus dem Garten.

Er tat es aus Neid—he did it out of envy.

Material:
Ein Stuhl aus Stahl.

Origin:
Ein Herr aus London.

Motive:
aus diesem Grunde—for this reason.

Nachrichten aus der ganzen Welt—news from all over the world.

bei

Proximity:

Neuß bei Düsseldorf—(the town of) Neuß near Düsseldorf. *Die Schlacht bei Waterloo*—the battle of Waterloo.

Occupation:

Er ist bei der Arbeit. Sie sitzen beim Wein (Bier, Kaffee, &c.).

In the case of, in connexion with:

Bei Goethe war es anders—in Goethe's case it was different. *Er war bei vielen Veranstaltungen tätig*—he took an active part in many functions.

At the house of:

Bei uns. Bei Müllers.

(For further examples of the use of *bei*, see Grammar Section, 142.)

entgegen

As separable prefix:

Sie kam mir lachend entgegen —she came towards me, laughing.

Contrary to:

deinen Anweisungen entgegen or *entgegen deinen Anweisungen* —contrary to your instructions.

gegenüber

Facing, opposite to:

Dem Park gegenüber or *Gegenüber dem Park steht das Hotel.*

Towards (used figuratively):

Mir gegenüber war er immer sehr freundlich.

nach

Movement (often involving a journey) to a named objective:

Er reist nach Berlin. Wie komme ich nach der Reuterstraße? Wann fahren Sie wieder nach Belgien?

According to:

Meiner Meinung nach wird es regnen.
Nach Baedekers Reiseführer ist dies die allerschönste Route—according to the Baedeker guidebook this is the most beautiful route of all.

zu

Short movements:

Er kam zu mir. Sie ging zur Tür.

Use with *sagen*:

Dann sagte er zu mir: „Danke schön."
„Komm her!" sagte die Mutter zu ihrem Kind.

Attitude to:

Was sagt ihr zu meiner Idee? Er war immer sehr freundlich zu mir.

Purpose:

Wasser zum Trinken. Wozu soll ich das wissen? Why (What . . . for) should I know that?

Location of ancient, famous buildings:
> *Der Dom zu Köln. Das Rathaus zu Münster.*

Inn names:
> *Zum Goldenen Löwen. Zum Roten Adler* (i.e. 'at the sign of . . .').

Group (ii)

bis

until:
> *bis Montag, bis Dezember.*

by:
> *Wir müssen bis Dienstag wieder zu Hause sein.*

bis + another preposition: 'as far as', 'up to', 'down to', 'until the', &c.
> *bis zum letzten Tag(e)*—until the last day.

durch

Means:
> *Durch eisernes Sparen konnte er sich ein Eigenheim kaufen.* By resolute saving he was able to buy a home of his own.

gegen/wider[1]

Opposition:
> *Er kämpfte gegen die Türken.*

Antidote:
> *Haben sie ein Mittel gegen Husten?* Have you anything for a cough?

Mode of travel:
> *zu Fuß gehen; zu Wasser und zu Lande fahren*—to travel by water and by land. (N.B. **mit** *dem Autobus,* **mit** *dem Auto,* **mit** *dem Zug,* &c., *fahren.*)

Price:
> *Äpfel zu 50 Pfg. das Pfund*—apples at 50 Pfennig a pound.

> *Sie gingen bis auf einen hinaus.* They all went out but one.
> *Das Wasser stieg bis in die Häuser, bis auf die Dächer.*
> *Bis nach London, bis an die Grenze hat man uns begleitet.* They accompanied us as far as London, as far as the frontier.

Approximate time:
> *Gegen sieben Uhr verdunkelte sich der Himmel.* About seven o'clock the sky grew dark.

[1] *wider*, which expresses only opposition, is rarely found nowadays except in certain stock expressions, e.g. *wider Willen*—against one's will, *wider Erwarten*—contrary to expectations.

Group (iii)

an

Position at an edge, limit:
> *Das Bild hängt an der Wand.*

> *Der Herr stand an der Tür.*
> *Wir wohnten an der See.*

To a position at an edge, limit:

Bitte hängen Sie das Bild an die Wand.

Der Herr ging langsam an die Tür.

Wir fahren morgen an die See.

auf

Position where:

Das Buch liegt auf dem Tisch.

To a position:

Er legte das Buch sorgfältig auf den Tisch.

Manner:

Auf diese Weise—in this way.

Sagen Sie es auf deutsch.

Wir sind auf du und du—i.e. we are very friendly, we are on a 'du' footing with each other.

Certain expressions of position,

'At' an institution:

Sie ist Lehrerin an dieser Schule.

Fritz studiert an (or *auf*) *der Universität.*

Er arbeitet als Arzt an dem städtischen Krankenhaus.

often implying height and/or authority:

Er wohnt auf Zimmer 99 in jenem Hotel.

Der Herzog wohnt auf seinem Schloß.

Sie war auf der Weltausstellung in Brüssel tätig. She was employed at the World Exhibition in Brussels.

Auf der Universität hat er Jura (law) *studiert.*

Ich möchte so gern auf dem Lande wohnen.

in

Position where:

Eine alte Frau ging im Garten umher.

To a position:

Die alte Frau ging nach dem Abendessen in den Garten.

'In/To' with feminine-gender countries or provinces; and

with forest or mountain districts:

Er lebte in der Schweiz (der Türkei, der Tschechoslowakei; in der Provence; im Schwarzwald; im Odenwald; in den Bergen; in den Alpen).

Er fuhr in die Schweiz (etc.); in die Provence; in den Schwarzwald (etc.).

über

Position where:

Hoch über dem Deck weht die Flagge.

To a position:

Hoch über das Deck hat man die Flagge gehißt (hoisted).

Via:

Fährt der Zug nach Innsbruck über Augsburg, meine Heimatstadt? (note the case).

Authority over:

Zwanzig Jahre lang herrschte der König über das englische Volk (note the case).

unter

Position where:

Die Wasserleitung lag unter der Erde. The water-pipe was below ground.

To a position:

Man verlegte die Wasserleitung unter die Erde. The water-pipe was put below ground.

Accompaniment:

Unter brausendem Beifall fiel

Excess:

Einen neuen Wagen kaufen? Das geht leider über meine Geldmittel (financial means, plur.; note the case).

der Vorhang. The curtain fell to thunderous applause.

Amongst:

Unter allen meinen Freunden ist David der beste.

Der Zauberer trat unter die Zuschauer und verteilte Karten. The conjurer went amongst the audience and distributed cards.

Group (iv)

trotz

N.B. *trotzdem*—in spite of that, nevertheless; *trotz allem*—in spite of everything.

As in English, many German verbs, participles, and adjectives followed by particular prepositions form one unit of meaning: to look forward *to*, to be satisfied *with*, to think *of*, to be proud *of*, to think *about*, to be wrong *about*, &c. It is necessary to pay particular attention to these usages in German, and to the cases which the prepositions govern in each instance. The majority—but by no means all—of the constructions involving prepositions of Group (iii) govern the *accusative*, e.g. *sich freuen auf*—to look forward to, *denken an*—to think of, *stolz sein auf*—to be proud of, *denken über*—to think about, *im Unrecht sein über*—to be wrong about. Some govern the *dative*, e.g. *Freude haben an*—to take pleasure in, *weinen vor*—to weep for (joy, &c.), *sterben an*—to die of. A moment's thought will often make the reason for the case clear; e.g. *sich freuen auf* suggests a movement, a projection of one's thoughts *into* the future, *on to* the thing desired; whereas *Freude haben an* suggests pleasure taken in something close at hand.

The question of these forms is dealt with in greater detail in Topics 12 and 16, pp. 81–83 and 105–6; see also Grammar Section, 32 and 89.

Topic 3. Country Life

REVISION OF PREPOSITIONS

An Alpine Village

In den hohen Gebirgen unseres Vaterlandes steht ein Dörfchen mit einem kleinen, aber sehr spitzigen Kirchturme, der mit seiner roten Farbe, mit welcher die Schindeln bemalt sind, aus dem Grün vieler Obstbäume hervorragt und wegen derselben roten Farbe in dem duftigen und blauen Dämmern der Berge weithin sichtbar ist. Das Dörfchen liegt gerade mitten in einem ziemlich weiten Tal, das fast wie ein länglicher Kreis gestaltet ist. Es enthält außer der Kirche eine Schule, ein Gemeindehaus und noch mehrere stattliche Häuser, die einen Platz gestalten, auf welchem vier Linden stehen, die ein steinernes Kreuz in ihrer Mitte haben.

Es gehen keine Straßen durch das Tal, sie haben ihre zweigleisigen Wege, auf denen sie ihre Felderzeugnisse mit einspännigen Wäglein nach Hause bringen, es kommen daher wenig Menschen in das Tal, unter diesen manchmal ein einsamer Wanderer, der ein Liebhaber der Natur ist, eine Weile in der bemalten Oberstube des Wirtes wohnt und die Berge betrachtet, oder gar ein Maler, der den kleinen, spitzen Kirchturm und die schönen Gipfel der Felsen in seine Mappe zeichnet. Daher bilden die Bewohner eine eigene Welt, sie kennen einander alle mit Namen und mit den einzelnen Geschichten von Großvater und Urgroßvater her;[1] trauern alle, wenn einer stirbt; wissen, wie er heißt, wenn einer geboren wird; haben eine Sprache, die von der der Ebene draußen abweicht; haben ihre Streitigkeiten, die sie schlichten; stehen einander bei und laufen zusammen, wenn sich etwas Außerordentliches ereignet.

ADALBERT STIFTER (1805–68): *Bergkristall* (adapted)

[1] 'dating back to the time of grandfathers and great-grandfathers'.

A Lonely Christmas

Meta stand in der Haustür und sah den beiden nach, wie sie gegen Westen den Fußsteig nach dem Bach hinabgingen. Das Dunkel der Heide hatte sie[1] bald ihren Blicken entzogen; nach einer Weile aber wurden sie noch einmal in der Ferne sichtbar, auf dem Hügel drüben; fast übernatürlich groß schienen ihr die Gestalten, wie sie sich schattenhaft gegen den schwachen

Schein des Abendhimmels abhoben. Endlich waren sie ganz verschwunden. Dann hörte sie noch unten vom Bach her das Geräusch der Fußtritte auf dem Stege, und dann war alles still. Sie war allein.

Nur im Stall in der Scheune waren die kleinen Ponys und die Kuh, und daneben in dem Verschlag saß schlafend das Federvieh auf seinen Leitern; hinter ihr im Hause strichen ein paar scheue Katzen durch die dunklen Räume. Leise drückte sie die Haustüre zu und ging in ihre Stube.

Mit trockenem Heidereis[2] und Torf brachte sie das Ofenfeuer wieder zum Brennen, daß es gesellig zu prasseln begann; dann, nachdem sie den Tisch abgeräumt und das Licht geputzt hatte, setzte sie sich in den Lehnstuhl und brach das Siegel ihres Weihnachtsbriefes. Sie las langsam und mit ganzer Andacht, und als sie an das Ende des Briefes kam, flog ein glückliches Lächeln über ihr Gesicht, und die Hand, welche ihn hielt, sank auf den Tisch. „Er kommt endlich, nach zehn langen Jahren!" rief sie vor sich hin.

THEODOR STORM (1817–88): *Abseits*

---

[1] *sie* is the direct object of the verb *hatte . . . entzogen*. Lit.: 'had withdrawn them from her gaze'—English equivalent?   [2] Storm is writing of the North German *Heide*, or moorland.

Bichlbach, nr. Reutte,
Tyrol
12 August

Dear Karl,

We arrived here yesterday towards seven o'clock in the evening. We flew to Basle and came by train as far as Innsbruck, where we caught a bus. In this way we were able to save time and get to our destination in nine hours. If you do the journey from London by rail you can hardly be here within a whole day.

The village lies in the middle of a fairly wide valley, whose eastern end is shut off by[1] the Zugspitze, on the German frontier. In the opposite direction it broadens out towards the town of Reutte,[2] one[3] of the most delightful places I have ever seen. Opposite me as I write this (for I am sitting on the balcony outside our room) the mountains forming one side of the valley tower up through dark-green pinewoods. Above these you can see the upland meadows[4] and cows moving slowly across them. Still farther up,[5] walls of rock stand out against a blue sky.

How still it is here. The silence does one good[6] after the noise and hurry of London. Everything I have seen[7] since our arrival has confirmed[8] what I had read about Tyrol. Amongst the many pleasant impressions I have had[9] so far, the one[10] I shall never forget is the friendliness of the local people.[11] Anyone who[12] has had enough of the city should come to Austria and talk to people like these: gentle and yet tough, hard-working and yet the sort who[13] always have time to help.

Enough for today. I shall be writing to you again at the end of the week.

Yours,
David

[1] *durch . . . abgeschlossen ist.*   [2] *gegen die Stadt . . . zu.*   [3] Take care with the apposition.   [4] upland meadow—*die Alm (-en)*.   [5] 'above' (adverb). [6] does one good—*tut wohl.*   [7] everything which . . ., nothing which . . .— *alles, was . . ., nichts, was . . .* See also Gram. 106 (*a*).   [8] to confirm—*bestätigen.*   [9] 'received'.   [10] The demonstrative pronoun 'the one' (followed by 'which . . .', 'who . . .', 'whom', &c.) is *der* (*die, das*, &c.) or *derjenige* (*diejenige, dasjenige*, &c.). See also Gram. 112.   [11] 'the village inhabitants'.   [12] anyone who . . .—*wer . . .* See also Gram. 112.   [13] 'such who . . .'

1. When we were travelling to the mountains last year, something extraordinary happened.
2. Contrary to all my expectations, the dialect varies from that of the plain.
3. I watched him go as he walked over the wooden bridge and disappeared in[1] the distance.
4. The life in Austria was too lonely for him, so he returned to Berlin.
5. I studied the peasants standing by the inn for a long time before I began to draw them in my sketchbook.
6. Who are those people up there on the side of the hill, and the others who have just moved behind them?
7. They came to the end of their walk and said 'Goodbye' to one another.
8. No one can settle such disputes if he does not understand those with whom he is dealing.[2]

[1] Dative.   [2] Cf. We are dealing with a difficult question. *Wir haben es mit einer schwierigen Frage zu tun.* Imitate this construction.

ESSAY

Ein Brief von einem Freund, der seine Ferien auf dem Lande verbringt.
Ein Bauer erzählt vom Leben auf dem Lande.
Ferien in Österreich.
Beschreiben Sie eine Wanderung, die Sie gemacht haben.

DISCUSSION

Was sind Ihrer Meinung nach die Vorteile des Landlebens gegenüber dem Stadtleben — oder umgekehrt?
Beschreiben Sie Dörfer, die Sie kennen, und berichten Sie
womöglich auch etwas über deren Einwohner.

GRAMMAR WORK

List 50 phrases involving the use of a preposition and noun
which have occurred in the German/English translation passages
of Topics 1-3, and explain the case usage for each. Vary the
examples as much as possible.

Topic 4

Use and Omission of the Article
Expressions of Time

1. Use and omission of the article

This is a question which requires careful attention, as the German usage often differs from the English. The points set out below are intended as a general guide for practical purposes; but competence in deciding whether to use or to omit the article in German can only be acquired through observation and practice.

Indefinite articles present less difficulty than definite articles. Generally speaking, they are used much as in English; but here, too, the student should take particular note of differences from English usage when he meets them.

(i) *The definite article is used:*

(*a*) Frequently with parts of the body, rather than a possessive adjective (see also Topic 18, pp. 118–19): *Der Fremde schüttelte mir die Hand. Sie hat sich den Fuß verrenkt.* She has sprained her foot. *Ich muß mir die Hände waschen.*

Note the use of the dative of the possessor (*mir; sich*) in the above examples—where the action in each case involves an *external* cause *affecting* the part of the body (moving, hurting, cleaning). But where the action is merely the *movement* of part of the body, no dative of the possessor is used: *Sie hob die Augenbrauen. Er legte die Hand auf den Tisch.* (For expressions of this kind involving the use of a preposition, see Topic 18, 1 (iii), pp. 118–19.) The article may (but need not) be used instead of the possessive adjective with articles of clothing: *Sie setzte den* (or *ihren*) *Hut auf. Er zog den* (or *seinen*) *Mantel aus.*

(*b*) Usually before abstract nouns (but the article is usually omitted where a preposition precedes the noun): *Sein größter Feind war die Angst.* His greatest enemy was fear. *Die Treue ist eine Tugend.* Loyalty is a virtue. *Der Ungehorsam wurde bestraft.* Disobedience was punished. But: *Er zitterte vor Angst.* He trembled with fear. *Durch Treue hat er die Liebe seines Königs gewonnen.* By (his) loyalty he has won the love of his king. *Bei Ungehorsam von seiten der Schüler pflegte er sehr ernst auszusehen.* In cases of disobedience on the part of the pupils he used to look very serious.

Where the article is needed in order to provide a suitable antecedent for a relative clause, it must of course be included: *Wegen der Angst, die er verspürte, konnte er sich nicht von der Stelle bewegen.* On account of the fear which he was experiencing he could not move from the spot.

(c) To make clear a case which might otherwise be obscure (especially important with genitives): *Ich ziehe Kaffee dem Tee vor.* I prefer coffee to tea. *Das bedarf der Überprüfung.* This needs to be checked (*bedürfen* governs the genitive). *Sie war der Sprache nicht mehr fähig.* She was no longer capable of speaking.

(d) With feminine and masculine names of countries and districts, names of streets and squares, dates, seasons, months, days of the week, parts of the day, meals: *Wir hatten eine Villa in der Schweiz. Sie wohnten in der Tschechoslowakei. Fährst du dieses Jahr in die Türkei? Die Bretagne und die Normandie liegen in Nordfrankreich. Der Iran liegt im mittleren Osten. Er herrschte über den Irak*—he ruled over Irak. (N.B. The gender of neuter countries—the majority of countries are neuter—is not normally stated, but *das Elsaß* is an exception to the rule: *Das Elsaß ist ein Teil von Frankreich.* Alsace is part of France.)

Damals hatte ich eine Wohnung in der Kaiserstraße (but: *damals wohnte ich Kaiserstraße 6*). *Mitten auf der Kaiserstraße steht eine hohe Säule* (column).

der zehnte Juli; am zwanzigsten Dezember; im Frühling; im Herbst; im Januar; im Juli; am Dienstag; der Freitag ist bei uns der Zahltag (pay-day); *am Morgen; am Nachmittag; am Abend; er hat das Mittagessen eben eingenommen* (or: *er hat eben zu Mittag gegessen*); *was gibt's zum Abendessen? Sie waren alle zum Abendessen bei Meyers eingeladen.*

(e) Before proper nouns preceded by an adjective: *der arme Heinrich; die alte Minna; das heutige Berlin; das alte Deutschland.* But: *armer Heinrich!* (exclamation).

(f) In many prepositional expressions where English uses an indefinite article or omits the article: *im Schritt gehen*—to go at a walking pace; *im Galopp reiten; im Nu*—in a trice;

mit dem Zug, dem Auto fahren; in der Lage sein, etwas zu tun—to be in a position to do s.th.; *über die Maßen*—beyond measure, beyond all bounds; *im Dreivierteltakt*—in 3/4 time; &c. These expressions should be specially noted as they occur.

(ii) *The article is omitted:*

(*a*) In the predicate to denote a profession, calling, condition: *Dieser Herr ist Arzt. Sie ist Krankenschwester. Er möchte Jurist werden. Hitler nannte sich „Führer und Reichskanzler". Ein Schweizer wurde Leiter der Expedition. Ich bin Besitzer eines Wirtshauses. Sind Sie Engländer?*

(*b*) and hence after *als* meaning 'in the capacity of': *Als Arzt kann ich das nicht gutheißen.* As a doctor I cannot approve of that. *Hillary und Tensing haben als erste den Mount Everest bestiegen.* Hillary and Tensing were the first to climb Mount Everest. *Als stellvertretender Geschäftsführer ist er in Abwesenheit des Chefs verantwortlich.* As deputy manager he is responsible in the absence of the chief. *Wir kennen ihn als erstklassigen Tennisspieler.*

(*c*) In groups of nouns related in their context: *Logen und Rang waren vollbesetzt.* The boxes and the circle were fully occupied. *Das Bundeshaus hat eine besondere Tribüne für Presse und Rundfunk.* The Federal Parliament has a special gallery for the press and radio. *Weder König noch Adel* (nobility) *kannten das Volk.*

(*d*) Often in adjectival phrases introduced by a preposition where the phrase denotes a distinctive individual feature of the thing or person described: *eine Treppe mit weißgemaltem Holzgeländer; ein Mann von hohem Wuchs* (stature). (But: *Ein Verkäufer mit einem großen Stoß Zeitungen*—a vendor with a great pile of newspapers; *eine Frau mit einem weinenden Kind*—a woman with a crying child. In these examples, the phrases are added to convey information which amplifies but does not imply a distinct, individual feature, i.e. the vendor is a seller of newspapers, and has a large pile of them; the woman has a child with her, and the child happens to be crying; whereas the white-painted wooden bannister is and remains part of the staircase as a characteristic detail.)

(*e*) In genitive expressions where a proper name precedes another noun: *Karls Buch; Annettes Fahrrad; Albert Schweitzers Krankenhaus; Professor Günthers Vorlesungen* (lectures).

2. Expressions of time

The following expressions of time should be especially noted:

DAY

(On) this, that day	an diesem Tage, an jenem Tage.
(On) the next day (On) the following day (On) the day after	am nächsten (folgenden, anderen) Tage, tags darauf.
(On) the day before	am vorigen Tage, tags zuvor.
All day Throughout the day The whole day (long)	den ganzen Tag (lang), (hindurch).
Every day	jeden Tag, täglich.
One day	eines Tages.
The day before yesterday	vorgestern.
The day after tomorrow	übermorgen.
At midday	um Mittag, zu Mittag.
At daybreak, at dawn	beim Tagesanbruch, beim Sonnenaufgang.
Day by day	Tag um Tag, Tag für Tag.
Day in, day out	tagaus, tagein.
In two or three days' time	in ein paar Tagen.
During the day	während des Tages, tagsüber.

N.B.

This morning	heute früh, heute morgen.
Tomorrow morning	morgen früh.

NIGHT. (These expressions follow the pattern of the 'day' expressions for the most part.)

(On) this, that night	in dieser Nacht, diese Nacht, in jener Nacht, jene Nacht.
One night	eines Nachts.
At midnight	um Mitternacht.
During the night, at nighttime	während der Nacht, in der Nacht, zur Nacht, nachts.
On the night of 24 March	in der Nacht zum 24. März (or: zum 25. März).
Tonight (this evening)	heute abend.
Tonight (during the night hours)	heute nacht.
Last night (yesterday evening)	gestern abend.
Last night (during the night hours)	gestern nacht.

TIME

This time	*diesmal.*
Every time	*jedesmal.*
Several times	*mehrere Male, mehrmals.*
Another time	*ein anderes Mal.*
The next time	*das nächste Mal, das nächstemal.*
For the first time	*zum ersten Mal, zum erstenmal.*
For the third time	*zum dritten Mal.*
All the time ⎱ The whole time ⎰	*die ganze Zeit.*
At that, this time (past)	*zu dieser Zeit, damals.*
At the same time (simultaneously)	*zur gleichen Zeit, gleichzeitig, in demselben Augenblick.*
At this time of year	*zu dieser Jahreszeit.*
At any time	*zu jeder Zeit, jederzeit.*
It is high time that . . .	*es ist höchste Zeit, daß . . .*
The remaining time	*die übrige Zeit.*
For a short time	*kurze Zeit, eine Zeitlang.*
For a long time	*lange, lange Zeit, seit langem.*[1]
For the time being	*vorläufig.*
In time (in the course of time)	*mit der Zeit.*
In time (e.g. arrive in time)	*rechtzeitig.*
Some time ago	*vor einiger Zeit.*
After a time	*nach einiger Zeit, nach einer Weile.*

MOMENT

At the moment	*zur Zeit.*
Just (wait) a moment!	*(Warten Sie) einen Augenblick, einen Moment!*
At the right moment	*im richtigen Augenblick.*
In a moment's time	*nach einem Augenblick, sogleich.*
In the next moment	*im nächsten Augenblick.*

[1] e.g. We have been in Germany for a long time. *Wir sind seit langem (schon lange) in Deutschland.*

Topic 4. 'Town' Vocabulary

USE AND OMISSION OF THE ARTICLE
EXPRESSIONS OF TIME

Berlin's Kurfürstendamm[1]

Der Kurfürstendamm, wohl die bekannteste von allen Straßen Westberlins, besitzt eine eigene Note[2] und einen eigenen Reiz. Da blickt man von einem Etagenrestaurant wie von einem

Luxusdampfer auf den Verkehrsstrom hinunter. Tag und Nacht strömt der Verkehr zwischen Gedächtniskirche und Halensee[3] den Kurfürstendamm herauf und herunter. Vorbei an den erlesenen Geschäften mit den verlockendsten Schaufenstern, vorbei an den Premieren-Kinos[4] and Theatern, auf deren Bühnen bekannte Stars stehen, vorbei an den Bierrestaurants, Schlemmerlokalen und Vorgarten-Cafés, in denen man wie auf einer Kurpromenade[5] sitzt, vorbei an den Reisebüros, Modesalons und Bücherläden, die nicht weniger internationale Würze haben als die Menschen selbst, die den emsigen Strom bilden. Ob vormittags als Geschäftsstraße, nachmittags als Korso[6] und abends als neonüberflammter Boulevard, immer wirkt[7] der Kurfürstendamm hoffnungsvoll und wird, obwohl er kaum Schlaf kennt, nicht müde zu lächeln.

[1] *der Kurfürstendamm*—lit. Elector's Causeway—but keep the name in its German form.   [2] *eine eigene Note*—a style all its own.   [3] *die Gedächtniskirche*—Memorial Church. A famous church on the Kurfürstendamm. *Halensee* —a lake near Berlin.   [4] *die Premiere*—first night of a play or film. [5] *Kurpromenade* : cf. *der Kurort*—spa.   [6] From Italian *corso* (a street of fashion and elegance). Use *corso* in translation.   [7] *wirken*—to create an impression, effect.

The Medieval City of Nuremberg today

Wer mit dem Zug in Nürnberg ankommt und auf den weiten Bahnhofsplatz hinaustritt, wird von zwei Eindrücken deutlich berührt: vom regen Leben, das hier vorbeipulst, und vom Anblick eines noch mittelalterlich wirkenden Stadtbildes.[1] Auffällig steht dem Ankommenden der große, runde Turm im Blickfeld,[2] von denen Nürnberg vier als weltbekannte Wahrzeichen[3] besitzt, die zu den starken und weitgehend erhaltenen Befestigungsanlagen gehören, die mit einer Ausdehnung von etwa vier Kilometern den historischen Stadtkern Nürnbergs umschließen und sich im Norden mit der Burg zu einer erhabenen Symphonie aus Stein und Kraft steigern. Dieser wuchtige Rundturm markiert einen Haupteingang zur Innenstadt. Man ist überrascht, sich dort plötzlich auf dem überaus lebhaften „Boulevard" Nürnbergs zu befinden. Moderne Geschäftshäuser, Cafés und andere Vergnügungsstätten prägen hier das Bild.[4]

[1] *Stadtbild*—tr. 'town'.   [2] *dem Ankommenden im Blickfeld*—lit. 'in the newcomer's field of vision'.   [3] *als weltbekannte Wahrzeichen*. Recast this sentence to avoid a stilted translation.   [4] *prägen hier das Bild*—'dominate the scene here' (lit. 'set their stamp on the scene here').

Extracts from travel brochures (adapted)
(Bund Deutscher Verkehrsverbände, e.V.)

A Visit to the Old Town

Mr. Meier was surprised to find[1] his old home town so well pre-
served. He had arrived in Neuburg by train the day before[2] and
had spent the night at the Station Hotel, which he had known
well before the war. At that time he had lived in the old part of
the city and used to walk down the hill from the castle at about
nine o'clock every morning and return home for lunch about
midday. In the afternoon he would visit business friends in the
suburbs[3] and take coffee[4] at a restaurant in Beethoven Street.
This morning he climbed the hill and paid a visit to the castle;
then—since it was high time to begin[5] the business[6] for which[7] he
had come to Neuburg—he wandered along Station Road, past
the two cinemas and the theatre, the bookshops, the business
houses, the bakers', greengrocers', and chemists' shops that he
had known before, towards[8] the Red Lion Hotel. He crossed the
street at the traffic lights and pushed his way through the busy
crowds that were staring in the windows of the big stores,[9]
and eventually reached his objective, which lay beyond the stone
railway bridge. At this time of year the chestnut trees were in
bloom outside the old building. Mr. Meier was pleased; in spite
of everything that[10] had happened, he had at last been able[11] to
make this visit. 'I shall spend the rest of the time here,' he
thought to himself.[12]

[1] 'find' in this context: *vorfinden*.   [2] Time—Manner—Place.   [3] suburb—
der Vorort.   [4] 'drink a cup of coffee'.   [5] Use: *beginnen mit*.   [6] *die Geschäfte*
(plur.).   [7] *um derentwillen* (see Topic 3, 2, p. 17).   [8] Use the noun *Richtung*
like a preposition; e.g. *der Zug fährt Richtung Köln*.   [9] *Warenhäuser*.   [10] *was*
(see note 7, p. 24, and note on *trotz*, p. 21).   [11] Use imperfect in German
in this context.   [12] *dachte er bei sich*.

1. Charles lived at No. 10 Maximilian St., in the old town
   centre.
2. The shops, theatres, and cinemas remained closed throughout
   the week; only the travel agency in the main shopping street[1]
   was open.
3. The older railway stations rarely create a beautiful impression
   as part of a city's architecture.[2]
4. Did you see young Werner over there? He is working as a
   waiter in this restaurant.
5. Last night a car with a British number-plate was standing in
   the station square.
6. They could meet each other for dinner at any time, but they
   always preferred Fridays.

7. The day after tomorrow we shall be hearing the President's speech from Berlin.

8. Is Johann's cousin going to the Westerwald or to Switzerland this year?

¹ Compound of *Haupt-*   ² Use *Stadtbild* to translate 'city's architecture'.

ESSAY

In der Großstadt.
Die zerstörte Stadt.
Ein Kind verirrt sich in der Geschäftsstraße. Berichten Sie über seine Erlebnisse.
Englische und ausländische Städte: ein Vergleich.

DISCUSSION

Was fehlt unserer Stadt (unserem Dorf, unserem Vorort)?
Wie möchten Sie London (Manchester, Liverpool usw.) umbauen lassen?

Topic 5

The Form of the Subjunctive: Revision
Conditional

1. The form of the subjunctive

Verbs in the subjunctive mood are conjugated in the present and the imperfect:

	Strong verbs				Weak verbs	
ich	*gehe*	*ginge*	*täte*[1]	*mache*	*machte*	*dächte*[2]
du	*gehest*	*gingest*	*tätest*	*machest*	*machtest*	*dächtest*[2]
er/sie/es	*gehe*	*ginge*	*täte*	*mache*	*machte*	*dächte*
wir	*gehen*	*gingen*	*täten*	*machen*	*machten*	*dächten*
ihr	*gehet*	*ginget*	*tätet*	*machet*	*machtet*	*dächtet*
sie/Sie	*gehen*	*gingen*	*täten*	*machen*	*machten*	*dächten*

[1] The imperfect subjunctive of strong verbs whose imperfect indicative forms have the vowels *-a-*, *-o-*, or *-u-* adds umlaut. [2] The rule for the imperfect subjunctive of mixed verbs and modal verbs is as follows: *bringen, denken, wissen* add umlaut to the indicative, as in 1 above; *brennen, kennen, nennen, rennen* become *brennte, kennte, nennte, rennte*; *senden* and *wenden* become *sendete, wendete*; and those modal verbs which have the umlaut in the infinitive keep it in the imperfect subjunctive (i.e. *dürfte, könnte, möchte, müßte.* But: *sollte, wollte*).

N.B. Certain strong verbs have an alternative form for the imperfect subjunctive: *hälfe* and *hülfe*; *stärbe* and *stürbe*; *verdärbe* and *verdürbe*; *wärbe* and *würbe*; *wärfe* and *würfe*; *gälte* and *gölte*; *schwämme* and *schwömme*; *stände* and *stünde*. Of these, only *stünde* is occasionally found nowadays.

2. Conditional

(i) *Mood*

The verb in the *wenn*-clause is expressed in the indicative or the subjunctive according to the sense of the statement. (Cf. in English: *if I am* and *if I were*.)

With verbs in the *Present* and the *Perfect*, the *Indicative* is used.
     ,,   ,,   *Imperfect* and the *Pluperfect*, the *Subjunctive* is used.

German and English tense usage in conditional statements are identical. Thus:

Wenn er das tut, ...	If he does that ...
Wenn er das getan hat, ...	If he has done that ...
Wenn er das täte, ...	If he did (were to do) that ...
Wenn er das getan hätte, ...	If he had done (were to have done) that ...

The verb of the main clause keeps the same *mood* as the subordinate clause:

Wenn er das tut, kommt er nicht mit.
Wenn er das getan hat, kommt er nicht mit.
Wenn er das täte, käme er nicht mit.
Wenn er das getan hätte, wäre er nicht mitgekommen.

(ii) *Use and avoidance of* würde + *infinitive in conditional statements*

Main Clause

würde + infinitive is frequently and increasingly used in modern German in preference to the (formerly more common) imperfect subjunctive in order to express the conditional mood of the verb in the main clause. However, *hätte* and *wäre, täte, dürfte, könnte, möchte, müßte, sollte* and *wollte* are nearly always preferable to *würde* . . . *haben, würde* . . . *sein,* &c. Similarly, in the perfect conditional, *hätte* . . . *gesehen, wäre* . . . *gekommen,* &c., are the normal usages.

würde + infinitive is generally used for *weak verbs* in the main clause, in order to distinguish them from their indicatives, i.e. *ich würde arbeiten, du würdest lachen,* &c., although choice language sometimes prefers the imperfect subjunctive of the weak verb where context clearly shows the conditional sense.

würde + infinitive also has the advantages: (*a*) that where a future sense is strongly felt, or where a 'future in the past' occurs, *würde* suggests the future auxiliary *wird* (see Grammar Section, 51).

Würdest du morgen reiten, wenn du könntest? rather than *Rittest du morgen, wenn du könntest?*
Ich wußte nicht, was er tun würde;

and (*b*) that it enables a speaker to avoid imperfect subjunctives which sound like other forms of the verbs, e.g. *er würde sprechen* rather than *er spräche; sie würden lesen* rather than *sie läsen; wir würden helfen* rather than *wir hälfen,* &c.

As an alternative to *würde* + infinitive, *könnte* or *möchte* +
infinitive may sometimes be used:

> *Wenn er deutsch spräche (sprechen würde), könnte (würde) ihn
> niemand verstehen.*
>
> *Möchtest (würdest) du morgen reiten, wenn du könntest?*

Subordinate Clause

In the subordinate clause (the *wenn*-clause), *strong verbs* and
modal verbs in imperfect hypothetical contexts (cf. *If he went . . .,
If you ran . . ., if she would like . . ., if I were allowed to . . .*) are
mainly expressed in the imperfect subjunctive form; and *weak
verbs* mainly in the form *würde* + infinitive: *wenn ich ginge*, but
wenn ich lachen würde. But here, too, strong verbs may be found
(especially in colloquial language) in the infinitive with *würde*;
and weak verbs (more especially in literary language) in the
imperfect subjunctive: *wenn er dich einladen würde (einlüde), . . .;
wenn er meinem Rat folgte (folgen würde), . . .*

As in the main clause, a modal verb (in this case *sollte*) +
infinitive may take the place of the imperfect subjunctive:

> *Wenn er dich einladen sollte, würdest du hingehen?* (*gingest du
> hin?*)

This is one means whereby an ugly doubling of the word *würde*
may be avoided.

It is also desirable to avoid, as far as possible, the tedious
repetition of the same vowel of imperfect subjunctive verbs:
Wenn er . . . käme . . . bäte . . . nähme . . . begänne . . ., &c.

(iii) *Alternative word-order*

An alternative word-order for conditional ideas is frequently
found (cf. *Had I . . ., were I . . .* in English):

> *Hätte ich die Zeit, so ginge ich heute ins Kino. Hätte ich die Zeit
> gehabt, so wäre ich heute ins Kino gegangen.*
>
> *Glaubte ich das, so würde ich ihm nicht helfen. Hätte ich das
> geglaubt, so hätte ich ihm nicht geholfen.*

This usage extends to all verbs, including modals. It is not
restricted to *haben* and *sein*.

Hätte ich . . . is more emphatic than *Wenn ich . . . hätte*, and
should be preferred where the *if*-clause is to be particularly
emphasized. An even more stressed form is: *Hätte ich doch . . .*
Oh, if only I had . . .

Topic 5. If things were different . . .

CONDITIONAL STATEMENTS

If only there were no Homework !

Wenn es keine Hausaufgaben gäbe — hätte man immer frei und brauchte gar nicht an die Schule zu denken, den ganzen übrigen Tag nicht mehr.[1] Seine Schulmappe würde man in die Ecke werfen und alle dummen Gedanken an die Schule dazu, und der ganze Nachmittag würde einem allein gehören wie in den Ferien. Am anderen Tag würde man viel besser aufpassen, und man würde es verstehen, daß Schule eben Schule sein muß. Und frischer und ausgeruhter würde man obendrein sein. Das sollten die Lehrer wissen — dann gäbe es viel bessere Zeugnisse, ja sogar gute Zeugnisse. Warum kommen sie einfach nicht auf diesen Gedanken? „Aber die Lehrer verstehen eben gar nichts von uns Schülern!"

Nehmen wir einmal an,[2] wir haben alle zusammen recht. Nichts verstehen die Lehrer und geben nur Hausaufgaben auf, weil sie einfach nicht zusehen können, daß wir unsere Ruhe haben.[3] Lehrer können einfach nicht mit ansehen, daß wir Kinder nichts tun. Als ob unsere Spiele nichts Gescheites wären! Was aber würden unsere Eltern sagen? Das kennen wir Kinder doch: „Weil du schon[4] keine Hausaufgaben hast, könntest . . . könntest du . . . könntest du . . . " Es ist ein Jammer auf dieser Welt: wenn wirklich die Lehrer uns verstehen, dann hören die Eltern auf, uns zu verstehen. Am Ende kommt es auf das gleiche heraus!

[1] N.B. There is no afternoon school in most German secondary schools (except for games).   [2] Let us assume for a moment . . .   [3] *seine Ruhe haben*—to be left in peace.   [4] Omit *schon* in translation.

What would happen if . . .

Was würde passieren, wenn über Nacht alle Straßen verschwänden? Wir bekämen am Morgen keine Milch, weil der Bauer die Milch ohne Straße nicht zur Molkerei und die Molkerei sie nicht zum Milchgeschäft schaffen könnte. So wie mit der Milch würde es mit allen Lebensmitteln gehen[1] und natürlich auch mit allen anderen Dingen, die wir zum Leben brauchen. Es wäre ein ganz undenkbarer Zustand.

Wie aber sähe ein Tag aus, wenn wir zwar[2] alle Arten von

Straßen und Verkehrswegen[3] hätten, über Nacht aber alle Verkehrsmittel, alle Autos, Lastwagen, Eisenbahnen, Schiffe und Flugzeuge verschwinden würden?[4] Das wäre wohl mindestens ebenso schlimm und undenkbar, denn dann würden wir unsere Milch auch nicht bekommen,[5] weil es ja kein Milchauto mehr gäbe. Ihr würdet zu spät in die Schule kommen,[6] weil plötzlich euer Fahrrad nicht mehr da wäre; die Väter kämen zu spät ins Büro, weil keine Straßenbahn, kein Zug und kein Auto sie dorthin bringen könnte. Das ganze Leben wäre plötzlich in Unordnung. Wir können uns heute eben ein Leben ohne die verschiedenen Verkehrswege und ohne die Verkehrsmittel Auto, Eisenbahn, Fahrrad, Schiff und Flugzeug nicht mehr vorstellen.

[1] Or: *ginge es* . . .   [2] *zwar* . . . *aber*—although (lit. indeed . . . but).   [3] *Verkehrswege*—transport routes.   [4,5,6] The author is careful to avoid a series of -*ä*- sounds by alternating between *würde* + infinitive and imperfect subjunctive.

Wunderbare Welt.

An Ideal State?[1]

What do you think of[2] the idea of a 'golden age',[3] when all human beings would live together without the dangers and temptations of civilization? How would it be if our complicated way of life[4] were to disappear?—If we could return to a natural state?

Since the eighteenth century many people have toyed with this thought. What would happen—so they have asked themselves— if one were to abolish,[5] for example, all means of transport, all factories, all cities, indeed[6] all governments? Would it then be possible to banish war[7] from the world? Would human beings[7] live peacefully and naturally together? Would we not then be like the inhabitants of the South Sea Islands;[8] laughing, friendly, peace-loving[9] people, who would bake their own bread, make their own clothes, and lead simple, innocent lives?[10]

Those who have thought in this way have often forgotten how much we owe to[11] our civilization. What would happen if our means of transport no longer existed? Or if the hospitals and doctors were suddenly no longer available? How could we travel? How could we keep ourselves fit? How could we visit friends if there were no railways, no buses, and no aeroplanes? How would one prevent disease?[12] What would one do[13] with one's leisure time[14] if one were suddenly to have the whole day free? Who would protect the population if we had got rid of the police?

We can hardly imagine such a condition; for we are[15] civilized

and cannot return to a 'simple' life. And when we think carefully
about it,[16] we have no desire to do so.[17]

[1] state—(in the meaning 'condition') *der Zustand.* [2] *halten von.* [3] age—
das Zeitalter. [4] *die Lebensweise.* [5] *abschaffen* (weak vb.). [6] indeed—
(here) *ja.* [7] Include definite article. [8] inhabitants of the South Sea
Islands—*die Südseeinsulaner.* [9] *friedliebend.* [10] Singular. [11] *verdanken*
(with dat. and no preposition). [12] Plural. [13] Use *anfangen.* [14] *die
Freizeit.* [15] Include *eben.* Cf. the usage of *eben* in the German–English passages of this Topic. [16] to think carefully about s.th.—*etwas genau betrachten.*
[17] Include *auch* ('either') in the sentence.

1. If I had the afternoon off I should go to the bookshops.
2. If it were not so I would have told you.
3. I'm sure you would get better reports if you went to a different school.
4. Had I been in his place[1] I should have hated all[2] that muddle.
5. No one would understand him if he spoke French.
6. She could have got the milk if the dairy had remained open.
7. If it had stopped raining sooner we should have played tennis.
8. If I am right I will let you know in a day or two.

[1] *an seiner Stelle.* [2] *ganz* (adj.).

ESSAY

Wenn ich meine Zeit zum zweitenmal hätte . . .
Was wäre anders geworden, wenn man nicht Maschinen erfunden
hätte?
Stellen Sie sich vor, Sie wären der einzige Mensch auf einer Insel
im Pazifik. Wie würden Sie sich am Leben halten?
Schreiben Sie einen Aufsatz, der mit folgenden Worten beginnt:
Wäre ich an jenem Tage die andere Straße gegangen, . . .

DISCUSSION

Wie wäre es, wenn Sie abends keine Hausaufgaben hätten?
Wie würden Sie tausend Pfund, die Sie gewonnen haben, ver-
wenden?

GRAMMAR WORK

Collect from your own reading further examples of conditional
statements. Observe carefully in what clauses *würde* + infinitive
or imperfect subjunctive are used.

Topic 6

The Subjunctive of Indirect Speech
The Subjunctive of Wish

1. The subjunctive of indirect speech

(i) Statements and questions in indirect speech require a verb in the subjunctive. The English rules of tense sequence (e.g. Indirect: He said that he *was* tired, corresponding to Direct: 'I am tired') do not, however, apply in German. The corresponding tenses of direct and indirect speech in German, *provided the subjunctive form is different from the indicative*, are as follows:

Direct	*Indirect*
1. Present	Present (colloquially, often Imperfect)
2. Imperfect	Perfect (colloquially, often Pluperfect)
3. Perfect	Perfect (colloquially, often Pluperfect)
4. Pluperfect	Perfect (colloquially, often Pluperfect)
5. Future	Future (colloquially, often Conditional)
6. Future Perfect	Future Perfect (colloquially, often Conditional Perfect)

Thus (numbers refer to tenses above):

1. *Ich bin müde.*   *Er sagte, er sei (wäre) müde.*
2. *Sie sang im Chor mit.*   *Man sagte, sie habe (hätte) im Chor mitgesungen.*
3. *Hat er mich gesehen?*   *Sie fragte, ob er sie gesehen habe (hätte).*
4. *Ich hatte alles gekauft.*   *Er sagte, er habe (hätte) alles gekauft.*
5. *Wird er das verstehen?*   *Sie fragte, ob er das verstehen werde (würde).*
6. *Er wird den Zug erreicht haben.*   *Man sagte, er werde (würde) den Zug erreicht haben.*

(ii) It is important that the subjunctive of indirect speech should, as far as possible, be seen and heard as such. Hence such subjunctives as *daß ich fahre, daß ich suche, daß wir haben, daß sie werden,* **which are identical with their indicative forms,** are replaced by the **imperfects:** *daß ich führe, daß ich suchte* (or *suchen würde*), *daß wir hätten, daß sie würden.* Thus:

Direct	*Indirect*
Wir haben ihn nicht gesucht.	*Wir sagten, wir hätten ihn nicht gesucht.*
Fahren Sie jedes Jahr in die Berge?	*Man fragte, ob ich jedes Jahr in die Berge führe.*
Sie arbeiten tüchtig.	*Er sagte, ich arbeitete tüchtig.*

N.B. Imperfect subjunctives of weak verbs have the same form as their imperfect indicatives (see p. 34). The context of indirect speech usually makes it clear that the subjunctive mood is intended.

It is considered good style in German to avoid the use of *daß* in indirect speech as far as possible.

There are 'borderline' situations where the factual content of what is written or said is felt to carry more weight than the need to represent the statement or question as indirect. Here, the indicative usage is preferred, and the notion of *fact* is usually introduced by the use of *daß*:

Ich sagte ihm, daß ich krank war.
Der Detektiv berichtete, daß er das gestohlene Geld gefunden hatte.

(iii) Other verbs of saying and asking, e.g. *behaupten* (assert, maintain), *erklären* (declare, explain), *sich erkundigen* (inquire), &c. are followed by the subjunctive where a fact, opinion, or question is to be understood as merely reported by the writer or speaker, whether referring to another person's utterance or to his own. The same applies to such verbs as *denken, meinen, glauben* where the situation is genuinely one of indirect speech. Compare the following:

Er meint, ich dürfe nicht länger bleiben   and
Ich meine, ich darf nicht länger bleiben.

Er behauptet, der neue Sportwagen könne nicht übertroffen werden.
He maintains that the new sports car cannot be excelled; and

Ich behaupte, der neue Sportwagen kann nicht übertroffen werden.

Sie möchte wissen, ob ihr Deutsch verständlich sei   and
Ich möchte wissen, ob mein Deutsch verständlich ist.

In colloquial usage, however, indicatives frequently take the place of indirect speech subjunctives.

2. The subjunctive of wish

The following usages should be noted:

(i) *Der Herr segne dich und behüte dich.* The Lord bless you and
    keep you.
    Es lebe der König! Long live the king!
    Es komme, was wolle, ich bleibe dabei. Come what may, I shall
    hold to this (see Grammar Section, 118, note 1).
    Nun, so sei es! Let it be so then!

(ii) *Nehmen wir an, er hat recht.* Let us assume he is right.
     Gehen wir hin! Let's go there!
     Machen wir jetzt Schluß. Let's finish off now.

Topic 6. Danger and Crime

THE SUBJUNCTIVE OF INDIRECT SPEECH
THE SUBJUNCTIVE OF WISH

A Baby is found¹

Bei der Erkundung² in etlichen Häusern am Eingang des Dorfes,
zu denen, wie sie bemerkt, keine der andern beiden Gruppen
hingegangen sei, hätten sie aus einiger Entfernung etwas gehört,
was sie zunächst für das Jammern einer Katze gehalten, dann
aber als das Schreien eines Kindes erkannt hätten. Daß sie's
überhaupt gehört, hätten sie nur dem eigentümlichen Umstand
zu verdanken gehabt, daß die Tür eines Hauses weit offen gestanden hätte, die der Kammern zu beiden Seiten der Vorstube
aber geschlossen gewesen wären. Geraume Zeit³ hätten sie
abwartend vor dem Hause verbracht, bis ihnen zur Gewißheit
geworden sei, daß tatsächlich in einer der Kammern ein Kind
schrie. Und alle Vorsichtsmaßnahmen zu beschreiben, unter
denen sie sich schließlich Eintritt in dem Haus verschafft hätten,⁴
reiche die Zeit einfach nicht aus. Sanavuori erwähnte nur, daß
er auf Suukselainens Rat den Hackklotz, der vor dem Hause
gestanden, mit einer Stange tiefer und tiefer in den Hausflur
geschoben hätte, um sicher zu gehen, daß nicht der Fußboden
vermint⁵ sei. Bei dem Gerumpel⁶ in seiner Nähe aber habe das
Kind nur noch lauter zu schreien begonnen. Als sie zu guter
Letzt sich bis ins Haus selber vorgewagt, hätten sie die ganze
Ärmlichkeit⁷ in wilder Unordnung, wie nach einem überstürzten
Aufbruch⁸ der einstigen Bewohner, vorgefunden. Im Lichtkegel

der Taschenlampe aber habe sich auch ein kleines Bett gezeigt, in welchem das Kind gelegen und laut geschrien habe.

EDZARD SCHAPER: *Das Christkind aus den großen Wäldern*
(abridged extract)

[1] Two Finnish soldiers are reporting to their comrades how they had found a baby abandoned in a village. The action of the story takes place in the last war. [2] *Erkundung*—reconnaissance. [3] 'For some time.' [4] *sich Eintritt verschaffen*—to gain access. [5] *vermint*—mined. [6] *das Gerümpel*—din. [7] *die ganze Ärmlichkeit*—'this scene of poverty'. [8] *ein überstürzter Aufbruch*—a hurried departure.

A Report on a Crime[1]

„Wie?" fragte er zerstreut, „noch einmal!"

Der Pfarrer von Kegel, antwortete Bexelius, habe die drei, nachdem sie von ihm gezogen seien, nicht wiedergesehen, doch habe er von ihnen vernommen, daß sie nach einer Schiffsgelegenheit, heimzukommen, aus gewesen seien,[2] und er habe ihnen bedeutet, an der Küste vor ihnen könnten sie um diese Jahreszeit wohl noch auf eine Gelegenheit hoffen. Er habe ihnen auch, um ihnen ein wenig beizustehen, erklärt, wie die Gegend beschaffen[3] sei und wo sie auf Hilfe und ein wenig Wegzehrung[4] rechnen könnten. Und dies — wiewohl Christenpflicht der Pfarrherrn — habe das Unglück wohl begünstigt. Die Spur der drei tauche erst wieder in Drostenholm auf, einem einsam gelegenen Waldgut im Hapsal'schen Kreis,[5] wo außer der Herrschaft und ihrer alten Bedienung[6] niemand mehr hause und wo man am St.-Martins-Tag alle Bewohner des Herrenhauses auf das grausamste erschlagen[7] und das ganze Haus geplündert vorgefunden habe. Die Übeltäter hätten sich als Martinsbettler[8] verkleidet Eintritt zu verschaffen gewußt. Dazu[9] hätten sie noch eine seetüchtige Schaluppe des Hofes entwendet und seien mit der nach verübter Missetat[10] davongefahren.   EDZARD SCHAPER: *Der Gouverneur* (adapted)

[1] The passage concerns an investigation into a crime committed by three soldiers of the Swedish army occupying Esthonia. The year is 1709. The three men had inquired of a padre how they might best pursue their journey. [2] *daß sie . . . aus gewesen seien*—that they had been looking for the chance of getting aboard some ship or other, in order to get home. [3] Cf. *die Gegend ist so beschaffen*—the area is like that, such is the character of the area. [4] *Wegzehrung*—food for the journey. [5] the district of Hapsal. [6] *die Herrschaft* and *die Bedienung*—the master and mistress of the house; and the servants. [7] *auf das grausamste erschlagen*—most brutally murdered. [8] 'St. Martin's beggars' (a local custom whereby alms might be begged on St. Martin's Day. This custom is still kept up, particularly in the Rhineland, for the sake of children). [9] *dazu . . . noch*—furthermore, in addition. [10] *nach verübter Missetat*—after committing the deed.

Too late !

One night in March the police in[1] the village of Rittershausen received a strange telephone call. They were simply informed[2] that they could capture[3] a well-known criminal at once if they cared to.[4] There was not sufficient time, so the caller[5] explained, to give all the details. He mentioned only the name of the lawbreaker and a manor-house near by, where, so[6] he asserted, a robbery was being committed at that moment. The police would need to make haste, the voice continued, for although the owners were not in that evening and the thief could therefore reckon on a good haul,[7] he was intending to get away quickly and would probably use a car.

To their question, who was speaking,[8] the police had received no reply.

The following day the police reported that they had made an entry into the manor-house. They had found several rooms in utter disorder, the report declared, but no trace had been found of the thief. They also reported that one of the two groups of policemen who had gone to the house had heard the noise[9] of a car engine when still some distance away. It was possible, so the report ended,[10] that it had been the car in which the thief had driven away.

In the village, they say it was the thief himself who rang up the police. But others think he was betrayed by a former accomplice.[11] Who can tell?

[1] Say: 'of the village (of) Rittershausen'.   [2] Translate in the active with *man*.   [3] *gefangennehmen*.   [4] to care to do s.th.—*Lust zu etwas haben*.   [5] *der Sprecher*.   [6] *so* or *wie*; but take care with the word-order.   [7] *die Beute*. Omit article.   [8] Use: *am Apparat sein*.   [9] *das Geräusch*.   [10] *schließen*.   [11] *der Komplize* (weak masculine: see Topic 11, pp. 72–73).

1. He asked me whether I could recognize the ship.
2. They said that the child had only cried all the louder when they had looked at it.
3. On the outskirts of the village we met a man who inquired whether a doctor lived near by.
4. I tried to explain to him what the region was like, but he did not listen to me.
5. Come what may, we shall stay here and not venture any farther.
6. The parson asked me whether the thieves had been disguised. I said I did not know.
7. Let us hope for better weather tomorrow.
8. We asked whom we had to thank for this unexpected gift.

ESSAY

Schreiben Sie einen Bericht über einen hitzigen Wortwechsel in der Straßenbahn, dessen Zeuge Sie waren.

Berichten Sie über den Inhalt einer Tischrede.[1]

Die Polizei erklärte gestern, man habe den am Sonntag ausgebrochenen Häftling[2] verhaftet . . .[3] — Setzen Sie den Bericht in der indirekten Rede fort.

Setzen Sie den Ausschnitt aus der Erzählung „Das Christkind aus den großen Wäldern" fort. (NB: Indirekte Rede beibehalten![4])

[1] *die Tischrede*—after-dinner speech.   [2] *der Häftling*—prisoner, convict.
[3] *verhaften*—arrest.   [4] keep.

DISCUSSION

Ein Klassenkamerad hat irgendein Verbrechen begangen. Er tüftelt mit einem Freund irgendeine Geschichte aus,[1] um ein Alibi aufzustellen. Die Klasse versucht durch Befragen zu beweisen, daß die Geschichte nicht stimmt.[2] Vorsicht beim Gebrauch der indirekten Rede!

Ein Deutscher (oder eine Deutsche) besucht Ihre Schule. Später haben Sie Gelegenheit, seine (ihre) Bemerkungen darüber zu hören. Erzählen Sie, wie *er* (*sie*) die Dinge bei Ihnen sieht.

[1] 'cooks up some tale or other'.   [2] 'does not tie up'.

Topic 7

Compound Nouns

(i) Compound Nouns occur very frequently in German. They usually consist of two nouns, an adjective and noun, an adverb and noun, or a verb stem and noun. Almost any compounds of nouns may be made up provided the elements constitute a single logical idea, but it is important to observe certain main traditions affecting the *form* of the first element (see below). Both true compounds and hyphenated compounds are found. See section (iii) below for notes on the use of the hyphenated compound.

(ii) The adaptability of the language in forming new compounds is evident from any rapid survey of news items in the German press: *Verkehrssicherheit*—road safety, *Regierungskurs*—government 'line', policy, *Preisüberwachung*—price control, *Bundesregierung*, *Bundeskanzler* (and scores of compounds of *Bundes-* —Federal), *Informationschef*, &c.

(iii) Compound nouns are hyphenated where there is felt to be some reason for keeping the elements separate. The hyphenated compound is formed, for example, (*a*) to avoid the threefold repetition of the same vowel: *Kaffee-Ersatz*—coffee substitute, *Tee-Ernte*—tea crop; (*b*) usually where the first element is a proper noun: *Churchill-Memoiren*, *Mercedes-Werk*. But note: *Lutherzeit*, *Goethezeit*, *Hitlerzeit*; (*c*) where the first element consists of the initials of some institution, firm, &c.: *UN-Generalsekretär*, *VW-Werk*; (*d*) to break up an otherwise excessively long compound: *Bundes-Fernverkehrsstraßennetz*—Federal Trunk Road System.

Types of Compound Nouns

(1) First element in its nominative singular form compounded with second element (a very large group, including many compounds implying a prepositional phrase: *Giebelhaus—Haus mit einem Giebel*; *Steinfliese—Fliese aus Stein*): *Seefahrt, Obstbaum, Dachzimmer, Fußtritt, Ofenfeuer, Lastwagen*, &c.

(2) First element a masculine or neuter noun, with a genitive

implied. The first element adds -*s* or -*es*: *Handelsstadt*, *Ver-kehrsstrom*, *Geschäftsstraße*, *Bahnhofsplatz*, *Freundeskreis*—circle of friends, *Jahresschluß*, *Tagesanbruch*.

(3) First element a feminine noun with an ending (-*heit*, -*keit*, -*ion*, -*ung*, -*schaft*, -*tät*; but not -*in*, -*ie*, -*ei*); first element adds -*s*: *Freiheitskrieg*, *Heiterkeitsausbruch*—outburst of merriment, *Informationsdienst*, *Empfehlungsschreiben*, *Landschaftsmaler*, *Universitätsgebäude*; but: *Königinmutter*, *Symphoniekonzert*, *Brauereiunternehmen*—brewery undertaking.

(4) First element thought of as a plural; plural form often used: *Premierenkino*, *Bücherladen* (but: *Buchhandlung*), *Damenkleidung*, *Herrenklub*, *Händewaschen*, *Pferderennen*.

(5) Where the first element is a feminine noun without an ending, various forms are found:

(*a*) As in group (1) above: *Stadtplan*, *Eisenbahnwagen*, *Ruhepause*. (But some feminine nouns add -*s*: *Liebesbrief*, *Liebeserklärung*, *Arbeitspause*, *Arbeitsschluß*.)

(*b*) Where a genitive or plural is implied, the feminine noun ending in -*e* usually adds -*n*: *Sonnenaufgang*, *Freudenruf*, *Kirchenlied*, *Lampenschirm*—lampshade, *Küchengerät*, *Düsenantrieb*—jet propulsion, *Wiesenweg*, *Kartenspiel*.

(*c*) Certain feminine nouns ending in -*e* drop this -*e* in compounds: *Schulgebäude*, *Schulfunk*—radio for schools, *Grenzbehörde*—frontier authorities (sing.), *Grenzpolizei*, *Wollhandschuhe*, *Wollstrümpfe* (woollen . . .), *Kirchturm*, *Kirchhof*.

(6) Weak masculine and masculine adjectival nouns (e.g. *der Knabe*, *ein Knabe*, and *der Arme*, *ein Armer*; see Topic 11, pp. 71–73) add the -*n* in compounds: *Ochsenwagen*, *Knabengymnasium*; *Fremdenheim*—guest house, *Armenheim*—home for the poor.

Mixed declension masculine nouns (e.g. *der Wille*, *des Willens*, *der Friede*, *des Friedens*, *der Name*, *des Namens*) in compounds implying a genitive add their genitive singular ending -*ens*: *Willensakt*, *Friedenskonferenz*, *Namenstag*. But where a plural is implied, the plural form is used: *Gedankengang*—train of thought.

(7) First element an adjective or adverb; no addition normally (i.e. the adjective remains uninflected). In most compounds of this type, the adjective is monosyllabic: *Frühjahr*, *Rundturm*, *Heißhunger*; *Wiederbelebung*—resuscitation, *Zusammenarbeit*—co-operation, *Außenpolitik*—foreign policy.

(8) First element a verb; only the verbal stem is used (not the whole infinitive): *Schwimmgelegenheit*—facilities for swimming, *Sehkraft*—power of sight, *Waschmaschine, Fernsehapparat, Prüfgerät*—testing device, *Sendepause* (note the form)—interval (between broadcasts).

N.B. The use of the hyphen in such forms as the following should be specially noted:

Wasch- und Nähmaschinen—washing and sewing-machines.

Musikfreunde und -kritiker—music lovers and (music) critics.

Where the first element of a compound noun ends with a double consonant which is the same as the initial letter of the second element, one of the three consonants is dropped, or in some cases, the compound is hyphenated: *Schiffahrt*—shipping; *Fußball-Länderspiel*—football international. However, where the second letter of the second element is a *consonant*, e.g. *Flamme, Plakat*, and not a vowel as in *Fahrt*, all three consonants appear in the compound: *Auspuffflamme*—exhaust flame, *Pappplakat*—cardboard placard.

Topic 7. Radio and Television

COMPOUND NOUNS

Evening Programme

Hier ist der Westdeutsche Rundfunk, Sender Köln. Guten Abend, verehrte Hörer. Zuerst die Zeitangabe: beim Gongschlag war es genau 18 Uhr 55 Minuten. Zunächst einige Hinweise auf unser heutiges Abendprogramm; anschließend hören Sie Nachrichten und Wettervorhersage.

Von 19.15 Uhr bis 19.50 Uhr bringen wir ein Konzert mit Werken von Mozart und Haydn. Es spielt das Kölner Rundfunk-Sinfonie-Orchester, unter der Leitung von Michael Gielen.

Dann folgen unsere Sportmeldungen, u. a.[1] der Bericht unseres Sportkorrespondenten über das Handball-Länderspiel Deutschland gegen die Tschechoslowakei.

Um 20.30 Uhr hören Sie „Das politische Forum": eine Diskussion zwischen Mitgliedern mehrerer politischer Parteien.

Den Nachrichten- und Wetterdienst bringen wir wieder um 21.00 Uhr. Danach legen wir eine kurze Sendepause ein.

Von 21.30 Uhr bis 22.50 Uhr spielt das Kölner Tanz- und Unterhaltungsorchester in der Sendereihe „Von Melodie zu Melodie". Dieser Sendung schließt sich auch der Südwestfunk an.

Wir wünschen allen Hörern eine angenehme Unterhaltung.

Radio Notes

Frankfurt eröffnet seine neue Hörspielreihe „Deutsche Funkregisseure" mit der von Wolfgang Schadewaldt übertragenen[2] und bearbeiteten Tragödie „König Oedipus" von Sophokles in der Regie von Christian Böhme Mo. 20 Uhr. In einer Aufnahme von den diesjährigen Maifestspielen Wiesbaden[3] sendet Frankfurt die Oper von Modest Mussorgski „Boris Godunow" in einer Aufführung der Belgrader Staatsoper Fr. 20 Uhr. Der NDR sendet im Hamburger Sinfoniekonzert Mo. 20 Uhr Beethovens Neunte Sinfonie in einer Übertragung[4] aus Kiel unter Hans Schmidt-Isserstedt. Das Hörspiel bringt Do. 20.20 Uhr „Der Spieler" nach Dostojewski,[5] bearbeitet von Fred v. Hoerschelmann in der Regie Gerd Westphals, den Alexei spricht Heinz Reinke. Das Hamburger Nachtprogramm behandelt Fr. 22.10 Uhr Jules Romains' Romanzyklus[6] „Die Menschen guten Willens".

Funknotizen (*Rheinischer Merkur*)

[1] *u. a.*: *unter anderem* (*und andere*)—including; amongst other things (and others). [2] *übertragen*—(here) translated. [3] Wiesbaden May Festival. [4] *Übertragung*—(here) broadcast. [5] *nach Dostojewski*—based on Dostoevsky. [6] Jules Romains' cycle of novels.

Commercials on British TV

Immer wenn die Liebesgeschichte ihrem Höhepunkt entgegengeht oder der findige Detektiv mit einem Stirnrunzeln ankündigt, daß er soeben den Schlüssel zu seinem besonders schwierigen Fall gefunden hat, wird ausgeblendet.[1] Liebespaar und Detektiv machen dem neuesten Hit auf dem Margarinemarkt oder einem glücklich machenden Eau de Cologne Platz.[2] Der britische Fernsehzuschauer muß sich ein paar Minuten gedulden, bis er am weiteren Schicksal seiner Bildschirmhelden[3] Anteil nehmen kann.[4] Bei jedem Spielfilm[5] erlebt er dieses Schauspiel[6] etwa dreimal.

Nicht alle britischen Fernsehzuschauer sind mit dieser Art der Programmgestaltung der kommerziellen ITV-Kette einverstanden. Manche schalten den Kanal gar nicht erst[7] ein und bleiben bei den zwei Programmen der staatlichen British Broadcasting Corporation (BBC), die keine Werbung macht.

Nicht nur die Fernsehwerbung ist in den Augen des Publikums fragwürdig. Eine Untersuchung des britischen Werbeverbandes[8] über die Meinung der Öffentlichkeit zur Werbung ergab, daß das Thema in seiner Wichtigkeit weit hinter dem Familienleben, der Politik, der Kindererziehung, Mode und Sport rangiert. Nur

neun Prozent halten es überhaupt für einen wichtigen Gesprächs-
stoff. Dieses knappe Zehntel allerdings hat entschiedene
Ansichten.

Von allen befragten Briten befürworten 67 Prozent die Werbung
generell, und nur 24 Prozent sind entschieden dagegen, wobei der
Anteil der Reklamefeinde[9] in den letzten drei Jahren um beinahe
die Hälfte[10] zugenommen hat. Besonders die Fernsehwerbung
fiel bei den Briten in Ungnade[11]: über 50 Prozent aller Befragten
lehnen sie ab.

GERD LÖHRER: *Die ungeliebten Spots* ([12]) (*Die Zeit*) (adapted)

[1] *ausblenden*—fade out, break off. *Es wird ausgeblendet*—the film breaks off.
[2] *Platz machen*—to make way for (+ dat. object in German).   [3] *der Bildschirm*
—screen.   [4] *Anteil nehmen an einer Sache*—to participate in s.th., follow the
fortunes of s.th.   [5] feature film.   [6] *Schauspiel*—(here) rigmarole,
farce, nonsense.   [7] See Gram. 123(*b*) and 126(*c*). Here, *gar nicht erst*—not
at all (i.e. in the first place).   [8] Advertising Association.   [9] German
frequently constructs compounds with *-feind* and *-freund*. Take care to find a
suitable English equivalent.   [10] The extent *by which* s.th. increases or de-
creases is registered in German by the use of *um*.   [11] *in Ungnade fallen*
—fall into disfavour.   [12] *der Spot*—TV ad., commercial.

Note on Radio Stations

Deutsche Rundfunksender

Folgende Liste enthält Bezeichnungen und Wellenlängen für
verschiedene Sender in der Bundesrepublik und der DDR
(Mittel- und Langwelle).

Kurzwellen- und UKW-Sender (Ultrakurzwellensender)[1] sind
in der Liste nicht aufgeführt.

Hessischer Rundfunk (Frankfurt)	506 m
Südwestfunk (Baden-Baden/Mainz)	295 m
Europa-Welle Saar (Saarbrücken)	211 m
Süddeutscher Rundfunk (Stuttgart)	522 m
Bayrischer Rundfunk (München)	187, 375 m
Deutschlandfunk (Köln)	195, 547, 1987 m
Westdeutscher Rundfunk (Köln)	189, 309 m
Norddeutscher Rundfunk (Hamburg)	
DDR-Sender	288, 383, 412 m

Stand: Juni 1977
Quelle: *Treffpunkt* (nach einem Artikel von Peter Heaney)

[1] *UKW* = VHF.

The Effect of Television

How much has television influenced our lives? It is a question which is often asked. It is probably true[1] to say that there are hardly any British families nowadays who do not possess a television set. And no doubt a fairly high proportion[2] of these families look in[3] evening by evening. What does the television public most enjoy? For many, soccer or rugby internationals, feature films or comedy programmes are perhaps the main attraction.[4] Others may prefer television plays or adaptations of novels. Others again will find most pleasure in[5] nature films or various outside broadcasts.[6] Certainly, though, few people have much time for television advertising, and many do not even bother to switch on to the commercial channel.

Television broadcasts can extend our range of ideas;[7] they can help us to understand what is happening in the world[8] or offer us a seat, so to speak, at[9] sporting events which we should otherwise not see—or simply fill up an occasional leisure hour.[10] But when one considers[11] how much time one can waste with television,[12] would it sometimes not be better to return to other forms of entertainment such as reading and conversation?

[1] 'correct'.   [2] a high proportion—*ein großer Teil*.   [3] *fernsehen* (sep. vb.) has established itself as the German equivalent of 'look in', 'view'.   [4] attraction (in this sense)—*die Attraktion*.   [5] to take pleasure in s.th.—*Freude haben an einer Sache*.   [6] *Außenaufnahmen*.   [7] *(der) Gesichtskreis*. [8] It is possible to render the phrase after 'understand' with a compound noun. [9] *bei*.   [10] to fill up a leisure hour—*eine freie Stunde ausfüllen*.   [11] consider —*bedenken* or *sich* (dat.) *überlegen* (insep.).   [12] *beim Fernsehen*.

1. Father always used to listen to early morning music[1] while he was shaving.
2. School broadcasting plays an important part[2] in the morning and the afternoon programmes.
3. A short interval was left[3] between the news broadcast and the radio play.
4. The thriller was just approaching its climax when they faded it out and the ads. began.
5. Many of my friends are keen on building radio sets,[4] but not one of them has ever tried to build a television set.
6. I did not hear the time given out before the nine o'clock news.
7. 'We are now presenting a discussion between a London[5] girls' school and a Berlin boys' school.'

8. Did you hear *Macbeth*, produced by Christian Böhme, in the series 'Great Tragedies'?

[1] *Frühmusik.*   [2] to play a part in s.th.—*eine Rolle bei etwas spielen.*   [3] See 'Evening Programme', p. 48.   [4] Use the noun *Radiobastler* (*basteln*—'to construct' in this sense).   [5] Adjectives derived from town names keep the capital letter and have the invariable ending -*er* (see also Gram. 87); e.g. *das Hamburger Nachtprogramm.*

ESSAY

Fernsehen: Segen oder Fluch?

Welche Möglichkeiten hat das Fernsehen oder das Radio noch nicht ausgenützt?

Beschreiben Sie einen Abend, den Sie beim Radiohören oder Fernsehen verbrachten.

Beschreiben Sie die Szene im Rundfunk- oder Fernsehstudio während der Aufführung eines Hörspiels bzw. eines Fernsehstücks.

DISCUSSION

Bietet das Fernsehen mehr als das Radio?

Was hören bzw. sehen wir am liebsten — und warum gerade diese Sendungen?

VOCABULARY WORK

Collect examples of different types of compound nouns from other sources (novels, newspapers, &c.).

Suggest translations for the following items from the *Fernsehen und Hörfunk* sections of a German newspaper:

Fernsehen

Programm-Vorschau.

Kennen Sie Kino?, ein Fernsehquiz für Kinogänger.

Ziehung der Lottozahlen; Anschließend: Tagesschau — Wetter.

Kurznachrichten.

Die Sportschau; u.a.: Deutsche Eisschnellauf-Meisterschaften in Inzell; Fußball-Regionalligen; Tischtennis: Bundesrepublik—China in Lübeck.

Wintersportwetter.

Aladin und die Wunderlampe — Scherenschnittfilm.

Herrschaft des Volkes im Zeitalter der Computer, drei Berichte über die parlamentarische Demokratie in drei westeuropäischen Ländern. 1.: in Deutschland: Werden wir richtig repräsentiert?

Hörfunk

Der Fall Mortain, Kriminalhörspiel.

Fußball-Länderspiel Deutschland — Polen in Hamburg, Übertragung der. 2. Halbzeit.

Das Deutschlandbild der Schweden und das Schwedenbild der Deutschen.

'Unsere Freunde — die Delphine.' Tatsachenbericht über ein merkwürdiges Säugetier.

Topic 8

Subjunctive in *als (ob)*—'as if ', 'as though'—clauses. Modal Auxiliary Verbs

1. Subjunctive in als (ob)—'as if', 'as though'—clauses

'as if ', 'as though' in German—*als* (or *als ob, als wenn*)—are usually followed by the imperfect or pluperfect subjunctive:

Der Wind blies so, als wollte er die Tür niederschmettern. The wind was blowing as if to smash the door down.

Tue so, als ob du es nicht bemerkt hättest. Pretend not to have noticed it.

After *als* with the meaning 'as if ', 'as though', the verb or auxiliary verb follows immediately as the second idea of the sentence (cf. main clause word-order). After *als ob* the usual subordinate clause word-order is used.

Modern literary style tends to prefer *als* to *als ob*, except in the expression *tun, als ob*—to pretend to—and in the exclamatory usage: e.g.

Als ob ich das nicht wüßte!

Als ob wir nicht schon die ganze Zeit mit diesem Gewackel gearbeitet hätten! (see *The Charlady*, p. 56).

Where the idea expressed in the *als (als ob)* clause is to be represented as a strong possibility, literary style often prefers the present or perfect subjunctive, whereas in spoken German the imperfect or pluperfect subjunctive is more common:

Er sah aus, als sei (wäre) er krank (als ob er krank sei (wäre)).

Sie grüßte mich, als habe (hätte) sie mich erkannt (als ob sie mich erkannt habe (hätte)). She greeted me as though she had recognized me: i.e. implying that although in fact she could not have recognized me she appeared to do so.

The present subjunctive may also be used where the verb has the same form in the imperfect indicative and subjunctive:

Er tat, als ob er ein Buch suche (suchte).

N.B. *Es war mir fast, als ob er mir das Haus hätte verkaufen wollen.* It almost seemed to me as if he would have wanted to sell me the house. The modal infinitive *must* be placed at the end of the construction (see Topic 2, p. 10).

2. Modal Auxiliary Verbs

The following less obvious usages should be known. Special attention should be paid to the meanings of imperfect and pluperfect subjunctives (*könnte* and *hätte* . . . *können*; *sollte* and *hätte* . . . *sollen*; &c.).

Dürfen

Es darf keinen dritten Weltkrieg geben. (Cf. *müssen* below.)

Können

Es kann sein. Maybe. *Sie kann schon heute ankommen.* She may even arrive today.
Er kann Französisch. He can speak French.
Man könnte fast sagen, daß . . . One might almost say that . . . (cautious statement). *Diese Frage könnte ich nicht beantworten* (conditional: 'could not', 'would not be able to').
So etwas hätte mein Freund nicht sagen können. My friend could never have said such a thing.

Mögen

Das mag wohl sein. That may well be so.
Möchtest du eine Tasse Kaffee trinken? Would you like to have a cup of coffee?
Ich hätte das Fleisch nicht essen mögen. I would not have liked to eat the meat.

Müssen

Das muß so sein. That must be so. *Das muß eine wunderschöne Stadt gewesen sein.* That must have been a wonderful city.
Du mußt nicht immer so früh aufstehen. You don't always have to get up so early (but: *Du darfst nicht immer so spät aufstehen!*).
Er müßte (or *sollte*) *das Examen bestehen.* He ought to pass the examination.
Ich hätte tüchtiger arbeiten müssen (or *sollen*). I ought to have worked harder.

Sollen

Du sollst nicht stehlen. Thou shalt not steal. (Note the implication of an outside authority in all these examples of *sollen*.)
Soll ich dich hinfahren? Shall I drive you there?
Das Treffen soll am Montag stattfinden. The meeting is (due) to take place on Monday.

Er soll zwei Meter hoch springen können. He is said (supposed) to be able to jump two metres.

Du solltest (or *müßtest*) *dir die Augen untersuchen lassen.* (See also Topic 4, p. 26, and Topic 18, p. 119.)
Er hätte mir ein so kostbares Geschenk nicht geben sollen. He ought not to have given me such an expensive present.

Wollen

Wollen wir gehen? Shall we go? (*Wollen wir hingehen?* Shall we go (there)?)
Ich wollte eben hinaus, als Hans zur Tür hereinkam. I was about to go out when Hans came in the door.

N.B. In subordinate clauses, care must be taken with the word-order of such phrases as *nicht hätte sagen können, hätte tüchtiger arbeiten müssen*:

Wenn er das nicht hätte sagen können, . . .
Obschon ich hätte tüchtiger arbeiten müssen, . . .

i.e. the modal infinitive *must* be placed at the end of the construction (see p. 53—*als ob,* and notes on word-order, Topic 2, p. 10).

Use of *vielleicht*: *vielleicht* is very commonly used in German to express, in conjunction with an indicative verb, what is expressed in English by 'may' or 'might': *Ich werde vielleicht einen kurzen Spaziergang machen.* I might take a short walk. *Ist er vielleicht den Kurfürstendamm hinuntergegangen?* Might he have walked down the Kurfürstendamm? *Ich habe es vielleicht verloren.* I may have lost it.

Where the idea of *probability,* rather than mere *possibility* (*vielleicht*) is to be expressed, *wohl* is often used: *Das wird wohl das Richtige sein.* That may (well) be the right thing to do. *Er ist wohl den Kurfürstendamm hinuntergegangen.* He may (well) have gone down the Kurfürstendamm.

Topic 8. Difficult People

REVISION OF THE SUBJUNCTIVE
REVISION OF MODAL VERBS

The Charlady

„Was soll denn das sein?" fragte Frau Hasenberger spöttisch und reichte uns einen Strohbesen dar. Er war allerdings schon etwas windschief geworden im Gebrauch. Strohbesen nehmen ja mit der Zeit etwas Verwegenes an[1] und kehren dann freilich nicht mehr ganz tadellos. Wir hatten uns bisher damit beholfen. Aber Frau Hasenberger behalf sich nicht, sie erhielt einen neuen. Sie erhielt die neuesten Putzlumpen und Fensterleder; die alten benutzten wir. Sie verlangte, daß der Stiel des Haarbesens festgemacht werde;[2] bei diesem Gewackel sei kein Arbeiten.[3] Als ob wir nicht schon die ganze Zeit mit diesem Gewackel gearbeitet hätten! Aber gut, ich machte den Stiel fest. Zum eigenen Gebrauch hätte ich ihn wahrscheinlich nur genagelt oder nachgeschraubt;[4] aber für Frau Hasenberger getraute ich mir das nicht, sondern nahm den Stiel ab, um ihn sauber zuzuschneiden und sorgfältig neu einzupassen.

Wir hatten uns das mit Frau Hasenberger eigentlich so gedacht,[5] daß sie uns Arbeit abnehmen sollte, damit wir uns in Ruhe anderen Arbeiten widmen könnten. Aber Frau Hasenberger hielt uns mit ihrer Arbeit so in Atem, daß wir zu einer eigenen gar nicht kamen.[6] Eins von uns beiden war ständig unterwegs, um drunten im Ort einzukaufen, teils für die Böden, teils für Frau Hasenberger selbst, die nicht gewohnt war, kalt zu speisen und im Kalten zu arbeiten. Zum Essen war Frau Hasenberger Bier gewohnt, nach dem Essen eine Tasse Kaffee und nach dem Kaffee eine Ruhepause, in der sie uns behaglich aus ihrem Leben erzählte ... Sie erzählte uns ihre Leiden, daß sie sehr empfindlich sei gegen Tabak und daß ihr Mann zeitlebens außer Haus gehen müsse, wenn er zu rauchen willens sei ...

Ernst Heimeran: Grundstück gesucht (abridged extract)

[1] *etwas Verwegenes*—an audacious air.   [2] Indirect speech subjunctive.
[3] *bei ... Arbeiten*—It was no good trying to work with this thing waggling all over the place; see Gram. 70.   [4] *nachschrauben*—to tighten up a screw (*die Schraube*).   [5] *Wir ... gedacht*—What we had had in mind with Frau H. was ...   [6] *zu etwas kommen*—(here) to get round to doing something.

Visitors

Bekannte hatten sich bei uns angesagt, Deutschamerikaner aus Chicago. Zuerst kam aus Rom ein Telegramm, worin die Leute uns mitteilten, sie würden in zwei Tagen bei uns sein. Dann kam aus Zürich ein Telegramm, worin sie uns ankündigten, sie würden am Morgen des folgenden Tages eintreffen. Dann kam ein Telephonanruf mit der Meldung, daß man jetzt nach unserm Haus abfahren werde. Dann — es war kurz nach zehn — erschienen sie bei uns.

Wir waren gerüstet. Meine Frau hatte zum Empfang ein vorzügliches Mittagessen geplant. Wir hatten ein Zimmer für die

Leute gerichtet; denn obwohl sie uns nicht mitgeteilt hatten, wie lange sie zu bleiben gedachten, rechneten wir mit mehreren Tagen. Wir erfuhren jedoch alsbald, daß sie noch am selben Tag weiterreisen wollten, da sie am Abend in Frankfurt sein mußten. So hatten wir denn umsonst das Zimmer gerichtet. Offenbar hatten die Leute es eilig.

Nun erzählten sie uns von ihrer Reise. Von Chicago waren sie nach Kalifornien geflogen, dann mit dem Flugzeug weiter nach Hawaii, dann mit dem Flugzeug nach Australien, dann nach Indien, dann Ägypten, dann Italien, alles auf dem Luftweg, und jetzt waren sie hier. Die Reise sollte von Frankfurt weitergehen nach Paris, von wo man nach New York fliegen wollte, um dort ein Flugzeug nach Chicago zu nehmen und somit die Weltreise zu beenden. Sie erklärten uns, daß sie sobald wie möglich zurück sein wollten, um sich noch einige Zeit in ihrem Landhaus etwa dreißig Meilen östlich von Chicago von den ungeheuren Strapazen dieser Reise zu erholen, ehe man sich wieder an die Arbeit machen müsse.

K. M.: 'Das Setzei des Kolumbus'
(abridged from the *Rheinischer Merkur*)

Last-minute Repairs[1]

Of course, I should have thought of it before. My wife had asked me several times when I was intending to fix the nail which held Aunt Emily's portrait. She had told me that it must be done in good time, for it had become weak, and that I must not leave it till the last moment. And now the portrait—admittedly no work of art—lay shattered on the dining-room floor. It would not have mattered if Aunt Emily had not told us that she wanted to come to lunch. 'It must be nearly twelve,' I said. 'Do you know what time she is to arrive?' 'Well, she said she might arrive on the twelve-thirty train. So she must have been[2] on her journey some time already,' my wife replied.

It was not as if[3] Aunt Emily were one of the most reasonable people. We had had to get a room ready for her and were prepared for[4] an uncomfortable week-end before she went on to visit Stephan and Anne. 'If only you had nailed it up[5] when I first mentioned it,' said my wife reproachfully, 'instead of hoping someone else[6] would take the work off your hands. If Aunt Emily sees that,' and here she pointed at the broken frame and fragments of glass,[7] 'she'll ask who was responsible for it—you know how she is; and if she doesn't see her picture on the wall, she'll want

to know why.'[8] I was about to object that the whole affair was
too ridiculous when my wife handed[9] me the hammer and nails
as a sign[10] that I should get to work without delay.

[1] *Reparatur in letzter Minute.*   [2] Use present, not perfect in German.
[3] Omit 'it was' in translation.   [4] to be prepared for s.th.—*auf eine Sache
gefaßt sein.*   [5] *annageln.*   [6] *jemand anders.* See Gram. 96.   [7] *Glasscherben.*
[8] End the sentence with *warum*, as though it were the first word in the implied
subordinate clause.   [9] to hand s.o. s.th. (here)—*jemandem etwas in die Hand
drücken.*   [10] *zum Zeichen.*

1. The charlady said I ought to get a new broom for her, since
   the old one was quite useless.
2. We were about to set off for Heidelberg when I received a
   postcard to tell me[1] that the visit was not necessary.
3. He looked as if he had just arrived from a journey round the
   world.
4. She is supposed to be able to speak Russian.
5. Although I could have managed with this book, the librarian
   suggested another I might use instead.[2]
6. Maybe we should have been able to hide the broken portrait
   if we had had more time.
7. All the players were asking me what time the match was due
   to begin.
8. Shall I drive you to the station as you are in such a hurry?

[1] 'which told me'. See Gram. 23.   [2] *statt dessen.*

Essay

Ein Familienstreit.
Eine Charakteristik[1] eines schwierigen Menschen.
Ein Tag aus dem Leben eines Weltreisenden.
Der Tag, an dem alles schiefging.

[1] Character-sketch.

Discussion

Darf man Putzfrauen kritisieren?
Ein Verwandter — etwa ein Onkel aus Amerika — lädt Sie zu
   einem Besuch bei sich ein. Was möchten Sie im Ausland tun
   und sehen?

Topic 9

Expressions commonly used in Debate and Discussion

Conversational German, like conversational English, has many phrases and particles (uninflected words such as adverbs and interjections) which may be used to indicate the standpoint of the speaker and/or the intensity of his feelings, to convey shades of opinion, or as an introduction to what he is about to express. Cf. in English the phrases 'Well, really!', 'Wouldn't it be true to say that . . .', or 'As I see it, . . .'

Not every such phrase can be translated directly into German. The attitude of the speaker may often be indicated by a stressed word-order, by an inflexion of the voice or by the use of an emotive particle (*doch, ja, schon, mal,* &c.). There are, however, many commonly used phrases which do correspond directly, or which bear a close resemblance to English forms. In developing his knowledge of conversational German, the student should pay special attention to these and practise using them, where they are appropriate, in discussions. But it is important to observe *where* such phrases are appropriate, and to use them sparingly, as one would do in English. Thus not every remark made in a discussion is prefaced by 'in my opinion', 'Well, . . .', or 'After all, . . .' and we rightly disapprove of speech which repeats *ad nauseam* some superfluous phrase such as 'I said' (*habe ich da gesagt*) or 'you know' (. . ., *wissen Sie*). It is particularly important not to use *eigentlich* in the same random fashion as English uses the word 'actually'. See Grammar Section, 121. The two words only correspond in the strict sense: 'in actual fact', 'properly speaking', &c., and a misplaced *eigentlich* may even create an impression of impertinence. Similarly, emotive particles should be avoided unless one is quite sure that they are appropriate to the context.

On the other hand, many situations arise in discussion where the speaker wishes to preface, reinforce or qualify what he has to say. Situations of this kind will be recognizable in the following notes, which are intended as an introduction to the means by which agreement and disagreement may be expressed in debate and discussion.

(i) *Expressing agreement*

Ich stimme mit Ihnen überein.	I agree with you.
Ich bin derselben Meinung wie Sie.	I am of the same opinion as you.
Ich bin ganz Ihrer Meinung.	I am entirely of the same opinion as you.
Ja, ich sehe es auch so.	Yes, that's the way I see it.
Ja, { *eben !* *gewiß !* *sicher !* *bestimmt !* }	Yes, of course, certainly, definitely.
Ja, da haben Sie vollkommen recht.	Yes, you're quite right there.
Das ist keine Frage.	There's no question about it.

(ii) *Expressing qualified agreement*

Nun ja, aber . . . *Na ja, aber . . .*	Well yes, but . . .
Ja, das schon, aber . . . *Ja, zugegeben, aber . . .* *Ja, freilich, aber . . .*	Yes, admittedly, but . . .

(iii) *Expressing disagreement*

Ich stimme nicht (ganz) mit Ihnen überein.	I don't (quite) agree with you.
Entschuldigung, ich sehe es anders.	I'm sorry, I don't see it like that.
Nun, da bin ich anderer Meinung.	Well, I'm of a different opinion.
Ich sehe nicht ein, warum . . .	I don't see why . . .
Ich muß sagen, . . .	I must say, . . . (I feel bound to say . . .)
Nun, dazu kann ich nur ein(e)s sagen: . . .	Well, there's only one thing I can say to that! . . .
Sie wollen doch nicht etwa sagen, . . .	Surely you're not trying to say . . .
Unsinn ! *Quatsch !*	Nonsense!

(iv) *Prefatory phrases*

Doch !	Yes! (replying to a negative question. Cf. French *si*.)

Wie ich es sehe, . . .	As I see it, . . .
Ich finde (meine), daß . . .	I think that . . .
Mir scheint (es), daß . . .	It seems to me that . . .
. . ., wie mir scheint, . . .	. . ., so it seems to me, . . .
Meiner Meinung nach . . .	
Meiner Ansicht nach . . .	
Nach meinem Dafürhalten . . .	In my opinion, view, . . .
Meines Erachtens . . .	
Wie wäre es, wenn . . .	How would it be if . . .
Wie wäre es mit . . .	How about . . .
Erlauben (Gestatten) Sie mir die Frage: . . .	Will you allow me to ask . . .
Offen gesagt, . . .	Frankly, . . .
Sagen Sie mal: . . .	Tell me—
Es ist ja klar, daß . . .	It's clear, isn't it, that . . .
Das ist es (ja) eben!	That's just the point!
Es versteht sich von selbst, daß . . .	It goes without saying that . . .
Man könnte fast sagen, daß . . .	One might almost say that . . .
Aber meinen Sie nicht, daß . . .	But don't you think that . . .

Topic 9. Agreement and Disagreement

EXPRESSIONS COMMONLY USED IN DEBATE AND
DISCUSSION

Shall they Dissolve the Club or not?

Herr Schön: Herr Vorsitzender, die Frage, mit der wir es heute zu tun haben, ist einfach die: ob der Klub bei solchen Schulden noch bestehen kann, oder ob wir nicht besser daran täten, ihn aufzulösen. Wir müssen es uns sorgfältig überlegen.

Vorsitzender: Nun, wie Sie wissen, meine Damen und Herren, bedeutet für die meisten Mitglieder unser Klub sehr viel. Es wäre zu schade, ihn einfach zum Tode zu verurteilen. Wie ich es sehe, haben wir die Pflicht, ihn auf jeden Fall am Leben zu erhalten. Zu diesem Zwecke . . .

Herr Bauer: Na ja, das ist alles schön und gut, aber sehen Sie nicht ein, daß Sie damit Unmögliches verlangen? Wo nehmen wir denn um Gotteswillen das Geld her? Ich muß Sie darauf aufmerksam machen, daß unsere Schulden insgesamt über 2000 Mark betragen.

Herr Runge: Nun, wie wäre es vielleicht mit einer weiteren

Anleihe bei der Bank? Meiner Ansicht nach könnten wir eine ohne allzu große Schwierigkeiten bekommen.

Herr Bauer: Aber sehen Sie doch! Wir stecken ja schon bis über beide Ohren in Schulden! Wie soll das weitergehen? Ich muß sagen, mein lieber Herr Runge, ich halte nicht viel von diesem Vorschlag.

Herr Runge: Als Mitbegründer dieses Tennisklubs, Herr Vorsitzender, verbitte ich mir solche Kritik an einem völlig ernst gemeinten Beitrag zur Diskussion!

Herr Bauer: Mit allem Respekt kann ich dazu nur eines sagen: Ihre langjährige Mitgliedschaft, Herr Runge, hat mit der Frage, um die es hier geht, überhaupt nichts zu tun. Wir wissen ja alle ganz genau, wie es um die finanzielle Lage des Klubs steht. Sicher *möchte* jedes Mitglied, daß wir unser Bestes tun, um die Auflösung des Klubs zu vermeiden, aber . . .

Herr Runge: Ganz offen gesagt, Herr Bauer . . .

Vorsitzender: Bitte, bitte, meine Herren! Es versteht sich von selbst, daß es unserem werten Vorstandsmitglied, Herrn Runge,[1] einzig und allein um das Wohl des Klubs zu tun ist. Meines Erachtens müßten wir seinen Vorschlag besprechen. Es wird sich wohl irgendein Ausweg aus unseren Schwierigkeiten finden lassen. Im schlimmsten Fall könnte ich vielleicht für die fehlende Geldsumme aufkommen . . .

---

[1] *unserem werten* . . . *Runge*—avoid a literal translation. The phrase could be rendered using a relative clause.

A Political Discussion

'What do you think of the political situation?'[1] asked Klein, as soon as we had sat down and the waitress had brought us the coffee.

'Hopeless, as ever,' replied Schmitz. 'In my opinion, no reasonable person can be much interested in politics. People would do better to devote themselves to[2] stamp-collecting[3] or other innocent hobbies. At any rate . . .'

'But look here!' Kluge interrupted him. 'Anyone who[4] does not take an interest in the political ideas of his time makes himself a guilty party[5] if extremist groups[6] come to power[7] in his country.'

'Nonsense!' retorted Schmitz. 'As I see it, everyone has the democratic right to be politically inactive.'

'Well, that's all very fine. But I must remind you that a politically uneducated nation represents a danger to world peace.[8]

And especially today, when,[9] after all, we have the chance of founding a West European federation of states,[10] we ought to be politically enlightened.'
'But do you believe that it will ever come to a federation of this sort?' Klein asked the others. 'I quite agree with you—we ought to have founded a single European federation long ago.[11] And if the worst comes to the worst, people may think of it as a solution. But normally the nations are too self-centred[12] to[13] see clearly what they ought to do in order to maintain peace.'
'How about another cup of coffee?' said Schmitz.

(Continued in Topic 16, p. 108.)

[1] *die politische Lage.*   [2] to devote o.s. to s.th.—*sich einer Sache widmen.*
[3] Include definite article.   [4] See Gram. 112.   [5] *sich mitschuldig machen.*
[6] *extremistische Gruppen.*   [7] *an die Macht kommen.*   [8] . . . *eine Gefahr für*
den Weltfrieden darstellt.   [9] *wo.*   [10] *der Staatenbund.*   [11] *schon längst.*
[12] *zu sehr auf sich bedacht.*   [13] too . . . to . . .—*zu . . ., um . . . zu . . .;*
see Gram. 22.

1. 'You didn't agree with him, I hope?'—'Yes, I did. Frankly, I think he is quite right.'
2. 'The question is simply this: can we find a way out or not?'
3. 'I shall certainly do my best to avoid the question. That goes without saying.'
4. 'How would it be if I were to pay the debts myself?'
5. 'It seems to me that this movement might be a danger to world peace.'
6. 'Surely you're not trying to say that she is not concerned about the good of the club?'
7. 'He was a good chairman, wasn't he?'—'Yes, admittedly, but I must say, I am glad we have Herr Schön now.'
8. 'They were asking the impossible, there's no question about that.'

ESSAY

Eine Konferenz.
Eine politische Auseinandersetzung[1] zwischen zwei Freunden.
Das Prinzip des „runden Tisches".
Die gute Ausrede.[2]

[1] argument.   [2] excuse.

DISCUSSION

Kann man ohne Vorurteile[1] sein?
Für oder gegen die Koedukation.

[1] *das Vorurteil*—prejudice.

Topic 10

The Passive in English and German

1. It is a mistake to imagine that every English passive is translatable by a corresponding German passive form. Often an active construction is the better parallel, sometimes with the direct object at the beginning of the sentence, or with the impersonal *man*.

Die besten Ergebnisse haben diejenigen erzielt, die die andere Methode gewählt haben. The best results were obtained by those who chose the other method.
Man hat mich gebeten, eine Zeitlang zu warten. I was asked to wait a while.

2. Need for care in forming the passive in German

(i) *Only* what can be the *direct object* in an active construction may become the *subject* of a passive construction. Verbs which govern a dative object may cause difficulty:

Mir wurde geholfen or ⎫
Es wurde mir geholfen ⎭ translates I was helped.
Man ist ihm begegnet translates He was met.

(For verbs governing a dative object, see Grammar Section, 13.)

N.B. The verb *fragen* may take a direct object of the person asked and a direct object noun clause: *Sie fragte mich,*—not *mir*—*ob ich die Zeitung gesehen hätte.* In the passive we therefore find:

Ich wurde gefragt, ob ich die Zeitung gesehen hätte.
But: *Mir wurde gesagt, ich hätte den Preis gewonnen.*

(ii) *Need for care with word-order in subordinate passive constructions:*

For word-order in the subordinate clause, see Topic 2, p. 10.

Er wollte fragen, ob alle Bücher schon zurückgebracht worden seien. He wanted to ask whether all the books had already been returned. N.B. This *worden* is sometimes omitted: *ob . . . zurückgebracht seien.*
Sagen Sie mir, wann die Bücher zurückgebracht werden müssen.

Passive infinitives also follow the usual rule for word-order:

Das braucht nicht gesagt zu werden. That does not need to be said.

Man weiß jetzt, daß dieses Problem gelöst werden kann. It is now known that this problem can be solved.

But after the verb *sein* an active infinitive is used to render the passive idea:

Dieses Buch ist leider nicht zu haben. This book is unfortunately not to be had.

Die Tatsachen in diesem Fall sind kaum zu glauben. The facts in this case are hardly to be believed. (Cf. Grammar Section, 45.)

3. Various translations of the English passive

(i) **man.** More frequent than English 'one'. See also Grammar Section, 101 (use of *einen*, *einem*, and *sein*).

Man spricht dieses Wort so: . . . This word is pronounced in this way: . . .

Man sagt ihm nach, er habe irgendein Verbrechen begangen. He is said to have committed some crime or other.

man does not specify the agent precisely, but does imply a personal agent (i.e. not a thing). It may imply some authority or institution:

Man hat uns aufgefordert, dem Ausschuß beizutreten. We were asked to join the committee.

(ii) *Passive.* Where the emphasis of the sentence is deliberately centred on the person or thing affected (i.e. the subject of the passive verb) rather than the agent, the passive is to be preferred; e.g. in the example below, the point of interest is what the city endured rather than the action of looting, although the two ideas are of course closely associated.

Die ganze Stadt wurde ausgeplündert. The whole city was looted.

Ich wurde vor Gericht geladen. I was summoned to appear in court.

Er ist zum Präsidenten ernannt worden. He has been appointed president.

(iii) *Reflexive usage.* The following special usage of the reflexive pronoun should be noted:

Solche Häuser vermieten sich leicht. Such houses are easily let.

Der Gebrauch des Wortes erklärt sich folgendermaßen: . . . The usage of the word is to be explained as follows: . . .

A reflexive pattern with *lassen* is frequently found:

> *Es läßt sich nicht behaupten, daß* . . . It cannot be asserted that . . .
>
> *Diese Deutung der Dinge läßt sich nicht widerlegen.* This interpretation of matters cannot be refuted. (Cf. Grammar Section, 46.)

4. Expressing the agent ('by . . .'): von or durch

von renders the idea of the direct doer of the action (i.e. in nearly every case a person or personified being). Where 'by' carries the meaning 'by means of' or 'through', *durch* should be used.

von

> *Der Brief wurde von meinem Vater geschrieben.*
>
> *Die neuen Briefmarken sind von allen Sammlern als besonders schön gepriesen worden.* The new stamps have been praised by all collectors as being particularly fine.
>
> *Ägypten wurde damals von vielen Plagen heimgesucht.* Egypt was visited by many plagues at that time. (Personified use of *Plagen*.)

durch

> *Das Leben in diesem Erdteil wird durch Hungersnöte erschwert.* Life in those parts is made more difficult by famines.
>
> *Das Schiff wurde durch eine Explosion schwer beschädigt.* The ship was severely damaged by an explosion.
>
> *Die Straßen werden durch Straßenkehrer reingehalten.* The roads are kept clean by road-sweepers. (N.B. Although the road-sweepers are the direct doers of the action of sweeping, *durch* is used here, because the sentence is meant to imply that the city authorities ensure clean roads *by the employment of*, *by means of* road-sweepers.[1])
>
> *Die neuen Kontinente wurden durch verschiedene große Seefahrer entdeckt.* The new continents were discovered by various great navigators. (N.B. Again, it is in fact the great navigators who were the direct doers of the action, but the implication of the sentence is that it was *through them* that the new continents became known.[1])

[1] *von* could of course be used here instead of *durch* if the emphasis were to be placed on the doer of the action.

5. Impersonal passive.

A passive usage which may appear puzzling at first sight is the impersonal *es wird gesungen, es wurde getanzt, es wird nicht geplaudert!* &c. These are translated in

English by 'there is singing', 'dancing went on', 'there will be no talking', &c. N.B. *Es wird nicht geplaudert = Es wird nicht geplaudert (werden)!*

6. Distinguishing between active and passive forms in English. Care must be taken not to read as an English passive what is really active. Cf.:

The whole town was surrounded by mountains (a state of affairs with the active verb *to be*). *Die ganze Stadt war von Bergen umgeben*; and
The whole town was surrounded in the course of the night (an action expressed in the passive voice). *Im Laufe der Nacht wurde die ganze Stadt umstellt.*

If, in translating, one is uncertain whether a verb is passive in the English, one can determine its voice by testing to see whether the sentence could be turned actively, supplying a subject where necessary. Thus: *Im Laufe der Nacht umstellten die Soldaten die ganze Stadt* renders the idea of the passive sentence above, whereas *Man umgab die ganze Stadt mit Bergen* is unthinkable.

Topic 10. Holiday Travel

THE PASSIVE IN ENGLISH AND GERMAN

Hitch-hikers

Noch immer ist Deutschland das klassische Wanderland. Überall sieht man während der Sommermonate die jungen Wanderer mit ihrem geschulterten Reisegepäck. Aber es sind nur noch selten die Naturschönheiten, die diese jungen Menschen hinauslocken. Heute ist es mehr der Ehrgeiz, touristische Sehenswürdigkeiten kennenzulernen. Deshalb wird heute jemand, der vom „Jugendwandern" spricht, leicht mißverstanden. Zu viele neue Formen des Reisens haben sich unter diesem Namen entwickelt.

Das Trampen steht dabei an erster Stelle.[1] Es ist jene internationale Art, kostenlos zu reisen, die sich aus den Verhältnissen der Kriegsjahre entwickelt hat. Heute wird sie sogar schon von Zwölf- bis Vierzehnjährigen als Vergnügungssport und zum Zeitvertreib geübt. Beim Trampen handelt es sich nicht nur darum, Fahrgeld zu sparen. Ein richtiger „Tramp" hat den Ehrgeiz, etwa die Route Kaiserslautern, Metz, Grenoble, Monaco, Nizza,[2] Marseille, Lyon, Paris, Brüssel, Aachen in nur

20 Tagen zurückzulegen und dabei von seinem Reiseetat —
150 DM[3] — noch etwas übrigzubehalten.
Die „Fußwanderer" sind selten geworden. Man schätzt ihre
Zahl auf ein Prozent der gesamten Wanderer. Viel häufiger
dient das Fahrrad als billiges Fortbewegungsmittel. Einzeln und
in Gruppen sieht man Jungen und Mädchen ihren Reisezielen
entgegenstrampeln.[4] Abends trifft man sie in den Jugendher-
bergen wieder.

Aber es ist merkwürdig: Gerade hier, wo man lebendige
Gespräche und Berichte über Fahrtenerlebnisse erwartet, gerade
hier findet man gelangweilte Gesichter. Aus irgendeiner Ecke
klingt die quäkende Melodie eines Kofferradios. Zwei Mädchen
spielen Federball, zwei Jungen Tischtennis. An vier Tischen
wird Skat[5] gespielt. Einige Jungen versuchen ihre Chancen bei
den Mädchen. Die übrigen Herbergsgäste wissen mit ihrer
Freizeit offenbar nichts anzufangen.[6] Dieser Eindruck wiederholt sich beinahe Tag für Tag. Er unterscheidet sich kaum von
irgendeiner Straßenecke in den Wohnvierteln einer Großstadt.

From: *Unsere Zeitung* (abridged extract)

[1] Lit. 'hitch-hiking stands in this connexion in the first place'. Find a suitable
English equivalent.   [2] Gram. 71.   [3] DM: *Deutsche Mark*—the phrase would
be read as '*150 Mark*'.   [4] 'pounding along towards their objectives'.   [5] *Skat*:
name of a card-game.   [6] *anfangen*—(here) 'do'.

On the Open Road[1]

During our journey through the Black Forest we got to know one
or two interesting people and had some amusing experiences. I
shall not forget, for example, the young couple who were hitch-
hiking from Konstanz to Rotterdam to visit relations. They had
been given lifts[2] by many people, but they had taken a whole
week to[3] cover the first fifty miles of their journey. However,
they did not seem to be especially troubled by this, and they
were still to be seen two days later in the village where we were
staying.[4] Whether they ever reached[5] Rotterdam we shall
never know; and we wondered whether they really intended to
do so.[6]

The same thing could not be said of the teenagers[7] we met.
They were obviously experienced hitch-hikers, whose only ambition it was to move on[8] as fast as possible. And although they
were not impressed by[9] the beauties of nature or places of interest, at least[10] they were to be admired for[11] their persistence.
One day a motorist was stopped by a group of thirteen- or
fourteen-year-olds. They stood in the middle of the street and

waved to him¹² as he approached. No doubt they had been told how dangerous that sort of thing¹³ can be, but they had evidently forgotten the warning.

Hitch-hiking is sometimes said to satisfy the spirit of adventure of young people, but it seemed to us that most of them looked bored and discontented. If this is the case, it would perhaps be better if they returned to¹⁴ genuine hiking.

¹ *Auf Fahrt.*   ² to give s.o. a lift—*jn. mitnehmen.*   ³ Use *brauchen* with *um . . . zu . . .*   ⁴ Avoid *bleiben.*   ⁵ Perfect tense.   ⁶ Use *wollen* with the direct object *es.*   ⁷ *die Jugendlichen.* Adjectival noun—care with the ending. See Topic 11, p. 71.   ⁸ *weiterkommen.*   ⁹ Use the verb *reizen* (to charm, fascinate, impress) in the active.   ¹⁰ Distinguish between *wenigstens* (at least = 'at any rate') and *mindestens* (at least = 'at the very least').   ¹¹ *wegen.*   ¹² to wave to s.o.—*jm. zuwinken.*   ¹³ *so etwas.*   ¹⁴ *zurückkehren zu.*

1. The total number of British visitors abroad¹ last year was estimated by one newspaper at over three millions.
2. When we arrived at² the customs we were asked to wait a while.
3. The Youth Hostel in Neustadt was built by means of generous gifts³ and was opened by the President only⁴ last year.
4. If you want to save travelling money, I advise you to hitch-hike.⁵ A pleasant holiday can be had in this way.
5. Could you tell me whether this word is pronounced in an English way⁶ or not?⁷
6. Dancing went on in the hotel until midnight.
7. When I was learning German I was greatly⁸ helped by⁹ my German friends.
8. Table-tennis and badminton are often played in German Youth Hostels, as in English ones.

¹ *Auslandsreisende*—adjectival noun—care with the ending.   ² *an . . . kommen* with accusative.   ³ *großzügige Geldspenden.*   ⁴ 'only' in a time sense. Not *nur.* See Gram. 123.   ⁵ Case after *raten*? As an alternative to *trampen*: *per Anhalter* (or *Autostop*) *fahren.*   ⁶ in an English way—*englisch* (adverb).   ⁷ *oder nicht?* should stand at the end of the sentence.   ⁸ *viel.*   ⁹ Avoid passive.

ESSAY

Ein Gespräch: „Ich fahre per Anhalter."—„Ich fahre lieber mit dem Rad."
Das Jugendherbergswerk.¹
Beschreiben Sie die Erfahrungen, die Sie auf Fahrt gemacht haben.
Wie verbringt man seine Ferien am besten?

¹ Youth Hostels Organization.

DISCUSSION

Meinen Sie, daß das „Trampen" zu rechtfertigen[1] sei?
Vorteile und Nachteile des Jugendwanderns.

[1] justify.

VOCABULARY AND GRAMMAR WORK

Collect from your own reading examples of German usages corresponding to English passive forms.

Topic 11

Masculine and Feminine Adjectival Nouns
Weak Masculine Nouns

1. Masculine and feminine adjectival nouns

Nouns derived from adjectives occur far more commonly in German than in English. They are of three kinds:

(i) Nouns derived from an ordinary adjective: *der Alte, die Alte*—the old man, the old woman; *der Einbeinige*—the one-legged man; *mein Lieber*—my dear fellow; *ein Deutscher, eine Deutsche, die Deutschen*—a German (man), a German (woman), the Germans. (N.B. *der Deutsche, die Deutsche,* &c., are the only nouns of nationality which are adjectival.)

(ii) Nouns derived from a present participle: *die Anwesenden*—those present; *der Handlungsreisende*—commercial traveller; *ein Sterbender*—a dying man; *alle Herumstehenden*—all the bystanders.

(iii) Nouns derived from a past participle: *der Kriegsgefangene*—the prisoner of war; *der Angeklagte*—the accused, the defendant; *ein Beamter* (formerly *Beamteter*)—a civil servant; *die hier-Versammelten*—those assembled here; . . . *der so Angeredete* . . .—. . . the man who had been addressed in this way . . .

The correct inflexion for the adjectival noun is of course found by treating the word as if it were the adjective preceding a noun with the appropriate gender, number, and case; e.g. *Kennst du viele Deutsche (Menschen)? Die so Angeredete (Frau) erwiderte: . . .; Ein Sterbender (Mensch) spricht die Wahrheit; Habt ihr mit dem Alten (Mann) gesprochen?*

It should be noted that certain commonly used adjectival nouns have come to be regarded rather as pronouns and are therefore written with a small letter; e.g. *der andere*—the other; *die beiden*—the two of them; *der erste, die erste*—the first (of them); *der zweite, die zweite,* &c.

Neuter adjectival nouns—which cannot refer to persons—are dealt with in Topic 14, pp. 93–94.

2. Weak masculine nouns

Weak masculine nouns denote persons or living beings and are so called because they take the weak ending *-en* in all cases, both singular and plural, *except the nominative singular*. They may be divided into the following groups:

(i) All masculine nouns ending in *-e* in the nominative singular (except those which are adjectival or which are of mixed declension—see Grammar Section, 69): *der Bote*—messenger; *der Genosse*—comrade (especially in left-wing usage); *der Hirte*—shepherd; *der Junge, der Knabe*—boy, lad; *der Schurke*—rogue; *der Zeuge*—witness; &c. (Feminines: *Botin, Genossin,* &c.)

N.B. A large number of nouns of nationality are of this type: *der Ire (die Irin); der Schotte (Schottin); der Franzose (Französin); ein Schwede; ein Pole; ein Russe; ein Chinese,* &c.

Note: *der Käse*—cheese, is not a weak noun.

(ii) A number of masculine nouns which do *not* end in *-e* in the nominative singular. The commonest of these are: *der Bär*—bear; *der Bauer*—peasant; *der Bayer*—Bavarian; *der Christ*—Christian; *der Fürst*—ruling prince; *der Gnom*—gnome; *der Graf*—count; *der Held*—hero; *der Herr*—gentleman, lord; *der Mensch*—human being; *der Narr*—fool; *der Oberst*—colonel; *der Pommer*—Pomeranian; *der Prinz*—(son of a *Fürst*); *der Spatz*—sparrow; *der Tor*—fool; *der Untertan*—subject (of a ruler).

Note the feminine forms *Bäuerin, Bayerin, Christin, Gräfin, Närrin, Törin.*

(iii) A large number of foreign nouns denoting persons and recognizable as weak masculines by their endings, which bear the main stress of the word: *der Intendant*—director of a theatre, *der Adjutant; der Photograph*—photographer, *der Biograph; der Patriarch, der Monarch; der Soldat, der Demokrat; der Student, der Patient; der Hornist*—bugler, *der Sozialist; der Philosoph, der Theosoph*—theosophist; *der Biologe, der Psychologe;* &c.

Feminines: *Photographin, Patientin,* &c.

N.B. *der Sextant, der Automat*—automatic machine, *der Paragraph, der Komet* and *der Planet,* although not denoting persons or living beings, belong to the weak masculines.

Note. Do not confuse adjectival nouns with weak masculine nouns. N.B. the distinction between the adjectival noun *Junge* (plural) in the sentence *die Katze hatte Junge*—the cat had (a litter of) young and the weak masculine noun *Jungen* (plural), as

for example in the sentence *Jungen essen immer gern.* Cf. also:
Die Katze holte ihr Junges aus dem Korb—the cat fetched her
kitten from the basket, and *Sie will ihren Jungen zum Mittagessen
holen*—she wants to fetch her boy for dinner.

Topic 11. The Law

MASCULINE AND FEMININE ADJECTIVAL NOUNS
WEAK MASCULINE NOUNS

Justice and Mercy[1]

Von dem ehemaligen New-Yorker Bürgermeister La Guardia
erzählt man sich folgende großartige Geschichte:

Eines Tages fungierte er, wie er zuweilen tat, als Polizeirichter.
Es war ein eisigkalter Wintertag. Man führte ihm einen zittern-
den alten Mann vor.

Anklage: Entwendung eines Laibes Brot aus einer Bäckerei.

Der Angeklagte entschuldigte sich damit, daß seine Familie am
Verhungern sei.

„Ich muß Sie bestrafen", erklärte La Guardia. „Das Gesetz
duldet keine Ausnahme. Ich kann nichts tun, als Sie zur Zahlung
von zehn Dollar zu verurteilen."

Dann aber griff er in die Tasche und setzte hinzu: „Nun, hier
sind die zehn Dollar, um Ihre Strafe zu bezahlen. — Und nun
erlasse ich Ihnen die Strafe."

Hierbei warf La Guardia die Zehndollarnote in seinen grauen
Filzhut.

„Und nun", setzte er mit erhobener Stimme fort, „bestrafe ich
jeden Anwesenden in diesem Gerichtssaal mit einer Buße von
fünfzig Cent — und zwar dafür, daß er in einer Stadt lebt, wo
ein Mensch Brot stehlen muß, um essen zu können! — Herr
Gerichtsdiener, kassieren Sie die Geldstrafen sofort ein und
übergeben Sie sie dem Angeklagten."

Der Hut machte die Runde. Und ein noch halb ungläubiger
alter Mann verließ den Saal mit siebenundvierzig Dollar fünfzig
Cent in der Tasche.

[1] Note the expression *Gnade vor Recht ergehen lassen*—to temper justice with
mercy.

There's still Justice in the World!

Es gibt natürlich viele Prozesse; doch ich schmeichle mir, das
Urbild[1] des Prozesses gefunden zu haben. Die Sache fängt ganz

unschuldig an: Ein wohlhabender Mr. Wilkins verlebte im Jahre 1892 seine Ferien in Neapel, bewunderte pünktlich die Sonnenuntergänge und unterhielt sich öfters mit einem Straßenbettler, dessen sanfter Christuskopf ihm aufgefallen war. Eines Tages erhält Mr. Wilkins eine gerichtliche Vorladung ins Hotel geschickt. Eine Vorladung, laut welcher[2] der Bettler 5000 Lire zurückverlangt, die er ihm, Mr. Wilkins, geliehen haben will.[3] Der Engländer findet die Sache sehr belustigend und erzählt sie beim Nachmittagskaffee dem britischen Konsul. Dieser wird sehr ernst und rät ihm, sogleich einen Advokaten zu nehmen.

Bei der Gerichtsverhandlung erklärt der Bettler mit dem sanften Christuskopf, er sei mit Mr. Wilkins befreundet gewesen und habe ihm mit 5000 Lire — seinen gesamten Ersparnissen — aus einer momentanen Geldverlegenheit geholfen.

„Und hier", fuhr er mit tragischer Handbewegung fort, „sind drei ehrenwerte Zeugen, die die Sache beeiden können!"

Tatsächlich: sogleich erhoben sich drei glutäugige Genossen des Bettlers und beschworen, daß sie selber gesehen hätten, wie der Engländer die 5000 Lire vom Bettler geborgt habe.

Nun erhob sich der Advokat des Engländers. Er war die Wahrheit selbst. Er stellte keineswegs in Abrede, daß sein Klient die 5000 Lire entliehen habe. Nein, er bezweifelte weder die Ehrlichkeit der Herren Zeugen, noch ihre Aufrichtigkeit! Doch er hatte seinerseits sechs nicht minder ehrenwerte Zeugen herbeizitiert.[4] Die erhoben sich jetzt wie ein Mann und beschworen, daß sie mit eigenen Augen gesehen hatten, wie der Engländer dem Bettler die 5000 Lire voll und ganz zurückbezahlt habe!

Die Klage wurde abgewiesen. Es gibt noch eine Gerechtigkeit.

---

[1] *das Urbild*—prototype. [2] *laut*—according to. *laut* governs the genitive.
[3] 'claimed to have lent . . .' [4] *einen Zeugen herbeizitieren*—bring a witness.

SIGISMUND VON RADECKI, *Das ABC des Lachens* (adapted)

Judges and Defendants

The following story is told of two English gentlemen who used to officiate alternately as magistrates in the court of a small town.

One day, summonses were issued to both for exceeding the speed-limit.[1] As no other magistrate was available,[2] the only possible solution was that each of them should try the case[3] of his colleague.

One magistrate[4] therefore took his seat on the Bench[5] and the other entered the dock.[6] The clerk of the court read out the charge. The defendant pleaded guilty[7] and the village constable appeared as witness.

'I must punish you,' said the magistrate. 'The law can tolerate no exceptions. I have no option but to fine you one pound.'

The defendant now rose from the dock and, to[8] the laughter of those present in the courtroom, took his seat[9] on the Bench, while the other became[10] the defendant. Again the charge was read out; again the officiating magistrate questioned[11] the village policeman as witness of the offence.[12] Turning to his colleague, he said severely:

'I must ask the accused: have you anything to say?'

'No, Your Honour,'[13] replied the one thus addressed; 'I plead guilty.'

'I shall fine you two pounds, then.'

'Here, just a minute!' retorted the defendant; 'I only fined you one pound!'

'I know,' said the judge. 'But I must make an example.[14] There's getting to be too much of this sort of thing nowadays.[15] You are the second one we've had this morning.'

---

[1] *wegen Überschreitens der Geschwindigkeitsbegrenzung.*   [2] *vorhanden.* [3] to try the case of a person—*jn. verhören.*   [4] Include the definite article ('the one magistrate'). Gram. 98.   [5] *der Richterstuhl.*   [6] to enter the dock—*auf die Anklagebank gehen.*   [7] to plead guilty—*sich schuldig bekennen.*   [8] i.e. 'to the accompaniment of'—what preposition? See Topic 3, p. 21.   [9] Include *seinerseits* ('in his turn', 'for his part').   [10] *werden zu.*   [11] to question s.o.—*jn. verhören.*   [12] *das Delikt.*   [13] What would be the equivalent title in German?   [14] *Ich muß aber ein Exempel statuieren.*   [15] *Dieser Unfug greift heutzutage immer mehr um sich.*

---

1. A German, a Frenchman, and an Englishman appeared before the international court and gave evidence.[1]

2. When the jury[2] discussed the case[3] they all said that they had never seen so pitiful a human being in court.[4]

3. Only rarely did the judge raise his voice. During the proceedings he usually addressed plaintiff, defendant, witness, and counsel in a soft tone.

4. The trial lasted three days. The public prosecutor[5] interrogated only two witnesses, a commercial traveller and a university student.

5. After a woman witness, a Bavarian, had spoken to the president, a civil servant was brought before him.

6. 'Do you consider me a fool?' asked the beggar. 'No, a[6] rogue,' replied the farmer's wife.

7. Is it really true that the rich are nowadays less rich than they were and the poor less poor?

8. We occasionally speak of[7] the 'British lion', the 'Russian bear', and the 'German eagle', but not as frequently as our fathers did.

[1] to give evidence—*aussagen.*   [2] *die Geschworenen.*   [3] *der Fall.*   [4] *vor Gericht.*   [5] *der Staatsanwalt.*   [6] Repeat the preposition of the preceding phrase. See Gram. 141.   [7] *sprechen von.*

Essay

Angeklagt!

Das Plädoyer eines Staatsanwalts vor Gericht.

Beschreiben Sie die Szene in einem Gerichtssaal.

Schreiben Sie, als Geschworener, einen Bericht über eine Gerichtsverhandlung.

Discussion

Sollte man die Todesstrafe wieder einführen?

Erzählen Sie aus dem Gedächtnis, was in den beiden deutsch-englischen Übersetzungsstücken geschieht!

Vocabulary Work

Compile a list showing all the phrases in the German–English passages of this topic which involve the use of a noun or pronoun in the dative.

Revision Topic 1

Mystery

A Body is Discovered

Alphons Clenin, der Polizist von Twann, fand am Morgen des dritten Novembers neunzehnhundertachtundvierzig dort, wo die Straße von Lamboing (eines der Tessenbergdörfer)[1] aus dem Walde der Twannbachschlucht[2] hervortritt, einen blauen Mercedes, der am Straßenrande stand. Es herrschte Nebel, wie oft in diesem Spätherbst, und eigentlich war Clenin am Wagen schon vorbeigegangen, als er doch wieder zurückkehrte. Es war ihm nämlich beim Vorbeischreiten gewesen,[3] nachdem er flüchtig durch die trüben Scheiben des Wagens geblickt hatte, als sei der Fahrer auf das Steuer niedergesunken. Er glaubte, daß der Mann betrunken sei,[4] denn als ordentlicher Mensch[5] kam er auf das Nächstliegende.[6] Er wollte daher dem Fremden nicht amtlich, sondern menschlich begegnen. Er trat mit der Absicht ans Automobil, den Schlafenden zu wecken, ihn nach Twann zu fahren und im Hotel Bären bei schwarzem Kaffee und einer Mehlsuppe nüchtern werden zu lassen; denn es war zwar verboten, betrunken zu fahren, aber nicht verboten, betrunken in einem Wagen, der am Straßenrande stand, zu schlafen. Clenin öffnete die Wagentür und legte dem Fremden die Hand väterlich auf die Schultern. Er bemerkte jedoch im gleichen Augenblick, daß der Mann tot war. Die Schläfen waren durchschossen. Auch sah Clenin jetzt, daß die rechte Wagentüre offenstand. Im Wagen war nicht viel Blut, und der dunkelgraue Mantel, den die Leiche trug, schien nicht einmal[7] beschmutzt. Aus der Manteltasche glänzte der Rand einer gelben Brieftasche. Clenin, der sie hervorzog, konnte ohne Mühe feststellen, daß es sich beim Toten um Ulrich Schmied handelte, Polizeileutnant der Stadt Bern.

FRIEDRICH DÜRRENMATT: *Der Richter und sein Henker*
(Rororo Taschenbuch-Ausgabe, Nov. 1959)

---

[1] *Tessenbergdörfer*—villages in the Tessenberg district. [2] *die Schlucht*—gorge.
[3] Cf. *es war mir, als ob* . . .—it seemed to me as though . . . [4] Note this usage: subjunctive for an *unfulfilled* assumption (i.e. he only *thought* it was so; *in fact* he was mistaken). See Gram. 48. [5] *ordentlich*—(here) plain, straightforward. [6] *das Nächstliegende*—the nearest, most obvious (thing, solution).
[7] See Gram. 128.

K. arrives at the Village

Es war spät abends, als K. ankam. Das Dorf lag in tiefem Schnee. Vom Schloßberg war nichts zu sehen, Nebel und Finsternis umgaben ihn, auch nicht der schwächste Lichtschein deutete das große Schloß an. Lange stand K. auf der Holzbrücke, die von der Landstraße zum Dorf führte, und blickte in die scheinbare Leere empor.

Dann ging er ein Nachtlager[1] suchen; im Wirtshaus war man noch wach, der Wirt hatte zwar keine Zimmer zu vermieten, aber er wollte, von dem späten Gast äußerst überrascht und verwirrt, K. in der Wirtsstube auf einem Strohsack schlafen lassen. K. war damit einverstanden. Einige Bauern waren noch beim Bier, aber er wollte sich mit niemandem unterhalten, holte selbst den Strohsack vom Dachboden und legte sich in der Nähe des Ofens hin. Warm war es, die Bauern waren still, ein wenig prüfte er sie noch mit den müden Augen, dann schlief er ein.

Aber kurze Zeit darauf wurde er schon geweckt. Ein junger Mann, städtisch angezogen, mit schauspielerhaftem Gesicht, die Augen schmal, die Augenbrauen stark, stand mit dem Wirt neben ihm. Die Bauern waren auch noch da, einige hatten ihre Sessel herumgedreht, um besser zu sehen und zu hören. Der junge Mensch entschuldigte sich sehr höflich, K. geweckt zu haben, stellte sich als Sohn des Schloßkastellans vor und sagte dann: „Dieses Dorf ist Besitz des Schlosses, wer hier wohnt oder übernachtet, wohnt oder übernachtet gewissermaßen[2] im Schloß. Niemand darf das ohne gräfliche[3] Erlaubnis. Sie aber haben eine solche Erlaubnis nicht oder haben sie wenigstens nicht vorgezeigt."

FRANZ KAFKA: Das Schloß

[1] a bed for the night. [2] gewissermaßen—as it were, in a certain sense.
[3] der Graf—count; and see Gram. 31.

An Unwelcome Guest

A few years ago a French friend of mine was travelling by car to Brittany to convalesce from a slight operation.[1] By eight o'clock in the evening he had still not reached his destination; it was getting dark and it was foggy. He therefore decided to break[2] his journey and spend the night in the next village. Within ten minutes he had found what he was looking for: through the fog an inn-sign could be seen. He left the car standing

by the roadside, for he knew that it would be safe there in[3]
this fog.

The door of the inn was open. My friend went straight in and
entered the small saloon, where the innkeeper was sitting with
some friends over a glass of wine and talking quietly to them.
They turned round[4] and surveyed the new arrival with curious
glances, as though it struck them as odd[5] to see a stranger in the
house.

At last the innkeeper got up and asked the traveller in an indifferent voice whether he could be of service[6] to him. My friend,
greatly surprised at this cool reception, replied that he would like
to have a room. He intended to stay only the one night here,
he added. Without a word, the innkeeper took him upstairs,
handed him the registration form[7] and left the room. He did not
even ask the guest whether he might need anything else.[8] My
friend thought the man must be slightly drunk, but he was too
tired to worry about[9] such treatment. He undressed and lay
down. As he fell asleep he heard movements outside his room
and a voice saying, 'He can't stay here, I tell you!'

He has never forgotten the events of that night . . .

[1] a slight operation—*eine leichte Operation*.   [2] *unterbrechen* (insep.).   [3] *bei*.
[4] to turn round—*sich umdrehen, sich umwenden*.   [5] it struck them as odd—*es
kam ihnen seltsam vor*.   [6] Cf. Can I be of service? What can I do for you,
sir?—*Womit kann ich dienen?*   [7] *der Meldezettel*.   [8] *sonst noch etwas*.
[9] *sich kümmern um*.

1. He walked up to the door with the intention of knocking, but
   then he turned round again and went back to the car.

2. Although it was forbidden to park in the main road it was not
   forbidden to wait there.

3. As landlord of the hotel he should perhaps have treated that
   guest in a more friendly way.

4. 'It's a matter of a short interrogation,' said the lieutenant of
   police, laying his hand on my arm.

5. I should like to ask him whether, as a straightforward man, he
   should have made that assertion.

6. Glancing briefly upwards, he noticed that the castle was no
   longer visible, for fog and darkness surrounded it.

7. I should have liked to ask whether there were any rooms to be
   let in the inn.

8. An official with a lean face, his hands in his trouser pockets,
   asked me to show my permit.

ESSAY

Setzen Sie *entweder* die Geschichte von Dürrenmatt *oder* von
   Kafka *oder* den ins Deutsche zu übersetzenden Text fort.
Das Werk eines bekannten Verfassers von Kriminalromanen.
Das geheimnisvolle Gefühl: „Ich war schon einmal hier!"
Die wunderbare Welt des kleinen Kindes.

DISCUSSION

Warum liest man gern Kriminalromane?
Ist es möglich, ein Leben ohne Angst zu führen?

Topic 12

Use of Prepositions after certain Verbs

The use of a preposition after certain verbs has already been mentioned (see Topic 3, p. 21). The following list contains the simpler verbs of this type which should be known at this stage, together with some of the more difficult examples which occur in Topics 1–11.

'Accusative' preposition

gelten für—to be considered—*Gilt er für einen Gelehrten?* (scholar).

halten für—to consider to be—*Hält sie mich für einen Narren?*

sich interessieren für—to be interested in—*Interessiert sie sich für Bücher?*

'Dative' prepositions

fragen nach—to ask, inquire about—*Immer wieder fragte sie mich nach ihrem Sohn.*

halten von—to think of, have an opinion about—*Was halten Sie von ihm?*

sprechen von—to talk about, discuss—*Wir sprachen eben von meiner Reise.*

gehören zu—to form part of, be one of—*Goethe gehört zu den großen Dichtern der Weltliteratur.*

sagen zu—to say to s.th.—*Was sagst du zu meinem Vorschlag?*

verurteilen zu—to condemn to—*Er wurde zu zehn Jahren Gefängnis verurteilt.*

'Accusative or dative' prepositions (the preposition governs the accusative except for examples marked (D)):

denken an—to think of—*Denken Sie an eine Zahl, etwa 5 oder 12 oder 23.*

sich erinnern an—to remember—*Erinnern Sie sich an mich?*

glauben an—to believe in—*Glaubst du an Gespenster?* (ghosts)

schreiben an—to write to—*Mein Vater wird heute an mich schreiben.*

(D) *vorbeigehen an*—to go past—*Er ging langsam an meiner Tür vorbei.*

antworten auf—to reply to (a letter, &c.)—*Ich muß noch heute auf den Brief antworten.*

blicken auf—to glance at—*Sie blickte auf die Armbanduhr und eilte weiter.*

sich freuen auf—to look forward to—*Wir freuen uns auf die Ferien.*

hoffen auf—to hope for—*Wir hoffen auf Ihre baldige Genesung!* (recovery).

sich vorbereiten auf—to prepare for—*Ich war auf seine Antwort nicht vorbereitet.*

warten auf—to wait for—*Hast du lange auf mich warten müssen?*

sprechen über—to speak about (a subject, &c.)—*Der Premierminister spricht heute abend im Radio über die politische Lage.*

nachdenken über—to think, ponder about—*Ich mußte lange über diese Frage nachdenken.*

weinen (lachen) über—to weep (laugh) at—*Ich wußte nicht, ob ich über seine Geschichte weinen oder lachen sollte.*

(D) *sich fürchten vor*—to be afraid of—*Du brauchst dich vor ihm nicht zu fürchten.*

(D) *retten vor*—to save from—*Ihre Warnung hat uns vor der Gefahr gerettet.*

(D) *schützen vor*—to protect from—*Die Berghütte hatte mich vor dem Sturm geschützt.*

(D) *weinen (lachen, zittern) vor*—to weep (laugh, tremble) for (with)—*Sie weinte und lachte vor Freude.*

N.B. Distinguish carefully between *halten von, denken an* and *nachdenken über*; also between *sprechen von* and *sprechen über*; and *weinen (lachen) über* and *weinen (lachen) vor.*

Notice the use of *auf* in expressions in this list relating to future events: *sich freuen auf, hoffen auf, sich vorbereiten auf, warten auf.*

Notice the use of *vor* in expressions relating to danger: *sich fürchten vor, retten vor, schützen vor.*

These expressions usually keep the preposition even where they are followed, not by a noun or pronoun, but by a clause or phrase. In such instances the words *danach, daran, darauf,* &c., must often be used:

Keiner hat danach gefragt, ob wir davon wissen. No one inquired whether we knew about it.

Ich hatte nicht daran gedacht, daß er krank war. I had not thought of the fact that he was ill.

Erinnern Sie sich bitte daran, daß er sie jahrelang nicht mehr gesehen hat. Please remember that he has not seen her for years.

Ich muß darauf warten, daß die letzten Antworten eintreffen. I must wait for the last replies to arrive.

Er freut sich darauf, die Ferien bei uns zu verbringen. He is looking forward to spending the holidays with us.

Warum sollte ich mich davor fürchten, hierzubleiben? Why should I be afraid of staying here?

N.B. *danach, daran, darauf,* &c., are sometimes omitted from such constructions where there is little need for them as a 'link' to the following clause or phrase. A similar 'link' is often provided in English by the use of such phrases as 'the fact that', 'such time as', 'the possibility of'; e.g. in the examples above, *Ich hatte nicht daran gedacht, daß er krank war; Ich muß darauf warten, daß die letzten Antworten eintreffen*—I must wait until such time as the last replies arrive; *Er freut sich darauf, die Ferien bei uns zu verbringen*—He is looking forward to the prospect of (the possibility of) spending the holidays with us.

It is not possible to lay down a precise rule for the omission of these link words; it is advisable to include them wherever a verbal construction of this kind is used. Only experience can show where the preposition may or should be omitted.

Nouns related to verbs followed by a particular preposition should also be followed by that preposition, e.g.

Ich habe kein Interesse dafür (or *daran*) . . .
Die Verurteilung zu einer Geldstrafe . . .
Die Antwort auf meinen Brief . . .
Mit einem raschen Blick auf die Uhr sagte er . . .
Meine Freude auf deinen Besuch . . .
Die Hoffnung auf Reichtum (wealth) . . .
Zuschriften an den Herausgeber . . .—letters to the editor . . .
Furcht vor Schmerzen . . .—fear of pain . . .
Rettung (or *Schutz*) *vor der Gefahr* . . .

Topic 12. The Press

The Times

Zum Unterschied von anderen englischen Zeitungen ist der Stoff in der *Times* so wohlgeordnet, daß der geübte Leser niemals im Zweifel darüber ist, wo er eine bestimmte Nachricht oder einen Kommentar zu suchen hat. Wohlgeordnet, ohne den leisesten Anflug von Sensationalismus in der äußeren Aufmachung,[1] in gedrängtem, fließendem Text bietet die Times ihren Lesestoff dar. Aber es ist eine Zeitung, an die man gewöhnt sein muß. Die Hauptnachrichten werden auf der ersten Seite gebracht. Danach aber werden auf besonderen Seiten die In- und Auslandsnachrichten in strenger Reihenfolge behandelt: auf die Inlandsnachrichten folgen die Seiten mit den Parlamentsdebatten, dann die Berichte über westeuropäische Angelegenheiten, Nachrichten aus Übersee, Sportberichte, Wirtschaftsteil, zum Schluß mehrere Seiten Inserate.

Die beiden inneren Seiten der Times enthalten das, was die eigentliche Tradition des Blattes ausmacht: auf der linken Innenseite die wichtigsten Korrespondentenberichte; auf der rechten Innenseite die Kommentare — zwei bis drei Leitartikel. Auf die Leitartikel folgen die wichtigsten Zuschriften an den Herausgeber, oft außerordentlich instruktive Abhandlungen oder Meinungsäußerungen von führenden Persönlichkeiten zu umstrittenen Tagesfragen,[2] die manchmal aufklärender und richtunggebender[3] sind als die Leitartikel.

Die erste, die Außenseite dieses inneren Bogens, befaßt sich ausschließlich mit kulturellen Nachrichten: zum Beispiel Konzert- und Opernbesprechungen, sowie Artikel von Theater- und Filmkritikern über die neuesten Vorstellungen auf Bühne und Leinwand. Die vierte Seite des inneren Bogens beginnt mit dem Hofzirkular und den Nachrichten aus der Gesellschaft, u.a. Geburts- und Heiratsannoncen. Dann folgen Nachrufe auf verstorbene Persönlichkeiten des In- und Auslandes, sowie verschiedene Sonderberichte, etwa[4] über die Versteigerung[5] von einem wertvollen Klavier bei Christie, oder Artikel von allgemeinem Interesse, die auf Informationen aus Fachzeitschriften[6] basieren.[7] Das ist die Tradition: ausführlichste unabhängige Berichterstattung über alles Politische,[8] richtungweisende[9] Kommentierung und Information über alles, was in den oberen

Schichten der Gesellschaft vor sich geht. Die Times ist die Zeitung einer Oberschicht, die sich aufs engste[10] mit der Regierung des Landes und seinen Geschicken verbunden fühlt.

Based on an article by CURT GEYER in the *Süddeutsche Zeitung*

[1] *die äußere Aufmachung*—presentation.   [2] *eine umstrittene Frage*—a vexed, controversial question.   [3] *richtunggebend*—authoritative (lit.: 'pointing the way').   [4] as, for instance.   [5] *Versteigerung*—auction sale.   [6] specialist journals.   [7] *basieren auf* (+ dat.)—to be based on.   [8] *alles Politische*—all political matters.   [9] *richtungweisend = richtunggebend.*   [10] *aufs engste verbunden*—most closely concerned, connected.

A German Newspaper

On Tuesdays my brother used to receive the weekend edition[1] of the *Frankfurter Allgemeine Zeitung*[2] direct from Germany. He was particularly interested in the political news and the leading articles, and I had to wait for him to finish reading these before I was allowed even to cast a glance at[3] the financial section, which chiefly interested me. I am afraid[4] that there was little in the paper which we could discuss together, for his understanding of[5] all political matters was much deeper than mine,[6] and he said he had neither time nor inclination[7] to concern himself with finance. But we both used to look forward to reading the letters to the editor, and once we even wrote to him ourselves about a particular sports report.

The *FAZ*, as it is called for short,[8] is one of the most quoted[9] German newspapers. Both in Germany and abroad[10] it is reckoned as an authoritative, well-informed paper.[11] The front page contains the main news items from all over the world, a short commentary on an important piece of news, and a fairly lengthy[12] essay on political events of the moment.[13] When we open the paper we find the familiar detailed accounts of political, social and economic matters, commentaries on controversial questions of the day, information on fashion and travel,[14] and reviews of films, plays, and recently published books.

[1] *die Wochenendausgabe.*   [2] See Gram. 67.   [3] even . . . a glance at— *auch nur einen Blick* (with the verb *tun* or *werfen,* and the preposition *in*).   [4] *leider.*
[5] understanding of—*(das) Verständis für.*   [6] Care with the pronoun inflexion.
[7] *(die) Lust.*   [8] for short—*kurz.*   [9] *meistzitiert* or *am meisten zitiert.*
[10] both . . . and—*sowohl . . . als auch.*   [11] An alternative to *die Zeitung?*
[12] fairly lengthy—*länger.* The comparative is frequently used in German to imply 'fairly . . .'. Cf. *ein älterer Herr*—an elderly gentleman; *die neueren Sprachen*— modern languages; *eine jüngere Dame*—a fairly young lady. See Gram. 76.
[13] *das politische Zeitgeschehen* (sing.).   [14] *Reisen* (plur.).

1. What do you consider the most interesting news item this week?
2. The small ads. appear always in strict alphabetical order.
3. I have not received an answer to my letter yet.[1]
4. What is the foreign press saying to the government's proposals?
5. The paper contained a detailed account of the trial and his conviction to ten years' imprisonment.
6. You have to be used to the layout of *The Times* in order to find what you want to read.
7. The news of the arts was followed by several pages of sport.
8. I am not in any doubt[2] that Müller prepared[3] that material for the press.

[1] not yet—(here) *noch keine (Antwort)*.   [2] Use *gar nicht*.   [3] Perfect tense. See Gram. 38 (ii).

ESSAY

Die Presse als Macht in der heutigen Welt.
Deutsche und englische Zeitungen: ein Vergleich.
Beschreiben Sie eine große Tages- oder Sonntagszeitung.
Ein Tag aus dem Leben eines Journalisten.

DISCUSSION

Nachrichten, die heute in der Zeitung stehen.
Was erwarten Sie von einer guten Zeitung?

VOCABULARY WORK

Collect from your own reading further examples of the use of particular prepositions after verbs (see this grammar topic).

Topic 13

Verbs of Movement
Types of Construction

The grammatical constructions found with different kinds of verbs of movement in German require special care. The following types of construction should be particularly noted:

(i) Simple verb of movement + prepositional phrase showing to what place, in what direction:

Preposition governing dative	*Preposition governing accusative*
Er kam zu mir.	*Er kam durch den Saal.*
Sie ging aus dem Haus.	*Sie ging um die Ecke.*
Wir fuhren nach London.	*Wir fuhren gegen ein anderes Auto.*
	Ich kletterte auf das Dach.

(ii) Separable verb of movement + prepositional phrase showing to what place, in what direction (the preposition is usually that of the separable prefix):

herauskommen (+ *aus*):   *Sie kam aus dem Zimmer heraus.*[1]
eintreten (+ *in*):   *Er trat ins Zimmer ein.*[2]
hinaufklettern (+ *auf*):   *Ich kletterte auf das Dach hinauf.*[3]
heranstolpern (+ *an*):   *Er stolperte an mich heran.*[4]

[1] The inclusion of *heraus* stresses the idea that the movement was towards me, the observer of the action.   [2] *hineintreten* would stress movement away from the observer, or draw attention to the significance of his entering the room, i.e. leaving his original position with some deliberate, significant intent: *Er trat leise in das Zimmer hinein, in der Hoffnung, das Dokument zu finden.* Again, *hereintreten* would show movement towards the observer.   [3] I clambered up on to the roof. *Ich kletterte auf das Dach hinaus*—I clambered out on to the roof.   [4] He stumbled up to me.

(iii) Separable verb of movement + prepositional phrase in the Dative, showing where the movement takes place or begins:

vorbeigehen or *vorübergehen, -laufen, -wandern, -kommen,* &c. + *an*:
   Sie gingen am Bahnhof vorbei. Er lief an mir vorüber, &c.

ankommen[1] *an, in, auf,* &c.:
   Wir sind spät am Bahnhof angekommen. Wann kommen wir in der Hauptstadt an? Auf welchem Flugplatz kommt man an?

herausnehmen, hervorziehen,[2] &c. + *von, aus, unter:*

> *Ich nahm den Schlüssel aus der Schublade heraus.*[3] *Wir haben die Tassen aus dem Eßzimmer herausgetragen. Er zog den Koffer unter dem Schrank hervor.*[4]

[1] *ankommen* always implies a journey of some length. Cf. *Guten Tag! Verzeihung, daß ich spät komme*—Hallo, sorry I'm late ('I've arrived late'); and *Erst um sieben Uhr kamen wir an das Haus*—Not until seven o'clock did we get to ('arrive at') the house; and *Heute bin ich etwas früher zur Schule gekommen*—I got to ('arrived at') school rather earlier today.   [2] pull out, pull forth (into view).   [3] I took the key out of the drawer.   [4] He pulled the case from under the cupboard.

(iv) Transitive verbs of movement, often of climbing and descending:

besteigen:	*Ich habe diesen Berg nie bestiegen.*[1]
erklettern:	*Der Junge hat den Fels erklettert.*[1, 2]
hinaufgehen:	*Ist er die Treppe hinaufgegangen?*[3]
herunterkommen:	*Sie war schon den Hügel heruntergekommen.*[3]

and:

betreten:	*Wir hatten das Zimmer betreten.*[4]
entlanggehen:	*Sie sind zusammen die Straße entlanggegangen.*[3]
entlangwandern:	*Ich bin den Waldweg entlanggewandert.*[3]
&c.	

[1] See also notes on Inseparable Prefixes, Topic 15, pp. 98–100.   [2] The boy has clambered to the top of the rock.   [3] *Die Treppe, den Hügel,* and *den Waldweg* in these examples are not direct objects of the verbs but *adverbial accusatives* of place. The verbs are therefore conjugated with *sein,* not with *haben.*   [4] We had entered the room.

(v) Inseparable transitive verbs of movement[1]

durchwandern:	*Wir haben den ganzen Schwarzwald durchwandert.*
durchwaten:	*Hat er den tiefen Bach durchwatet?*[2]
durchfliegen: &c.	*Ich habe dichte Sturmwolken durchflogen.*

überfahren:	*Er wurde von einem Auto überfahren.*
überfallen:	*Banditen überfielen die Reisenden.*
überholen: &c.	*Es ist unmöglich, ein so schnelles Auto zu überholen.*

umreisen:	*Sie haben die ganze Welt umreist.*
umgehen:	*Ich möchte diese Schwierigkeit umgehen.*[3]
umsegeln:	*Habt ihr die Insel umsegelt?*
&c.	

[1] The majority of verbs in this group are formed with *durch-*, *über-*, or *um-*. Since they are transitive, these verbs must be conjugated with *haben*. The idea of an action carried through to its completion (*durchwandern*—to hike right through, *umsegeln*—to sail right round) is an important feature of verbs of this type.   [2] Did he wade across that deep stream?   [3] I should like to get round (avoid) that difficulty.

(vi) Verbs of movement governing an object in the dative:

(*a*) Verbs with the prefix *ent-*:

entkommen:	*Er ist seinen Feinden entkommen.*[1]
entfliehen:	*Sie entflohen ihren Verfolgern.*[2]
entsteigen:	*Ein seltsamer Geruch entstieg den Schiffs-planken.*[3]
&c.	

(*b*) Separable verbs whose prefix is a preposition requiring the dative:

nachlaufen:	*Der Mann lief mir nach.*
beitreten:	*Ich bin dem Ausschuß beigetreten.*[4]
zufließen:	*Die Flüsse fließen dem Meer zu.*
&c.	

(*c*) The verb *sich nähern*—to approach:

Wir näherten uns langsam der Küste.
Ich habe mich ihm schnell genähert.

[1] He escaped from his enemies. But: *Er ist **aus** dem Gefängnis entkommen*—He escaped from prison.   [2] They evaded (escaped from) their pursuers. But: *Sie entflohen **aus** der Falle*—They escaped from the trap.   [3] A strange smell rose from the ship's boards.   [4] I have joined the committee.

Topic 13. Movement

TYPES OF MOVEMENT CONSTRUCTION

Painters get to Work

„Es wäre allenfalls ein Vorschlag", begann Herr Quichow und blickte mich aus seinem faltigen Gesicht blinzelnd an, „der Gartenzaun ist so lang, daß ich ihn allein nicht streichen kann.

Wenn Sie mir behilflich sein könnten, würden wir ihn zusammen streichen.“

Ich überlegte nicht lange und nickte zustimmend. Der bescheidene Mann lächelte, als ob etwas zu entschuldigen wäre. Dann stand er auf, sprang leichtfüßig die Stufen hinauf und verschwand in der „Waldesruh“.[1] Ich ging inzwischen zum Wagen und suchte die Kurbel. Als Herr Quichow zurückkam, nahm er mir die Kurbel nachsichtig aus der Hand, warf den Motor an und stieg ein. Mit einem Ruck schoß der Wagen vor und davon.

Der Wald wurde licht, und dann kamen Tannenschonungen, und dann fuhren wir schon an Maisfeldern vorbei. Eine Dorfkirche tauchte am Himmel auf, weiß mit nadelspitzem Turm, wir bogen in einen Feldweg ein, fuhren durch Fichtenwald und dann über einen Feldweg auf den Zaun eines langgestreckten Grundstücks zu. Hinter schwarzgrünen Fichten tauchten im Hintergrund des düsteren Gartens die Türme und das Schieferdach eines Landhauses auf. Herr Quichow sprang aus dem Wagen und öffnete das Gatter. Der Gartenzaun schien lange nicht mehr gestrichen worden. Ich schloß das Gatter und folgte dem Wagen, der unter den Tannen zu der kleinen Wellblechgarage fuhr. Wir näherten uns dem hohen, streichholzschachtelartigen Landhaus von der Rückseite. Über eine Treppe mit Eisengeländer stiegen wir in den Keller hinunter. Herr Quichow schloß eine Tür auf und ließ mich eintreten.

Ernst Kreuder: *Die Gesellschaft vom Dachboden*
(adapted)

[1] Name of a café.

Strange Shoppers

„Wir wollen gehen“, sagte er. Er nahm das Angelgerät und stand auf. Wir gingen den Weg am Ufer entlang, flußabwärts. Die Morgensonne erwärmte die kühle Luft. Nachdem wir unter der zweiten Brücke hindurchgegangen waren, stiegen wir die grasige Böschung hinauf und kamen auf die asphaltierte Straße, die zur Stadt führte.

„Hellgelb“, sagte ich, „sind hier die Straßenbahnen. Woanders sind sie blau oder grün.“

„Wir müssen nachher einen kleinen Umweg machen“, sagte Wilhelm. „Man soll uns nicht sehen, wenn wir hineingehen.“

In der Geschäftsstraße mit vielen Läden blieben wir vor einem vielstöckigen Kaufhaus[1] stehen.

„Am besten kaufen wir auch etwas dort drin“, sagte er. Ich

folgte ihm durch die Drehtüre. Das Warenhaus war erleuchtet.
Wir schoben uns langsam durch die Menge nach der Abteilung
„Bücher und Schreibwaren". In einem großen Kasten lagen
billige Bücher, antiquarisch. Sie kosteten 50 Pfennig. Wilhelm
erwarb eine „Anthologie jüngster[2] Lyrik"; ich kaufte den Detek-
tivroman „Der einzige Zeuge". Wir steckten die Bücher ein und
schoben uns einem der hinteren Ausgänge zu. „Hof" stand über
der Tür, durch die wir hinausgingen. In dem weiten Hinterhof
standen viele Kisten und Fässer. Wilhelm öffnete zwischen den
Fässern eine Lattentür und ließ mich in den Nachbarhof treten.
Als ich mich umwandte, sah ich, wie er das Angelgerät hinter
den Fässern verbarg.

ERNST KREUDER: *Die Gesellschaft vom Dachboden*

[1] *Kaufhaus* = *Warenhaus*—cf. note 9, p. 32.   [2] contemporary, recent.

The Chase

'A journalist has a difficult time of it[1] occasionally,' he began,
smiling short-sightedly at me. 'For example, I recently had to
report the arrival in London of one of these new film stars. At
Victoria Station[2] I had the very greatest difficulty[3] in pushing my
way through the crowd to the front.[4] She was already surrounded
by a throng of reporters and was just walking over to the car
which was to take her to some country-house or other. You can
imagine what trouble I had in getting back to the press car in
order to take up the pursuit.

'Fortunately she didn't escape me, either in the town or during
the rest of the journey. We did, in fact,[5] lose sight of her[6] a few
times; now and then it seemed as if they had made a detour and
we had lost track of them[7] altogether. Countless times we drove
past side-roads where they could have turned off,[8] and at one
point we had to stop abruptly when a car roared[9] out on to the
road just ahead of us.

'At last we saw that the people ahead[10] were slowing down, as if
they thought we wanted to overtake them. But then they turned
off to the left, driving along a narrow avenue. We continued the
chase beneath tall elms, towards the fence of a plot of land behind
which there emerged the outline of the country-house. By the
time[11] we had arrived at the house itself she had bounded nimbly
up the main steps and had disappeared through the door.'

[1] *es schwer haben.*   [2] *Am Victoria-Bahnhof.*   [3] *die allergrößte Mühe.*
[4] *nach vorne.*   [5] *zwar.*   [6] to lose sight of s.o.—*jn. aus den Augen verlieren.*
[7] to lose track of s.o.—*jemandes Spur verlieren.*   [8] Care with word-order. See
Topic 2, p. 10.   [9] to roar (in this sense)—*sausen.*   [10] *die da vorne.*   [11] *bis.*

1. He paced slowly across the room; then he turned and nodded in agreement.
2. I took the newspaper out of his hand and walked to the door.
3. Modestly he approached Herr Schulz and handed him the key.
4. A small boy was just pulling his brother up the embankment as the train thundered past.
5. They stepped aside[1] politely and allowed us to go ahead[2] through the swing-door.
6. The owner of the shop pulled out a few second-hand books from under the cupboard.
7. While we were driving past vineyards in the Rhineland, you were climbing mountains in Switzerland.
8. After we had gone through the third tunnel we knew that we should soon arrive at Innsbruck.

[1] to step aside—*zur Seite treten.*   [2] *vorangehen.*

Essay

Beschreiben Sie den Verlauf einer Panik bei einer Massenversammlung.

Mittagspause auf dem Schulhof.

Nach Geschäftsschluß[1] in der Untergrundbahn.

Setzen Sie entweder den ersten oder den zweiten deutsch-englischen Abschnitt fort.

[1] Lit. 'after the end of business'—i.e. rush hour.

Discussion

Beschreiben Sie ausführlich[1] — ohne Benützung des Texts — was in den beiden Auszügen geschieht.

Finden Sie nicht, daß die beiden Auszüge aus Kreuders Roman auf eine eigenartige Handlung schließen lassen?[2] Was ist Ihrer Meinung nach besonders eigenartig an Stil und Inhalt[3] dieser Auszüge?

[1] in detail.   [2] . . . that the two extracts from Kreuder's novel suggest a peculiar plot?   [3] *der Inhalt*—content.

Topic 14

Neuter Adjectival Nouns

(i) Masculine and feminine adjectival nouns have already been considered (Topic 11, p. 71). Whereas these denote *persons*, neuter adjectival nouns denote qualities or aspects, or those things to which these qualities or aspects apply. Compare:

der Gute	the good man, *and*
das Gute	the Good, the idea of the Good, that which is good, good things, &c.
die Alte	the old woman, *and*
das Alte	that which is old, old things, &c.

Thus:

Das Alte geht unter, und das Neue erscheint. Old things pass and new things appear.

Das Interessante an diesem Roman war für mich der Stil. The interesting aspect (part, &c.) of that novel for me was its style.

Wir wollen das Beste bis zuletzt lassen. We'll leave the best (part, things, &c.) till the end.

Present and past participles may similarly be used as neuter adjectival nouns:

Das Bleibende in der Zeit. That which is enduring in the flow of time.

Der Kellner brachte das Bestellte. The waiter brought what they had ordered.

It is important not to confuse *die Alten, die Starken, die Kleinen,* &c. (the old people, the strong, the small children, &c.) with *das Alte, das Starke, das Kleine,* &c. (old things, strong things, little things, &c.).

The neuter adjectival noun must follow the rules for adjective inflexions:

Altes und Neues wurde gespielt. Both old and new things were played.

Über dem Komischen der Lage vergaßen wir das Gefährliche daran. On account of the comic aspect of the situation we forgot the dangerous aspects of it. .

(ii) Neuter adjectival nouns must be used in expressions of quantity after such pronouns as *etwas, nichts, allerlei, viel, wenig*:

etwas Wichtiges	something important (N.B. *statt etwas Wichtig*em: dative—not genitive).
nichts Schlimmes	nothing serious
allerlei Neues	all kinds of new things
viel Schönes	many lovely things
wenig Besseres	little that was better
&c.	

In the above examples the adjectival nouns have an inflexion which was formerly a partitive genitive (cf. modern French: *quelque chose d'important, rien de sérieux*, &c.). This partitive sense is now completely lost, and the inflexion of the adjectival noun is governed simply by the case in which the noun stands in its context:

Ist er mit etwas Wichtigem verschwunden? Has he disappeared with something important?

Ich habe von nichts Schlimmem gehört. I have not heard of anything serious.

Care must be taken with expressions of quantity involving *alles, manches*, or any other pronoun of quantity which has a variable inflexion. The neuter adjectival noun following these must be inflected according to the normal rules for adjective inflexions (see Topic 1, pp. 1–3, for inflexion of adjectives after *manch-* and *solch-*):

Sie wünschten mir alles Gute. They wished me all the best.

Sie interessierte sich für alles Alte. She was interested in all old things.

Er war ein Feind von allem Halben. He was opposed to everything half-hearted.

N.B. In some common expressions the capital letter for the adjectival noun is dropped:

Er war alles andere als faul. He was anything but lazy.

Das ist nichts anderes als ein Meisterwerk. That is nothing short of a masterpiece.

Wir waren aufs genaueste unterrichtet. We were most precisely informed.

Sie waren aufs engste miteinander verbunden. They were very closely associated.

Topic 14. Human Qualities

NEUTER ADJECTIVAL NOUNS

A Married Couple

Ein Mann hatte das Gut seiner Eltern übernommen, welches durch die nachlässige Wirtschaft[1] des Vaters heruntergekommen war, und hatte es durch unermüdliche Tätigkeit im Lauf der Jahre wieder hochgebracht. Die Familie war in früheren Zeiten sehr angesehen gewesen. Sein Ehrgeiz ging dahin,[2] daß er einmal wieder so in der Achtung der Nachbarn dastehen wollte[3] wie seine Vorfahren, und daß seine Nachkommen in der Gegend wieder so angesehen sein sollten, wie die Familie sonst gewesen.

Wie es einem solchen Manne leicht geschehen kann, daß er das Menschliche über dem Wirtschaftlichen vergißt, war er erst spät zum Heiraten gekommen. Er hatte eine gute und stille Frau gewählt, die viel jünger war als er und fast seine Tochter hätte sein können. Er liebte sie in seiner Art, in der Art eines tüchtigen und verständigen Mannes, der das Seine hat zusammenhalten müssen und immer an seine Arbeit gedacht hat, und die junge Frau hätte sich gewiß über nichts beklagen können bei ihm, wenn sie überhaupt von der Art gewesen wäre, welche klagt. Sie hatte eine feine und durchsichtige Gesichtshaut, die leicht errötete, und hatte als Mädchen gern gelesen. Nun eilte sie mit leichten Füßen die Treppen auf und ab, sorgte für Hühner und Garten, richtete die Stuben schön ein und hielt sie gut, und zuweilen sah sie mit sehnsüchtigen Blicken ins Weite, wo vielleicht Dinge geschahen und Verhältnisse waren, welche den Erzählungen der Bücher glichen . . .

PAUL ERNST: *Das zweite Gesicht*[4]

[1] *nachlässige Wirtschaft*—neglectful management.   [2] It was the object of his ambition . . .   [3] *in der Achtung der Nachbarn dastehen*—to occupy a position in the regard of his neighbours.   [4] second sight. (N.B. *das Gesicht*, pl. *die Gesichter*—face; *das Gesicht, die Gesichte*—vision, apparition.)

Franz Kafka

Für den ersten Anschein war Kafka ein gesunder junger Mensch, allerdings merkwürdig still, beobachtend, zurückhaltend. Seine geistige Richtung[1] ging durchaus nicht auf das Bizarre, Groteske, sondern auf das Große der Natur, auf das Gesunde, Festgefügte,[2] Einfache.

Ich habe es immer wieder erlebt, daß Verehrer Kafkas, die ihn nur aus seinen Büchern kennen, ein ganz falsches Bild von ihm haben. Sie glauben, er müsse auch im Umgang[3] traurig, ja verzweifelt gewirkt[4] haben. Das Gegenteil ist der Fall. Es wurde einem wohl[5] in seiner Nähe. Die Fülle seiner Gedanken, die er meist in heiterem Ton vorbrachte, machte ihn zu einem der unterhaltendsten Menschen, denen ich je begegnet bin — trotz seiner Bescheidenheit, trotz seiner Ruhe. Er sprach wenig, in großer Gesellschaft nahm er oft stundenlang nicht das Wort. Aber wenn er etwas sagte, machte es sofort aufhorchen. Denn es war immer inhaltsvoll, traf den Nagel auf den Kopf. Und in vertrautem Gespräch löste sich ihm manchmal die Zunge auf ganz erstaunliche Art, er konnte begeistert und hingerissen sein, des Scherzens und Lachens war dann kein Ende; ja er lachte gern und herzhaft und wußte auch seine Freunde zum Lachen zu bringen. Mehr als das: in schwierigen Lagen konnte man sich seiner Weltklugheit, seinem Takt, seinem Rat, der kaum je das Richtige verfehlte, ohne Bedenken aufatmend anvertrauen. Er war ein wundervoll helfender Freund. Nur für sich selbst war er ratlos, hilflos . . .

MAX BROD: *Franz Kafka. Eine Biographie*
(abridged extract)

---

[1] His intellectual inclinations.   [2] *festgefügt*—firmly established.   [3] *im Umgang*—amongst others, in his social contacts.   [4] *wirken* (+ adverb)—to create an impression, to have an effect.   [5] Cf. *mir ist wohl*—I feel at ease, content.

A Friendship

The Meyers[1] had been living in the village for two years before the wife met Fräulein Seghers. She was one of the most prosperous and respected landowners of the district, whereas Frau Liese Meyer was anything but wealthy. Modest and reticent in her social contacts, Frau Meyer was often considered sad, if not unfriendly. Her quiet exterior,[2] however, concealed[3] a gay and observant mind, as Fräulein Seghers soon realized. For her, the interesting thing about Frau Meyer was her ability to comment on[4] comic and serious aspects of village life in a humorous yet kindly manner,[5] talking[6] enthusiastically about everything new or unusual that occurred.

At first sight, Fräulein Seghers was a proud, aristocratic, humourless woman. Her ambition was directed mainly towards the development of the farms on the family estate, whose welfare[7] she advanced[8] with unflagging energy. And although people trusted her advice, which hardly ever went wide of the mark,[9] it was said that she forgot the human side for business considerations.[10]

In the course of the years there developed[11] a deep friendship between the two women. Only Frau Meyer, it was said, knew how to make her friend laugh. People wondered[12] whether they had always had a completely false impression of Fräulein Seghers.

[1] *Meyers* or *die Meyers.*　　[2] *das Äußere* (adjectival noun).　　[3] *verbergen.*
[4] to comment on s.th. (in this sense)—*etwas kommentieren.*　　[5] in a humorous manner—*auf humorvolle Weise.*　　[6] Use a subordinate clause introduced by *wobei.*　　[7] *das Wohl.*　　[8] *fördern.*　　[9] Cf. German–English text (Max Brod).
[10] Cf. German–English text (Paul Ernst).　　[11] Reflexive verb.　　[12] *Man fragte sich . . .*

1. I have heard many good things about this man.
2. On[1] my departure they wished me all the best.
3. The aged often prefer[2] old things to new.
4. The sad part was that nobody said anything[3] kind to him.
5. He was only interested in the best. He did not want anything[4] cheap.
6. The mysterious is especially important in the works of that author.
7. Let us forget what is past;[5] let us think about new things.
8. The two men were intimately associated in business.[6]

[1] *bei.*　　[2] *vorziehen* (with direct and indirect objects; but no preposition!).
[3] *etwas.*　　[4] *nichts.*　　[5] to pass (in this sense)—*vergehen.*　　[6] Use the adverb *geschäftlich.*

ESSAY

Eine Charakteristik eines Freundes oder einer Freundin.
Ein kluger Mensch.
Schreiben Sie ein Zeugnis[1] für einen Bekannten, der sich um eine Stelle bewirbt.[2]
Was sind Ihrer Meinung nach die besten Eigenschaften,[3] die ein Mensch haben kann?

[1] testimonial.　　[2] . . . who is applying for a post.　　[3] qualities.

DISCUSSION

Wer ist Ihrer Meinung nach der bedeutendste Mensch unserer Zeit? Wie begründen[1] Sie Ihre Wahl?
Was erwarten Sie von einem guten Freund?

[1] *begründen*—justify, give reasons (*Gründe*) for.

VOCABULARY WORK

Compile a list of 15 desirable and 15 undesirable human qualities. List also the adjectives which relate to the nouns you find.

Topic 15

The Inseparable Prefixes
be-, ent- (emp-), er-, ver-, zer-

Inseparable verbs require careful study. They occur frequently and cause difficulty because the root idea contained may no longer be clearly felt: e.g. whereas the connexion between *binden*—to tie and *verbinden*—to bandage is evident, the English student may not easily find the connexion between *stehen* and *bestehen*—to exist, to endure. Moreover, some inseparable verbs have a root which is not easily identified with other German words the student knows: e.g. *verlieren, erlauben*.

The prefix *zer-* always renders the idea of destruction, dissolution. But each of the prefixes *be-, ent- (emp-* before *f-), er-, ver-* is used with varying significance in different verbs.

The following notes deal with some aspects of the significance which the different inseparable prefixes may carry. The student should pay careful attention to all inseparable verbs as he meets them, and think not only of their English equivalents but try also to see the meaning conveyed by the prefix.

N.B. For inseparable verbs beginning with a preposition, see Grammar Section, 4–6.

be-

(i) *Intransitive changed to transitive verb:*

antworten—beantworten, herrschen—beherrschen, steigen—besteigen, siegen (win victory)—*besiegen* (defeat).

(ii) *Transitive verb formed from another transitive verb or verb governing dative* (marked D). The new verb often intensifies the meaning of the original verb, focusing attention on a particular object:

denken—bedenken (consider—s.th.), *lehren—belehren* (teach—s.o. a lesson), *halten—behalten* (keep), *dienen* (D)—*bedienen* (serve—customers).

(iii) *Formation of verb from adjective or noun.* The significance of the prefix here varies. It is often 'to make . . .', 'to provide . . .', 'to cover with . . .':

> *befreien, begrenzen* (limit), *beneiden* (envy—*der Neid*), *beschmutzen* (soil), *beleuchten* (illuminate).

ent- (emp-)

(i) *Signifying beginning, change, development:*

> *entstehen* (arise, develop), *entstammen* (originate, hail from),[1] *entschlummern* (drop off to sleep), *entfachen* (fan up—fire), *entwickeln* and *sich entwickeln* (develop—Eng. trans. and intrans. meanings).

(ii) *Signifying separation, removal, withdrawal:*

> *entreißen* (snatch away),[2] *entbehren* (do without, dispense with), *entkommen* (escape),[3] *entdecken* (discover), *entladen* (unload), *entwirren* (unravel), *entscheiden* (decide).[4]

N.B. Verbs with the prefix *ent-* often denote the opposite of verbs with *ver-*: e.g. *verdecken* (obscure), *verladen* (load up), *verwirren* (confuse).

[1] to originate from s.th.—*einer Sache* (D) *entstammen.*   [2] to snatch s.th. away from s.o.—*jemandem etwas entreißen.*   [3] to escape from s.o.—*jemandem entkommen.* But: to escape from a place—*aus einem Ort entkommen.*   [4] *entscheiden* is explained by the idea it contains of removing various possibilities until only one (the decision) is left.

er-

(i) *Signifying the idea of a process, an attaining:*

> *erreichen, ersteigen* (climb to the top of), *erdenken* (think out), *erfinden* (invent), *erkämpfen* (get by fighting), *ertrotzen* (get by defiant insistence), *ermöglichen* (make possible), *erröten* (blush), *erblinden* (go blind), *erzittern* (start to tremble), *erziehen* (educate).

N.B. Some verbs with the prefix *er-* lay the stress on the beginning, not the end, of the process: e.g. *erzittern.*

ver-

(i) *Signifying:*

> (*a*) *Wastage, consumption, loss, dispensing with:*
> *verwüsten* (lay waste), *verspielen* (gamble away—money), *verbrauchen*—(use up—supplies), *verlieren, verwerfen* (reject).

(b) *Error, wrong or improper doing:*

sich verlaufen (lose one's way), *sich versprechen* (make a slip of the tongue), *sich verschreiben* (make a slip of the pen), *verpassen* (miss—train, opportunity, &c.).

(ii) *Reversal of meaning of root verb:*

verkaufen, verleiten (lead astray), *verlernen* (forget how to do), *verachten* (despise; *achten*—respect), *verblühen* (fade, wither).

(iii) *Formation of verb from adjective or noun:*

verlängern (trans. vb. lengthen), *vertiefen* (deepen, accentuate), *veröffentlichen* (publish), *vereisen* (freeze over), *verkörpern* (embody), *verteilen* (distribute).

(iv) *Signifying 'away', 'forth':*

verreisen (go away on a journey), *verjagen* (chase away), *vertreiben* (drive away—s.th.), *verstecken* and *verbergen* (hide), *versetzen* (transfer, pawn), *vertagen* (postpone), *vergehen* (pass away), *verbluten* (bleed to death).

(v) *Intensifying the meaning of the root verb:*

versinken (intrans. vb. sink), *verlassen* (abandon, leave), *verändern* (trans. vb. alter, change), *verhören* (interrogate), *versprechen* (promise).

zer-

Signifying destruction, disruption, dissolution, &c.:

zerreißen (tear up), *zerpflücken* (pluck to pieces), *zerlegen* (dissect), *zerbrechen, zerstören, zertreten* (trample to pieces), &c.

N.B. Verbs with the prefix *zer-* may be made up at will.

It will be evident from the examples given above that certain verbs may be grouped under different headings, e.g. *beantworten* belongs to both (i) and (iii), *verblühen* to both (ii) and (iv).

Topic 15. Exploration and Discovery

INSEPARABLE PREFIXES

The Voyages of Discovery of the Zeno Brothers

Die Brüder entstammten dem alten Patriziergeschlecht[1] der Zeno; im Jahre 1380 oder 1390 rüstete Nicolo, um sich Ehre und Ruhm zu erwerben, ein Schiff aus, durchsegelte die Straße von

Gibraltar und steuerte nordwärts, um England und Flandern zu besuchen, wurde aber durch einen Sturm verschlagen und geriet augenscheinlich auf eine der Färöer, die einem nordischen Frei-beuter untertan war. Er ließ seinen Bruder nachkommen; die beiden führten nun teils im Auftrage, teils in Gesellschaft des Freibeuters mehrere Reisen aus, die sie vermutlich nach Kanada und dem Gebiet der USA brachten. Antonio schrieb Briefe von diesen Unternehmungen nach Hause, die zunächst unbeachtet im Familienarchiv der Zeno liegenblieben; dann aber, über 100 Jahre später, gerieten sie in die Hände eines Knaben, des 1515 geborenen Nicolo Zeno, des jüngeren, der sie las, aber ihren Wert nicht erkannte und sie zum Teil zerriß. Erst in reiferen Jahren suchte er die Bruchstücke zusammen und entwarf mit Hilfe seiner Erinnerung an das, was er als Junge gelesen, und den unversehrten Stücken eine neue Beschreibung jener Reisen, die im Jahre 1558 bei[2] Francesco Marcolini in Venedig veröffentlicht wurde. Ihr Inhalt ist in Kürze folgender.

Der (bereits erwähnte) Sturm verschlug das Schiff Nicolos an die Insel Frieslanda, es scheiterte, aber Mannschaft und Ladung konnten gerettet werden. Der Beherrscher der Insel, der Zichmi hieß, nahm sie freundlich auf, freute sich, daß sie Venezianer seien und behielt sie in seinen Diensten, da sie ihm als Seefahrer nützlich sein könnten. Zeno wurde dem Befehlshaber einer Flotte von 13 Schiffen unterstellt, die nach Westen segelte und verschie-dene Inseln der Herrschaft Zichmis unterwarf.

ANTON MAYER: *Tausend Jahre Seefahrt*

[1] Patrician family.   [2] 'by' in the sense: 'at the publishing house of'.

Preparations for Captain Scott's journey to the South Pole

Dazwischen[1] wagen sie kleine Vorstöße. Sie proben ihre Auto-mobilschlitten, sie lernen Skilaufen und dressieren die Hunde. Sie rüsten ein Depot für die große Reise, aber langsam, ganz langsam blättert nur der Kalender ab bis zum Sommer (dem Dezember), der ihnen das Schiff durch das Packeis bringt mit Briefen von Hause.[2] Kleine Gruppen wagen schon auch jetzt inmitten des grimmigsten Winters abhärtende Tagesreisen,[3] die Zelte werden geprobt, die Erfahrung befestigt. Nicht alles gelingt, aber gerade die Schwierigkeiten geben ihnen neuen Mut. Wenn sie zurückkommen von ihren Expeditionen, erfroren und abgemüdet,[4] so empfängt sie Jubel und warmer Herdglanz, und dies kleine behagliche Haus im 77. Breitengrad[5] scheint ihnen nach den Tagen der Entbehrung der seligste Aufenthalt der Welt.

Aber einmal kehrt eine Expedition von Westen zurück, und ihre Botschaft wirft Stille ins Haus. Sie haben auf ihrer Wanderung Amundsens Winterquartier entdeckt: mit einem Male weiß nun Scott, daß außer dem Frost und der Gefahr noch ein anderer ihm den Ruhm streitig macht,[6] als erster das Geheimnis der störrischen Erde entrafft zu haben: Amundsen, der Norweger. Er mißt nach[7] auf den Karten. Und man spürt sein Entsetzen aus den Zeilen nachschwingen,[8] wie er gewahr wird, daß Amundsens Winterquartier um[9] hundertzehn Kilometer näher zum Pole postiert ist als das seine. Er erschrickt, aber ohne darum zu verzagen. „Auf zur Ehre meines Landes!" schreibt er stolz in sein Tagebuch.   STEFAN ZWEIG: 'Der Kampf um den Südpol'
(*Sternstunden der Menschheit*)

[1] Meanwhile (Zweig has been describing life in the base camp).   [2] or: *von zu Hause.*   [3] single-day toughening journeys.   [4] or: *ermüdet.*   [5] the 77th degree of latitude.   [6] *jemandem etwas streitig machen*—to challenge s.o.'s right to s.th.   [7] *nachmessen*—to check up (by measuring).   [8] *nachschwingen*—lit. to go on vibrating, continue to resound. Tr. 'We catch the echo of his dismay . . .'
[9] *um*—by, to the extent of.

The Great Discoverers

In our time, when the whole world is known, it may be difficult to imagine the thoughts of the old explorers who first sailed out[1] to discover new territories, to cross untravelled seas, in spite of all the dangers and privations which they might encounter. The spirit of adventure which inspired[2] the great discoverers of bygone ages, the desire[3] to acquire new knowledge,[4] to undertake advances into the unknown, pales[5] perhaps in an age when science is every year achieving enormous progress.

But we should remember how intrepid the great adventurers were when they made their voyages of discovery in order to wrest their secrets from the remotest parts of the earth. Certainly, the voyages of a Columbus,[6] a Drake,[6] or a Captain Cook[6] have something romantic about them.[7] But the successes which they achieved often had to be paid for with human lives;[8] for years they had to give up[9] family and homeland; they had to learn to despise[10] hunger, cold, exhaustion; they could not comfort themselves with the thought that they would certainly soon be returning to publish their accounts of their travels.

It is easy to recognize the value of such men's achievements. What they discovered made possible a whole series of further developments in many spheres[11] of knowledge.[12] However, we should always bear in mind[13] that they[14] were resolute[15] men who were prepared to lose much in order to gain much.

[1] Perfect tense, in order to establish the link between *our* thoughts and *theirs*. Cf. Gram. 38.   [2] inspire—(here) *beseelen* or *anspornen*.   [3] *das Verlangen*.   [4] *Kenntnisse* (plur.).   [5] *verblassen*.   [6] ... *eines Kolumbus, eines Drake oder eines Kapitän Cook.* (But: *Kolumbus' Reisen*; *Drakes Entdeckungen*; *Kapitän Cooks Schiffe.* See also Gram. 64.)   [7] Omit 'about them'.   [8] *mit Menschenleben.*   [9] *verzichten auf* (accus.).   [10] *Sie mußten lernen, ... zu* + infinitive; or: *Sie mußten ... infinitive + lernen.*   [11] sphere (in this sense)—*das Gebiet*; used with the preposition *auf*.   [12] *Wissenschaft.*   [13] bear in mind—*beachten.*   [14] *es ... waren.*   [15] *entschlossen.*

1. After their return the explorers drew up a long account of their travels.
2. I should not miss the opportunity of taking part in[1] the expedition.
3. For days on end the travellers sailed through a narrow, frozen channel.
4. The diary of the journeys found its way into the hands of Nicolo.
5. The discoverers escaped from the natives[2] but soon lost their way again.
6. 'A barren, deserted land,' we read in the description of the journey; 'shall we ever conquer it?'
7. Only[3] a century ago our knowledge of large parts of Africa was very limited.
8. Robinson Crusoe was cast up[4] on a desert island and had to think out means of preserving his life.

[1] to take part in—*teilnehmen an* (dat.).   [2] native (in this sense)—*der Wilde.*   [3] *noch.*   [4] *verschlagen.*

ESSAY

Schreiben Sie einen Auszug aus dem Tagebuch eines Entdeckungsreisenden.
Eine große Forschungsreise unserer Zeit.
Christoph Kolumbus und die Entdeckung Amerikas.
Vorbereitungen für eine Entdeckungsreise.

DISCUSSION

Hat es einen Zweck, die großen Himalaja-Berge zu besteigen?
Würden Sie lieber ein unerforschtes Gebiet im Polarkreis oder in Äquatorialafrika durchreisen?

VOCABULARY WORK

Collect from previous chapters in this book further examples of verbs with inseparable prefixes which may be grouped under the headings given in the notes on pp. 98–100.

Make a list of verbs with an inseparable *prepositional* prefix (*unternehmen, überholen, umschließen, durchsegeln,* &c.) from this and previous chapters.

Topic 16

Use of Prepositions after certain Verbs and Past Participles

The list below gives further verbs which are followed by particular prepositions. The verbs are grouped according to sense. In some instances the verb and preposition governs an object (the 'prepositional object' form); cf. English:

I rely on you (*Ich verlasse mich auf dich*) and
Don't bother about him (*Kümmern Sie sich nicht um ihn*).

In other instances, the preposition following the verb or past participle is rather to be thought of as introducing an adverbial phrase; cf. English:

He turned to them (*Er wandte sich an sie*) and
I was occupied with my studies (*Ich war mit meinen Studien beschäftigt*).

For all practical purposes no distinction need be drawn between such prepositional object and adverbial phrase constructions. What is important is the use of the appropriate preposition after the verb or past participle.

'Accusative or Dative' prepositions govern the *accusative* except for those marked (D).

For further notes on the use of prepositions following verbs, see Grammar Section, 32; following adjectives and past participles, Grammar Section, 89.

(i) Denoting concern, worry, grief:

sich kümmern um[1]	to bother about
sich sorgen um	to worry about, be concerned about
trauern um	to mourn for
weinen um	to weep for

(ii) Denoting relationships between people:

verwandt mit	related to
sich verloben mit	to become engaged to
sich verlieben in	to fall in love with
vertrauen auf	to trust in[2]
sich verlassen auf	to rely on[2]
zählen auf	to count on[2]

(iii) Denoting concentration (preoccupation, interest, participation, attention, &c.):

sich konzentrieren auf	to concentrate on
bedacht sein auf	to be intent on
achten auf	to pay attention to
sich befassen mit ⎫ *sich beschäftigen mit* ⎭	to busy, occupy, concern o.s. with
(D) *teilnehmen an*	to take part in

(iv) Denoting seeking, striving, longing (towards):

suchen nach	to seek for
streben nach	to strive for
sich sehnen nach	to long for
greifen nach	to reach for
dürsten nach	to be thirsty for
hungern nach	to be hungry for
graben nach	to dig for
fischen nach	to fish for

(v) Denoting direction:

zeigen auf ⎫ *deuten auf*[3] ⎭	to point to
hinweisen auf[4]	to point to, to point out
anspielen auf	to allude to
sich beziehen auf	to relate to, refer to
sich wenden an[5]	to turn to
sich umwenden nach ⎫ *sich umdrehen nach* ⎭	to turn (right) round to

(vi) Denoting possession, loss, &c. ('having' and 'not having'):

herrschen über	to rule over
verfügen über	to have at one's disposal
(D) *fehlen an*[6] ⎫ (D) *mangeln an*[6] ⎭	to be lacking in
verzichten auf	to forgo, renounce
(*jn.*) *um etwas bringen*	to cheat, defraud (s.o.) of s.th.
ums Leben kommen	to lose one's life

---

[1] As in English (to bother about) *sich kümmern um* is found mainly in a negative sense: *Kümmere dich nicht um ihn.*   [2] These verbs may also be used to denote a relationship with things: *Vertraue auf diese Landkarte! Verlaß dich auf meine Uhr! Können wir auf gutes Wetter zählen?*   [3] Also figuratively, *to point to, indicate*: *Alles deutet auf Regen.*   [4] Usually in the figurative sense, *to point out, draw attention to*: *Ich muß darauf hinweisen, daß Sie sich irren* (I must point out that you are wrong).   [5] Also figuratively, to turn to (s.o.) for help.   [6] Impersonal verbs: *Es fehlt* (or *mangelt*) *ihm an Interesse.*

Topic 16.   Men and Politics

USE OF PREPOSITIONS AFTER CERTAIN VERBS AND PAST PARTICIPLES

Sir Winston Churchill

Wie ungemein schwer ist es, die Größe dieses Mannes in zutreffende Worte zu fassen! Wie einfach wäre es, und doch wie falsch, zu sagen, daß das britische Volk mit Liebe auf seinen greisen Ministerpräsidenten[1] blickt. Niemand weiß besser als Churchill, daß er die schwindelerregende Höhe, von der er heute auf sein Schaffen herabschaut, nicht seiner Popularität verdankt. Wohl kein anderer Staatsmann hat in seinem Leben soviel Feindseligkeit und so viele Rückschläge erlitten wie der Mann, der sein Volk zum Siege führte, nachdem er ihm gesagt hatte: „Ich habe nichts, was ich Ihnen bieten könnte, als Blut, Schweiß, Mühsal und Tränen.“[2] Und vielleicht haben wenige andere geschichtliche Persönlichkeiten so bitter unter den Anfeindungen gelitten, denen er sein Leben lang ausgesetzt war, wie Winston Churchill.

Er hat diese latente Feindseligkeit gegen sich nie begreifen können. Sie hat ihn immer tief geschmerzt, wenn er diesem Gefühl auch nur selten Ausdruck verliehen hat. Und man kann sagen, daß seine Größe in seiner fast prometheischen[3] Einsamkeit liegt, in seiner Unfähigkeit, die ganzen Ausmaße seines Charakters und seines Intellekts den bescheideneren Proportionen seiner Zeitgenossen anzupassen. In seiner eigenen Partei ist die Verehrung für ihn mit Scheu und Furcht vor seinem impulsiven und unberechenbaren Temperament gepaart. Seine sozialistischen Gegner haben nie aufgehört, ihn als einen typischen Vertreter der Aristokratie, einer arroganten herrschenden Klasse, zu betrachten. Seit dem Tage im Jahre 1901, als der junge konservative Abgeordnete Churchill in seiner Jungfernrede im Unterhaus, dem damals herrschenden Burenhaß[4] und der fanatischen Antiburenpolitik der konservativen Regierung zum Trotze,[5] dem Kampfgeist und der Heimatliebe der Buren einen großzügigen Tribut zollte,[6] ist Winston Churchill der Schrecken der Parteifunktionäre[7] geblieben, die nichts so entsetzt wie Unbotmäßigkeit.

Churchill hat nie ein Hehl daraus gemacht,[8] daß er Parteien als Mittel zu einem höheren Zweck, nie aber als Selbstzweck betrachtet hat. Er hat sich nie dafür entschuldigt, daß er vom

Konservativen zum Liberalen[9] und zum Bewunderer Lloyd Georges wurde, um schließlich wieder den Weg zur konservativen Partei zurückzufinden. Obgleich er ohne Zweifel der größte Parlamentarier ist, den England seit den Tagen von Pitt und Fox besessen hat — er selbst bezeichnet sich gern als „ein Kind des Unterhauses" —, so ist er doch das krasse Gegenteil des typischen Parteipolitikers.

STEPHAN W. POLLACK: 'Fürst der Paradoxe—
Zu Winston Churchills 80. Geburtstag.' (*Rheinischer Merkur*)

[1] The article was published in November 1954. Churchill was Prime Minister at the time.   [2] The reference is to Churchill's famous appeal to the nation after the fall of France: 'I have nothing to offer you but blood, toil, tears, and sweat.'   [3] Promethean.   [4] *Burenhaß*—hatred of the Boers (this was the period of the Boer War).   [5] *Einer Sache . . . zum Trotze*—in spite of s.th., in defiance of s.th.   [6] *jm.* or *einer Sache Tribut zollen*—to pay tribute to s.o. or s.th.   [7] *der Parteifunktionär*—party official.   [8] *ein Hehl aus etwas machen*—to make a secret of s.th. (cf. also the verb *verhehlen*—to conceal, make a secret of).   [9] *der Konservative* and *der Liberale* are adjectival nouns (cf. the adjectives *konservativ* and *liberal*); *der Sozialist*, *der Kommunist*, &c., are weak masculine nouns.

A Political Discussion (continued)[1]

'Anyway, I don't see why you are not concerned about these questions,' said Kluge. 'You, for example,' he added, turning[2] to Schmitz, 'ought to be more interested in politics; especially in the political careers of the great personalities of the present time.[3] Then perhaps you would understand that they are intent on preserving peace, and that they are always[4] seeking for means to this end. Not every conference they take part in leads to set-backs and hostility; they do what they can, and they deserve the confidence of the electors. In recent weeks, everything has been pointing to an improvement.'

'Nobody doubts[5] the abilities of these men,' said Klein. 'One can even say that they long for peace as much as the nations they represent. But they are[6] often arrogant and incalculable men whom we should regard as a possible danger. Or they are men who desire peace but who are not willing to renounce war as a political means. They do not lack character, even[7] greatness, but often merely[7] imagination. They have enormous power[8] at their disposal, and therefore concentrate more on political successes than on international goodwill.[9] A single man is capable of cheating a whole nation out of its security and happiness.'

Schmitz said nothing, but beckoned the waitress across[10] and ordered more coffee.

[1] See English–German passage, Topic 9. [2] Translate with a clause; or, if the participle is used, place it at the end of the phrase. [3] the present (time)—*die Gegenwart*. [4] 'always' in the sense of 'constantly'—*ständig*. [5] to doubt s.th.—*zweifeln an* (D) or *bezweifeln* (trans. verb). [6] *es sind* . . . [7] Repeat the preposition. See Gram. 141. [8] Power—*die Macht*. [9] *der gute Wille*. [10] to beckon s.o. across—*jn. heranwinken*.

1. The committee consisted of[1] conservatives, liberals, and socialists.
2. The Prime Minister paid generous tribute to all who had helped him.[2]
3. Our member of parliament made a very good maiden speech in the House of Commons yesterday.
4. Churchill's book *Great Contemporaries* is one of his most popular works.
5. All his life he was exposed to bitter hostility.
6. How difficult it would be to prove that he is wrong!
7. The party made no secret of the fact that they had suffered a set-back.
8. She never apologized for not writing to me.

[1] to consist of—*bestehen aus*. [2] Take care with the order of direct and indirect objects.

Essay

Ein großer Staatsmann.

Vorteile und Nachteile der politischen Laufbahn.

Schreiben Sie einen Brief an Ihren Abgeordneten, in dem Sie ihm Ihre Meinung sagen zu einer Rede, die er im Unterhaus gehalten hat.

„Ich habe nichts, was ich Ihnen bieten könnte, als Blut, Schweiß, Mühsal und Tränen."

Discussion

Wer sind Ihrer Meinung nach die glücklichsten Menschen? Sorgen sich Ihre Eltern zu sehr um Sie?

Vocabulary and Grammar Work

Many verbs in English are followed by the word 'to' and a noun or pronoun. Collect from the German–English translation

passages of Topics 15 and 16 two lists of expressions corresponding to English expressions involving 'to': (*a*) those which in German include a preposition (e.g. *Die Flotte segelte nach Westen;
er führte sein Volk zum Siege*). (*b*) those which do not (e.g. *Er
wurde dem Befehlshaber einer Flotte unterstellt;* . . . *die Anfeindungen, denen er ausgesetzt war* . . .).

Topic 17

Translation of the English Present Participle and Gerund

It is often difficult to choose a correct equivalent in German for what is expressed in English by a present participle or gerund (verbal noun with the ending -ing). A German present participle, for example, could not be used in the following phrases:

> By studying hard he was able to pass the examination. (*Durch fleißiges Studium konnte er das Examen bestehen.*)
> We saw them coming towards us. (*Wir sahen sie auf uns zu-kommen.*)
> She contented herself with sending a postcard. (*Sie begnügte sich damit, eine Postkarte zu schicken.*)

It is important for the student to study this question thoroughly in his reading, for it is a major problem of translation—not only in 'prose composition' passages, but also in German–English translation. Here the use of the English present participle often converts what would otherwise have been a stilted version into an idiomatic and stylistic rendering of the German phrase.

The following types of construction corresponding to English present participles should be noted:

(i) Participle used as adjective or noun:

> *die singenden Kinder; lachende Menschen; funkelnder Wein.*
> *der Sterbende; die Herumstehenden; das Kommende.*
> *eine Zeitung lesende* (or *zeitunglesende*) *Putzfrau; ein glück-bringendes Geschenk.*
> *ein nie zu lösendes Problem* (cf. *dieses Problem ist nicht zu lösen*).

(ii) Participle used like an adverb:

> „*Gott sei Dank!*", *sagte er aufatmend.*
> *Keuchend erreichte er als erster das Ziel.* Panting, he arrived first at the winning-post.
> *Stirnrunzelnd blickte er mich an.* He glanced at me, frowning.

Ein blendendweißes Licht erschien. A blinding white light appeared.

Sie spricht immer so verwirrend schnell. She always speaks so bewilderingly fast.

(iii) Use of subordinate clauses:

(*a*) **während, indem, wobei:**

während: to indicate that two or more actions occur simultaneously: *Während sie die Kleider bügelte, sang sie leise vor sich hin.* Whilst ironing the clothes she sang quietly to herself.

indem: frequently found with the meaning *während*; but properly indicates that one action takes place *within* the duration of the other. Another important usage of *indem* is to show the *means by which*, i.e. 'by -ing':

Indem er dies sagte, stand er auf. So saying, he stood up (*Time*).

Man gibt seine Stimme ab, indem man ein Kreuz auf den Stimmzettel zeichnet. One votes by making a cross on the ballot paper (*Means*).

N.B. *indem* is also found introducing clauses which show an *attendant circumstance*, i.e. some action which is intimately related to what follows or precedes the *indem*-clause. In some instances the *indem*-clause is more akin to the idea of time, in others to that of means:

Von Zeit zu Zeit blickte er, indem er die Augenbrauen hob, um sich her. From time to time he glanced around him, raising his eyebrows as he did so (*Time*). (See p. 115.)

Indem wir die neueren Sprachen studieren, erweitern wir unsere Kenntnisse der Geschichte und der Geographie. By (in) learning modern languages we extend our knowledge of history and geography (*Means*).

wobei: English 'and in so doing', 'and as (he) did so', 'meanwhile . . . -ing', &c. Denotes an accompanying action to what has just been mentioned:

Er stand neben ihr und drehte an seinem Schnurrbart, wobei er leise vor sich hinpfiff. He stood near her, twisting his moustache and whistling softly to himself. (See p. 114.)

(*b*) Relative clause:

Ein Mann, der der Beschreibung entspricht, ist hier gesehen worden. A man corresponding to the description has been seen here.

Diejenigen, die Bücher mitnehmen wollen, sollen sich hier melden. Those wishing to take books with them are to report here.

(*c*) **wie-** and **daß-**clauses:

Ich sah, wie er das Angelgerät hinter den Fässern verbarg. I saw him hiding the fishing tackle behind the barrels (p. 91, *Strange Shoppers*). (See also (vi) below.)

Haben Sie je bemerkt, daß er mit ihr gesprochen hat? Did you ever notice him talking to her?

(*d*) **als-, bevor- (ehe-)** and **nachdem-**clauses:

Als wir in die Seitenstraße einbogen, erblickten wir das Auto. Turning (i.e. when we turned) into the side-street, we caught sight of the car.

Similarly:

Bevor (or ehe) wir in die Seitenstraße einbogen, . . . Before turning . . .

Nachdem wir in die Seitenstraße eingebogen waren, . . . After turning . . .

(iv) Main clauses joined by *und*:

Wir bogen in die Seitenstraße ein und erblickten das Auto. Cf. *Als wir . . . einbogen, . . .* Turning into . . .

Er nahm das Buch in die Hand und schlug die Titelseite auf. Picking up the book, he turned to the title-page.

(v) Infinitive used as noun (corresponding to the English gerund):

Das Summen der Bienen—the humming of the bees; *das Quaken der Frösche*—the croaking of the frogs; &c.

Durch Schwimmen erhielt sie sich gesund. She kept fit by swimming.

Im Vorbeigehen nickte er mir zu. He nodded to me in passing.

N.B. The use and omission of articles after prepositions in such phrases is a matter of idiom. Generally speaking, the article is included.

(vi) Infinitive after *sehen* and *hören* (see also Topic 18, pp. 119–20):

Wir sahen sie aus dem Zimmer kommen. Wir hörten sie zusammen flüstern. (Perfect tense: *Wir haben sie aus dem Zimmer kommen sehen. Wir haben sie zusammen flüstern hören.*) These sentences may also be expressed: *Wir sahen, wie sie aus dem Zimmer kamen. Wir hörten, wie sie zusammen flüsterten.* Similarly, the sentence in (iii) (*c*), *Ich sah, wie er das Angelgerät hinter den Fässern verbarg*, may be expressed: *Ich sah ihn das Angelgerät hinter den Fässern verbergen.*

N.B. This use of the infinitive is not possible after other verbs implying seeing and hearing, e.g. *erkennen* (to recognize), *vernehmen* (to perceive, hear); these require a *wie*-clause:

Ich erkannte, wie er das Angelgerät hinter den Fässern verbarg.
I spotted him hiding the fishing tackle, &c.
Wir vernahmen, wie sie zusammen flüsterten.

(vii) Use of the past participle after the verb *kommen*:

Die beiden Jungen kamen die Treppe herunter gelaufen. The two boys came running down the stairs. *Das Kind kam in die Stube gesprungen.* The child came bounding into the parlour.

Topic 17. Description of People

ENGLISH PRESENT PARTICIPLES

A Visit to the Artist's Studio

Sie mochte etwa so alt sein wie er, nämlich ein wenig jenseits der Dreißig. In ihrem dunkelblauen, fleckigen Schürzenkleide saß sie auf einem niedrigen Schemel und stützte das Kinn in die Hand.[1] Ihr braunes Haar, fest frisiert und an den Seiten schon leicht ergraut, bedeckte in leisen Scheitelwellen ihre Schläfen und gab den Rahmen zu ihrem brünetten, slawisch geformten, unendlich sympathischen[2] Gesicht mit der Stumpfnase, den scharf herausgearbeiteten Wangenknochen und den kleinen, schwarzen, blanken Augen. Gespannt, mißtrauisch und gleichsam gereizt,[3] musterte sie schiefen und gekniffenen Blicks[4] ihre Arbeit . . .

Er stand neben ihr, hielt die rechte Hand in die Hüfte gestemmt[1] und drehte mit der Linken eilig an seinem braunen Schnurrbart. Seine schrägen Brauen waren in einer finsteren und angestrengten Bewegung, wobei er leise vor sich hinpfiff, wie gewöhnlich. Er war äußerst sorgfältig und gediegen gekleidet, in einen Anzug[1] von ruhigem Grau und reserviertem Schnitt. Aber in seiner durcharbeiteten[5] Stirn, über der sein dunkles Haar so

außerordentlich simpel und korrekt sich scheitelte, war ein nervöses Zucken, und die Züge seines südlich geschnittenen Gesichts waren schon scharf, während sein Mund so sanft umrissen, sein Kinn so weich gebildet erschien . . . Nach einer Weile strich er mit der Hand über Stirn und Augen und wandte sich ab.
„Ich hätte nicht kommen sollen", sagte er.

THOMAS MANN: Tonio Kröger (adapted)

¹ Note the case. The movement which produced the state is still felt, although the movement itself has now ceased.   ² *sympathisch*—likeable.   ³ irritated.
⁴ Adverbial genitive; cf. *mit einem . . . Blick.*   ⁵ laboured.

The Man in the Square

Da¹ begegnete ich ihm, und ich habe ihn, während ich schreibe, mit außerordentlicher Deutlichkeit vor Augen. Er war kaum mittelgroß und ging schnell und gebückt, während er seinen Stock mit beiden Händen auf dem Rücken hielt. Er trug einen schwarzen, steifen Hut, hellen Sommerüberzieher und dunkelgestreifte Beinkleider.² Aus irgendeinem Grunde hielt ich ihn für einen Engländer. Er konnte dreißig Jahre alt sein, vielleicht auch fünfzig. Sein Gesicht, mit etwas dicker Nase und müdeblickenden, grauen Augen, war glattrasiert, und um seinen Mund spielte beständig ein unerklärliches und ein wenig blödes Lächeln. Nur von Zeit zu Zeit blickte er, indem er die Augenbrauen hob, forschend um sich her, sah dann wieder vor sich zu Boden, sprach ein paar Worte mit sich selbst, schüttelte den Kopf und lächelte. So ging er den Platz auf und nieder.

An dem Abend, den ich im Sinne habe, hatte eine Militärkapelle konzertiert. Ich saß an einem der kleinen Tische, die das Café Florian weit auf den Platz hinausstellt, und als nach Schluß des Konzertes die Menge, die bis dahin³ in dichten Strömen hin und wieder gewogt war, sich zu zerstreuen begann, nahm der Unbekannte, auf abwesende Art lächelnd wie stets, an einem neben mir freigewordenen Tische Platz.

Ich las, indem ich meinem Nachbar⁴ den Rücken zuwandte, in meiner Zeitung und war eben im Begriff, ihn allein zu lassen, als ich mich genötigt sah,⁵ mich halb nach ihm umzuwenden; denn während ich bislang³ nicht einmal das Geräusch einer Bewegung von ihm vernommen hatte, begann er plötzlich zu sprechen.

THOMAS MANN: Enttäuschung (abridged extract)

¹ (In this context) then.   ² *Beinkleider*—nowadays, *Hose.*   ³ *bis dahin; bislang; bisher*—up till now, up till then, &c.   ⁴ alternatively: *Nachbarn.*
⁵ *ich sah mich genötigt*—I was compelled.

Fellow Travellers

John sat down in a corner-seat[1] and made himself comfortable.[2] Having nothing to read, he began looking at the other people in the compartment. Opposite him was sitting a small fat gentleman with likeable features, dressed in a blue suit and holding an umbrella between his knees. He was humming quietly away to himself with his eyes on the floor and tapping with his foot in time with the tune.[3] After a while he passed his hand over his face, yawned, leaned back, and nodded off to sleep.[4]

The young lady sitting next to him was anything but sleepy. With her head resting on her hand she was looking impatiently out of the window, scrutinizing the crowds who surged past on the platform. She was wearing an elegant light-grey dress and a small pink hat. She was of medium build, with dark-brown, well-dressed hair in gentle waves. Opening her handbag, she took out a cigarette-case and lighter and lit a cigarette, drawing in[5] the smoke in a tense, irritated manner. Suddenly she stood up, opened the window and called, 'Karl!'

A young man was passing the carriage. He was walking with a stooping gait, smiling absent-mindedly to himself as he went. He looked around him inquiringly on hearing her voice, raising his eyebrows as he did so, almost as if he were not expecting to meet anybody.

'Oh, there you are,[6] Julie,' he said. 'Karl,' said the girl, frowning at him. 'I thought you were never coming. Where are the others?'

---

[1] *der Eckplatz.*   [2] *machte es sich bequem.*   [3] *im Takte der Melodie.*   [4] to nod off to sleep—*einnicken.*   [5] to draw in smoke—*Rauch einziehen.*   [6] '. . . *da bist du ja!'*

---

1. By sitting down at the next table I was able to observe the stranger.
2. He was rather over forty, with weary eyes and greying hair.
3. Turning away from me, he suddenly started talking to his neighbour.
4. After the end of the concert we saw the musicians packing away[1] their instruments.
5. There was a nervous twitching in his eyebrows, as if he were afraid of telling the truth.
6. He walked slowly along the street, smoking a cigarette.
7. They are not even putting out the tables on the square tonight, so threatening does the sky look.

8. For some reason or other she has the habit of constantly shaking her head while speaking.

      [1] to pack s.th. away—*etwas einpacken.*

ESSAY

Ist die Porträtmalerei langweilig?
Beschreiben Sie die Mitglieder Ihrer Familie.
Der sonderbarste Mensch, dem ich je begegnet bin.
Beschreiben Sie einen wirklichen oder erfundenen Dorfpfarrer *oder* Dorflehrer.

DISCUSSION

Beschreiben Sie so ausführlich wie möglich Bilder oder Photographien von Menschen verschiedener Typen.
Beschreiben Sie gemeinsam einen Menschen,[1] indem jedes Klassenmitglied Einzelheiten[2] über Aussehen und Kleidung beiträgt.

    [1] 'Make up together a description of a person.'   [2] *die Einzelheit*—detail.

Topic 18

Movements of the Body
Verbs followed by an Infinitive without *zu*

1. Movements of the body

The following lists contain a number of common phrases denoting movements of the body. These and similar expressions often cause difficulty to English students, either because the verbs, although simple in themselves, are unfamiliar, or because the way in which the phrases are constructed is not understood (e.g. the use of reflexive verbs, the article, or prepositions). Cf. Topic 4, 1 (i) (*a*), p. 26: use of the definite article with parts of the body.

(i) *Reflexive verbs.* N.B. Not all verbs in this list are reflexive in English (see Grammar Section, 7–11).

Ich erhebe mich (vom Stuhl). Ich lege mich (auf das Bett) hin. Ich lehne mich (in den Sessel) zurück. Ich recke mich, strecke mich, dehne mich—stretch. *Ich rekele mich (im Stuhl)*—sprawl, lounge. *Ich verbeuge mich, verneige mich (vor ihm)*—bow. *Ich wiege mich (hin und her)*—rock (to and fro).

(ii) *Actions done to or with parts of the body:*

Ich balle die Faust—clench my fist. *Ich drehe, wende, den Kopf um. Ich kratze mir das Ohr*—scratch my ear. *Ich lasse die Arme fallen. Ich lasse den Kopf hängen. Ich reibe mir die Augen*—rub my eyes. *Ich rümpfe die Nase (über eine Sache)*—screw, turn up my nose (at s.th.). *Ich schlage die Beine übereinander*—cross my legs. *Ich schüttele den Kopf. Ich schüttele, gebe ihm die Hand. Ich spreize die Finger*—spread out, extend my fingers. *Ich strecke die Arme (nach etwas) aus*—stretch out my arms (to s.th.). *Ich verschränke, kreuze, die Arme*—fold, cross, my arms. *Ich vertrete mir die Beine*—stretch my legs (by taking a walk). *Ich verziehe das Gesicht*—pull a wry face. *Ich ziehe die Brauen zusammen, runzele die Stirn*—frown, knit my brows.

(iii) *Expressions involving a preposition:*

Ich fahre (mir) mit der Hand durchs Haar, über das Gesicht, &c. Ich klappere mit den Zähnen—my teeth chatter. *Ich klopfe mir (or*

mich) auf den Schenkel—I slap my thigh. *Ich nicke (mit dem Kopf)*
—I nod (my head). *Ich schlage dir (or dich) auf die Schulter*—slap
you on the shoulder, the back. *Ich schlage mit der Faust auf den
Tisch. Ich stütze das Kinn in die Hand. Ich trommle mit den
Fingerspitzen*—drum with my fingers. *Ich winke mit der Hand*—
wave my hand. *Ich zittere in den Knien.*

2. Verbs (other than modal verbs) which are followed by an infinitive without zu

Certain verbs other than the modal verbs are followed by an
infinitive without *zu*. The most important of these are:

brauchen (but in written German it is preferable to use *zu*
before the infinitive here)—to need, *fühlen, helfen, hören,
lassen,*[1] *lehren, lernen, machen, sehen.*

For example:

Er braucht nicht länger (zu) warten.
Ich fühlte die Erde beben. I felt the earth quake.
Sie half ihm aufstehen. Sie half ihm das Buch lesen.
Hörst du die Kinder singen?
Er ließ mich zu sich kommen. He had me sent for. *Die Mutter
ließ dem Kind das Haar schneiden.*[1] The mother had the
child's hair cut. *Ich muß mir das Haar schneiden lassen. Er
ließ sie die Stuhllehne greifen.* He got her to take hold of the
arm of the chair.
Er lehrte mich deutsch sprechen.
Ich lernte deutsch sprechen.
Nichts würde mich das glauben machen. Nothing would make me
believe that.
Sie sah uns kommen.

After an infinitive, the past participle of the verbs *brauchen,
lassen*[2] and *sehen* has the infinitive form (cf. modal verbs):

Er hätte nicht länger (zu) warten brauchen. He need not have
waited (would not have needed to wait) any longer.
Er hat sie die Stuhllehne greifen lassen.
Sie hat uns kommen sehen.

---

[1] For passive infinitive, see Gram. 45–46.   [2] N.B. *Er hat das Buch
liegenlassen* or *liegengelassen.* He left the book behind; and *Er hat die Vase fallen
gelassen.* He dropped the vase.

As with modal verbs (see Topic 2, p. 10), these infinitives used as past participles must stand at the end of the clause, even when they are subordinate:

Obschon er nicht hätte warten brauchen, . . .
Als er sie die Stuhllehne hatte greifen lassen, . . .
Nachdem sie uns hatte kommen sehen, . . .

The usage with *hören* varies:

Hast du die Kinder singen hören ? (Or: *Hast du die Kinder singen gehört ?*)

Other verbs in the list above tend nowadays to take the usual past participle when they occur with an infinitive:

Ich habe die Erde beben gefühlt (or: *Ich habe gefühlt, wie die Erde bebte*).
Sie hat ihnen aufstehen geholfen (or: *Sie hat ihnen geholfen, aufzustehen*).
Er hat mich deutsch sprechen gelehrt (or: *Er hat mich gelehrt, deutsch zu sprechen*).

Topic 18. Movements of the Body

EXPRESSIONS DENOTING MOVEMENTS OF THE BODY
VERBS FOLLOWED BY AN INFINITIVE WITHOUT *zu*

A Blind Girl learns to see[1]

Abdias fing nun an, Ditha sehen zu lehren. Er nahm sie bei der Hand, daß sie fühle, daß das dieselbe Hand sei, die sie so oft an der ihrigen im Zimmer oder im Garten herumgeführt habe. Er hob sie von dem kleinen Sessel empor. Der Arzt und drei Diener des Hauses standen dabei. Er führte sie einen Schritt von dem Sessel weg, dann ließ er sie die Lehne greifen, die ihr so lieb geworden war, dann die Seitenarme des Stuhles, die Füße und anderes — und sagte, das sei ihr Sessel, auf dem sie immer gerne gesessen sei. Dann ließ er sie ihre eigene Hand, ihren Arm, die Spitze ihres Fußes sehen — er gab ihr den Stab, dessen[2] sie sich gerne zum Fühlen bedient hatte, ließ sie ihn nehmen und die Finger um ihn herum schlingen — er gab ihr ein Stückchen Lein-wand, führte ihre Hand darüber hin und sagte, das sei das Linnen, welches sie so liebe und gerne befühlt habe. Dann setzte er sie wieder in den Sessel zurück, kauerte vor sie hin, zeigte mit den

zwei Zeigefingern seiner Hände auf seine Augen und sagte, das
seien die Dinge, mit denen sie nun alles, was um sie herum sei,
sehe, wenn auch hundert Arme aneinandergefügt zu kurz seien,
es zu greifen. Er wies ihr nun, da sie sah, alle Dinge des Zimmers,
die sie sehr gut kannte, und sagte ihr, wie sie dieselben gebraucht
habe. Um ihr dann den Raum[3] zu weisen, führte er das wider-
strebende Mädchen, weil es anzustoßen fürchtete, durch das
Zimmer zu den verschiedenen Gegenständen, von einem zum
anderen und zeigte, wie man Zeit brauche, um zu jedem zu
gelangen, obgleich sie auf einmal in dem Auge seien. Er blieb
den ganzen Tag bei ihr in dem Zimmer.

ADALBERT STIFTER:[4] Abdias (abridged extract)

[1] The blind girl Ditha has suddenly acquired the faculty of sight. Her father,
Abdias, is teaching her to use the new power.   [2] The verb *sich bedienen*—to
make use of—governs the genitive. See Gram. 15.   [3] space.   [4] It should be
noted that the style of Adalbert Stifter (1805–68) is excessively mannered and particularly far removed from present-day conversational style.

The Hamster is fooled by the Winter Sun

Vorsichtig hatte er die rosenrote Nase hinausgestreckt und lange
geschnuppert, ehe er sich weiter vorwagte; schließlich aber hatte
ihn die warme Luft doch hinausgelockt. Eine ganze Weile blieb
er regungslos vor seinem Loch sitzen[1] und lauschte und witterte,[2]
ehe er sich noch einmal ausgiebig kratzte und seinen bunten Pelz
mit den langen gelben Zähnen und den scharfen Krallen in
Ordnung brachte, und noch viel länger dauerte es, daß er sich
getraute, sich an der jungen Saat zu laben und sich die Backen-
taschen[3] damit vollzustopfen, um für die häßlichen Tage ein
wenig frisches Futter zu haben.

Als er aber die zehnte Fuhre in seine Kammer geschafft hatte
und die folgende holen wollte, schien die Sonne nicht mehr; ein
barscher Wind pfiff über den Acker, und ehe der Hamster noch
flüchten konnte, klatschte ihm eine dicke nasse Schneeflocke auf
die Nase, daß er erschreckt zurückprallte, schleunigst[4] die
Ausfahrt zuscharrte und ärgerlich brummend in seinen Kessel[5]
rutschte, wo er sich über seine neuen Vorräte hermachte[6] und
dann schwer schnaufend schlief, bis die Sonne ihn wiederum
weckte und nochmals anführte.

HERMANN LÖNS: 'Der Geizhals', from Tiergeschichten

[1] *sitzen bleiben*—to remain sitting. (N.B. *stehen bleiben*—to remain standing;
stehenbleiben—to pause, to stop walking.)   [2] *wittern*—(of an animal) to scent,
sniff the air.   [3] pouches.   [4] as quickly as possible.   [5] *der Kessel*—(here)
den.   [6] *sich über eine Sache hermachen*—to fall upon, set about s.th.

Visiting the Zoo

In what does the fascination of the zoo consist?[1] Particularly during the spring and summer months endless visitors pass[2] along the walks,[3] stop at cages, pools, and glass partitions, watch[4] monkeys swinging from tree to tree as in the jungle, penguins diving into the water and snakes slithering across stones and through grass.

There is[5] a family, for example, standing in front of the monkey-house. Some of the monkeys are busying themselves with food, others are hanging from the roof or clinging to the bars.[6] One is sitting on the floor, supporting its head in one hand; from time to time it nods wisely, so it seems, and stretches out its other hand to a heap of apples, or thoughtfully scratches its fur. Meanwhile a female[7] and her young reach out for the new supply of straw[8] which the keeper is having brought[9] into the cage.

The human family moves on. In the lions' cage the big cats are moving restlessly to and fro, growling angrily. One lies down, sniffs at[10] the bars, then lies motionless for a while. Another[11] raises a paw, spreading its claws and scenting the air— is the keeper soon coming with food?[12]

When the family has visited seals and elephants, when they have been shown giraffes and ostriches, they go perhaps to the restaurant, where they can rest[13] their weary limbs and have refreshments brought to them. No doubt they will discuss the afternoon's experiences, and some of them may wonder whether the animals themselves sometimes take a dim interest in[14] their human visitors. . . .

---

[1] to consist in—*bestehen in* (+ dative).   [2] *ziehen.*   [3] *die Alleen.*   [4] Verbs other than *sehen* (e.g. *beobachten*—to observe) will require a subordinate clause. See Topic 17 (vi), p. 114.   [5] *Da ist* . . .   [6] *das Gitter*, or *die Gitterstäbe* (plur.).   [7] *ein Weibchen.*   [8] Compound noun.   [9] See Gram. 46.   [10] *an* (dat.).   [11] *Eine zweite.*   [12] *(das) Futter. Nahrung* is food for human consumption.   [13] *ausruhen.*   [14] *ein dunkles Interesse nehmen an* (dat.).

1. He leaned back in the chair, crossed his legs, and lit his pipe.
2. They need not have taken us to the zoo!
3. When she had had her hair dressed she went to the cinema.
4. 'Shall we stretch our legs a bit?' he said, getting up.
5. The speaker banged his fist on the table and sat down, whilst the audience[1] clapped enthusiastically.
6. Folding his arms and frowning severely, the father waited. His son could only hang his head.

7. Are you going to teach him to speak Italian?
8. He took the blind man by the hand and led him gently across the road.

> [1] *die Zuhörer. die Audienz* refers only to an interview with an august personage.

ESSAY

Beschreiben Sie, was sich auf einem öffentlichen Kinderspielplatz zuträgt.[1]

Ein Blinder macht seinen Morgenspaziergang im Dorf. Beschreiben Sie, was er dabei erlebt.

Das Spiel eines jungen Hundes oder eines Kätzchens im Garten.

Die Bedeutung der Bewegung für das Drama.

> [1] *sich zutragen*—to happen, go on.

DISCUSSION

Führen Sie einander eine Reihe Bewegungen vor. Die Zuschauer in der Klasse beschreiben nachher genau, welche Bewegungen gemacht wurden.

Die Klasse nimmt eine Szene aus irgendeinem deutschen Theaterstück durch. Die Klassenmitglieder besprechen, was für Bewegungen geeignet sind,[1] um die Bedeutung der Szene hervorzuheben.[2]

> [1] *geeignet*—suitable, appropriate.   [2] *hervorheben*—bring out.

Revision Topic 2

Holidays and the Family

One short ![1]

Der Marsch zum Bahnsteig, zum Zuge beginnt. „Bahnsteig sieben!" ruft Vater noch der Mutter zu. Sie macht mit Fiete die Führerin, während Vater mit mir die Nachhut bildet. Es ist aber unmöglich, in geschlossener Formation zu marschieren. Immerzu drängen sich Leute dazwischen. Wir sammeln uns erst wieder am Häuschen des Billettknipsers. Vater zeigt das Fahrscheinheft[2] and läßt uns vorangehen, während er die Häupter seiner Lieben zählt.[3] Plötzlich stößt er einen Schrei aus. „Louise!" ruft er über die Sperre fort. „Wir müssen doch sieben sein und sind nur sechs! Wo ist Eduard?"

„Ede?!" ruft die Mutter. „Ede!! Er war doch vorhin noch da! Hast du ihn denn nicht auf der Treppe gesehen?"

„Ich weiß nicht!" ruft Vater und sieht sich verzweifelt um.

„Los! Los!" ruft der Billettknipser. „Machen Sie hier keine Verstopfungen! Sie müssen die Sperre frei machen!"

„Wann hast du Ede zum letztenmal gesehen?" ruft Vater.

„Ich weiß doch nicht! Als wir zur Treppe gingen, war er noch da — glaube ich!"

„Also jetzt 'raus oder 'rein!"[4] wird dem Vater energisch gesagt. „Ihretwegen können wir nicht den ganzen Betrieb[5] stillegen!"

„Ich suche den Jungen!" ruft der Vater wie ein letztes Vermächtnis.[6] „Nehmt immer[6] eure Plätze ein!"

Und er stürzt sich wie ein Schwimmer in die Fluten.

Sehr bedrückt gehen wir den endlosen Zug entlang. Mutter versucht durch Befragen festzustellen, wann wir Ede zum letztenmal gesehen haben, als ob das jetzt noch irgendeine Bedeutung hätte! „Ist denn sein Handkoffer da? Nein? Auch nicht! Ach Gott, der Junge, der Junge! Was er nur immer anstellt![7] Er wird doch nicht[8] schlechten Leuten in die Hände gefallen sein! Und der arme Vater! Er hat es so gerne, wenn alles still und glatt zugeht! Und heute klappt[9] rein gar nichts . . ."

HANS FALLADA: *Damals bei uns daheim*

---

[1] The author is recalling a childhood memory of a family holiday. The period is the first decade of the present century.   [2] book of tickets.   [3] The phrase is an allusion to a Berlin parody of a line from Schiller's 'Lied von der Glocke'.

The parody runs: 'Er zählt die Häupter seiner Lieben, Und sieh! es fehlten ihm nur sieben.'   [4] i.e. *heraus oder herein. Heraus, herunter, herauf,* &c., are frequently used in colloquial speech to mean *hinaus, hinunter, hinauf,* &c.; e.g. *Gehen wir hier 'rauf?*—Shall we go up here?   [5] *Betrieb*—(here) 'works', traffic.
[6] *immer* implies here *immerhin*—anyway.   [7] *etwas anstellen*—to get up to s.th. (mischievous).   [8] Surely he hasn't . . .   [9] *klappen*—(colloquial) to work, work out, go right.

The End of the Holidays

Die letzten Tage, die allerletzten Tage! Jedes von uns hat ein Bedürfnis, sich abzusondern, heimlich und ganz allein geliebte Stellen aufzusuchen. Ich weiß da eine kleine Lichtung im Kiefernhochwald, zu der gehe ich nun. Es ist heiß, fast Mittagstunde. Ich werfe mich auf den trockenen Waldboden, lege den Kopf zurück und blinzele mit halbgeschlossenen Lidern in die strahlende Höhe. Über mir ist ein großer Kiefernast, zwischen den Nadeln, zwischen den Seitenzweigen sehe ich das Himmelsblau. Es flimmert vor Hitze. Eine kleine weiße Wolke steht darin, regungslos.

Wieder meine ich, das dumpfe Sommersummen des Waldes zu hören, es schwillt an und ab wie das Atmen in meiner Brust, wie das Meer es tut, und wie der Wind bläst, es schwillt und sinkt wie alles Lebendige. Mehr nicht? Nein, sonst nichts. Nur Stille und ein fern dahinstreichendes[1] Sausen. Meine Glieder werden schlaff, sie scheinen von der Sonne gelöst, sie möchten hineinwachsen in den sommerwarmen Sand. Eltern und Geschwister, Schule und die Stadt Berlin sind nicht mehr, nur der Sommer . . .

Dann sitzen wir wieder im Zug, der uns heimwärts trägt. Heimwärts? Berlin ist kein Heim, Berlin ist nur ein Wohnort, ein Aufenthalt, nie ein Heim. Aber seltsam, je weiter uns das Rollen des Zuges von unserer Sommerfrische[2] entfernt, um so leichter trennen sich die Gedanken von dem zurückbleibenden Ferienglück, wenden sich der Stadt zu. Ich denke daran, wie lange ich meine Bücher nicht in der Hand gehabt habe. In den Ferien ist mir eingefallen, daß ich sie nach einem ganz neuen Prinzip ordnen könnte, nicht alphabetisch nach Verfassernamen, sondern nach dem Inhalt: Entdeckungsreisen für sich, Märchen für sich, Indianergeschichten für sich. Ich sehne mich plötzlich danach, sie zu ordnen, und plötzlich fällt mir auch ein, daß ich vor den Ferien ein neues Buch zu lesen anfing. Endlich kann ich es zu Ende lesen!

HANS FALLADA: *Damals bei uns daheim*
(Abridged extract)

[1] *fern dahinstreichend*—sweeping along in the far distance.   [2] *die Sommerfrische*—holiday resort.

Nostalgia

'Do you still remember how we used to go out in the evening at that little holiday-place to visit the harbour? How we used to run down the stone steps and clamber into the boats? And when we saw the fisherman coming, how we lay down as quickly as we could, trembling at the knees and hoping he wouldn't notice us?— And even then we didn't always manage to escape from him!'

'And how father lost[1] us once for such a long time that at last he had the police searching for us? Afterwards he gave us a thorough[2] scolding—as if we had really been in danger! Anyway,[3] how long is it since we were last there?'

'Ten years ago? The holidays simply flew past in those days, and we never lacked for ideas. How is it that one never enjoys holidays as fully as one did when a child?[4] The simple things about those days are quite unforgettable. We used to seek out our own favourite spots, get up to all kinds of stupid pranks,[5] and hardly spent a penny in doing it—and yet we had a wonderful time. When I think back to all that it seems to me almost like a dream. I often long for that childlike innocence . . .'

'Well, we weren't as innocent as all that,[6] you know! But I do know[7] what you mean. And it wasn't only our adventures which made[8] all the beauty of such times. Everything living seems to have been lovelier then: the sky was always blue, the sea always enticing, and trees, seagulls, fish somehow more significant. Early in the morning everything pointed to a wonderful, exciting day. And now—it seems as if one always has to be contented with[9] half-pleasures . . .[10] But perhaps all these memories are nothing but romantic nonsense.'

[1] to lose (in this sense)—*vermissen*.   [2] *tüchtig*.   [3] Anyway (in the sense 'by the way', 'incidentally')—*übrigens*.   [4] *als man noch ein Kind war*.   [5] *dumme Geschichten*.   [6] *. . ., so unschuldig waren wir nicht, . . .*   [7] I do know (in this sense)—*ich weiß schon*.   [8] *ausmachen*.   [9] *sich begnügen mit*.   [10] half-pleasures—*halbe Freuden*.

1. The whole valley was shimmering with heat as we entered it.
2. Suddenly it occurred to me that we had not been there for a long time.
3. Will you please have the tickets sent to my office?[1]
4. I like everything to go smoothly when I travel on holiday.[2]
5. You need not have waited for me, for I could have come by the next train.
6. While he was standing on deck[3] someone came up and slapped him on the shoulder.

7. Perhaps we ought not to waste any more time,[4] but travel home at once.
8. Since my last visit this resort has developed considerably.

[1] *mir . . . ins Büro.*   [2] *in Urlaub fahren* or *in die Ferien fahren.*   [3] *an Deck.*   [4] to waste time—*Zeit verlieren* or *Zeit vergeuden.*

ESSAY

Frühe Ferienerinnerungen.
Ferienvorbereitungen.
Rückkehr von den Ferien.
Die Familie reist in die Ferien.

DISCUSSION

Stimmen Sie mit den Ansichten überein, die im englisch-deutschen Übersetzungsstück dargelegt sind?
Fahren Sie lieber mit der Familie in Urlaub oder mit gleichaltrigen Freunden?

PART II

PROSE PASSAGES AND POEMS FOR TRANSLATION

A New Guest in an Alpine Village

Kaum daß man am Urlaubsort angekommen ist und seinen Koffer ausgepackt hat, da stürzt man sich schon, um ja nichts zu versäumen, in die verheißene Gegend.[1] Es ist gar nicht so leicht, sich zurechtzufinden. Zwar hat man schon kurz nach Weihnachten begonnen, die einschlägigen Prospekte[2] zu studieren, man kennt — aus dem Reiseführer und aus den Drucksachen des Verkehrsvereins — bereits die Namen der wichtigsten Aussichtspunkte und Ausflugsziele, man hat sich sogar schon eine Art Plan zusammengebastelt, nach dem man nun alles Sehenswerte einzusammeln[3] beabsichtigt, aber nun — an Ort und Stelle[4] — sieht alles ganz anders aus. Der Urlauber steht, mit der Karte in der Hand, auf irgendeiner Straße und blickt sich ein wenig hilflos um. Ist das nun die Mühlgasse,[5] durch die man gehen muß, um auf den Weg in die Höllenschlucht[5] zu gelangen? Und welcher der vielen Pfade führt auf die Winterhalde?[5]

Der weniger selbstherrliche Urlauber faltet die Karte resigniert zusammen und fragt. Einen Einheimischen um Auskunft anzugehen, hat im allgemeinen wenig Zweck. Die wissen am wenigsten Bescheid,[6] weil sie keine Ausflüge machen. Oder sie sagen: „Da gehen Sie am besten bis zum Riederhof[5] und dann . . .“ Oder: „Gleich hinter der Kuhwiese führt ein Pfad . . .“ Man ist also genauso schlau[7] wie vorher. Man hat keine Ahnung, wo der Riederhof oder die Kuhwiese liegt. Und weiterzufragen verbietet sowohl der Urlauberstolz wie die Eile des Eingeborenen, der, mit einer Sense über der Schulter, seinem Acker zustrebt.

HEINZ REIN: 'Fremd in Oberwiesenau':
Rheinischer Merkur (adapted)

---

[1] 'the promised region' (cf. *das verheißene Land*).   [2] the prospectuses on the subject.   [3] 'to take in'.   [4] *an Ort und Stelle*—on the spot.   [5] Do not translate.   [6] *Bescheid wissen*—to know (the answer to an inquiry).   [7] *schlau*—(here) 'wise'.

The Pleasures of a Country Life

Mein Landleben[1] unterscheidet sich von meinem Stadtleben zunächst einmal[2] dadurch, daß ich täglich größere Wegstrecken zurücklege. Ich muß jeden Morgen eine halbe Stunde zu Fuß gehen und dann noch eine halbe Stunde mit der Bahn und der Straßenbahn fahren, um an die Stätte meiner Berufsarbeit zu kommen. Denn Landleben ist ja an sich noch kein Beruf.[3] Abends habe ich denselben Weg noch einmal. Während ich früher in der Stadt nur um die Ecke bog, um an meine Arbeitsstätte zu gelangen, verwende ich jetzt täglich mehrere Stunden auf den Weg.

Man kann demnach feststellen, daß Landleben zu einem großen Teil in Anmarsch besteht. Das scheint ja gerade kein Vorteil[4] zu sein, besonders wenn es regnet. Bei schönem Wetter springen mir Steinchen in die Schuhe, so ist der Weg nun einmal beschaffen;[5] ich muß früher aufstehen und früher zu Bett gehen als in der Stadt. Ich verliere mit dem Landleben viel Zeit, so könnte man meinen. In Wirklichkeit gewinne ich sie für mich. In der Stadt war ich viel zu schnell daheim; ich hatte kaum Zeit, mich auf das Nachhausekommen zu freuen und die Berufsgedanken abzuschütteln. Jetzt fallen sie unterwegs ganz von selber ab, und ich gewinne Platz für eigenes Nachdenken.

Und dann der Blick. Nicht weil er mich fortwährend fesselt, im Gegenteil, daß er mich in Ruhe läßt in seiner Weite, das ist das Schöne an ihm. In der Stadt sehe ich fortwährend etwas, was meine Aufmerksamkeit in Anspruch nimmt. Auf dem Lande sehe ich derartiges nicht. Ich habe mich so daran gewöhnt, daß da unten der See liegt und drüben das Gebirge, daß ich in aller Ruhe meinen häuslichen Beschäftigungen nachgehen kann, ohne daß ich fürchten muß, etwas zu versäumen.

ERNST HEIMERAN: *Die Freuden des Landlebens* (adapted)

---

[1] The author used to be a city-dweller. [2] *zunächst einmal*—a common phrase meaning 'in the first place', 'to begin with'. [3] . . . is, after all, not a job in itself. [4] not exactly an advantage. [5] that's just the nature of the lane. *Nun einmal*: an emotive particle (cf. *doch, ja*) implying a resigned acceptance of the inevitable.

1. In fine weather the tourists spent most of the day out of doors.
2. She looked around rather helplessly and asked me the way.
3. By four o'clock they had seen everything worth seeing.
4. He never tried to shake off his troubles. On the contrary, he worried more and more.

5. Let's not waste time here. One might think we had all day free!
6. After my day's work I always look forward to getting home.
7. 'You had best turn left at the police-station and catch a bus at the corner.'
8. Do you think you will be able to find your way without me?
9. The fine thing about it was that we learnt the language on the spot.
10. The less enterprising holiday-makers simply followed the guide.

A Man and his Dog

Gern, wenn ich, auf meinem Stuhl in der Mauerecke des Gartens oder draußen im Gras, den Rücken an einen bevorzugten Baum gelehnt, in einem Buche lese, unterbreche ich mich in meiner geistigen Beschäftigung, um etwas mit Bauschan zu sprechen und zu spielen. Was ich denn zu ihm spreche? Meist sage ich ihm seinen Namen vor, den Laut, der ihn unter allen am meisten angeht, weil er ihn selbst bezeichnet, und der darum auf sein ganzes Wesen elektrisierend wirkt, — stachle und befeuere sein Ichgefühl,[1] indem ich ihm mit verschiedener Betonung versichere und recht zu bedenken gebe,[2] daß er Bauschan heißt und ist; und wenn ich dies eine Weile fortsetze, kann ich ihn dadurch in eine wahre Verzückung, eine Art von Identitätsrausch versetzen,[3] so daß er anfängt, sich um sich selber zu drehen und aus der stolzen Bedrängnis[4] seiner Brust laut und jubelnd gen[5] Himmel zu bellen. Oder wir unterhalten uns, indem ich ihm auf die Nase schlage, und er nach meiner Hand schnappt wie nach einer Fliege. Dies bringt uns beide zum Lachen — ja, auch Bauschan muß lachen, und das ist für mich, der ebenfalls lacht, der wunderlichste und rührendste Anblick von der Welt.

THOMAS MANN:· *Herr und Hund*

[1] his ego.　　　[2] *jm. etwas recht zu bedenken geben*—to impress s.th. upon s.o.
[3] put him into a kind of intoxication with his own identity.　　[4] (here) fullness.
[5] *gen*: an old form of *gegen*; found only in the expression *gen Himmel*—heavenwards—in modern German.

The End of the Journey

Als der Zug seine Geschwindigkeit verminderte und langsam über die große Flußbrücke fuhr, die unmittelbar vor der Endstation lag, trat Robert an das Fenster des Abteils und warf noch einen Blick auf das zurückliegende Land. Endlich am Ziel!

Aufatmend sah er unter sich das tiefe Bett des Stromes, der die Grenze bildete. Zu beiden Seiten der Fahrtrinne dehnten sich breite Streifen mit verschlammten Geröllsteinen, die der vorzeitige Sommer ausgetrocknet hatte. Über allem lag das triefende Zwielicht[1] der frühen Morgendämmerung.

Robert hatte die Nacht in einem Zustand zwischen Schlaf und Halbwachen verbracht, der ihm die Reise noch länger hatte erscheinen lassen. Während der Zug in die verhältnismäßig kleine Bahnhofshalle einlief, vergewisserte er sich, wie schon so oft auf der Fahrt, des Schreibens der Stadtverwaltung,[2] das ihn aufgefordert hatte, hierherzukommen. Er steckte es griffbereit[3] neben die Brieftasche, bevor er seinen Koffer aufnahm und ausstieg. Durch einen Tunnel gelangte er mit den zahlreichen Fahrgästen des Zuges an die Zollschranke, wo ein untersetzter Beamter mit mürrischer Gleichgültigkeit die Papiere prüfte. Auch dem Inhalt des Gepäcks, das die notwendigen Gegenstände für Übernachtung und kurzen Aufenthalt enthielt, schenkte er nur flüchtige Beachtung. Dann aber stutzte er. Robert wies das Schreiben der Präfektur vor. „Passiert!" rief der Wächter und gab ihm mit einer ausladenden Geste den Weg frei.

HERMANN KASACK: *Die Stadt hinter dem Strom*

[1] rain-soaked half-light.   [2] *vergewisserte er sich . . . des Schreibens der Stadtverwaltung*—he looked to see he had the letter from the municipal authority. Gram. 15.   [3] *griffbereit*—ready to hand.

1. His name does not concern me.
2. I asked him to come here as soon as possible.
3. The dog began to turn round and round himself.
4. During the journey the train never reduced speed once.
5. He always had the dictionary ready to hand on his desk.
6. With a sigh of relief he cast a last glance over the bridge.
7. This is the strangest sight in the world.
8. We continued our conversation for a while.
9. At long last she reached the customs, where an official checked her papers.
10. When the dog snaps at my hand like that it always makes me laugh.

Adventures of an Otter

Glitsch, der Otter, reckte sich und streckte sich, kratzte sich hier und da und gähnte von Herzen; aber dann verschwand er blitzschnell in dem Strudel, gerade rechtzeitig genug, daß der Schrotschuß, den der Jäger ihm zugedacht hatte,[1] dahin traf, wo Glitsch sich eben gerekelt hatte. Aber als der Jäger, der zufällig des Weges gekommen war, noch da stand und ein dummes Gesicht machte, war der Otter schon unter Wasser ein ganzes Ende[2] stromaufwärts geschwommen, hatte, wenn ihm die Luft ausging, unter dem hohlen Ufer die Nasenspitze herausgehalten und schließlich einen Graben angenommen,[3] der in den Bach mündete.

Dieser Graben war breit und tief, dicht mit Büschen bestanden und roch ausgezeichnet, nämlich nach[4] Forellen; von allen Fischen schätzte Glitsch diese am meisten. So schwamm er weiter, tauchte ab und zu auf, um zu atmen, wodurch er hier den Eisvogel ärgerte, der auf einer Weidenrute saß und auf Ellritzen wartete, und da eine Krähe, die am Ufer auf eine Maus lauerte und beinahe auf den Rücken fiel, als der Otter vor ihr aufging, so daß sie vor Schreck fast vergaß, daß sie Flügel hatte, um endlich unter Schreckensgequarre[5] von dannen[6] zu taumeln, worüber Glitsch entsetzt untertauchte und erst dann wieder aufkam, als das Wasser ihm ganz nahe Forellenwitterung[7] zutrug.

HERMANN LÖNS: 'Glitsch' (adapted, from *Tiergeschichten*)

[1] had intended for him (note the verb).   [2] *ein ganzes Ende*—quite a distance.
[3] *annehmen*—(here) 'take to' (hunting jargon).   [4] *riechen nach*—to smell of.
[5] Gram. 70.   [6] *von dannen = hinweg*—away.   [7] scent of trout (hunting jargon).

Conspiracy[1]

Die Offiziere traten zusammen. Lapie sah von einem zum andern. Dann sagte er mit gedämpfter Stimme, doch so, daß seine Worte von der ganzen Gruppe vernommen werden konnten: «Maintenant! Messieurs, ce serait le moment!»

Jeder verstand ihn. Jeder wußte, welcher Augenblick gekommen war und welche Tat er verlangte; und das, obgleich nie von einem solchen Augenblick und von einer solchen Tat die Rede gewesen war,[2] zum mindesten[3] nicht in einem so großen Kreise. Lapie vertraute darauf, der Gedanke werde kaum einen ungestreift[4] gelassen haben. Wer aber weder Gedanken noch Worte gewagt hatte, sah jetzt den Kaiser westwärts jagen und die Armee — Trümmer und Überreste — im Stich lassen.

„Dieser Mann hat es sich selbst zuzuschreiben",[5] sagte finster einer der Kompaniechefs. Sprach man damals vom Kaiser, so wurde er als „cet homme" bezeichnet.

Sie berieten die Ausführung.[6]

„Kann man uns kommen sehen?"

„Nein", sagte Lapie. „Die Stube, in der gedeckt ist, liegt nach der Gartenseite."

Es waren noch einige Einzelfragen zu lösen. Man einigte sich auf folgenden Plan. Eine Kompanie dringt[7] ins Haus, eine andere besetzt den rückwärtigen Ausgang. Der Mameluck[8] wird niedergestoßen, man ist im Eßzimmer. Zwei Gruppen werfen sich sofort auf die rückwärtige Zimmertür, niemand darf entkommen. Von diesen Gruppen bleibt eine an der Innenseite der Tür, die andere dringt weiter in den Korridor, um etwa[9] sich einmischende Leute, vielleicht von den servierenden Ordonnanzen[10] oder vom Küchenpersonal, unschädlich zu machen.

WERNER BERGENGRUEN: *Der Augenblick* (abridged extract)

[1] The passage describes how, during the retreat from Moscow, a group of French officers plan to assassinate Napoleon while he is at breakfast. [2] Cf. *davon kann keine Rede sein*—there can be no question of that. [3] *zum mindesten = mindestens*. [4] Cf. *der Gedanke streifte ihn*—the thought passed through his mind. [5] 'That man has only himself to blame' (*jm. etwas zuschreiben*—to ascribe, attribute s.th. to s.o.). [6] i.e. *die Ausführung des Plans*. [7] The present tenses in what follows imply what is to happen, according to the plan. [8] The Mameluke: Napoleon's North African servant. [9] *etwa* means 'as, for example', 'say, for the purposes of argument'. Here, ignore *etwa* and translate the phrase with 'might interfere'. [10] *die Ordonnanz*—orderly.

1. Don't leave us in the lurch now!
2. Above the overhanging bank a crow was lying in wait for a mouse.
3. There are still a few letters to be answered.
4. Of all the German authors I have read I am most fond of Eichendorff.
5. The whole house smelt of fish.
6. There had never been any question of it.
7. The otter disappeared like lightning when the huntsman happened to walk past.
8. Can they see us coming?
9. He gave a hearty yawn and stretched.
10. Their voices were so muffled that none of the answers could be heard.

On Horseback in the Caucasian Steppes

Als wir gegen vier Uhr morgens losritten, lag dichter Nebel über der Landschaft. Es war nicht kalt. Der Kaukasus ist ein schmales Gebirge. Wir waren, da wir fast am Fuße des Gebirges entlangritten, von seinem Kamm höchstens fünfzig Kilometer entfernt. Von jenseits des Gebirges brachte der Südwind mit dem Nebel zugleich Wärme mit. Chamidjia,[1] wo ich Major Fabricius zu treffen hoffte, lag nur sechs Kilometer westlich von unserem Quartier. Dazwischen war ein kleiner Flußlauf, der von Süden in den Terek mündete,.auf der Karte eingezeichnet. Über diesen kleinen Fluß mußten wir hinüber.

Die Flüsse der kaukasischen Steppe sind mit unseren Flüssen nicht zu vergleichen. Was ein Fluß überhaupt ist, das lernten wir erst hier. Das Tal des Terek[2] ist mehrere Kilometer breit. Die steilen Ränder, von denen das Tal gesäumt ist, sind dreißig bis fünfzig Meter hoch. Sie erzählen ein Stück Erdgeschichte. In gewaltigen Hochwasserkatastrophen hat das Wasser sich im Lauf der Jahrtausende in breitem Strom tief in den weichen Lößboden[3] hineingefressen. In ruhigen Zeiten ist das Tal von lieblicher Schönheit. Zwischen Strauch- und Bauminseln, von unzähligen Vögeln belebt, schlängelt sich der Fluß in einem wunderbaren smaragdenen Grün in ständig wechselnder Richtung friedlich dahin. Es gibt viele Furten, durch die man ihn durchschreiten kann. Bei Hochwasser reißt er die Brücken weg.

PETER BAMM: *Die unsichtbare Flagge*

[1] What would be an equivalent English spelling for the Russian word? [2] *des Terek*—the genitive -*s* is sometimes omitted with foreign proper names. [3] loess —a fine quartz dust containing lime, formed during the Ice Age and deposited on the edge of mountain ranges by the action of wind. Loess is a very rich soil.

Noises of the Night

Die Mutter richtete sich von ihrem Kopfkissen empor und blickte nach dem Lager des Kindes hinüber. Rund um die Stadt Neustadt in den Büschen und am Rande der Gewässer[1] regten sich die Nachtvögel; des Nachtwächters rauhe Stimme erschallte bald näher, bald ferner; die Uhren der beiden Kirchen zankten sich um die richtige Zeit und waren sehr abweichender Meinung; sehr lebendig waren alle Neustädter Fledermäuse und Eulen, die ihre Stunden ganz genau kannten und sich um keine Minute irrten; Mäuse zirpten hinter der Wand der Kammer, und e i n e Maus raschelte unter dem Bett der Frau Christine; eine Brumm-fliege, welche auch nicht schlafen konnte, summte bald hier, bald da, stieß mit dem Kopf bald gegen das Fenster, bald gegen die Wand, und versuchte vergeblich einen Ausweg; es knackte in der Stube der Großvaterstuhl hinter dem Ofen, und auf dem Hausboden trappelte und schlich es so schauerlich und gespen-stig, daß es schwerhielt,[2] den beruhigenden Glauben an „Katzen"

festzuhalten. Die Frau Christine Unwirrsch, welche als eine
ahnungsvolle Seele[3] sonst ein scharfes, ängstliches Ohr für alle
Töne und Laute der Nacht hatte und an dem Hereinragen der
Geisterwelt[4] in ihre Kammer nicht im mindesten zweifelte, hatte
in dieser Nacht nicht Zeit, darauf zu horchen und die Gänsehaut
darüber zu bekommen. Ihr Herz war zu voll von anderen Dingen,
und die Gespenster, die zwischen Erd' und Himmel wandeln
und mit den Nerven der Menschen ihr Spiel treiben,[5] hatten
keine Macht über sie.

WILHELM RAABE: *Der Hungerpastor* (adapted)

[1] Gram. 70.   [2] *daß es schwerhielt* . . .—that it was difficult . . .   [3] a fanciful soul.   [4] the intrusion of the spirit world.   [5] play their tricks.

1. Do your neighbours often squabble like that?
2. I got goose-flesh several times over the last scene of the play.
3. I don't doubt it in the least.
4. About seven o'clock in the evening we rode off.
5. The swallows are not out by a single day when they fly south.
6. The members of the committee were of very divergent opinion.
7. Sitting up in bed, I looked over to the window.
8. They said that the plain was at most twenty kilometres away.
9. This mountain range is not marked on any map.
10. You can cross the river by one of the many fords.

The Early Life of Friedrich Nietzsche

Friedrich Wilhelm Nietzsche wurde am 15. Oktober 1844 als
Sohn des Pfarrers Karl Ludwig Nietzsche in dem Dorfe Röcken
bei Leipzig geboren. Die Mutter stammte aus dem Pfarrhaus
von Pobles bei Weißenfels. Friedrich war das erste Kind; im
Jahre 1846 wurde seine Schwester Elisabeth geboren. Der von
der ganzen Familie verehrte und geliebte Vater starb im Juli 1849
an einer Gehirnaffektion, die er sich durch einen unglücklichen
Sturz zugezogen haben soll. Im April des folgenden Jahres
siedelte Frau Nietzsche mit ihren beiden Kindern nach Naumburg über. Hier trat Nietzsche 1854 in das Gymnasium ein; im
Oktober 1858 kam er in die Landesschule Pforta.[1] Er verließ
die Anstalt, in der er lebenslängliche Freundschaft mit Carl von
Gersdorff und Paul Deussen geschlossen hatte, im September
1864 und bezog die Universität Bonn. Zwei Semester lang hörte

er bei dem Kunsthistoriker A. Springer, dem Philologen und Archäologen O. Jahn und dem Philologen F. Ritschl. Im letzten Studienjahr 1866/67 trat ihm Erwin Rohde besonders nahe. Von 1867 bis 1868 diente Nietzsche als Einjähriger[2] bei der Feldartillerie in Naumburg. Wegen einer Wunde, die er sich beim Sprung aufs Pferd zugezogen hatte, mußte er eine langwierige Kur auf sich nehmen. Im Herbst 1868 kehrte er nach Leipzig zurück; dort machte er am 8. November die persönliche Bekanntschaft mit Richard Wagner. Im Februar 1869, noch vor der Doktorpromotion,[3] erhielt er einen Ruf als außerordentlicher Professor[4] der klassischen Philologie an die Universität Basel.

Abridged from the note on Nietzsche's life in the Kröner edition of
Also sprach Zarathustra

[1] The Landesschule in Pforta (a famous royal foundation). [2] *als Einjähriger*—as a one-year conscript (a privilege of the wealthier classes: the normal term was from two to three years). [3] *Doktorpromotion*—the awarding of the degree of doctor. N.B. *promovieren*—to be awarded a doctorate. [4] *außerordentlicher Professor*—assistant lecturer.

A Midnight Visitor

Gleich darauf ereignete sich ein ganz andersgeartetes[1] Abenteuer. Riccardo, der besonders in den Sommermonaten häufig an Schlaflosigkeit litt, pflegte dann, um der stickigen Luft in dem niedrigen Zimmer zu entgehen, auf dem Hausflur zu schlafen, wo zu diesem Zweck immer ein mit Maishaar[2] gefüllter Sack lag. Das erklärte er auch diesmal tun zu wollen, als ich ihm die beschwerliche Treppe hinaufhelfen wollte, und ohne irgendwelches Bedenken, da ich seine Gewohnheiten kannte, ließ ich ihn auf seiner Matratze hinter der Haustür. Riccardo fiel sogleich in einen festen Schlaf, aus dem er aber schon nach wenigen Minuten, wie es ihm schien, erwachte. Er hatte die Empfindung, von einem Geräusch erweckt zu sein, und horchte in das Haus hinauf,[3] wo aber alles still blieb; als er sich aufrichtete und durch die Tür auf die Straße hinausblickte, sah er an der gegenüberliegenden Seite der Gasse, dicht der Mauer entlang, etwas durch die Dunkelheit huschen; der Mond war schon hinter den Häusern untergegangen. Zuerst schlug er ein Kreuz in der Meinung, daß es eine arme Seele sei, die die Stätte ihrer Irrsale[4] wieder aufsuchte; als er sich aber weiter vorbeugte und schärfer hinsah, erkannte er Torquato, den Bruder des Jurewitsch.[5] Er mußte erfahren haben, daß der Schuster Bonalma gelegentlich der Wallfahrt[6] von Hause fort war, und wollte den Umstand dazu benutzen, den Laden auszuplündern, wenigstens hielt er gerade dort an und schwang sich an dem niedrigen Fenster empor.

RICARDA HUCH: *Aus der Triumphgasse* (abridged extract)

[1] What is the root of the second half of this word? [2] maize hair. [3] Care with the translation; *hinaufhorchen* implies not only attentive listening but also direction. [4] *Irrsale = Sünden.* [5] Yurevitch. [6] on account of the pilgrimage.

1. The parson was the son of a university professor and was born in 1860.
2. He recognized Misha, the brother of Yurevitch, on the other side of the road.
3. She had the feeling of having escaped a great danger.
4. Do you know when he made the acquaintance of the great archaeologist?
5. Has the moon set yet?
6. He received an invitation to lecture at the University of Bonn.
7. During recent months I have been suffering from insomnia.
8. I entered the grammar school six years ago.
9. Thinking that we were away, he tried to burgle the house.
10. He died of an illness which he is said to have caught in Africa.

An Old House

Das Haus selbst war ein altes unregelmäßiges Gebäude mit Seitenflügeln, kleinen Höfen und Hinterhäusern, voll von Mauern und kleinen Treppen, von geheimnisvollen Durchgängen, wo kein Mensch welche[1] vermutete, von Korridoren, Nischen, tiefen Wandschränken und Glasverschlägen. Es war ein durchaus künstlicher Bau, an dem Jahrhunderte gearbeitet hatten, um ihn für späte Enkel so schwierig und unverständlich als irgend möglich zu machen. Und doch sah er im ganzen[2] betrachtet behaglich aus und umfaßte mit seinen Mauern eine große Welt voll Menschen und Interessen. Der ganze Raum unter dem Gebäude und unter seinen Höfen war zu Kellern gewölbt und bis an die Gewölbegurte mit Waren gefüllt; das ganze Parterre gehörte der Handlung und enthielt außer den Kontorzimmern fast nichts als Warenräume. Darüber lagen im Vorderhause die Säle und Zimmer, in denen der Kaufherr selbst wohnte.

GUSTAV FREYTAG: *Soll und Haben*

[1] Gram. 102. [2] *im ganzen*—the capital letter for the neuter adjectival noun is dropped in this expression, because it is felt to be an adverb.

The Meaning of Christmas[1]

Es wird gut sein, wenn wir uns heute noch einmal an jenes tiefe Weihnachtserlebnis der Kriegszeit erinnern. Denn wir sind schon wieder im Begriff, es zu vergessen. Zwar[2] äußerlich hat sich unsere betriebsame Zeit des Festes eifrig angenommen.[3] Schon lange vor dem Heiligen Abend brennen in den Schaufenstern die Christbäume, ein hochgetriebener Geschäftsverkehr bemüht sich um die Weihnachtsgeschenke, viele schöne Sachen werden angeboten und verkauft. Man bäckt wieder Kuchen und Plätzchen wie in der Vorkriegszeit. Das alles sieht recht festlich aus, und doch, ist es uns nicht, als gehe über diesen allzulauten, allzugrellen Vorbereitungen der Weihnacht die Weihnacht selbst unter, die Botschaft von dem Kind, in dem Gott Mensch geworden? Ja, diese Botschaft, täuschen wir uns nicht, sie wird weithin überhört oder überhaupt nicht mehr verstanden. Weihnachten ist für viele eine weltliche Veranstaltung geworden, die viel Geld kostet und viel Geld einbringt, das Kind von Bethlehem aber steht fremd und obdachlos geworden vor den Türen unserer Häuser wie einst seine Eltern vor der Herberge zu Bethlehem.

GERTRUD VON LE FORT: *Das kleine Weihnachtsbuch*

[1] The author has been writing of the rediscovery of the true meaning of Christmas which many people experienced in the privations and tragedy of the war.
[2] *zwar*—Gram. 132.   [3] Gram. 15.

1. There were partitions in the cellars where you would not have suspected any.
2. I'll have to be seeing to the presents for the family.
3. The box contained hardly anything but old newspapers.
4. Why did she take such a keen interest in the festival?
5. He tried to make the test as difficult as possible.
6. Let us not deceive ourselves, the message is often not understood at all.
7. It was long before Christmas Eve that the parcels were brought.
8. Are you still working at that motor?
9. The house itself was a thoroughly comfortable home.
10. In pre-war days there were less Christmas trees with lights in the shop windows.

The Election of the Federal President

. . . Seine Wahl obliegt der Bundesversammlung,[1] die nur zu diesem Zweck zusammentritt. Sie wurde gebildet aus den 402 Abgeordneten des Bundestages[2] und ebenso vielen Abgesandten, die von den Volksvertretungen[3] der elf Bundesländer[4] gewählt wurden.

Die Wahl erfolgte am 12. September 1949, nach Artikel 54 des Grundgesetzes,[5] und im zweiten Wahlgang wurde

Professor Dr. Theodor Heuss

zum ersten Bundespräsidenten der Bundesrepublik Deutschland gewählt.

Der Präsident des Bundestages, der die Sitzung leitete, gab das Wahlergebnis bekannt. Dann fragte er den Gewählten, ob er das hohe Amt annehme. Als er dies bejaht hatte, leistete Bundespräsident Dr. Theodor Heuss den Eid auf die Verfassung vor dem im Sitzungssaal anwesenden Deutschen Bundestag und Bundesrat.[6] Dabei wurde ihm das Original unserer Verfassung, des Grundgesetzes, vorgelegt.

Der Eid des Bundespräsidenten lautet:

„Ich schwöre, daß ich meine Kraft dem Wohle des deutschen Volkes widmen, seinen Nutzen mehren, Schaden von ihm wenden, das Grundgesetz und die Gesetze des Bundes wahren und verteidigen, meine Pflichten gewissenhaft erfüllen und Gerechtigkeit gegen jedermann üben werde, so wahr mir Gott helfe."

Nach diesem feierlichen Akt sprach der Bundespräsident zum erstenmal zu den versammelten Abgeordneten und zugleich über den Rundfunk zum deutschen Volk. Er schloß seine Rede mit den Worten: „Im Bewußtsein meiner Verantwortung vor Gott trete ich dieses Amt an und stelle unsere gemeinsame Arbeit unter das Wort:

,Gerechtigkeit erhöhet ein Volk'."[7]

From: *Die Bundesrepublik Deutschland*, issued by the panel 'Der Bürger im Staat', Stuttgart

[1] Federal Assembly: a body which is convoked only for the election of a Federal President.   [2] The lower house of the Federal parliament. Do not translate.
[3] *Volksvertretungen*—provincial parliaments.   [4] Federal Länder (the constituent provincial areas of the *Bundesrepublik*).   [5] *das Grundgesetz*—the Basic Law: the official designation of the constitution of the Federal Republic.
[6] *Bundesrat*—the upper house of the Federal parliament, consisting of representatives of the provincial parliaments. Do not translate.   [7] See Proverbs xiv. 34.

A Lonely Walk

Es gibt nichts Verlasseneres in der Welt als eine kleine Bahnstation bei Nacht, auf der nur ein einzelner aussteigt. Es gibt nichts Einsameres als eine dunkle Landstraße, an der die Drähte simmern.[1]

Ein junger Mensch mit aufgestelltem Mantelkragen stapfte allein die leere Landstraße entlang, die von der isoliert gelegenen Bahnstation Neumarkt-Köstendorf nach der Ortschaft Alt-Köstendorf hinaufführt. Er schleppte mühsam sein Gepäck, einen alten, mit einem Strick zugebundenen Handkoffer und eine große, bis zum Platzen vollgestopfte Ledermappe. Es war dunkel und kalt, die Straße mit verharschtem Eisschlamm bedeckt, der Wind trieb Schloßen wäßrigen Schnees vor sich her und pfiff dem jungen Mann durch den dünnen Mantel und das lange, strähnige Haar, denn er trug weder Hut noch Mütze. Der Schnee beschlug seine Brillengläser, die Kälte mußte seine Ohrmuscheln zerbeißen, aber da er beide Hände voll hatte, konnte er sich nicht schützen oder reiben, sondern machte nur mit seinen eckigen Schultern hilflose, zuckende Bewegungen. Der Zug hatte natürlich wieder Verspätung gehabt, es war schon tiefe Nacht, die Bauernhöfe hockten vermummt im Finstern, die kahlen Bäume und Telegraphenstangen am Wegrand seufzten, klapperten im Wind, die Drähte sirrten[2] und simmerten. Weit und breit war kein Licht zu sehen, nur am niedern, wolkenzerklüfteten Himmel der rote Funkenstreif, den die Maschine des ostwärts weiterstampfenden Bummelzuges[3] aus ihrem Schlot spie.

CARL ZUCKMAYER: *Der Seelenbräu*

[1] *simmern = summen.*   [2] *sirren*—to 'sing'.   [3] *Bummelzug = Personenzug—* local train.

1. For what purpose is the council meeting this evening?
2. The president has to take the oath on the constitution.
3. A young man with an upturned collar was rubbing his hands by the fire.
4. The beginning of the speech is as follows: . . .
5. There's nothing more empty than a country station at night.
6. The parliament was elected by the people in 1961.
7. That local train is going to be late again, I think.
8. Only a single person got out at the next halt.
9. The assembled delegates elected the candidate as president.
10. Plodding along the road to the village was a lonely traveller.

The General's Château

Eine unsichtbare Uhr schlug elf helle Schläge, als Thomas vor der Schloßtreppe stand. Das Schloß war nicht mehr als ein großes Gutshaus, mit einem hohen braunen Dach über zwei Flügeln. Doch lag es breit und stattlich über der Seebucht, und der Efeu, der bis an die Fenster des oberen Stockwerks rankte, ließ es alt und ganz auf sich zurückgezogen erscheinen. Das Wappen über der schweren Tür war so verwittert, daß es nicht mehr als eine gepanzerte Faust erkennen ließ, die etwas trug, aber es konnte ein Lilienstengel wie eine Streitaxt sein. Der Park hinter dem Hause mußte gleich in den Wald übergehen, hinter dem Hof aber hob sich gerade der dünne Nebel über dunklen Feldern, die erst vom Horizont begrenzt schienen. Ein blaues Tor tat sich zwischen den ziehenden Wolken auf, und ein heller Schein fiel auf die regennasse Erde, auf die leuchtenden Dächer und auf die Spitze der Fahnenstange, die sich über der Mitte des Hauses erhob.

Dann stieg Thomas die Stufen hinauf. Er läutete an einem alten Glockenzug, und die schwere Tür wurde von einem Riesen in altertümlicher Uniform geöffnet. Thomas meinte, sie müsse aus der Zeit Friedrichs des Großen stammen, mit weißem Lederzeug und verschnürtem Rock, doch trug der Mann keine Bärenmütze, sondern kurz verschnittenes Haar,[1] sah auch so aus, als hätte man ihn eben vom Pfluge fortgeholt und er hätte sich dort wohler befunden[2] als in seinem gegenwärtigen Amt.

„Der Herr General lassen bitten",[3] sagte er düster und half Thomas aus dem Mantel. Es klang, als liege der General im Sterben.

ERNST WIECHERT: *Das einfache Leben*

[1] short-cropped hair.   [2] *sich befinden*—(here) to feel oneself.   [3] 'The General will see you.' The plural form of the verb in formal address in conjunction with a rank or title is now obsolete.

The Attempt to lay the First Submarine Cable across the Atlantic

Von den beiden Schiffen ist der „Niagara"[1] die Aufgabe zugefallen, vom Festland aus das Kabel bis in die Mitte des Meeres zu legen. Langsam, vorsichtig steuert die amerikanische Fregatte dahin, wie eine Spinne aus ihrem gewaltigen Leibe den Faden ständig hinter sich zurücklassend. Langsam, regelmäßig rattert an Bord die Auslegemaschine — es ist das alte, allen Seeleuten wohlbekannte Geräusch eines abrollenden Ankertaues, das sich von der Winde niederdreht. Und nach wenigen Stunden achten die Leute an Bord auf dies regelmäßig mahlende Geräusch ebensowenig wie auf ihren eigenen Herzschlag.

Weiter, weiter hinaus in die See, ständig, ständig das Kabel hinab hinter dem Kiel. Gar nicht abenteuerlich scheint dieses

Abenteuer. Nur in einer besonderen Kammer sitzen und horchen die Elektriker, ständig Zeichen mit dem irischen Festlande tauschend. Und wunderbar: obwohl man längst die Küste nicht mehr erblickt, funktioniert die Übertragung auf dem Unterwasserkabel genauso deutlich, als ob man von einer europäischen Stadt zur andern sich verständigte. Schon sind die seichten Wasser verlassen, schon das sogenannte Tiefseeplateau, das hinter Irland sich erhebt, teilweise überquert, und noch immer läuft wie Sand aus der Sanduhr regelmäßig die metallene Schnur hinter dem Kiel herab, gleichzeitig Botschaft gebend und Botschaft empfangend.

STEFAN ZWEIG: 'Das erste Wort über den Ozean'
(*Sternstunden der Menschheit*)

¹ Ships' names are normally feminine in German. See Gram. 58 (*c*).

1. The ivy climbed up as far as the windows of the second story.
2. The spider was moving steadily, leaving a long thread behind her.
3. The coat of arms must have dated from the period of Frederick the Great.
4. A grey mist was rising over the lake as we approached the château.
5. The task of writing all the letters fell to me.
6. They were able to communicate on the submarine cable from one continent to another.
7. The morose servant helped me out of my coat and led me in.
8. What seaman does not know that sound?
9. The wet roofs, shining in the bright light, were suddenly visible.
10. Above the east wing of the stately manor-house was a white flagpole.

A Gardener's Joys

Der Rentner Karl Altenpohl wohnte in Honnef am Rhein, wo der Weg nach Menzenberg seitab in die Weinberge geht. Da hatte er sein kleines Haus im Garten und einen Zaun aus geflochtenem Draht rundum, daß ihm die Hasen im Winter nicht den Kohl fräßen oder die jungen Obstbäume benagten; denn seitdem er nicht mehr bei der Post war, hätte er nicht leben gemocht, ohne in seinem Garten basteln zu können.

Einmal im Juni morgens so gegen neun Uhr hatte er gerade

ein Gläschen von seinem Stachelbeerwein getrunken und saß
mit der Zeitung am Fenster, weil draußen ein Sprühregen herge-
weht war, der ihm den Garten freundlich begoß. Er sah den
Salat, der schon zu köpfen begonnen hatte, sah die grünen Reihen
der Erbsen schön in die Schnüre gewachsen, die mit Papier-
schnitzeln gegen die Spatzen gespannt waren, sah den Spinat und
das Beet mit den krausen Mohrrübenbüscheln; er sah das Werk
seiner fleißigen Hände, das er mit Mist und künstlichem Dünger
betan hatte, sah den freundlichen Regen und wie drüben hinter
dem Rodderberg¹ schon wieder der blaue Himmel herauskam:
Wir müssen zusammenhalten, dachte er, der Himmel, der
Mensch und die Erde; gutes Wetter muß sein und emsige Arbeit
und ein Boden, auf dem es sich lohnt, den Rücken zu krüm-
men!

Denn in der Zeitung stand mit großen Lettern quer über die
Seite „Der Mord von Serajewo"² gedruckt. Der Rentner Karl
Altenpohl aber hatte auch bei der Post nie Händel gehabt, und er
begriff nicht, daß so viel Feindschaft in der Welt sein konnte,
einen Erzherzog mit seiner Frau totzuschießen.

, WILHELM SCHÄFER: *Der Mord von Serajewo* (adapted)

¹ Name of a hill.   ² The murder, at Serajevo, of the Archduke Franz Ferdinand of Austria and his wife, by Serbian nationalists, was the immediate cause of
the outbreak of war in 1914.

The Unemployed

Er war in diesen naßkalten Februartagen des Jahres 1892 viel auf
der Straße, in der Erwartung großer Ereignisse. Unter den
Linden¹ hatte sich etwas verändert, man sah noch nicht, was.
Berittene Schutzleute hielten an den Mündungen der Straßen
und warteten auch. Die Passanten zeigten einander das Aufgebot
der Macht. „Die Arbeitslosen!" Man blieb stehen, um sie
ankommen zu sehen. Sie kamen vom Norden her, in kleinen
Abteilungen und im langsamen Marschschritt. Unter den Linden
zögerten sie, wie verwirrt, berieten sich mit den Blicken und
lenkten nach dem Schloß ein. Dort standen sie stumm, die
Hände in den Taschen, ließen sich von den Rädern der Wagen
mit Schlamm bespritzen und zogen die Schultern hoch unter
dem Regen, der auf ihre entfärbten Überzieher fiel. Manche
von ihnen wandten die Köpfe nach vorübergehenden Offizieren,
nach den Damen in ihren Wagen, nach den langen Pelzen der
Herren, die von der Burgstraße herschlenderten; und ihre Mienen
waren ohne Ausdruck, nicht drohend und nicht einmal neugierig,

nicht, als wollten sie sehen, sondern als zeigten sie sich. Andere aber ließen kein Auge von den Fenstern des Schlosses.[2] Das Wasser lief über ihre hinaufgewendeten Gesichter. Ein Pferd mit einem schreienden Schutzmann trieb sie weiter, hinüber oder bis zur nächsten Ecke — aber schon standen sie wieder, und die Welt schien versunken[3] zwischen diesen breiten hohlen Gesichtern, die fahler Abend beschien, und der starren Mauer dort hinten, auf der es dunkelte.

HEINRICH MANN: *Der Untertan*

[1] *Unter den Linden*—name of a famous street in Berlin, leading from the Brandenburger Tor to the former Schloß. Tr. 'On the Unter den Linden'.
[2] *Schloß*—the (Imperial) Palace. Do not translate. [3] 'seemed to have passed into oblivion . . .'

1. It is hardly worth while working so busily in such a poor garden.
2. As they turned off towards the palace I could not even see the end of the procession.
3. Are you going to water the lettuces again this evening?
4. My new coat was splashed with mud by a passing car.
5. He could not understand that it was possible for such things to happen.
6. They hesitated and turned their heads to watch the mounted police.
7. About ten o'clock the wind had brought a shower over the hills.
8. The pensioners have a small garden of their own in which they grow carrots, spinach, peas, and other vegetables.
9. The unemployed stood about in the streets, staring at the passers-by.
10. A crowd of young men came strolling along from the direction of the Alexanderplatz.

Working in a DDR Factory[1]

Über all den Aufregungen hatte sie ihre eigenen Ängste und Beklemmungen vergessen. Sie konnte sich jetzt darauf verlassen, daß sie früh zur richtigen Minute erwachte, daß sie mit geschlossenen Augen wußte, wann sie aus der Bahn zu steigen hatte. Immer an der gleichen Stelle traf sie in der Pappelallee immer die gleichen Leute, und die Mittags- und Feierabendzeit erkannte sie an einem Dutzend untrüglicher Zeichen.

Meist war sie jetzt mit Hänschen allein im Wagen. Meternagel kam manchmal, wenn er sich bei den anderen erschöpft und heiser geredet hatte, um bei ihnen zu verschnaufen. Sie zeigten ihm ihre Arbeit, er nickte und setzte sich müde auf die noch rohen Holzsitze des Wagens. Sie beide nahmen ihm gegenüber Platz — soviel Zeit hatten sie immer —, ließen ihn in aller Ruhe rauchen und kümmerten sich nicht um das Fluchen der Elektriker, die ihre dicken Kabel durch das Fenster zogen und kreuz und quer im Wagen verlegten, auch nicht um die Lackierer, die über ihren Köpfen an der Decke herumturnten. Sie saßen mit Meternagel zusammen und schwiegen meist. Sein Gesicht wurde immer hagerer, nur die Augen traten stark daraus hervor, eisblau, intensiv strahlend. Manchmal gab er Rita kleine Aufträge, die sie gewissenhaft ausführte. Sie ging jetzt ohne Scheu in jeden Winkel des Werkes und sprach jeden beliebigen Menschen an.

CHRISTA WOLF: *Der geteilte
Himmel* (adapted)

[1] The main character of the novel, Rita, works in a factory producing railway coaches. (Notice the many prepositional usages in the passage!)

A Boy and a Library

Bücherfreude und Lesetrieb hatten bei mir früh begonnen, und in den ersten Jugendjahren war die einzige große Bibliothek, die ich kannte und benutzen durfte, die meines Großvaters. Der weitaus[1] größte Teil dieser gewaltigen Bibliothek von vielen tausend Bänden war mir gleichgültig und blieb es immer, ich konnte gar nicht begreifen, wie man in solchen Mengen Bücher dieser Art anhäufen könne: historische und erdkundliche Jahrbücher in langen Reihen, theologische Werke in englischer und französischer Sprache, englische Jugendschriften und Erbauungsbücher mit Goldschnitt, endlose Fächer voll gelehrter Zeitschriften, sauber in Karton gebunden oder jahrgangweise in Packen verschnürt. Das alles schien mir recht langweilig, staubig und kaum des Aufbewahrens wert zu sein.

Aber nun hatte diese Bibliothek, wie ich allmählich entdeckte, auch andere Abteilungen. Zunächst waren es einige einzelne Bücher, die mich anzogen und mich veranlaßten, das Ganze dieser so öde scheinenden Bücherei allmählich zu durchstöbern und das für mich Interessante herauszufischen.

Es war da namentlich ein „Robinson Crusoe" mit ganz ent-
zückenden Zeichnungen von Grandville, und eine deutsche
Ausgabe von „Tausendundeine Nacht", zwei schwere Quart-
bände aus den dreißiger Jahren,[2] ebenfalls illustriert. Diese
beiden Bücher zeigten mir, daß es in diesem trüben Meere auch
Perlen zu fischen gebe, und ich ließ nicht nach, die hohen
Bücherregale des Saales abzusuchen, oft saß ich dabei stundenlang hoch oben auf einer Leiter, oder lag bäuchlings am Boden,
wo überall unzählige Bücher gestapelt lagen.

HERMANN HESSE: *Eine Bibliothek der Weltliteratur*

[1] Gram. 79.   [2] Gram. 145 (*a*).

1. He always sat down at the same place, opposite me.
2. When we were young we were never allowed to use grand-
   father's library.
3. The more I rummaged through the various sections, the
   more I discovered.
4. You can rely on him to talk to anyone in the factory.
5. He gave her a little job to do, which she carried out con-
   scientiously.
6. I always wake up in the morning just at the right moment.
7. For hours on end we stacked up books in German and
   Russian.
8. By far the largest part of the books seemed hardly worth
   preserving.
9. I did not give up studying these volumes until I had passed
   the examination.
10. You'll recognize him by his lean face and hoarse voice.

The Old Cook

Eilig packte sie ihre Sachen zusammen, als habe unsere Unter-
haltung schon die zulässige Dauer eines Gespräches zwischen
Herrn und Magd überschritten. Dann verschwand sie mit
Zitherkasten, Korb und Hund, schwerfällig trippelnden Ganges[1]
unter den Lärchen. Ich sah ihr nach. Sie trug in der rechten
Hand einen abgeschnittenen Ast als Stock. Da sie aber meinen
Blick im Rücken zu spüren schien, benützte sie die Stütze nicht,
als schäme sie sich. Während ich weiterspazierte, wunderte ich
mich darüber, daß ich soeben das erste längere[2] Gespräch mit
Teta geführt hatte. Sie diente schon beinahe zwanzig Jahre im
Hause Argan.[3] Ich war ihr in der Stadt wie in Grafenegg[4] immer

wieder begegnet. Wir hatten stets nur einen Gruß getauscht. Das gleichgültige Gespräch dieses Nachmittags aber klang in mir fort. Irgend etwas Festes und Abgeschlossenes[5] spürte ich an der alten Magd, das mich packte. Freilich, wenn mir jemand gesagt hätte, ich würde mich einmal wochenlang mit Teta beschäftigen, ich hätte ihn nicht verstanden.[6] Und doch, schon jetzt beschäftigte ich mich mit Teta. Das Bild, wie sie, den blinden Hund dicht neben sich, eilig und schwerfällig im Walde verschwunden war, wich nicht von meinen Augen.[7] Ich dachte daran, daß Teta eine unerreichte Meisterin ihres Faches war, was alle Freunde und Gäste des Hauses Argan wohl wußten, und daß man mit Fug und Recht[8] von der „Koch-Kunst"[9] spricht und nicht vom „Koch-Handwerk". Denn diese wie jede andere echte Kunst — sie ist die Musik des Geschmackssinns — beruht auf dem Zusammenwirken von Begabung, Formgefühl, hingegebenem Fleiß und echter Persönlichkeit.

FRANZ WERFEL: *Der veruntreute Himmel*

---

[1] Adverbial genitive: 'with short, ponderous steps'.   [2] Gram. 76.   [3] 'in the Argans' household'.   [4] The name of the Argans' family estate.   [5] 'a certain air of firmness and finality'.   [6] Gram. 118 (c), note 1.   [7] Avoid a too literal translation. Take care to find a suitable English equivalent.   [8] *mit Fug und Recht*—with every justification.   [9] Normally: *Kochkunst*. The author hyphenates here in order to emphasize his meaning.

A Boy Climbs a Mountain

Bald kam auch die Zeit, daß ich mich den Wolken nähern, zwischen sie treten und manche aus ihrer Schar von oben betrachten durfte. Ich war zehn Jahre alt, als ich den ersten Gipfel erstieg, den Sennalpstock, an dessen Fuß unser Dörflein Nimikon liegt. Da sah ich denn zum erstenmal die Schrecken und die Schönheiten der Berge. Tiefgerissene Schluchten, voll von Eis und Schneewasser, grüngläserne Gletscher, scheußliche Moränen, und über allem wie eine Glocke hoch und rund der Himmel. Wenn einer zehn Jahre lang zwischen Berg und See geklemmt gelebt hat und rings von nahen Höhen umdrängt war, dann vergißt er den Tag nicht, an dem zum erstenmal ein großer, breiter Himmel über ihm und vor ihm ein unbegrenzter Horizont lag. Schon beim Aufstieg war ich erstaunt, die mir von unten her wohlbekannten Schroffen und Felswände so überwältigend groß zu finden. Und nun sah ich, vom Augenblick ganz bezwungen, mit Angst und Jubel plötzlich die ungeheure Weite auf mich hereindringen. So fabelhaft groß war also die Welt! Unser ganzes Dorf, tief unten verloren liegend, war nur noch ein kleiner heller Fleck. Gipfel, die man vom Tale aus für eng benachbart hielt, lagen viele Stunden weit auseinander.

HERMANN HESSE: *Peter Camenzind*

1. The permitted limit must not be exceeded.
2. Even as we were approaching the clouds, the rain began to fall.
3. We had only ever exchanged an occasional letter.
4. I am surprised that you have never run into him in town.
5. If anyone had told me that he was an unsurpassed master in his craft I should not have believed him.
6. The well-known peaks are in fact not close neighbours, but are miles apart.
7. From the top of the mountain we seemed to have a limitless horizon.
8. The village was now only two hours away.
9. Modern languages are rightly regarded as an important subject.
10. I only knew the range from below. When I had climbed to the top of the mountain everything looked different.

The Burial of Mozart

Es schneite in den Regen, als Mozart die letzte von seinen vielen irdischen Wohnungen so kläglich verließ. Der Wind wehte den Schnee gegen den Sarg, daß die Bretter bald von der Nässe glänzten; nur in den Rillen setzte sich eine weiße Spur an, als ob das Wetter den kahlen Sarg schmücken wollte. Die[1] dem traurigen Trupp begegneten, nahmen den Hut ab; aber es war der Tod, nicht der Mann, dem sie die Ehrfurcht bezeigten. Es fragte auch keiner, wen sie da trügen, weil es sichtbar ein Armer war, der verscharrt werden sollte.

In den Kaffeestuben saßen die Bürger, von ihrem Alltag zu schwatzen; in den Läden wurde gefeilscht und hinter verronnenen Fenstern über das Wetter geklagt; die Handwerker regten die Hände ihrer Gewerbe,[2] und die Bankherren rechneten an Zahlenreihen den Gewinn oder Verlust ihrer Geschäfte aus; die Soldaten in den Kasernen putzten an ihren Monturen, und die Leutnants spielten Karten, weil das Wetter ihnen nicht zu flanieren erlaubte; in der dunklen Hofburg[3] standen die Lakaien herum, auf das Licht der Kerzen zu warten, und der, dem die Kerzen angesteckt werden sollten, der Kaiser Leopold, hatte böse Post[4] aus Paris bekommen, wo seine Schwester Marie Antoinette im Schrecken der Revolution noch auf ihre Flucht

hoffte: Von all den vielen tausend Herzen in Wien fühlte nicht
eins das Ereignis, davon eine Trauer über die Stadt hätte ausgehen sollen, daß Mozart tot war, und daß zwei Männer seinen
Leichnam auf einer Bahre zum Armenbegräbnis hinaustrugen.

WILHELM SCHÄFER: *Mozarts Begräbnis*

¹ *die = diejenigen, die.*   ² *regten die Hände ihrer Gewerbe*—'set about the
work of their various crafts'.   ³ *Hofburg*—the Imperial Palace in Vienna.
Do not translate.   ⁴ *böse Post = schlechte Nachrichten.*

The Last Apollo

Mit einer fast dreistündigen Verspätung, hervorgerufen¹ durch
einen Computer-Irrtum, der die Startvorbereitungen unterbrach,
hob am Donnerstagmorgen voriger Woche in Kap Kennedy eine
Saturn-Rakete mit Apollo 17 zum längsten und vorerst² letzten
bemannten Mondflug ab. Umlauf,³ Einschießen auf Reisekurs
und Einschwenken in die Mondumlaufbahn verlief trotz kleinerer
Defekte reibungslos.⁴ Am Montag um 20.55 Uhr MEZ⁵ setzten
die Astronauten Eugene Cernan und Harrison Schmitt ihre
Fähre *Challenger* im sogenannten Taurus-Littrow-Tal auf.
75 Stunden Aufenthalt und drei je⁶ siebenstündige „Ausflüge"
sollen wichtige Aufschlüsse und Ergebnisse bringen.

Die Raumfahrtbehörde NASA erwartet von dem Geologen
Schmitt, dem ersten mitfliegenden Zivilisten, besonders wertvolle
Erkenntnisse. Astronaut Ronald Evans soll bis zum Rückstart
am Freitag in seiner Kommandokapsel *America* den Erdtrabanten⁷
umkreisen, kartographisch weiter vermessen und nach Spuren
von Wasser forschen. Die Landung — „Wasserung" — ist für
den 19. Dezember südlich von Samoa im Pazifik vorgesehen.

Das Tauros-Littrow-Gebiet wurde ausgewählt, weil die
Geologen hier das älteste und auch das jüngste Mondgestein zu
finden hoffen. Apollo 17 bietet die vorerst letzte Chance, die
Entstehung des Mondes an Hand von⁸ Gestein zu enträtseln.

DIE ZEIT, 15 December 1972

¹ *hervorrufen*—cause.   ² *vorerst*—provisionally, for the present.   ³ orbit.
⁴ without a hitch (*Reibung*—friction).   ⁵ *MEZ*—*mitteleuropäische Zeit.*
⁶ Gram. 149 (*a*).   ⁷ *der Trabant*—satellite (like *der Satellit*, a weak masc.
Note the other weak masc. nouns in the passage.)   ⁸ *an Hand von*—on the
basis of.

1. Mozart's body was carried through the rain in a bare coffin
   to a pauper's grave.
2. It was the geologist's job to look for traces of water.

3. The two 'moonwalks' of two hours each brought important results.
4. The passers-by showed their respect by doffing their hats.
5. The death of Mozart was an event which should have been mourned throughout Vienna and the whole world.
6. Splashdown is due to take place in the South Pacific tonight.
7. The preparations went off without a hitch.
8. On the basis of this rock we may be able to puzzle out the problem.
9. The merchants sat at long tables calculating profits and losses.
10. Don't complain about the weather. The snow is far worse than this rain.

A Message from the Examining Magistrate[1]

K. war telephonisch verständigt worden, daß am nächsten Sonntag eine kleine Untersuchung in seiner Angelegenheit[2] stattfinden würde. Man machte ihn darauf aufmerksam, daß diese Untersuchungen regelmäßig, wenn auch vielleicht nicht jede Woche, so doch häufiger[3] einander folgen würden. Es liege einerseits im allgemeinen Interesse, den Prozeß rasch zu Ende zu führen, anderseits aber müßten die Untersuchungen in jeder Hinsicht gründlich sein und dürften doch wegen der damit verbundenen Anstrengung niemals allzulange dauern. Deshalb habe man den Ausweg dieser rasch aufeinanderfolgenden, aber kurzen Untersuchungen gewählt. Die Bestimmung[4] des Sonntags als Untersuchungstag habe man deshalb vorgenommen, um K. in seiner beruflichen Arbeit nicht zu stören. Man setze voraus, daß er damit einverstanden sei, sollte er einen anderen Termin wünschen, so würde man ihm, so gut es ginge, entgegenkommen. Die Untersuchungen wären beispielsweise auch in der Nacht möglich, aber da sei wohl K. nicht frisch genug. Jedenfalls werde man es, solange K. nichts einwende, beim Sonntag belassen. Es sei selbstverständlich, daß er bestimmt erscheinen müsse, darauf müsse man ihn wohl nicht erst[5] aufmerksam machen. Es wurde ihm die Nummer des Hauses genannt, in dem er sich einfinden solle, es war ein Haus in einer entlegenen Vorstadtstraße, in der K. noch niemals gewesen war.

FRANZ KAFKA: *Der Prozeß*

[1] 'Examining magistrate'—*Untersuchungsrichter*. In serious cases, which are due for trial before a high court, the Public Prosecutor requests a preliminary examination by an 'examining magistrate'. This practice is normal in German law, but does not exist in England.   [2] (here) 'case'.   [3] Cf. Gram. 76. The same principle applies for certain adverbs.   [4] Cf. *einen Tag bestimmen*—to fix, arrange a day.   [5] Gram. 123 (*b*).

Running Away

Verfolgung während der Fahrt hatte Etzel nicht zu befürchten. Er wußte, daß der Vater erst am Donnerstag von seiner Dienstreise zurückkehrte, bis dahin war er in Berlin. Die Frage war nur: was dann? wo Unterschlupf finden? wo sich verbergen? Daß die Bitte, die er in dem Abschiedsschreiben an den Vater gerichtet, er möge[1] ihm nicht nachstellen lassen, unerfüllt bleiben würde, darüber gab er sich keiner Täuschung hin.[2] Er mußte aber den Rücken frei haben und sich nach Erfordernis bewegen können, sonst taugte die ganze Geschichte[3] nichts. In jedem Gasthaus, in jeder Pension, in jeder Herberge mußte er polizeilich gemeldet werden. Es unter falschem Namen zu tun, würde vermutlich wenig Erfolg haben, da sie doch, wenn sie ihn suchten, seine Personbeschreibung hatten und in diesen Dingen gewitzt waren. Bekannte hatte er dort nicht, keine Menschenseele, an die er sich wenden konnte, außer vielleicht . . . Melchior Ghisels. Allein es war ohne weiteres anzunehmen, daß ein Melchior Ghisels sich um so niedrige Angelegenheiten nicht kümmern konnte, falls er sich um einen Etzel Andergast überhaupt zu kümmern geneigt war. Wohin also? Es war eine große Sorge.

JAKOB WASSERMANN: *Der Fall Maurizius*

[1] Gram. 27 (*b*). [2] *sich keiner Täuschung hingeben*—to entertain no illusions.
[3] *die ganze Geschichte*—the whole business.

1. My attention was drawn to the fact that I must definitely appear.
2. Etzel had written to his father with the request that he should not have him followed.
3. I visit her quite often, if not every week, at least two or three times a month.
4. Surely I don't need to tell you that!
5. I'm afraid I shall not be back till Tuesday.
6. I entertain no illusions about his interest in this whole business.
7. Shall we leave it at Monday unless I hear from you?
8. There was no one to whom I could turn in difficulties.
9. We will do our best to oblige you, in order not to disturb you too much.
10. I am not at all inclined to advise him in this matter.

The Church in the Medieval Town

Welche Bedeutung die Kirche — sowohl die geistige Gemein-
schaft wie auch ihr Gehäuse, das Bauwerk — im Bewußtsein und
im täglichen Leben jedes einzelnen Menschen noch vor zwei-
hundert Jahren hatte, das kann man sich heute nicht einmal mehr
in ausgesprochen[1] religiösen Kreisen vorstellen — und schon gar
nicht[2] ihre Bedeutung in den Zeiten vor der Reformation. Der
einzelne war beruflich bei weitem nicht so spezialisiert, die
Interessen der Bürger einer Stadt waren nicht so zersplittert wie
heute, wo jeder nur sein eigenes, hochentwickeltes Fach versteht;
das gegenseitige Verständnis war viel stärker, das Bewußtsein
der Zusammengehörigkeit viel größer. Über allen aber stand,
als gemeinsame beschirmende und höchste Macht: die Kirche.
Zudem lagen alle öffentlichen Aufgaben, die heute ausschließlich
durch die Amtsstellen der Erziehungsdirektionen[3] und Schulen
— von der Primarschule bis zur Universität — erledigt werden,
aber auch die der Gesundheitsdirektionen, der Fürsorgeämter[4]
usw. — in der Hand der Kirche, und zwar finanziert aus frei-
willigen Beiträgen. Nur so kann man verstehen, welche Bedeutung die Kirche im Bilde der mittelalterlichen Städte einnimmt.
Sie ist der Mittelpunkt, die Stätte der täglichen Andacht und
der Feste, ein unablässiges Gebet, zugleich auch der Stolz und
der Prunkbau[5] der Stadt, mit dem kein anderes Bauwerk wett-
eifert, riesenhaft emporragend über das Gewinkel[6] der kleinen,
bis ins 16. Jahrhundert meist hölzernen Häuser der Bürger,
vertraut und fremdartig zugleich . . .

PETER MEYER: *Kunst in der Schweiz* (adapted)

[1] *ausgesprochen*—(adverb) markedly, distinctively.   [2] Gram. 126 (c).
[3] local education authorities.   [4] national assistance boards.   [5] showpiece,
show building.   [6] intricate angular maze.

Conversations with the Artist

Gianluca liebte es, während des Malens zu reden und auch mich
zum Sprechen zu bringen, damit sich, wie er sagte, meinen
Zügen eine größere Lebendigkeit mitteile. Er erzählte mir viel
von seiner Arbeit und von seinen Reisen, von den Städten, die er
besucht, und den der Erinnerung werten Menschen, mit denen
er Umgang gehabt hatte; und er tat es in einer glänzenden und
lebhaften Art, so wie ich zeit meines Lebens[1] keinen anderen
habe erzählen hören, und oft auch voll einer Heiterkeit, wie sie
wenigen Menschen gegeben ist. Und obwohl ich ihm immer

hätte zuhören mögen, so nötigte er mich doch auch, ihm von meinem Leben und von allerlei städtischen Vorkommnissen zu berichten. Ich tat dies erst mit Zurückhaltung, denn ich meinte, ein Mann wie er könne doch nicht gut an so kleinen Dingen Gefallen finden; und doch machte es mich glücklich, daß er mich reden hören wollte, wenn ich mir auch sagen mußte, daß er mich vielleicht nur seiner Arbeit zuliebe² zum Erzählen aufforderte. Aber nun verstand er es, durch sein Zuhören, durch seine Ausrufe und Zwischenfragen, durch seine Blicke und Mienen dem von mir Erzählten eine Bedeutung zu geben, die ich selber meinem Dasein nie beizumessen gewagt hätte. Ich möchte wohl sagen, ich habe alle diese Zeit wie in einer Verzauberung hingelebt, und ich hätte nichts anderes wünschen mögen, als daß es immerfort so angedauert hätte.

WERNER BERGENGRUEN: Der Turmbau

¹ *zeit meines Lebens*—ever in my life.   ² *seiner Arbeit zuliebe*—for the benefit of his work.

1. Both the individual and the community have rights and duties.
2. 'In this factory it is important that each employee should know his job.'
3. The artist would never have attributed so great an importance to his work.
4. We shall not be able to see to these tasks without bigger voluntary contributions.
5. How can I get him to talk?
6. I should always have liked to listen to him for he usually talked a lot about his travels.
7. No one else could have competed with the painter.
8. The people he had had to do with were mainly artists.
9. The church was the centre of municipal affairs in the Middle Ages.
10. People cannot imagine such a thing nowadays.

The Trade Routes of the Middle Ages

Das Mittelalter, das heißt die Zeit bis zur Entdeckung der neuen Seewege über den Ozean, kannte nur zwei Hauptadern des Welthandels. Die eine ging über das Mittelmeer, die andere durch die Ostsee in die Nordsee. Jene führte dem Abendland die Waren von Vorderasien und Indien zu, diese vermittelte den Austausch mit der weiten russischen Tiefebene. Bestanden hatte sie wohl von jeher, aber recht eigentlich lebendig wurde sie erst, als die Eroberung der Ostseeküsten durch die Deutschen begann. Man darf ihre volkswirtschaftliche Bedeutung nicht danach schätzen, was der Ostseehandel etwa in neueren Zeiten gewesen ist; da trat er gegenüber dem mächtigen transozeanischen Verkehr immer mehr zurück. Ehe aber diese neuen Straßen erschlossen wurden, darf man seinen Wert wohl annähernd dem auf dem Mittelmeer gleichstellen. Eine ganze Reihe der notwendigsten Rohstoffe wurde über die Ostsee entweder aus ihren Küsten- ländern — Preußen, Polen, Livland, Schweden — oder aus dem ungeheuren russischen Hinterland nach dem Westen geführt: Getreide, Flachs und Hanf, Wachs, Honig, Butter, Häute, Fett und Talg, Holz, Harz, Teer, Asche, Eisenerz, Kupfer und Pelzwerk und schließlich — um einen Hauptartikel zuletzt zu nennen — Fische. Umgekehrt waren die Ostseeländer ein dank- bares Absatzgebiet[1] für die Industriewaren des Westens, vor allem Tuche,[2] dazu Salz und Wein und alles das, was durch Vermittlung[3] der westlichen und südlichen Länder aus dem Orient kam.

JOHANNES HALLER: *Die Epochen der deutschen Geschichte*

---

[1] market (for goods).   [2] N.B. the plural *Tuche* (as distinct from *Tücher*— cloths) connotes different types of cloth; hence 'cloth'.   [3] *durch Vermittlung*— via (*vermitteln*—to mediate; to act as middleman).

A Weather Phenomenon

Die vorherrschenden Luftströmungen in Frankreich und Süd- westdeutschland sind die mit den atlantischen Tiefdruckwirbeln[1] kommenden Südwestwinde. Sie treffen ungefähr senkrecht auf den Wall des Wasgenwaldes,[2] der sie zum Aufsteigen zwingt. Die Westseite und die Kammhöhe dieses Gebirges sind dement- sprechend feucht, wasser- und flußreich. Von den Vogesen[2] herunter fällt die Luft in die breite Furche des Rheintals, innere Reibung und Druck erwärmen diese fallenden Winde. Die Wolken lösen sich auf — und während die Westseite schlechtes Wetter hat, herrscht auf der Ostseite und im ganzen Rheintal der schönste Sonnenschein. Er reicht bis zum Westfuß des Schwarz- walds. Da dessen[3] Berge viel steiler emporragen als die Westseite der Vogesen, so ist hier die Lufthebung viel plötzlicher und darum auch die Wolkenbildung noch ausgesprochener. Und der Reisende im Rheintal hat an sichtigen Tagen das merk- würdige Schauspiel, daß er unter einem heitern Himmel dahin- fährt, während die Schwarzwaldhänge in dunklen Wolkenballen

stecken und über den Vogesenkamm ununterbrochen die Nebel-
schwaden sich wie breite, langsam fließende Wasserfälle wälzen,
um sich in einer für den Unkundigen ganz rätselhaften Weise im
Rheintal zu verflüchtigen.

HENRY HOEK: *Wetter, Wolken, Wind*

[1] depressions. [2] *der Wasgenwald* or (more often) *die Vogesen*—the Vosges.
[3] *dessen* is preferred to *seine* here for the sake of clarity. Cf. Gram. 104 and 15.

1. One route lay across the Mediterranean, the other across the North Sea.
2. No doubt this trade had existed from time immemorial.
3. The prevailing air-currents in this part of the country are the south-westerly winds.
4. The value of this exchange of goods cannot be compared with any other.
5. Cloud-formation is even more pronounced on the northern side of the mountains.
6. Grain, skins, tar, and iron ore—to mention only some of the chief articles—were imported from the east.
7. What a remarkable spectacle one has when the sun shines on the hills!
8. The rampart of the Vosges forces the warm air upwards.
9. What are the most necessary raw materials for modern industry?
10. Do you see how the clouds are clearing over the ridge of the hills?

The Importance of the Present Moment

Jeder Zustand, sagte Goethe einmal zu Eckermann, ja jeder
Augenblick ist von unendlichem Wert, denn er ist der Repräsen-
tant einer ganzen Ewigkeit. Jeden Moment des Lebens hielt
Goethe für selbständig und in sich selbst geschlossen und voll-
endet. Er ist nicht Vorbereitung und auch nicht Abschluß. Ja,
auch das Werk eines großen Künstlers ist nach Goethe in jedem
Stadium seiner Entwicklung schon fertig, so wie die Natur mit
jeder ihrer Produktionen schon am Ziele ist und auch der kleinste
Teil einer Pflanze um seiner[1] selbst willen und nicht zu einem
Endzweck da ist. Diese Stellung zu Vergangenheit und Zukunft,
diese unbedingte Vergöttlichung des gegenwärtigen Augenblicks
war für seine Dichtung ganz entscheidend. Sie kam nicht aus der
Sehnsucht, wie die der Romantiker. Ein Gedicht des Königs
von Bayern über Weimar wurde von Goethe als zu subjektiv

gescholten: es sei gar nicht poetisch, die Vergangenheit so tragisch
zu behandeln, statt reinen Genusses und Anerkennung der
Gegenwart, und jene erst totzuschlagen, um sie besingen zu
können. Vielmehr müsse man die Vergangenheit wie in den
römischen Elegien behandeln. Weil die Menschen die Gegenwart nicht zu würdigen, zu beleben wüßten, schmachteten sie
so nach einer besseren Zukunft, kokettierten sie so mit der Vergangenheit.   FRITZ STRICH: *Deutsche Klassik und Romantik*

¹ Gram. 90.

A Crime Story¹

Die an sich kurze Erzählung Schillers beginnt mit einer unge-
wöhnlich breiten theoretischen Einleitung, die sich mit der
Psychologie des Verbrechens und des Verbrechers beschäftigt.
Offensichtlich hat Schiller das Bedürfnis, seine Kriminalgeschichte
als Beitrag zur Seelenkunde und zur moralischen Bildung zu
rechtfertigen. Der Verbrecher interessiert ihn nicht so sehr
wegen der spannenden Begebenheit, sondern wegen der psycho-
logischen und soziologischen Probleme, die mit seinem Dasein
verknüpft sind und die tief in die Welt des moralischen Be-
wußtseins hineinreichen. Um Sensation ist es Schiller nicht zu
tun.² Trotzdem steckt in seinem Interesse am Verbrecher auch
etwas Naives. Es ist gewiß kein Zufall, daß fast alle Schillerschen
Dramen in ihrem Grundriß als Kriminalstücke gebaut sind. Der
radikal zugespitzte³ Rechtsfall gibt besondere Möglichkeiten,
extreme Situationen oder auch extreme Charaktere und Affekte
darzustellen, die für Schiller von früher Jugend an besonders
anziehend waren. Der Verbrecher fesselt ihn vom Standpunkt
der Menschenkunde aus; ja, der Mensch erreicht nach Schillers
geheimster Meinung erst dort seine eigentliche Bedeutung, wo er
im Bösen oder im Guten, als Held oder als Opfer das Außer-
ordentliche, das Ungewöhnliche verwirklicht.

BENNO VON WIESE: *Die deutsche Novelle*

¹ The author is writing about Schiller's story 'Der Verbrecher aus verlorener
Ehre'.   ² Cf. *Es ist mir sehr darum zu tun,* . . .—I am very concerned about . . .;
I am very interested in . . . (doing).   ³ *zugespitzt*—pointed, accentuated.

1. Even the work of a great artist may contain weaknesses.
2. The author was interested in the criminal from the psycho-
   logical point of view.
3. There is no need to treat the subject so tragically. It has its
   comic side, after all.

4. The story was, in itself, of little interest.
5. Does a work of art require precision and attention at every stage?
6. Clearly he feels obliged to justify his actions.
7. It was certainly not a coincidence that his contribution only reached us this morning.
8. These journalists are not concerned with news but only with sensations.
9. His poems were of infinite value for those who believed in the principle 'Art for Art's sake'.
10. There is no point in longing for a better future if we do not work to achieve it.

Die Schatzgräber

Ein Winzer, der am Tode lag,
Rief seine Kinder an und sprach:
„In unserm Weinberg liegt ein Schatz:
Grabt nur danach!" — „An welchem Platz?"
Schrie alles laut den Vater an.
„Grabt nur!" — O weh! da starb der Mann.

Kaum war der Alte beigeschafft,
So grub man nach aus Leibeskraft.
Mit Hacke, Karst[1] und Spaten ward
Der Weinberg um und um gescharrt.
Da war kein Kloß, der ruhig blieb;
Man warf die Erde gar durchs Sieb
Und zog die Harken kreuz und quer
Nach jedem Steinchen hin und her.
Allein da ward kein Schatz verspürt,
Und jeder hielt sich angeführt.

Doch kaum erschien das nächste Jahr,
So nahm man mit Erstaunen wahr,
Daß jede Rebe dreifach trug.
Da wurden erst die Söhne klug
Und gruben nun jahrein, jahraus
Des Schatzes immer mehr heraus.

GOTTFRIED AUGUST BÜRGER (1747–94)

[1] der Karst = die Erdhacke.

Die stille Stadt

Liegt eine Stadt im Tale,
Ein blasser Tag vergeht;
Es wird nicht lange dauern mehr,
Bis weder Mond noch Sterne,
Nur Nacht am Himmel steht.

Von allen Bergen drücken
Nebel auf die Stadt;
Es dringt kein Dach, nicht Hof noch Haus,
Kein Laut aus ihrem Rauch heraus,
Kaum Türme noch und Brücken.

Doch als den Wanderer graute,[1]
Da ging ein Lichtlein auf im Grund;
Und durch den Rauch und Nebel
Begann ein leiser Lobgesang
Aus Kindermund.

RICHARD DEHMEL

[1] Gram. 100 (c). *mir graut davor* is more common than *mich graut davor*.

Aus der Kinderzeit

In alten Briefen saß ich heut' vergraben,
Als einer plötzlich in die Hand mir fiel,
Auf dem die Jahresziffer mich erschreckte,
So lange war es her, so lange schon.
Die Schrift stand groß und klein und glatt und kraus
Und reichlich untermischt mit Tintenklecksen:
„Mein lieber Fritz, die Bäume sind nun kahl,
Wir spielen nicht mehr Räuber und Soldat,
Türk hat das rechte Vorderbein gebrochen,
Und Tante Hannchen hat noch immer Zahnweh,
Papa ist auf die Hühnerjagd gegangen.
Ich weiß nichts mehr. Mir geht es gut.
Schreib bald und bleibe recht gesund.
Dein Freund und Vetter Siegesmund." —

„Die Bäume sind nun kahl", das herbe Wort
Ließ mich die Briefe still zusammenlegen,
Gab Hut und Handschuh mir und Rock und Stock
Und drängte mich hinaus in meine Heide.

DETLEV VON LILIENCRON

Abseits

Es ist so still: die Heide liegt
Im warmen Mittagssonnenstrahle,
Ein rosenroter Schimmer fliegt
Um ihre alten Gräbermale;
Die Kräuter blühn; der Heideduft
Steigt in die blaue Sommerluft.

Laufkäfer hasten durchs Gesträuch
In ihren goldnen Panzerröckchen,
Die Bienen hängen Zweig um Zweig
Sich an der Edelheide[1] Glöckchen;
Die Vögel schwirren aus dem Kraut —
Die Luft ist voller Lerchenlaut.

Ein halbverfallen niedrig Haus
Steht einsam hier und sonnbeschienen;
Der Kätner[2] lehnt zur Tür hinaus,
Behaglich blinzelnd nach den Bienen;
Sein Junge auf dem Stein davor
Schnitzt Pfeifen sich aus Kälberrohr.[3]

Kaum zittert durch die Mittagsruh
Ein Schlag der Dorfuhr, der entfernten;
Dem Alten fällt die Wimper zu,
Er träumt von seinen Honigernten. —
Kein Klang der aufgeregten Zeit
Drang noch in diese Einsamkeit.

THEODOR STORM

[1] bell-heather.　　[2] *Kätner*—cottager.　　[3] chervil.

Auf dem Canal Grande[1]

Auf dem Canal Grande betten
Tief sich ein die Abendschatten,
Hundert dunkle Gondeln gleiten
Als ein flüsterndes Geheimnis.

Aber zwischen zwei Palästen
Glüht herein die Abendsonne,
Flammend wirft sie einen grellen
Breiten Streifen auf die Gondeln.

In dem purpurroten Lichte
Laute Stimmen, hell Gelächter,
Überredende Gebärden
Und das frevle Spiel der Augen.

E i n e kurze, kleine Strecke
Treibt das Leben leidenschaftlich
Und erlischt im Schatten drüben
Als ein unverständlich Murmeln.

C. F. MEYER

[1] The *Canal Grande* in Venice. Do not translate.

Das Schilf

„Stille, er schläft, stille, stille!
Libelle, reg die Schwingen sacht,
Daß nicht das Goldgewebe schrille,
Und, Ufergrün, halt gute Wacht,
Kein Kieselchen laß niederfallen.
Er schläft auf seinem Wolkenflaum
Und über ihn läßt säuselnd wallen
Das Laubgewölb der alte Baum;
Hoch oben, wo die Sonne glüht,
Wieget der Vogel seine Flügel,
Und wie ein schlüpfend Fischlein zieht
Sein Schatten durch des Teiches Spiegel.
Stille, stille! er hat sich geregt,
Ein fallend Reis hat ihn bewegt,
Das grad[1] zum Nest ein Hänfling[2] trug;
Su, su! breit', Ast, dein grünes Tuch —
Su, su! nun schläft er fest genug."

ANNETTE VON DROSTE-HÜLSHOFF

[1] *grad—gerade.*   [2] linnet.

Gewitter im Urwald

Die Nacht ist ganz von Blitzen hell
Und zuckt in weißem Licht
Und flackert wild, verstört und grell
Über den Wald, den Strom und mein bleiches Gesicht.
Am kühlen Bambusstamm gelehnt
Steh' ich und schaue unverwandt
Über das regengepeitschte, blasse Land,
Das sich nach Ruhe sehnt,

Und aus der fernen Jugend her
Blitzt mir aus regentrüber
Verdüsterung[1] ein Freudenschrei herüber,
Daß doch nicht alles leer,
Daß doch nicht alles schal und dunkel sei,
Daß noch Gewitter sprühen
Und an der Tage ödem Zug vorbei
Geheimnisse und wilde Wunder glühen.
Tief atmend lausche ich dem Donner nach
Und spüre feucht den Sturm in meinem Haar
Und bin für Augenblicke tigerwach
Und froh, wie ich's in Knabenzeiten
Und seit den Knabenzeiten nie mehr war.

HERMANN HESSE

[1] *aus regentrüber Verdüsterung*—'from rain-dim gathering gloom' (*sich verdüstern*—to become gloomy).

Der Falter

Nacht stand bis ans Fenster dicht.
In den kleinen Kreis von Licht,
den ich eng um mich gezogen,
kam ein Falter wild geflogen.

Schwirrte poltertaumlig[1] flatternd,
rauschte im Papierschirm knatternd,
schrecklich in sein Schicksal rennend,
sich zerstürzend, sich verbrennend . . .

Griff ich plump ihn, menschenhändig,[2]
schlug er wie ein Herz lebendig,
angstvoll in Verzweiflung wütend —
hilflos war ich, ihn behütend.

Dreimal warf ich ihn im harten
Schwunge in den schwarzen Garten.
Doch er sah im Glanz sein Glück,
dreimal schwirrte er zurück,

bis er tappend, blind durchs Zimmer
torkelte, um still zu enden . . .
Aber mir an meinen Händen
blieb des feinsten Goldes Schimmer.

EUGEN ROTH

[1] *poltern*—to make a noise, din; *taumeln*—to reel, stagger.   [2] *plump . . . menschenhändig*—'with clumsy human hand'.

PASSAGES FOR PROSE COMPOSITION

In the Austrian Province of Vorarlberg

Some years before the war I paid my first visit to the north-west part of Vorarlberg, in Austria, and ever since[1] I have kept a nostalgic memory of[2] that charming country.

When I returned there last spring, it was with mixed feelings; I wondered whether I might not be disappointed, as happens so often in such cases. My fears were unfounded—the[3] Vorarlberg has remained exactly as it was so many years ago—delightful and unspoilt.

The small town of Dornbirn would be a good centre[4] from which to visit the region.[5] It has not the character and the originality of Feldkirch, farther south, but it is more centrally placed.[6]

There is a new and very comfortable hotel here. If you do not care to stay in a town, then five or six miles away, up in the mountains at Bödele, there is one of the most delightful hotels I know.

You cannot even call this place a village. There is a tiny chapel, three or four houses, and this hotel. The old hotel, which was burned down to the ground[7] some time ago,[8] has been replaced by a modern and very pretty building, half wood, half stone,[9] in the traditional style and in a better position than the old one. On the one hand one can see across to the high mountains of Germany[10] and on the other the view over the Bodensee to Switzerland is equally lovely although quite different.

PIERRE D'HARCOURT: 'Unspoilt Austria' (from the *Observer*)

[1] Use *seitdem* and *immer* with Present tense.   [2] See Topic 12, p. 83.
[3] Omit the article in German.   [4] *der Ausgangspunkt.*   [5] 'for walks in the region'.   [6] *zentraler gelegen.*   [7] Use the verb *abbrennen* in the active voice.
[8] *vor einiger Zeit.*   [9] 'half of wood, half of stone'. Cf. Gram. 134.   [10] *das deutsche Hochgebirge.*

The Pleasures of a Country Life

'See here,'[1] he said, 'let us say[2] you clear up[3] five hundred a year from[4] this farm——'

'You exaggerate——' I interrupted.[5]

'Do I?' he laughed; 'that makes my case all the better.[6] Now, isn't it possible to rise from that?[7] Couldn't you make a thousand or five thousand, or even fifty thousand a year?'

'I suppose I might,' I said, 'but do you think I'd be any better off[8] or happier with fifty thousand a year than I am now? You see, I like all these surroundings[9] better than any other place I ever knew. That old green hill over there with the oak on it is an intimate friend of mine. I have a good cornfield in which every year I work miracles.[10] I've a cow and a horse and a few pigs. I have a comfortable home. My appetite is perfect, and I have plenty to eat.[11] I sleep every night like a boy,[12] for I haven't any troubles. I enjoy the mornings here in the country: and the evenings are pleasant. Some of the neighbours have come to be my good friends.[13] I like them, and I am pretty sure they like me. Inside the house over there I have the best books ever written, and I have time in the evenings to read them—I mean *really* read them. Now, the question is, would I be any better off, or any happier, if I had fifty thousand a year?'

John Starkweather laughed.

'Well, sir,'[14] he said, 'I see I've made the acquaintance of a philosopher.'[15]

DAVID GRAYSON: *Adventures in Contentment* (adapted)

[1] '*Sehen Sie mal*'.   [2] See Topic 6, p. 42.   [3] *einen Reingewinn ziehen* (*aus*). [4] *aus*.   [5] Include the direct object 'him'.   [6] 'that only strengthens my case (*meine These*).   [7] 'to earn more'.   [8] *besser daran sein*.   [9] 'this whole environment'.   [10] to work miracles—*Wunder wirken*.   [11] *ich habe reichlich zu essen*.   [12] 'like a child'.   [13] 'have become good friends of mine' (*von mir*). [14] Omit 'sir' in translation. There is no satisfactory German equivalent.   [15] Weak masculine noun. See Topic 11, 2 (iii), p. 72.

A Man and his Dog

The sun is high, the cuckoo is shouting over the valley, and the woods are calling to[1] unknown adventures. . . . Chum knows that I am in a good mood.[2] I think he feels[3] that,[4] in spite of my work, at any moment I may speak the magic word 'Walk'. What a[5] word that is. No sleep so sound that it will[6] not penetrate its[7] depths and bring him to his feet.[8] He would sacrifice the whole dictionary for that one electric[9] word. That[10] and its brother 'Bones'. Give[11] him these good, sound, sensible words, and he will gladly forgo all the fancies of the poets and all the rhetoric of the statesmen. . . . Yes, Chum knows very well that I am thinking about him and thinking about him[12] in an uncommonly kindly way. That is the secret of the strange friendship between us.

We may love other animals and other animals may return[13] our affection. But the dog is the only animal who has an intelligence that may be compared with ours. Stroke a cat or a horse and it will have a certain bodily pleasure, but go to Chum and call him 'Good dog'[14] and he experiences a spiritual pleasure. He is pleased because you are pleased.

A. G. GARDINER (adapted)
O. & C. S.E.B., A.S. Level, 1951

[1] *locken zu.*   [2] *guter Laune sein.*   [3] *ahnen.*   [4] Include *ich* immediately after *daß.*   [5] Use *welch ein.* Gram. 111.   [6] Gram. 50.   [7] Gram. 104.   [8] *auf die Beine bringen.*   [9] Cf. 'A Man and his Dog', p. 130.   [10] 'For that and for its brother "Bones".' Cf. Gram. 141.   [11] If the imperative is used here it must be in the familiar (sing.) form.   [12] Include *und zwar.* Gram. 132 (c).   [13] *erwidern.*   [14] Cf. Gram. 74, note 1.

The End of the Journey

Now they were in the tunnel. Daniel stared out into the darkness, waiting for the first sight of Dullchester at the other end. Yes, there it came. A loud whistle; the tunnel opened,[1] the smoke gradually cleared,[2] and there they were: castle, cathedral, river, and ships, and the voice of a porter calling out, 'St. Rood's. Change here for[3] Dullchester.' Daniel got out, said good-day to[4] his companion, and started to cross to the other train. But suddenly he decided to walk. It would only take half an hour. So he left his bag[5] at the station, strolled down into St. Rood's and made for[6] the great stone bridge, beneath which the river flowed sluggishly to the sea. Here the wind, that had come[7] past meadows and old-fashioned windmills, filled[8] the red and brown sails of barges[9] and brought the scent of seaweed[10] drying on the muddy banks. From here[11] he could already see the shady High Street[12] on the further side, and the great white clock that sticks out over the pavement. Its black hands showed half past three, and the cathedral bells were ringing. Daniel stopped, went to the edge of the bridge, leant over and gazed down at the water. 'I wonder[13] how many people will remember me?' he asked himself. 'Is there anyone left here who knew[14] me when I was a boy?'[15]

R. THORNDIKE (adapted)
O. & C. S.E.B., A.S. Level, 1954

[1] Gram. 9.   [2] *sich verflüchtigen* or *sich auflösen.*   [3] *nach.*   [4] *sich verabschieden von.*   [5] *den Koffer abgeben.*   [6] 'went in the direction of'.   [7] *herkommen.*   [8] *blähen.*   [9] barge—*der Lastkahn.*   [10] seaweed—*der Seetang.*   [11] Gram. 140.   [12] *Hauptstraße* or *Hohe Straße.*   [13] Use *wohl* to express 'I wonder'. Gram. 130.   [14] Perfect.   [15] 'as a boy'. Care with the case.

A Young Otter's Play

While swimming in this happy way, he noticed the moon. It danced on the water just before his nose. Often he had seen the moon, just outside the hollow tree, and had tried to touch it with a paw. Now he tried to bite it, but it swam away from him. He chased it. It wriggled[1] like a silver fish and he followed to[2] the sedges[3] on the far[4] bank of the river, but it no longer wriggled. It was waiting to play with him. Across the river Tarka could hear the mewing[5] of his sisters, but he set off after[6] the moon over[7] the meadow. Farther and farther from the river he ran, the moonlight gleaming on his coat.[8]

As he stopped to listen to[9] the bleat of lambs, a moth whirred[10] by his head and tickled him. While he was scratching, a bird flying with irregular wingbeats[11] and gliding like a hawk took[12] the moth in its gaping beak and flew out of[13] sight. Tarka forgot the moon-play. He crouched in the grasses, which rose above his head like the trees of a forest, whispering and swaying. Tarka was glad to hear his mother calling him.[14] He mewed. He listened and her whistle was nearer,[15] so he ran away in the wet grasses. The cub[16] did not know how alarmed his mother was nor did he know that a bird with great eyes and wings spanning a yard[17] was flying upon him.[18]

HENRY WILLIAMSON: *Tarka the Otter* (adapted)

[1] *sich winden.* Gram. 9.   [2] See Topic 3, p. 19: *bis* + another preposition.
[3] sedges—*das Schilf.*   [4] *jenseitig.*   [5] *das Miauen.*   [6] *sich auf die Jagd machen (nach).*   [7] *über . . . hin.*   [8] coat—*das Fell.* See also Topic 17, (iii) (*a*), p. 112.   [9] Gram. 14.   [10] *schwirren.*   [11] wingbeats—*der Flügelschlag.*   [12] *fangen.*   [13] *außer.*   [14] 'to hear his mother's call'.
[15] 'had come nearer'.   [16] 'the young otter'.   [17] 'with wings which measured (*umspannten*) a metre'.   [18] to fly upon s.th.—*auf etwas zufliegen.* Cf. Gram. 140.

An Attempt on the Life of the Prime Minister

Mr. Pitt handed Roger a dirty piece of paper[1] covered on both sides with pencilled writing.[2] The script was very faint,[3] and so full of[4] alterations that it was most difficult to read. Roger glanced carelessly through[5] the first two or three lines; then he gave a gasp, pulled the lamp towards[6] him, and began to study the paper in earnest.

The thing was[7] nothing less than[8] a proposal to assassinate the Prime Minister—Mr. Pitt,[9] the man who was sitting on the other side of the table. The writer of the paper seemed[10] to be offering to do the deed himself, and the manner in which he hoped to accomplish it was set forth in full. He was to[11] call at the Prime Minister's house late in the evening, give some name at the door which would procure him admission,[12] and so reach the great man's presence. That was all that was necessary; once there, he would act.[13] As Mr. Pitt rose to greet him he would take out a pistol from his pocket and shoot him through the head. His own life did not matter; but to be sure,[14] he would do his best to get out of the house and escape. A horse would be waiting outside, and lest[15] any of the servants or bystanders should recognize him later, he would be wearing a beard which could afterwards be shaved off.

M. PEACOCK: *The House on the Cliff* (adapted)

[1] *das Blatt.*　　　[2] to cover with writing—*beschreiben.* See Topic 15, p. 99. [3] *undeutlich.*　　[4] Gram. 154.　　[5] *überfliegen* (insep.).　　[6] *heranziehen* (*zu*). [7] *es handelte sich um.*　　[8] *nichts weniger als.*　　[9] Care with the apposition if *Herr* is used.　　[10] Rephrase: 'It seemed as if . . .'　　[11] Modal verb.　　[12] (*ihm*) *Eintritt verschaffen.* Cf. 'A Report on a Crime', p. 43.　　[13] *handeln.*　　[14] *freilich.* Gram. 132.　　[15] 'in order that none of the . . . should recognize him . . .' Use the modal verb.

A Soldier in Flight

After a while I got up and started[1] along the bank. I knew there was no bridge across the river until Latisana. I thought I might be opposite San Vito. I began to think out what I should do. Ahead there was a ditch running into[2] the river. I went toward it.[3] So far I had seen no one and I sat down by some bushes along the bank of the ditch and took off my shoes and emptied them of water. I took off my coat, took my wallet with my papers and my money all wet in it[4] out of the inside pocket[5] and then wrung the coat out. I took off my trousers and wrung them too, then my shirt and underclothing. I slapped and rubbed myself and then dressed again.[6] I had lost my cap.

I started up the bank of the canal. It was daylight and the country was wet, low and dismal-looking.[7] The fields were bare and wet; a long way ahead I could see a campanile[8] rising out of the plain. I came up on to a road. Ahead I saw some troops coming down the road. I limped along the side of the road and they passed me and paid no attention to me.

That day I crossed the Venetian plain. It is a low level country[9] and under the rain it is even flatter. Toward the sea[10] there are salt-marshes and very few roads. The roads all go along the river mouths to the sea and to cross the country you must go along the paths beside the canals. I was working across[11] the country from the north to the south and had crossed two railway lines and many roads and finally I came out at the end of a path on to[12] a railway line where it ran beside a marsh. It was the main line from Venice to Trieste.[13]

ERNEST HEMINGWAY: *A Farewell to Arms* (abridged extract)

[1] *sich auf den Weg machen.* [2] *münden in.* [3] Gram. 140. [4] 'which was quite soaked through (*durchnäßt*)'. [5] *die Innentasche.* [6] See Topic 2, 1 (iv), p. 9. [7] 'sad'. [8] *der Kampanile.* [9] *die Gegend.* [10] Gram. 140. [11] *sich arbeiten durch.* [12] to come out on to (in this sense)—*stoßen auf.* [13] Venice; Trieste—Gram. 71.

Noises of the Night

At half past six that night Tom and Sid were sent to bed as usual. They said their prayers, and Sid was soon asleep. Tom lay awake and waited in restless impatience. When it seemed to him that it must[1] be nearly daylight,[2] he heard the clock strike ten! This was despair.[3] He would have tossed and fidgeted[4] as his nerves demanded,[5] but he was afraid he might wake Sid. So he lay still and stared up into the darkness. Everything was dismally still.[6] By and by, out of the stillness,[7] little, scarcely perceptible noises began to emphasize themselves. The ticking of the clock began to bring itself into notice. Old beams began to crack[8] mysteriously. The stairs creaked[9] faintly. Evidently spirits were abroad.[10] A measured, muffled snore issued from[11] Aunt Polly's chamber. And now the tiresome chirping of a cricket began. Next the ghastly ticking of a death-watch beetle in the wall at the bed's head made Tom shudder—it meant that somebody's days were numbered.[12] Then the howl of a far-off dog rose on[13] the night air, and was answered by a fainter howl from a remoter distance. Tom was in an agony.[14] At last he was convinced that time had ceased and eternity begun; he began to doze; the clock chimed eleven, but he did not[15] hear it.

MARK TWAIN: *The Adventures of Tom Sawyer* (adapted)

[1] Gram. 48 (i). [2] 'day'. [3] *Es war zum Verzweifeln.* [4] to toss and fidget—*sich unruhig herumwälzen.* [5] Supply the direct object *es.* [6] 'Everything lay in dismal stillness'. [7] *aus . . . heraus,* in order to render the idea of emergence. [8] Cf. 'Noises of the Night', p. 134. [9] *knarren.* [10] *umgehen* (sep. vb.). [11] *drang aus . . . her.* Cf. 7 above and Gram. 3. [12] German uses the same expression. Active or passive? See Topic 10, p. 67, 6. [13] Case? [14] *Tom stand Todesängste aus (ausstehen—*to endure). [15] Include *mehr* (i.e. 'no longer').

Tolstoy

Count Leo Tolstoy (1828–1910), the greatest name in Russian literature, was born on the family estate at Yasnaya Poliana[1] and educated at Kazan University. He fought in the Crimean War[2] and was present at the storming of Sebastopol.[3] He then retired from the army, and after travelling in Germany and Italy he married and settled down[4] on his estates, where he wrote the long succession of books which have made his name world-famous. But about 1880 he resolved to hand over[5] his property to his wife and family and to live like a peasant of the soil.[6] Besides novels, he wrote first-rate essays and works of a philosophic, religious, and social character,[7] which had world-wide circulation and influence,[8] as well as a series of plays, which rank among[9] the best of Russian dramatic work; so that, when his whole achievement is taken into account,[10] he stands quite unrivalled.[11]

His greatest novel perhaps is *War and Peace*, a very long work presenting the lives of two Russian families during a period of more than a dozen[12] years, and including the Napoleonic invasion. It is a marvellous production[13]—a landmark no one can afford to miss[14] who wishes to understand Russia or its literature. As Maurice Baring has said: 'For the first time in an historical novel, instead of saying: "This is very likely true" or "What a wonderful work of historical reconstruction!" we feel that we were ourselves there, that we knew those people; that they are a part of our very own past.'

JOHN DRINKWATER (editor): *The Outline of Literature*

[1] *Jasnaja Poljana.* [2] Compound noun. Cf. Gram. 73. [3] *Sewastopol.* [4] *sich niederlassen.* [5] *überlassen* (insep.). [6] 'as a simple peasant'. [7] *das Gepräge.* [8] 'which won and influenced (*beeinflussen*) a world-wide (*weltweit*) reading public (*Leserschaft*)'. [9] *zählen zu.* [10] *in Rechnung stellen.* [11] 'unsurpassed'. [12] Use *ein Jahrzehnt.* [13] *das Werk.* [14] *ein Markstein, an dem vorüberzugehen sich niemand leisten darf, der* . . . The position of the infinitive (*vorüberzugehen*) in relation to the relative pronoun should be specially noted.

The Sleep-walker

I suppose[1] I had slept for about four hours when I woke[2] suddenly thinking I heard a noise in the garden. And, immediately, cold terrible fear seized me—not fear of something that[3] was happening,[4] like the fear I had experienced in the wood, but fear of something that might happen.

Our room was on the first floor, looking out on to the garden—or terrace, it was rather[5] a wedge-shaped[6] piece of ground covered with roses and vines, and intersected with[7] little asphalt paths.[8] It was bounded on the small side[9] by the house; round the two long sides[10] ran a wall, only three feet[11] above the terrace, but with a good twenty feet drop over it into the yards beneath.[12]

Trembling all over,[13] I stole[14] to the window. There, pattering up and down the asphalt paths, was something white. I was too much alarmed to[15] see clearly; and in the uncertain light of the stars the thing took on[16] all manner of curious shapes. Now[17] it was a great dog, now an enormous white bat, now[17] a mass of quickly travelling cloud. It would bounce like a ball, or take[18] short flights like a bird, or glide slowly like a wraith. At last the obvious explanation occurred to me. I realized that Eustace had got out of bed, and that we were in for something more.[19]

E. M. FORSTER: *The Story of a Panic* (adapted)

[1] Gram. 130.   [2] Gram. 12.   [3] Gram. 106 (*a*).   [4] 'that was happening in reality'.   [5] Gram. 131.   [6] *keilförmig*.   [7] *durchkreuzt von*.   [8] Compound noun.   [9] *die Schmalseite*.   [10] *die Längsseiten*.   [11] Gram. 151 (*b*).   [12] 'but a good twenty feet above the surrounding yards'. See also Gram. 84.   [13] *am ganzen Körper zitternd*.   [14] Use *sich stehlen*.   [15] Gram. 22.   [16] *annehmen*.   [17] Gram. 134, note 1.   [18] *machen*.   [19] Cf. What are we in for now?—*Was steht uns jetzt bevor?*

Sherlock Holmes

One summer night, a few months after my marriage,[1] I was seated by my own hearth smoking a last pipe and nodding[2] over a novel, for my day's work had been an exhausting one.[3] My wife had already gone upstairs, and the sound of the locking of the hall door some time before told me[4] that the servants had also retired. I had risen from my seat and was knocking out the ashes of my pipe, when I suddenly heard the clang of the bell.

I looked at[5] the clock. It was a quarter to twelve. This could[6] not be a visitor at so late an hour. A patient, evidently, and possibly an all-night sitting.[7] With a wry face I went out into the hall and opened the door. To my astonishment, it was Sherlock Holmes who stood upon my step.

'Ah, Watson,' said he, 'I hoped that I might not be too late to catch you.'[8]

'My dear fellow,[9] pray come in.'

'You look surprised, and no wonder! Relieved, too, I fancy! Hum! you still smoke the Arcadia mixture of your bachelor days,[10] then! There's no mistaking that fluffy ash upon your coat. It's easy to tell[11] that you've been accustomed to wear a uniform,[12] Watson; you'll never pass as a pure-bred[13] civilian as long as you keep that habit of carrying your handkerchief in your sleeve. Could you put me up tonight?'

'With pleasure.'

'You told me you had bachelor quarters for one,[14] and I see that you have no gentleman visitor[15] at present. Your hat-stand proclaims as much.'[16]

Sir Arthur Conan Doyle: 'The Crooked Man',
from *The Memoirs of Sherlock Holmes*

[1] Distinguish between: *die Heirat*—marriage; *die Ehe*—state of marriage, married life; and *die Trauung*—marriage ceremony.   [2] *einnicken.*   [3] 'for I had an exhausting day behind me'.   [4] 'through the locking . . . I knew . . .'   [5] *blicken nach* or *sehen nach.*   [6] Indicative; cf. Gram. 26.   [7] i.e. consultation— *Beratung.*   [8] „*Ich hoffte, Sie noch auf zu finden.*"   [9] Adjectival noun.   [10] *Junggesellenzeit.*   [11] *Man sieht es Ihnen leicht an.*   [12] Omit article.   [13] 'genuine'.   [14] *ein Junggesellenzimmer für eine Person.*   [15] *Herrenbesuch.*   [16] *bezeugt es.*

Getting to know each other

She sat on the little bench before the spinet and gently and softly started to play 'In a Country Garden'.[1]

George closed his eyes and listened. When the tinkling sounds[2] from the cheery little country garden had stopped, he said, 'Please play it again.'

'You like it?' she said. 'All right. I will play it again.'

When she had finished, he turned to her. 'Where did you learn to play?'[3]

'In Vienna,' she said.

'Are you from Vienna?'

'Yes, that is where I was born.'

'Do you remember my name?' he said.

'Yes, it is George Zapolski.'

He smiled. 'I don't remember yours.'

'Excuse me,' she said. 'My name is Mona—Mona Travor.'

'Why did you come to America?'

Her eyes widened a little. 'Everyone wants to come to America,' she said.

'How old are you, Mona?'

'Twenty-two.'

'You look about seventeen,' he said.

She smiled. 'Maybe that is because[4] I am small. I don't know why I am so small. My parents weren't small.'

'Are your parents still in Austria?'

'No, they are dead. I have only an old aunt left there. She gave me the money to come[5] to America.'

'Do you mind if I ask you these questions?' he said.

She laughed. 'No. Why should I mind?'

'Well, you see, I'm a lawyer—or at least I'm trying to be. So I guess asking questions[6] is just second nature.'[7]

'You are a lawyer?' she said. 'Then I shall be your witness. You may ask me any question you like.'

HARRY T. MADDEN: *Date with a Stranger* (adapted)

[1] '*Im ländlichen Garten*'.   [2] *die glockenhellen Klänge*.   [3] See Topic 18, 2, p. 119.   [4] *Das kommt vielleicht daher, daß . . .*   [5] Gram. 23.   [6] Compound noun or infinitive phrase.   [7] *. . . liegt eben im Wesen meines Berufes*.

The Crossing

When I went back to the cottage I found the curate had just come across from the south island, and had had a worse passage than any[1] he had yet experienced.

The tide was to[2] turn[3] at two o'clock, and after that it was thought the sea would be calmer, as the wind and the waves would be running from the same point.[4] We sat about in the kitchen all the morning, with men coming in every[5] few minutes to give their opinion whether the passage should be attempted, and at what points the sea was likely to be at its worst.

At last it was decided we should go, and I started for the pier in a wild shower of rain with the wind howling in the walls.[6] The schoolmaster and a priest who was to have gone with me[7] came out as I was passing through the village and advised me not to make the passage;[8] but my crew had gone on[9] towards the sea, and I thought it better to go after them. The eldest son of the family was coming with me, and I considered that the old man, who knew the waves[10] better than I did, would not send out his son if there was more than reasonable danger.[11]

I found my crew waiting for me under a high wall below the village, and we went on together. The island had never seemed so desolate. Looking out over the black limestone through the driving rain to[12] the gulf of struggling waves, an indescribable feeling of dejection came over[13] me.

J. M. SYNGE: *The Aran Islands*

[1] *alle*.   [2] What modal verb?   [3] Cf. the tide turns—*der Strom kentert*.
[4] 'coming from the same direction'.   [5] *alle*.   [6] 'in (*bei*) a wind which . .'
[7] 'who had intended (*wollen*) to accompany me'.   [8] 'advised me not to attempt the passage'. See also Gram. 13.   [9] 'gone ahead'—*war vorausgegangen*.
[10] 'the sea here'.   [11] 'if one were to run (*an*) unreasonable risk in doing so'.
[12] What preposition?   [13] *überkommen* (insep.).

A Girls' Camp

In the United States of America school holidays begin in June, and so does[1] the camping season[2] for thousands[3] of boys and girls. The camps are mostly situated on the shores of a lake, for this provides fine opportunities for[4] safe bathing and boating.

Treetop is a typical New England girls' camp. The site[5] is a hilly one, densely covered with pine trees, maples, and birch trees. The ground rises from the shores of a lake and there are exciting-looking[6] trails winding through the bilberry bushes and bracken. At the end of a sandy road there is a picturesque timber building and inside is a big recreation room[7] with an open fireplace at one end. Under this roof are the camp offices,[8] kitchens, and dining-room.

The camp is on a permanent site[9] with some solidly constructed buildings, like wash and shower houses, recreation rooms, and hospital. It is open for two and a half months, and most of the hundred and fifty girls, who range in age[10] from eight to sixteen, come for[11] two weeks. Nearly all the staff are students training[12] to be teachers[13] or to work with[14] youth organizations. Their jobs at summer camps during the long vacation give them[15] useful experience which counts in their favour[16] when later on they apply for posts.

C. H. FALCON: *How Girls Camp in the U.S.A.* (adapted)

---

[1] and so does—*ebenso wie.*   [2] *die Lagersaison.*   [3] Gram. 146.   [4] opportunities for—*Gelegenheiten zu*; *zu* implying aim, purpose.   [5] *der Lagerplatz.*
[6] 'adventurous'.   [7] *der Tagesraum.*   [8] *die Büros der Lagerverwaltung.*
[9] 'It is a permanent site (*Standlager*)'.   [10] 'whose age ranges (*sich bewegen*) between . . .'   [11] *für.*   [12] *sich ausbilden.*   [13] 'for the teaching profession' (*der Lehrberuf*).   [14] 'or for (the) work in . . .'   [15] 'Through their work . . . they gain (use *sammeln*) useful experience' (plur. in German).   [16] to count in s.o.'s favour—*jm. zugute kommen* (sep. vb.).

There is a door in our factory which is constantly being used. The men who work in the room into which the door leads want it to stay shut, so every month one of them gets a new piece of string, ties it to the door handle, passes it through the hook at the top of the door and down to a lump of iron. When the door is opened the weight of the iron slowly pulls it shut again. Once I asked whether it wouldn't be easier to fix a spring to the door. But they would not listen to me. They had always done it that way. It was no trouble, really, said the apprentice, taking his penknife out of his pocket.

V. WILLIAMS

The prisoners were then carried back to their dungeon. The Governor himself had not really the power of life and death over the people in his district, but he could if he chose send them to the capital and have them hanged there. I proposed therefore that the prisoners should be threatened with this fate. The answer of the Governor made me feel ashamed of my effeminate suggestion. He said that if I wished it he would willingly threaten them with death, but he added that if he threatened he would also execute the threat. Thinking at last that nothing was to be gained by keeping the prisoners any longer in confinement, I requested that they might be set free. To this he finally acceded.

A. W. KINGLAKE
London, A Level, Summer 1957

The Dormouse's Story

The Dormouse slowly opened his eyes. 'I wasn't asleep,' he said in a hoarse, feeble voice:[1] 'I heard every word you fellows were saying.'

'Tell us a story!' said the March Hare.

'Yes, please do!' pleaded[2] Alice.

'And be quick about it,' added the Hatter, 'or you'll be asleep again before it's done.'[3]

'Once upon a time there were three little sisters,'[4] the Dormouse began in a great hurry; 'and their names were Elsie,[5] Lacie,[5] and Tillie;[5] and they lived at the bottom of a well——'

'What did they live on?'[6] said Alice, who always took a great interest in questions of eating and drinking.[7]

'They lived on treacle,' said the Dormouse, after thinking a minute or two.

'They couldn't have done that, you know,' Alice gently remarked; 'they'd have been ill.'

'So they were,'[8] said the Dormouse; 'very ill.'

Alice tried to fancy to herself what such an extraordinary way of living would be like, but it puzzled her too much,[9] so she went on: 'But why did they live at the bottom of a well?'

'Take some more tea,' the March Hare said to Alice, very earnestly.

LEWIS CARROLL: Alice in Wonderland

[1] Omit article. [2] eindringlich bitten. [3] aus; or zu Ende. [4] Cf. the traditional opening to the fairy story in German (note the word-order): Es war einmal ein König, der hatte drei schöne Töchterlein. [5] Do not translate. [6] leben von. [7] Omit 'questions of'. [8] 'Das waren sie auch'. [9] sehr or viel? Gram. 127.

An Unwelcome Visitor

It was a few nights later. It was overcast and pitch dark, and Torstein had placed the paraffin lamp just by[1] his head, so that[2] the night watches should see where[3] they were treading when they crept in and out. About four o'clock Torstein was woken[4] by the lamp tumbling over[5] and something cold and wet which was flapping about his ears. 'A flying fish,' he thought, and felt for[6] it in the darkness to throw it away. He caught hold of something long and wet that wriggled like a snake, and let it go as if he had burned himself. The unseen visitor twisted itself away[7] and over to Herman, while Torstein tried to get the lamp alight.[8] Herman started up too, and this made me wake thinking of the octopus which came up at night in these waters.[9] When we got the lamp alight, Herman was sitting[10] in triumph, with his hands gripping the neck[11] of a long, thin fish which wriggled in his fists like an eel. It was over three feet long, as slender as a snake, with dull[12] black eyes and a long snout with a greedy jaw full of sharp teeth. The teeth were as sharp as knives and could be folded back[13] into the roof of the mouth to make way for what it swallowed.

Bengt too was woken at last by all the noise, and we held the lamp and the long fish under[14] his nose. He sat up drowsily in his sleeping-bag and said solemnly:

'No, fish like that don't exist.'[15]

With which[16] he turned over quietly and went to sleep again.

THOR HEYERDAHL: The Kon-Tiki Expedition (adapted)

[1] *in nächste Nähe.*   [2] Result or Purpose? (*so daß* or *damit?*)   [3] *wohin.*
[4] Gram. 12.   [5] Use the verb *umschlagen* (to tumble over) as a gerund (verbal noun).   [6] *tasten nach.* Cf. Topic 16 (iv), p. 106.   [7] *sich loswinden.*   [8] Cf. 'A Lonely Christmas', p. 23.   [9] Gram. 70. Plural noun.   [10] *dasitzen.*   [11] 'whilst with his hands he was gripping (*umklammern*, insep.) the neck . . .'   [12] Use *glanzlos-* or *stumpf-.*   [13] Use *lassen.* See Topic 10, 3 (iii), pp. 65–66.   [14] With accus.   [15] Gram. 18.   [16] *worauf.*

Across the Yorkshire Moors[1]

At last the horses began to go more slowly, as if they were climbing uphill, and presently there seemed to be no more hedges and no more trees. She could see nothing, in fact, but a dense darkness on either side. She leaned forward and pressed her face against the window just as the carriage gave a big jolt.[2]

'We're on the moor now sure enough,'[3] said Mrs. Medlock.

The carriage lamps shed a yellow light on a rough-looking road which seemed to be cut through[4] bushes and undergrowth which ended in the great expanse of dark[5] apparently spread out before and around them. A wind was rising and making a singular, wild, low, rushing sound.[6]

'It's—it's not the sea, is it?'[7] said Mary, looking round at her companion.

'No,' answered Mrs. Medlock. 'Nor is it fields or mountains, it's just miles and miles and miles[8] of wild land[9] that nothing grows on but heather and gorse and broom, and nothing lives on but wild ponies and sheep.'

On and on they drove through the darkness, and though the rain stopped, the wind rushed by and whistled and made strange sounds. The road went up and down, and several times the carriage passed over a little bridge beneath which water rushed very fast with a great deal of noise. Mary felt[10] as if the drive would never come to an end, and that the wide, bleak moor was a wide expanse of black ocean[11] through which she was passing on a strip of dry land.

'I don't like it,' she said to herself. 'I don't like it.'

FRANCES HODGSON BURNETT: *The Secret Garden* (adapted)

[1] *das Heideland von Yorkshire.*   [2] *einen Ruck tun.*   [3] *richtig.*   [4] *geschlagen durch.*   [5] Use *weit ausgedehnt* to render 'great expanse'.   [6] Cf. 'The End of the Holidays', p. 125.   [7] Include the emotive particle *doch.*   [8] Use *meilenweit* like an adverb.   [9] wild land—*Ödland.*   [10] *Marie* (dat.) *war es, als ob . . .*   [11] 'an infinitely wide, dark (*finsterer*) ocean'.

Gulliver and the Cat

During dinner, my mistress's favourite cat leapt into her lap. I heard a noise behind me like that of [1] a dozen stocking-weavers at work; and turning my head, I found it came from[2] the purring of this animal, who seemed to be three times as big as an ox, as I estimated from[3] the size of her head and one of her paws, while her mistress was feeding and stroking her. The fierceness of this creature's face thoroughly upset my composure,[4] even though I was standing at the farther end of the table, over fifty feet away, and my mistress was holding her fast for fear she might[5] make a spring and seize me in her claws. In fact, however, there was no danger; for the cat took not the least notice of me[6] when my master placed me within three yards of her. And as I have always been told, and found true by experience in my travels, that running away or showing fear when faced with[7] a fierce animal inevitably causes it to pursue or attack you, I resolved to show no concern whatsoever.[8] I walked boldly five or six times in front of the very head of the cat, and approached to within[9] half a yard of her: whereupon she drew back, as if she were afraid of me.

JONATHAN SWIFT: *Gulliver's Travels* (adapted)

[1] Use *von*. Gram. 143 (*d*).   [2] Use *herrühren von*. Gram. 3.   [3] *an* with dat.
[4] to upset s.o.'s composure—*jn. aus der Fassung bringen*.   [5] *aus Furcht, sie könnte* . . .   [6] to take notice of s.o.—*jm. Aufmerksamkeit schenken*.   [7] when faced with—*gegenüber*. See Topic 3, pp. 17, 18.   [8] 'not the slightest fear'.
[9] *bis auf*.

If you will not admit that the earth is an island, since it is sur-rounded not by water but by air, you must at least agree that all the dry land on earth consists of islands. Most of these, however, are islands to dream about rather than to inhabit. I myself prefer life on a mainland, where newspapers arrive every morning and where there are shops selling the twenty or thirty things to which civilization has accustomed me. I should not like to have to row a mile across a storm-swept sea every time I had forgotten to provide myself with a box of matches. If I had been wrecked on a lonely island I should, like Crusoe, have taken the first available boat home.   R. LYND

'Why won't you talk about your book, Will? Can I help you?'

'No, Dick,' the judge answered, 'to tell you the truth, I haven't really begun.'

'But why not? The material's complete?'

'I suppose so. Yes—so far as material for a book of that kind can ever be said to be complete.'

The judge was silent. His brother encouraged and goaded him, saying that he had now been retired two whole years; that the great book, which he alone was equipped to write, lay open, waiting to be written; that if he did not begin now, he might never see the end.

'I know,' Dick said, 'that if the book were mine, I could die happy, having written it.'

CHARLES MORGAN

London, A Level, Autumn 1957

A Boy on a Farm

When he awoke at dawn the barnyard back of the house also awoke. In the house people stirred about.[1] Eliza Stoughton the half-witted girl was poked in the ribs[2] by a farm-hand[3] and giggled noisily, in some distant field a cow bawled[4] and was answered by the cattle in the stables, and one of the farm-hands spoke sharply to[5] the horse he was grooming by the stable door. David leaped out of bed and ran to a window. All of the people stirring about excited his mind,[6] and he wondered what his mother was doing in the house in town.

From the windows of his own room he could not see directly into the barnyard where the farm-hands had now assembled to do[7] the morning chores,[8] but he could hear the voices of the men and the neighing of the horses. When one of the men laughed, he laughed also. Leaning out at the open window, he looked into an orchard where a fat sow wandered about with a litter[9] of tiny pigs at her heels.[10] Every morning he counted the pigs. 'Four, five, six, seven,' he said slowly, wetting his finger and making straight up and down marks on the window ledge. David ran to put on his trousers and shirt. A feverish desire to get out of doors took possession of him. Every morning he made such a noise coming downstairs that Aunt Sallie, the housekeeper, declared he was trying to tear the house down.[11]

SHERWOOD ANDERSON: *Winesburg, Ohio*

[1] to stir, stir about—*sich regen.*   [2] to poke s.o. in the ribs—*jm. in die Rippen stoßen.*   [3] farm-hand—*der Knecht.*   [4] *brüllen.*   [5] *sprechen zu.*   [6] 'excited him'.   [7] *(Arbeiten) verrichten.*   [8] *die üblichen Morgenarbeiten.*   [9] *der Wurf.*   [10] 'behind her(self)'.   [11] to tear down (in this sense)—*einreißen.*

The Man in the Library

I cannot remember my first visit to the British Museum Reading Room. I remember feeling somewhat lost there, and oppressed by[1] the heavy warm air, all scented with[2] floor polish and old books. The attendant[3] at the Cloak Room had won the Victoria Cross at[4] the defence of Rorke's Drift, but I was warned not to ask[5] him about it, because (so I was told) 'he couldn't see why people made such a fuss about it'.[6] After passing him, I went into the Rotunda,[7] chose a seat and then slowly began to find my way about,[8] and to learn[9] to use what[10] was there.[11]

Often in those mornings I used to notice a most unusual man, whom I knew at once to be an exceptional being. Often I sat near him, and felt the extraordinary attraction[12] of his strangeness. Often I saw him walking slowly and sedately to the door, or to some Reference bookshelf.[13]   I saw that he was a visionary, always seeming to be looking at something very clear to him just above the level of his eyes, and to be smiling at what he saw, while nothing else much mattered. I was very young; it was not for me[14] to begin a conversation, but sometimes I wished that the strange man would speak to me. Once, as it fell, he did speak to me. I was leaving the Room,[15] and found that he was following. I held open the door so that he might pass; his face lit up with a smile to me,[16] as he thanked me and passed on. Later, I knew that this strange being was Lenin.

JOHN MASEFIELD: *So Long to Learn*

---

[1] *bedrückt durch.*   [2] Omit 'all'. Use *stark riechen nach.*   [3] *der Beamte.*
[4] *bei.*   [5] *ausfragen* or *fragen nach.*   [6] to make a fuss about (in this sense)—*viel Aufhebens machen von.*   [7] The name of the British Museum Reading Room. Do not translate.   [8] to find one's way about (in this sense)—*sich gründlich umsehen.*   [9] See Topic 15, verbs in *er-*, p. 99.   [10] 'to learn the use of what was there'.   [11] *vorhanden.*   [12] *die Anziehungskraft.*   [13] Reference bookshelf—*das Regal mit Nachschlagewerken.*   [14] *Mir kam es nicht zu,* . . .
[15] *das Lesezimmer.*   [16] Omit 'to me' in translation.

Marley's Ghost

After walking up and down the room several times, he sat down again. As he threw his head back in the chair, his glance happened to rest upon[1] a bell that hung in the room, and communicated[2] for some purpose now forgotten with a chamber in the highest story of the building. With great astonishment, and with a strange, inexplicable dread, he saw[3] this bell begin to swing.[4] It swung so softly in the outset that it scarcely made a sound; but soon it rang out[5] loudly, and with it every bell in the house.

This might have lasted[6] half a minute, or a minute, but it seemed an hour. The ringing was succeeded by a clanking noise,[7] deep down below; as if someone were dragging a heavy chain over the casks in the wine-merchant's cellar. Scrooge then remembered to have heard[8] that ghosts in haunted houses were supposed to drag chains.

The cellar door flew open[9] with a booming sound, and then he heard the rattling noise much louder, on the floors below; then coming up the stairs; then coming straight towards his door.

'It's humbug still!'[10] said Scrooge. 'I won't[11] believe[12] it.'

His colour changed though, when, without a pause, it came on[13] through the heavy door, and passed into the room before his eyes. Upon[14] its coming in, the dying flame leapt up, as though it cried 'I know him! Marley's ghost!' and fell again.[15]

CHARLES DICKENS: A Christmas Carol (adapted)

[1] happened to rest upon—*fiel zufällig auf.*   [2] to communicate with (in this sense)—*in Verbindung stehen mit.*   [3] . . . *sah er, daß* . . .   [4] *schwingen.* [5] See Topic 15, verbs in *er-*, p. 99.   [6] *mochte* + perfect infinitive. Cf. Gram. 27.   [7] Active voice: *Dem Läuten folgte* . . .   [8] Gram. 21.   [9] *auffliegen.* [10] *doch* (emotive particle): *Es ist doch Unsinn!*   [11] *wollen.*   [12] Gram. 13, note 5.   [13] *heran.*   [14] *bei.*   [15] Use *in sich zusammensinken.*

A Strange Incident[1]

About this time there occurred a strange incident which hardly anyone was able to understand. One night at about[2] twelve o'clock there was[3] a loud crash in the yard, and the animals rushed out of their stalls. It was a moonlit night.[4] At the foot of the end wall of the big barn, where the Seven Commandments were written,[5] there lay a ladder broken in two pieces.[6] Squealer,[7] temporarily stunned, was sprawling[8] beside it, and near by there lay a lantern, a paint-brush, and an overturned pot of white paint. The dogs immediately made[9] a ring round Squealer, and led him back to the farm-house as soon as he was able to walk. None of the animals could form any idea[10] as to what this meant, except old Benjamin, who nodded in a sly manner, and seemed to understand, but would say nothing.

But a few days later Muriel, reading over the Seven Commandments to herself, noticed that there was yet another of them which the animals had remembered wrong. They had thought that the Fifth Commandment was:[11] 'No animal shall drink[12] alcohol',[13] but there were two words that they had forgotten. Actually[14] the Commandment read:[15] 'No animal shall drink alcohol *to excess*.'[16]

GEORGE ORWELL: Animal Farm (adapted)

[1] On Animal Farm, which is run by the animals as a collective enterprise in accordance with Seven Commandments, the pigs and dogs are arranging things to suit themselves.   [2] See Topic 3, p. 19.   [3] Use *erschallen.*   [4] *eine mondhelle Nacht.*   [5] *geschrieben standen.*   [6] *mitten durchgebrochen.*   [7] to squeal— *quieken.*   [8] to sprawl (in this sense)—*lang hingestreckt liegen.*   [9] *bilden.* [10] to form an idea—*sich vorstellen.* Ignore 'any'.   [11] Gram. 48 (i).   [12] *genießen.* [13] The most satisfactory way of avoiding the word-order difficulty which arises in translation here is to assume that the Fifth Commandment was written on *two* lines, with 'shall' at the end of the first line.   [14] 'in reality'.   [15] *lauten.* [16] *im Übermaß.*

'I'm sorry to disturb you at this late hour, Campbell, but I wanted to ask you if I might use your telephone. I've had rather an unpleasant experience.'

'Come in, Captain. Would you like a cup of tea?'

The old lady rose from her chair, astonished. Her son had actually asked the visitor to have a cup of tea without waiting for her to invite him! She went into the kitchen, looking like Lady Macbeth walking in her sleep.

'I'd better ring Donald up before I tell you what has happened,' said Waggett. 'I want him to call for me in a car.'

'At half past two in the morning?'

'They're on duty all night, aren't they?'

COMPTON MACKENZIE

To avoid the various foolish opinions to which mankind is prone, no superhuman genius is required. A few simple rules will keep you, not from *all* error, but from silly error. Many matters may be settled by your own observation. Aristotle could have avoided the mistake of thinking that women have fewer teeth than men, by merely asking Mrs. Aristotle to keep her mouth open while he counted. He did not do so because he thought he knew. I believe myself that pigs eat coal, because I have been told that they do; but if I were writing a book on the habits of these curious animals, I should make no such statement until I had seen one enjoying such an unappetizing meal.

BERTRAND RUSSELL (adapted)

London, A Level, Summer 1958

Anticipation

It was[1] longer than the squire[2] imagined ere we were ready for the sea,[3] and none of our first plans—not even[4] Dr. Livesey's, of keeping me beside him[5]—could be carried out[6] as we intended. The doctor had to go to London for[7] a physician to take charge of his practice; the squire was hard at work[8] at Bristol; and I lived on at the Hall[9] under the charge of old Redruth, the gamekeeper, almost a prisoner, but full of sea-dreams and the most charming anticipations of[10] strange islands and adventures. I brooded by the hour together over the map, all the details of which I well remembered. Sitting by the fire in the housekeeper's room, I approached[11] that island in my fancy[12] from every possible direction; I explored every acre of its surface; I climbed a thousand times to that tall hill they call the Spyglass, and from the top enjoyed the most wonderful and varied prospects. Sometimes the isle was thick with[13] savages, with whom we fought; sometimes full of dangerous animals that hunted us; but in all my fancies nothing occurred[14] to me so strange and tragic as our actual adventures.

R. L. STEVENSON: *Treasure Island* (adapted)

[1] Avoid *sein*.   [2] *der Gutsherr*.   [3] *seeklar*.   [4] Gram. 128.   [5] Care. To whom does 'him' refer?   [6] See Topic 10, 3 (iii), pp. 65–66.   [7] Use *ausfindig machen*.   [8] *war vollauf beschäftigt*.   [9] *das Gutshaus*.   [10] *Vorahnungen von*.   [11] *anlaufen*.   [12] *die Phantasie*.   [13] to be thick with—*wimmeln von*.   [14] Meaning?

The Viper

My brother and I were playing one evening in a sandy lane in the neighbourhood of the military camp,[1] our mother was a short distance away. All of a sudden a bright yellow, and, to[2] my childish eye, beautiful and glorious object appeared at the top of the bank[3] from between[4] the thick bushes, and, gliding down, began to move across the lane to the other side, like a line of golden light. Uttering a cry of pleasure,[5] I sprang forward, and seized it nearly by the middle. A strange sensation of numbing coldness seemed to pervade my whole arm, which[6] surprised me all the more[7] as the object appeared so warm and sunlike.[8] I did not drop it, however, but, holding it up, looked at it intently, as its head dangled about a foot[9] from my hand. It made[10] no resistance; I felt not even the slightest movement; but now my brother began to scream and shriek like one possessed.[11] 'O mother, mother!' he said, 'the viper! my brother has a viper in his hand!' He made a frantic effort to snatch the creature away from me.[12] The viper now began to hiss viciously, and raised its head, in which were eyes like hot coals, menacing, not myself, but my brother. I dropped my captive,[13] for I saw my mother running towards me; and the reptile, after standing for a moment nearly erect, and still hissing furiously, made off,[14] and disappeared. The whole scene is now before me, as vividly as if it had occurred only yesterday—my terrified brother, my agitated mother, and a frightened hen clucking[15] under the bushes: and yet I was not three years old.

GEORGE BORROW: *Lavengro* (adapted)

[1] *das Militärlager*.   [2] *für*.   [3] *die Böschung*.   [4] See Topic 13 (iii), pp. 87–88.   [5] See Topic 17, pp. 111–14.   [6] Gram. 106 (*b*).   [7] Gram. 78.   [8] *leuchtend*.   [9] Adverbial accusative.   [10] 'offered'.   [11] Adjectival noun.   [12] See Topic 15, verbs in *ent*-, (ii), p. 99.   [13] *meine Beute*.   [14] Use *entschlüpfen*.   [15] *gackern*.

A Dangerous House

'If it hadn't been for the legacy of this house,'[1] he began, 'nothing would have happened. The other, my predecessor, would have stayed in his Rectory, and I . . . I should never have come on the scene at all. Although it must be confessed that he, my predecessor, was not happy in his Rectory. He met with unfriendliness, suspicion. That was why he first came to this house—just as a trial,[2] you see.[3] It was bequeathed to him empty: simply the house—no furniture, no money—and he came and put in[4] one or two things—this table, this bench, a few kitchen things,[5] a folding bed upstairs. He wanted, you see, to try[6] it, first. Its remoteness appealed to him, but he wanted to be sure about it in other ways.[7] Some houses, you see, are safe, and some are not, and he wanted to make sure that this was a safe house before moving into it.'[8] He paused and then said very earnestly: 'Let me advise you, my friend, always do that when you contemplate[9] moving into a strange house: because some houses are very unsafe.'

I nodded. 'Quite so!'[10] I said. 'Damp walls, bad drainage, and so on.'

He shook his head. 'No,' he said, 'not that. Something much more serious than that. I mean the spirit of the house. Don't you feel'—his gaze grew more piercing than ever[11]—'that this is a dangerous house?'

I shrugged my shoulders. 'Empty houses are always a little queer,' I said. MARTIN ARMSTRONG: *The Pipe Smoker*

[1] '*Wäre die Erbschaft . . . nicht gewesen*', . . .   [2] *probeweise.*   [3] '*. . ., sehen Sie.*'   [4] *hineinstellen.*   [5] *Küchengeräte.*   [6] *ausprobieren.*   [7] *in anderer Hinsicht.*   [8] 'before moving in (*einziehen*) here'.   [9] 'think of'.   [10] See Topic 9 (i), p. 60.   [11] *. . . denn je.*

An Attempt at Rescue

He was stunned, and he lay sprawling with his hands out[1] and his mouth full of sand. Then he pulled himself together;[2] he was not really hurt[3]—it had not been very far to fall—only his ankle hurt him rather. But he limped across to the place where Traill lay. He bent over him.[4] Traill was lying on his face, so Perrin pulled very gently his shoulder down[5] and rolled him over.[6] His face was cut and bleeding and very white, and one leg was crumpled[7] beneath him in a way that showed it was broken. Perrin opened his coat and waistcoat and undid his shirt; his heart was beating—very faintly[8]—but Traill was alive. Then he scooped[9] with his hands and brought some water and rubbed Traill's forehead; but he did not stir—he probably had concussion of the brain,[10] Perrin thought. Then Perrin sat down on the sand with his back to the rock, and made Traill as comfortable as he could[11] against him. He rested his poor, bleeding head on his chest, and took his hands and rubbed them, and then looked about him and wondered what was next to be done.[12] The little cove was very quiet and still, but the sea was touching[13] his feet—every moment it was rising higher—and only behind him was the black cliff, frowning,[14] uncompromising.[15]

HUGH WALPOLE: *Mr. Perrin and Mr. Traill*

[1] Adverbial accusative. Omit 'with' in translation.   [2] *sich zusammenraffen.*
[3] *verletzt.*   [4] Case?   [5] *zog ihm ... die Schulter herab.*   [6] *drehte ihn herum.*
[7] *lag verbogen.*   [8] 'weakly'.   [9] *schöpfen.*   [10] *eine Gehirnerschütterung.*
[11] *so* as a conjunction is NOT followed by *wie*. Gram. 135.   [12] See Topic 10, 2 (ii), p. 65.   [13] *spülte schon bis an ...*   [14] *finster.*   [15] uncompromising (i.e. implacable)—*unerbittlich.*

'Well, I must confess I'm disappointed. I had hoped you would live with us when Norman left us,' said Mrs. Macleod. 'But we want you to be happy. When do you intend to get married?'

'In the summer holidays, if George's mother doesn't make it too difficult.'

And as Catriona said that, poor George was being greeted by his mother with the information that she knew all.

'I'm sorry,' he stammered, 'I was going to tell you last night, but you seemed so anxious to go to bed.'

'The bed I have made for myself and on which I must lie,' Mrs. Campbell said in tones that the prophet himself might have envied. 'This comes of spoiling my only child.'

COMPTON MACKENZIE

My rule was that no label must be covered by another. I loved them not only for the meaning they had for me, but also, in some measure, because of the effect they had on other people. Travelling in the train, with my luggage beside me, I enjoyed the silent interest which my labels aroused in my fellow-passengers. If the compartment was so full that my case had to be put on to the rack, I would always, in the course of the journey, take it down and pretend to be looking for something I had put into it. It pleased me to see from beneath my eyelids the respectful wonder and envy evoked by it. No one suspected that the labels had been carefully collected.   MAX BEERBOHM

London, A Level, January 1959

A Changed Social Position

Kitty, coming to Hong Kong on her marriage, had found it hard[1] to reconcile herself to[2] the fact that her social position was determined by her husband's occupation. Of course everyone had been very kind to her and for two or three months they had gone out to parties almost every night; when they dined at Government House[3] the Governor[4] took her in as[5] a bride; but she had understood quickly that[6] as the wife of the Government bacteriologist[7] she was quite an insignificant personage. It made her angry.

'It's too absurd,' she told her husband. 'There's[8] hardly anyone here one would bother about at home.[9] Mother wouldn't dream[10] of asking any of them to dine at our house.'[11]

'Don't let that worry you,' he answered. 'It doesn't really matter, you know.'[12]

'Of course it doesn't matter, it only shows how stupid they are, but it is rather funny when you think of all the people who used to come to our house at home that here we should be treated like dirt.'

'From the social standpoint the man of science[13] does not exist,' he smiled.

W. SOMERSET MAUGHAM: *The Painted Veil* (adapted)

[1] Cf. I find it difficult—*es fällt mir schwer*.   [2] *sich mit etwas abfinden.*
[3] *im Hause des Gouverneurs.*   [4] 'the latter'.   [5] *als*.   [6] *sie* should follow *daß* immediately. Why?   [7] *der Regierungsbakteriologe.* See Topic 11, 2 (iii), p. 72.
[8] *Es ist* . . . Gram. 18.   [9] Add 'in England'.   [10] 'think of', reinforced by 'at all' or 'for a moment'.   [11] *zu uns zum Abendessen einladen.*   [12] *ja.* Care with the position of the word.   [13] *der Wissenschaftler.*

Boyhood

Like most youngsters, Charlie Chaplin led[1] a dual existence. Outside, there was[2] all the excitement of gang warfare,[3] in[4] which he incited his playmates like a young Napoleon against the enemy that lurked in the next backyard; the glory[5] of playing truant[6] from the school he hated, of swimming in the Kennington baths whenever[7] he could afford the entrance money, of attending[8] the magic lantern shows[9] at the Baxter Hall, where a penny would entitle him to[10] coffee and cake as well as[11] a fascinating exposition[12] of the Crucifixion or the Flight into[13] Egypt. There was the illicit fun of pilfering from street stalls; and the stimulus of escaping from the heavy-footed policeman whenever two of the local toughs[14] started fighting in the street, or a chance[15] ball broke a window.

Then there was the endless fascination of the streets and the shops, like bright caverns filled with unimaginable treasures. The hungry little boy pressed his nose against the pastry-cook's window, feeding[16] his empty stomach with the warm smell of bread and the sight of succulent cakes and pastries covered with icing and stuffed with fruit and cream. Old bookshops fascinated him even though he could not read. It was enough for him[17] to look at prints and engravings and illustrations for his imagination to be led into other worlds.

PETER COTES and THELMA NIKLAUS: *The Little Fellow* (adapted)

[1] *führen.*   [2] Use *man hatte . . .*   [3] *der Gangsterkrieg.*   [4] *bei.*   [5] *das herrliche Gefühl.*   [6] to play truant—*die Schule schwänzen.*   [7] *jedesmal, wenn . . .*   [8] *besuchen.*   [9] *die Laterna-magica-Vorstellungen.*   [10] to entitle s.o. to s.th.—*jm. das Recht auf eine Sache verschaffen.*   [11] both . . . and . . .—*sowohl . . . als auch . . .*   [12] *die Darstellung.*   [13] *nach.*   [14] *die ortsansässigen Rowdys.*   [15] Treat as an adverb.   [16] 'filling'.   [17] 'Prints and engravings . . . were enough (*genügen*) to lead his imagination . . .' (*um . . . zu führen*).

The Stage-coach Goes By

As the coach rolls swiftly past the fields and orchards which skirt the road, groups of women and children, piling the fruit in sieves, or gathering the scattered[1] ears of corn, pause for an instant from[2] their labour, and shading[3] the sun-burned face with a[4] still browner hand, gaze upon the passengers with curious eyes, while some stout urchin,[5] too small[6] to work, but too mischievous to be left at home, scrambles over the side of the basket in which he has been deposited for security,[7] and kicks[8] and screams with delight. The reaper stops in his work, and stands with folded arms, looking at the vehicle as it whirls past; and the rough[9] cart-horses bestow[10] a sleepy glance upon the smart coach team,[11] which says as plainly as a horse's glance can, 'It's all very fine to look at,[12] but slow going, over a heavy field, is better than warm work[13] like that, upon a dusty road, after all.'[14] You cast a look behind you, as you turn a corner of the road. The women and children have resumed their labour; the reaper once more stoops to his work; the cart-horses have moved on; and all are again in motion.

CHARLES DICKENS: *The Pickwick Papers*

[1] *verstreut.*   [2] *in.*   [3] *beschatten.*   [4] Omit article. Cf. Topic 4, 1 (ii) (*d*), p. 28.   [5] *Kerlchen* or *kleiner Bengel.*   [6] Include 'still'.   [7] *zur Sicherheit stecken.*   [8] *strampeln.*   [9] *plump.*   [10] *schenken.*   [11] *das Gespann.*   [12] Reflexive verb. See Topic 10, 3 (iii), pp. 65–66.   [13] *schweißtreibende Arbeit.*   [14] Gram. 122 (*b*); or use the emotive particle *doch.*

The Six Old Ladies

'It was already late in the afternoon, and the nights of winter were closing in fast.[1] On a dark, windy road, we set out[2] towards[3] the lonely house of Colonel Hawker,[4] perhaps the queerest cortège[5] that ever made its way up that or any other road. To[6] every human eye we were six very respectable old ladies in black dresses and antiquated bonnets; and we were really five criminals and a clergyman.

'I will cut a long story short.[7] My brain was whirling like a windmill as I walked, trying to think of some manner of escape.[8] To cry out, so long as we were far from houses, would be suicidal, for it would be easy for the ruffians to knife me or to gag me and fling me into a ditch. On the other hand, to attempt to stop strangers and explain the situation was impossible, because of the frantic folly[9] of the situation itself. Long before I had[10] persuaded the chance postman[11] or carrier[12] of so absurd a story, my companions would certainly have got off themselves, and in all probability would have carried me off, as a friend of theirs who had[13] the misfortune to be mad or drunk. The last thought, however, was an inspiration;[14] though a very terrible one. Had it come to this,[15] that the Vicar of Chuntsey must pretend to be mad or drunk? It had come to this.'

G. K. CHESTERTON: *The Club of Queer Trades* (adapted)

[1] 'were becoming longer and longer'.　　[2] *sich in Bewegung setzen.*　　[3] *in Richtung auf.*　　[4] Gram. 63.　　[5] *der Trauerzug.*　　[6] *für.*　　[7] *sich kurz fassen.*　　[8] Compound noun: 'possibility of flight'.　　[9] frantic folly—*die Verrücktheit.*　　[10] i.e. 'before I could have'.　　[11] *den zufällig vorbeikommenden Briefträger.*　　[12] *der Laufbursche.*　　[13] Gram. 47.　　[14] *eine Eingebung.*　　[15] *War es so weit gekommen, . . .?*

An ancient car crawled up the hill towards the lonely farm-house. The driver was a little, elderly man. Every Wednesday he called at all the farms in the neighbourhood with his car, which was really a shop on wheels; it was crammed with household goods— mainly soap, brushes, saucepans, and china—and with cardboard boxes containing stockings, shirts, handkerchiefs, and gaudy ties. Somehow he always succeeded in persuading people to buy. But, on the other hand, if you had more eggs than you needed, or an unusually heavy crop of apples, he was always ready—if he liked you—to give you a few shillings for them. He lived by himself in a tiny cottage on the outskirts of the market-town and did his own cooking and washing, though there was no doubt that he was quite well off. Lately he had bought himself a new suit, and

had taken to visiting the farm up on the hill twice or even thrice
a week. Its owner had died some years before; his widow kept
the place on, however, but she obviously found it hard to make
ends meet. 'What she needs,' people said, 'is a man who under-
stands business. By far the most sensible thing for her would be
to get married again.' Judging by the frequency of his visits, the
dealer was of the same opinion.

O. & C. S.E.B., A.S. Level, 1957

Travelling Down to Glebeshire

Katherine and Philip, although they saw no one but one another,[1]
were aware of the day[2]—it was as though it had been arranged
especially[3] for them. The rise and fall[4] of their voices had a sleepy
rhythm, as though they were keeping time with[5] the hum[6] of the
train:

'I'm so glad,' said Katherine, 'that your first view of Glebe-
shire will be on a day like this.'

'I'm a little afraid,' he answered. 'What will you say if I don't
like it?'

She seemed really for an instant to be afraid. 'But, of course,
of course, you will.'

'Everyone doesn't. Someone told me the other day that either
it was desolate enough to depress you for a lifetime[7] or stuffy
like a hot-house, and that the towns were the ugliest in the United
Kingdom.'[8]

Katherine sighed and then smiled.

'I expect they'd think Manchester the loveliest place on earth,'[9]
she said. Then, looking at him very intently, she asked him: 'Do
you regret Russia—the size and the space and the strangeness?
I daresay you do. Do you know, Phil, I'm rather jealous of [10]
Russia, of all the things you did before I knew you, I wonder
whether I'd have liked you[11] if I'd met you then, whether you'd
have liked me. I expect you were very different. Tell me about[12]
it. I'm always asking[13] you about Moscow, and you're so mysterious[14]—yes, I believe I'm jealous.'

HUGH WALPOLE: The Green Mirror

---

[1] 'only had eyes for one another'. Gram. 92.   [2] Cf. Gram. 90, note 1.
[3] *eigens hergerichtet.*   [4] *das Auf und Ab.*   [5] *Takt halten mit.*   [6] *das Rollen.*
[7] *ein Leben lang.*   [8] *das Vereinigte Königreich.*   [9] *auf Erden.* Gram. 69.
[10] Gram. 89.   [11] Use *sympathisch sein*, e.g. *Er ist mir sehr sympathisch*—I like him,
he appeals to me, very much.   [12] *erzählen von.*   [13] *ausfragen.*   [14] *du tust
so geheimnisvoll.*

Country-side and Sea

The warm sun of the stormy August day was out[1] again and it beat down[2] upon them. Here in the sheltered drive, with the oak-trees between them and the marshes,[3] they did not feel the wind from the sea. Through the wrought-iron[4] gate in the wall the man could see the golden and orange glow of autumn flowers, the tall and gracious trees of an old garden, and, beyond, the irregular roof of the house. He had chosen to walk from the station instead of taking a taxi. He had asked his way[5] in Radford and taken the coast road through the marshes carrying his bag, a thing the doctor had forbidden him to do, but the beauty of the walk[6] had made him forget the weight of it. To his right the marshes had been splashed with colour[7] like a painter's palette; to his left, just at the corner of the lane that led down from the high-road,[8] there had been a cornfield bending[9] beneath the wind.[10] On the horizon he had seen the silver line of the sea and the estuary, with the cliffs of the Island beyond, at one moment[11] half hidden in mists[12] of driving rain, remote and far away,[13] at the next leaping out[14] under the sun in such[15] clear distinctness that they looked like the longed-for[16] Celestial Mountains at the end of the unending way. Then he had reached the harbour, with wild sea-asters growing beside the harbour wall and fishing-boats and yachts rocking peacefully at anchor.[17]

ELIZABETH GOUDGE: *The Heart of the Family*
(abridged extract)

[1] Use *hervorkommen*. [2] *herabstechen*. [3] Singular. Gram. 61.
[4] Gram. 86 (*b*). [5] *nach dem Weg fragen*. [6] *der Weg*. [7] *mit Farben betupft*. [8] *die Landstraße*. ˙ [9] Gram. 9. [10] *im Winde*. [11] Gram. 134.
[12] *Schwaden*. Cf. 'A Weather Phenomenon', p. 155. [13] *in weit entrückter Ferne*.
[14] *hervorbrechend*. [15] Use *solch* uninflected. [16] *ersehnt-*. Cf. Topic 15,
p. 99. [17] *vor Anker schaukeln*.

A Surprise

A little before nine o'clock, I descended to the ground floor of the house. The solemn manservant whom I had seen the night before[1] met me wandering[2] among the passages and showed me the way to the breakfast room.

As the man opened the door, my eyes fell on a well-furnished[3] breakfast table, standing in the middle of a long room with many windows. I looked from the table to the window farthest from me and saw a lady standing at it, with her back turned towards me. The instant[4] my eyes rested on her, I was struck by the rare

beauty of her form, and by the unaffected[5] grace of her attitude.
Her figure was tall, yet not too tall; comely and well-developed,
yet not fat; her head set[6] on her shoulders easily and pliantly, yet
firmly. She had not heard me enter the room; and I allowed
myself the pleasure of admiring her for a few moments, before I
moved[7] one of the chairs near me, in order to attract her attention
in the least embarrassing way.[8] She turned towards me[9] immediately. The natural elegance of every movement of her limbs
and body as soon as[10] she began to advance from the far end
of the room, set me in a flutter of expectation[11] to see her face
clearly. She approached nearer—and I said to myself (with
a sense of surprise which words fail me to express[12]): The lady
is ugly!

WILKIE COLLINS: The Woman in White (adapted)

[1] 'on the previous evening'.   [2] irren.   [3] reichgedeckt.   [4] Recast with
'instantly'.   [5] ungekünstelt.   [6] saß.   [7] rücken. ˋ   [8] in der unauffälligsten
Art—lit. in the least obtrusive way.   [9] Sie wandte sich mir zu (or zu mir hin).
[10] Gram. 135.   [11] Cf. 'A Man and His Dog', p. 130. Translate: 'set me in a
state of excited (erregt-) expectation'.   [12] 'for which I cannot find words'.

A Call to a Sick-bed[1]

At this time he[2] was a civil servant with a small circle of con-
ventional and unimaginative friends, and was living with a
married cousin and her husband in a flat near Baker Street. At
present they were away, and on this particular evening he had
been dining out[3] in Chelsea. When he returned, rather late, to
the silent flat he found a telegram waiting[4] for him. It was
characteristic of him[5] to open it not[6] with his finger but with a
paper-knife. The telegram was to say that[7] Violet had been taken
ill;[8] would he[9] come at once. He rushed out of the house, not only
without an umbrella but without a hat—such was his agitation—
then got into a taxi and directed the driver to a rectory in Cam-
berwell. Violet was the rector's daughter and she and Henry
were virtually[10] engaged, but he did not expect to be able to marry
her until his sick old rich uncle was dead. . . .

Violet was indeed ill, but not dangerously,[11] and Henry was
allowed to sit and hold her hand for an hour or so. Then she fell
asleep, so he tiptoed out of the room and after a short conversation with her mother he left the house. Although it was very late,
it had occurred to neither of them that he might have spent the
rest of the night there, and it did not occur to him until[12] he was
out of the house that the chance of finding a taxi thereabouts[13]

at such a time was very slight, that the tubes had stopped running,[14] and that if there were still any buses they would be going in strange[15] directions to remote termini.[16]

WILLIAM PLOMER: *The Night before the War* (abridged extract)

[1] *Ruf an ein Krankenbett.*   [2] The story concerns the experiences of a fastidious young man named Henry.   [3] *auswärts essen.*   [4] to find . . . waiting—*vorfinden.*   [5] Gram. 89.   [6] Gram. 124.   [7] 'informed him that'.   [8] *erkranken.*   [9] . . .; *ob er* . . .   [10] *so gut wie.*   [11] *schwerkrank* or *ernstlich (krank).*   [12] Cf. Gram. 123 (a).   [13] *hier in der Nähe.*   [14] the tubes have stopped running—*die U-Bahn hat ihren Betrieb schon eingestellt.*   [15] in strange directions—*in ausgefallene Richtungen.*   [16] terminus—*die Endstation.*

At that time George was living with his parents and waiting for a cottage to fall vacant for him and his young wife. However bad the weather, he travelled to and from his work by motor cycle. On that particular evening he had had to work late. The rough, narrow road was ice-coated; there was a thick mist; and he was probably going much faster than he ought to have done. He was within half a mile of home when he caught a glimpse of something huge in the beam of his headlamp, right in front of him. Too late, he realized that it was a cow that had somehow strayed on to the road. Next moment he had hit it. When he recovered consciousness, he was lying on his back. The cow had vanished. He felt as though every bone in his body was broken, but he managed to get on his feet and, after carefully testing his arms, chest, and legs, he decided there was nothing much wrong with him. The motor cycle lay on its side a few yards away; it seemed to be more or less undamaged, and the lamp was still burning. All the same, he thought it wiser to take no further risks; he dragged the machine to the edge of the road, picked up his scattered parcels, and started off to walk the remainder of the way.

O. & C. S.E.B., A.S. Level, 1959

ESSAY SUBJECTS

DESCRIPTIVE

1. Beschreiben Sie eine ausländische Stadt oder Landschaft, die Sie kennen.
2. Sie fahren auf einem großen Ozeandampfer nach New York. Berichten Sie über Ihre Erlebnisse.
3. Beschreiben Sie, was sich bei einem Erdbeben in einer Stadt ereignen kann.
4. Abend im Park.
5. Ein Kanalschwimmer erzählt von seinem Versuch, einen neuen Rekord aufzustellen.
6. Sommer in der Großstadt.
7. Erzählen Sie von einer peinlichen Szene, der Sie beiwohnen mußten.
8. Sie nehmen an einer Außenministerkonferenz teil. Berichten Sie darüber.
9. Geben Sie Ihre Eindrücke von einem Hafen wieder, den Sie besichtigt haben.
10. Bei einem Unfall verliert ein Freund von Ihnen das Gedächtnis. Schreiben Sie einen Bericht über seine späteren Abenteuer.

POLITICAL

1. Welche Rolle wird Deutschland voraussichtlich in der europäischen Politik der nächsten zehn Jahre spielen?
2. Was sind Ihrer Ansicht nach die „demokratischen Grundrechte"?
3. China und der Westen.
4. Wäre eine politische Föderation aller europäischen Staaten wünschenswert oder möglich?
5. Leben die Briten zu sehr „auf der Insel", um je „gute Europäer" zu werden?
6. „Politik ist die Kunst des Möglichen."
7. „Wir wollen Vermenschlichung des Staates, nicht Verstaatlichung des Menschen." Pestalozzi.
8. Was verstehen Sie unter „Faschismus"?
9. Beschreiben Sie, wie die allgemeinen Wahlen in England durchgeführt werden.
10. Welches ist Ihrer Meinung nach das glücklichste Land Europas? Wie begründen Sie diese Wahl?

ART

1. „Die Literatur von heute muß engagiert sein!" Nehmen Sie
   Stellung zu dieser Aussage.
2. Das Werk eines deutschen Malers.
3. Der schönste Film dieses Jahres.
4. Für oder gegen Hörspiele (oder Fernsehstücke).
5. Meinen Sie, daß internationale Ausstellungen (oder Sport-
   treffen) den Frieden fördern?
6. Die Kunst Ihres Lieblings-Filmkomikers.
7. Beschreiben Sie die Leistungen eines großen Architekten.
8. Was erwarten Sie von einem guten Kriminalroman?
9. Sie sollen drei berühmte Gemälde geschenkt bekommen.
   Welche werden Sie sich wählen — und warum gerade
   diese?
10. Das Werk eines großen Komponisten unserer Zeit.

MISCELLANEOUS

1. Ziele des Jugendklubs.
2. Schreiben Sie einen Brief an einen österreichischen Hotel-
   besitzer, in welchem Sie ihn bitten, für eine englische
   Jugendgruppe eine Unterkunft zu reservieren, und erkundigen Sie sich nach Ausflugs- und Unterhaltungsmöglich-
   keiten in der näheren Umgebung.
3. „Jeder Student sollte, bevor er auf die Universität geht,
   sich mindestens ein Jahr in der wirklichen Welt umtun."
4. Was erwarten Sie von einer guten Schule?
5. Die Weltraumfahrt: heute und morgen.
6. „Wohlstand für alle." — Ist das ein leerer Traum?
7. Schreiben Sie einen Brief an einen Freund, worin Sie ihm
   Ratschläge geben, wie er, ohne ins Ausland zu fahren, sein
   Deutsch verbessern kann.
8. Gefahr auf den Straßen.
9. Beschreiben Sie die Arbeit der „Samariter" oder einer
   ähnlichen Hilfsorganisation.
10. Gegen die Frauen (die Männer).

GRAMMAR SECTION

(*Note.* A number in square brackets after an example refers to the *page* on which the example occurs. References to Topics are given by the number of the Topic and the page; where a Topic is divided into sections, the appropriate section is referred to. Other numbers refer to *articles* of the Grammar Section.)

VERBS

TYPES OF VERB

Separable verbs

1. The range of meanings covered by the prepositional prefix of a separable verb may be very wide. It is especially important to note the different meanings which the various prepositional prefixes may have, e.g.

> *aussteigen*—alight; *ausrechnen*—work out, calculate; *sich ausruhen*—rest; *ausrüsten*—equip.
> *einzeichnen*—mark in; *einnicken*—nod off to sleep; *sich einfinden*—put in an appearance.
> *aufnehmen*—take in, accommodate; *aufschließen*—unlock; *aufkommen* (*für*)—be responsible for, find (e.g. money).

2. It is clear from the above examples that the familiar prepositional prefixes sometimes convey a figurative meaning, e.g. *sich ausruhen*, *aufkommen* (*für*). Verbs of this sort are most likely to cause difficulty and need to be carefully learned as they are met.

3. Verbs with the prefixes *hin-* and *her-* also show a wide range of meaning. Usually the sense conveyed by *hin* is 'away', but it can also denote 'down', e.g. *sich hinlegen, sich hinsetzen.* The prefix *her* always denotes 'towards', but it frequently occurs in the figurative sense of 'originating from', 'hailing from', e.g. *herleiten*—derive; *herrühren* (*von*)—arise, result (from).

Accuracy in the use of separable verbs is a question of constant observation and practice.

Inseparable verbs with prepositional prefix

4. **Only** the prepositions *durch-, über-, um-, unter-* (very rarely, *hinter-* and *wider-*) are found as both separable and inseparable prefixes. *All other prepositions used as prefixes form part of separable verbs.*

The vast majority of inseparable verbs with prepositional prefix are *transitive*.

5. Just as the *stress* of the inseparable verb falls on the verb, not on the prefix, the emphasis in *meaning* is also given by the verb rather than by the prefix: *unter***höhlen**—under**mine**; *über***setzen**—trans**late** (i.e. **carry** across); *durch***waten**—**wade** through. (But: **unter***gehen*—go **under**, be ruined; **über***laufen*—desert, go **over** to the enemy; **durch***kommen*—come **through** safely.)

6. Where a verb has both separable and inseparable usages, there is usually a difference in meaning, e.g.

Sie zieht den Faden durch. She pulls the thread through.
Sie durchzogen das Land. They travelled right through the country.
Der Fährmann setzte mich über. The ferryman took me across.
Ich übersetzte das Gedicht. I translated the poem.

Some verbs are either separable (in some of their parts) or inseparable with no difference of meaning, e.g. *überführen*—convict; *übersiedeln*—move (one's home); *widerhallen*—re-echo. It is safest to treat these and other verbs in the same category as inseparable.

Reflexive verbs not reflexive in English

7. Many reflexive verbs are common to both German and English, e.g. *sich vorstellen*—to introduce oneself; *sich benehmen*—to behave oneself; *sich verletzen*—to injure oneself; *sich anstrengen*—to exert oneself.

8. However, the English equivalents of many German reflexive verbs need not be expressed in a reflexive way:

Er kleidete sich schnell an. He dressed (himself) quickly.
Sie sorgt sich zu sehr um ihn. She worries (herself) about him too much.
Ich muß mich waschen. I must wash (myself).

9. In most instances it is true to say that English verbs which are felt, in their context, to have a reflexive sense (e.g. He dressed quickly, &c., above) are expressed as reflexive verbs in German. But it is frequently the case that English verbs which are *not* felt, in their context, to have a reflexive sense must be translated by a reflexive verb in German if they are verbs which *could be used transitively* in other contexts. Thus:

He moved slowly	must become		*Er bewegte* **sich** *langsam.*
It has developed	„	„	*Es hat* **sich** *entwickelt.*
They dispersed	„	„	*Sie zerstreuten* **sich**.

10. Many German reflexive verbs, however, have no hint of reflexive or even transitive sense in English. These should be particularly noted as they are met. The following examples are taken from Part I:

> *Er . . . unterhielt sich mit einem Bettler.* [74] (to converse)
> *Ich sehne mich plötzlich danach, sie (die Bücher) zu ordnen.* [125] (to long)
> *Die junge Frau hätte sich über nichts beklagen können.* [95] (to complain)

11. Some reflexive verbs in German are 'genuine' reflexives, i.e. the verb itself (e.g. *schämen*) can only stand in conjunction with a reflexive pronoun (*ich schäme mich*—I am ashamed); others are not genuine reflexives, as the verb may be applied to an object other than the subject idea, e.g. *sich fürchten* (*ich fürchte mich*; but also: *Ich fürchte das Dunkel*). Genuine reflexive verbs are intransitive, and the verb must be expressed in quite a different way if it is to be given transitive force, e.g.

> *Ich habe mich geirrt.* I made a mistake; *but*:
> *Ich habe dich irregeführt.* I misled you.
> *Ich weigerte mich hinzugehen.* I refused to go there; *but*:
> *Ich verweigerte ihm die Antwort.* I refused him an answer.
> *Sie sorgt sich zu sehr.* She worries too much; *but*:
> *Sie will dich nicht in Sorge bringen.* She does not want to worry you.

12. Intransitive and transitive verbs often confused

Certain intransitive verbs with the root vowels *-a-*, *-i-* and *-ie-* have a corresponding transitive form with the vowel *-e-* or *-ä-*. The following list contains some verbs which are frequently confused:

dringen	force[1]	*drängen*	squeeze, press
erblinden	go blind	*blenden*	blind, dazzle
ertrinken	drown	*ertränken*	drown (s.o.)
erwachen	wake, awake	*wecken*	wake (s.o.)
fallen	fall	*fällen*	fell (trees)
hängen[2]	hang	*hängen*	hang (up)
liegen	lie	*legen*	lay
sinken	sink, drop	*senken*[3]	lower
sitzen	sit, be sitting	*setzen*	place
springen	jump, leap	*sprengen*	blow up

N.B. also:

fortfahren	continue[4]	*fortsetzen*	continue
steigen	rise	*steigern*	raise, accentuate

[1] Normally found as a separable or inseparable verb and/or followed by a preposition, e.g. *eindringen in, durchdringen, dringen durch*, &c.   [2] *hängen* has replaced the former *hangen* as the intransitive verb. Its principal parts are: *hängen—hängt—hing—hat gehangen*.   [3] to sink a ship—*ein Schiff versenken*.   [4] 'Now,' he continued, . . .—*„Nun", fuhr er fort*, . . . She continued her reading—*Sie setzte ihre Lektüre fort* (or: *Sie fuhr* **mit** *ihrer Lektüre fort*.)

THE USE OF THE VERB

13. Verbs governing a dative object whose English equivalents govern an accusative object

The following are common verbs governing a dative object (usually a person) where an accusative object might be expected. Impersonal verbs are marked *, e.g. **es** *gelingt mir*—I succeed.

ähneln	resemble	**glücken*	succeed
antworten	answer[1]	*gratulieren*	congratulate
begegnen	meet[2]	*helfen*	help
beistehen	support, stand by	*huldigen*	pay homage to
		lauschen	listen intently to
beistimmen	agree with (s.o.)		
		mißfallen[6]	displease
danken	thank	**mißlingen*[6]	not to succeed, fail
dienen	serve		
drohen	threaten	*mißtrauen*[6]	mistrust
entfliehen	escape from[3]	*nachgeben*	give in, yield
entsprechen	correspond to	*nachlaufen*	pursue, run after
fluchen	curse[4]		
folgen	follow	*nahen*	approach
gefallen	please	*sich nähern*	,,
gehorchen	obey	*nutzen* ⎫	be of help to
*gehören	belong	*nützen* ⎭	
*gelingen	succeed	*raten*	advise
*genügen	be enough for, suffice	*schaden*	harm
		schmeicheln	flatter
glauben	believe[5]	*trauen*	trust
gleichen	resemble	*trotzen*	defy

unterliegen	be defeated	*widersprechen*	contradict
	by[7]	*widerstehen*	resist
vergeben	forgive[8]	*zuhören*	listen to
verzeihen	forgive[8]	*zustimmen*	agree to/with,
weichen	yield to.		vote for

[1] *Ich antwortete ihm.* But: *Ich antwortete auf den Brief* or *Ich beantwortete den Brief.*   [2] *begegnen* always means 'to meet by chance'; *treffen* means 'to meet' whether by chance or by appointment.   [3] See Topic 15, p. 99: Inseparable Prefixes.   [4] To curse s.o. or s.th.—also *verfluchen* with an accusative object.   [5] Distinguish between: *ich glaube ihm*—I believe him; *ich glaube es*—I believe it; and *ich glaube an ihn*—I believe in him.   [6] *mißfallen, mißlingen,* &c., are inseparable.   [7] Inseparable. *Sie unterlagen dem Feind.*   [8] *Vergib mir! Verzeihe mir!* But: *Ich kann es ihm nicht vergeben (verzeihen).*

14. Separable verbs whose prefix is a preposition governing the dative and which show a relationship of reference, advantage, or disadvantage generally govern a dative object, e.g. *ausweichen, beistehen, nachlaufen, zuhören,* &c. above. But where the prefix merely reinforces the meaning of a transitive verb, the verb takes an accusative object:

Füllen Sie bitte dieses Formular aus.
Wir müssen hier die indirekte Rede beibehalten.

15. Verbs governing a genitive object

Only very few verbs govern a single object in the genitive, e.g.

sich annehmen	befriend, interest o.s. in
sich bedienen	make use of
bedürfen	require, have need of
sich bemächtigen	get control of, secure
sich enthalten	abstain from, refrain from
sich entledigen	rid o.s. of
sich erwehren	restrain, suppress, ward off[1]
gedenken	commemorate
sich rühmen	pride o.s. on
sich vergewissern	assure o.s. of

[1] e.g. *Ich konnte mich dieses Eindrucks nicht erwehren*—I could not help having this impression.

Thus:

. . . vergewisserte er sich . . . des Schreibens der Stadtverwaltung [note 2, 131]
Zwar äußerlich hat sich unsere betriebsame Zeit des Festes eifrig angenommen [138]
Er bedarf meiner nicht. He has no need of me.

16. Certain expressions used in connexion with the law require both an accusative and a genitive object, e.g. *jn. eines Mordes überführen*—to convict s.o. of a crime; *jn. eines Diebstahls beschuldigen*—to accuse s.o. of a theft.

17. Omission of the participle

Das Bild, wie sie, den blinden Hund neben sich, . . . verschwunden war . . . [147]
Das Kinn in die Hand gestützt, sah er mich lange an.

The form of the adverbial phrase in such sentences (English: with . . .) is to be explained by the omission of a present participle, e.g. *. . . neben sich (habend); das Kinn in die Hand gestützt (haltend).*

18. 'There is', 'there are' in German

When translating 'there is' or 'there are' into German, it is important to distinguish between statements denoting *position*, where it is generally necessary to recast the sentence with *stehen, liegen, sich befinden,* &c., and statements of *fact*. In such a statement of fact as 'There was no time for me to finish the book', a recasting is necessary, e.g. *Ich hatte keine Zeit, das Buch zu Ende zu lesen*; but at the beginning of the sentence, *es ist* or *es sind* is frequently used in contexts corresponding to 'there is' or 'there are' in English, provided that the sense is a purely local and demonstrative, e.g. 'There is cheese in the cupboard'— *Es ist Käse im Schrank.* Since the function of *es* in such sentences is really that of a temporary subject, *es* disappears when it is no longer needed to introduce the sentence, e.g. *Gestern war kein Käse im Schrank.* The translation *es gibt* (followed by the accusative!) should only be used where the statement of fact implies in a *general* (not a local) sense that the subject of the English sentence 'exists':

Fish like that don't exist [174]. *Solche Fische gibt es nicht.*
If there were no homework. *Wenn es keine Hausaufgaben gäbe . . .* [37]
There is cheese in boxes and tubes. *Es gibt Käse in Schachteln und in Tuben.*
There is cheese production in all European countries. *Es gibt Käseproduktion in allen europäischen Ländern.*

19. Other verbs and verbal expressions may be translated by 'there is':

Es besteht keine Gefahr. There is no danger.

Kein anderer Richter war vorhanden. There was no other magistrate *or* No other magistrate was available. [74]

. . . *als ob etwas zu entschuldigen wäre* [90]. . . . as though there was something to apologize for.

20. German infinitive verb as translation of the English present participle or gerund

German must often use an infinitive where English uses a present participle or a gerund (see also Topic 17, pp. 111–14). Examples from Part I:

(Der Kurfürstendamm) wird . . . *nicht müde zu lächeln* [31]— does not weary of smiling.

. . . *dann hören die Eltern auf, uns zu verstehen* [37]—our parents stop understanding us.

. . . *jene internationale Art, kostenlos zu reisen* [67]—. . . of travelling.

. . . *trat mit der Absicht ans Automobil, den Schlafenden zu wecken* [77]—. . . of waking . . .

. . . *entschuldigte sich* . . ., *K. geweckt zu haben* . . . [78]—. . . for waking . . .

21. Infinitive phrase with zu instead of subordinate clause

After a verb denoting an *attitude of mind,* where the remaining part of the sentence has the *same subject* as this verb, it is better to avoid using a subordinate clause; a dependent infinitive phrase with *zu* should be used instead:

Wir hofften, dich hier zu finden. We hoped to find you here (that we should find you here).

Wieder meine ich, das dumpfe Sommersummen des Waldes zu hören [125]. Again I think I hear (seem to hear, have the impression of hearing, &c.) . . .

Das erklärte er auch diesmal tun zu wollen . . . [136]

Where the subject of the second part of the sentence is *not* the same as that of the main verb, a subordinate clause *must* be used:

Wir hofften, daß du noch hier bist. We hoped *you* were still here.

Wieder meine ich, daß das Summen aufgehört hat. Again *I* think that *the humming* has stopped.

Other verbs and verbal expressions to note in this connexion:

denken, glauben, behaupten, bestehen auf, froh sein, erstaunt sein.

. . ., um . . . zu . . .

22. The following less obvious usages of . . ., *um . . . zu . . .* should be noted:

> . . ., *um schließlich wieder den Weg zur konservativen Partei zurückzufinden* [108]—only to find his way back at last to the Conservative Party.
> *Das ist zu schön, um wahr zu sein.* That is too good to be true.
> *Die Fabrik erzeugt allerlei Waren: um nur die wichtigsten zu nennen, Schokolade und Kakao.*

23. . . ., *um . . . zu . . .* cannot be used where the subject of the phrase is different from that of the main verb:

> I sent a letter to tell them that . . . *Ich schickte einen Brief, um ihnen zu sagen, daß . . .*

but:

> I received a letter to tell me that . . . *Ich erhielt einen Brief, in dem man mir sagte, daß . . .*

24. Where the verb *gehen* is closely associated with another verb in the sense 'to be on one's way to', . . ., *um . . . zu . . .* is omitted:

> „*Wo gehst du hin?*" — „*Ich gehe schwimmen.*"
> *Dann ging er ein Nachtlager suchen.* [78]

FURTHER USES OF MODAL VERBS
Cf. also Topic 8, pp. 53–55

(*a*) Indicative; (*b*) Subjunctive:

25. Dürfen

(*a*) *Man darf annehmen, daß . . .* One is entitled to assume that . . .
(*b*) *Das dürfte (wohl) richtig sein.* That might (possibly) be true (very cautious statement; cf. *könnte, möchte*).

26. Können

(*a*) *Was kann man dafür?* What can be done about it? (i.e. nothing.)
Das kann mein Freund nicht gesagt haben. My friend cannot have said that. (Note strong stress on *kann.*)
Er konnte dreißig Jahre alt sein [115]. (Cf. *mochte.*)
Die Brücke konnte jeden Augenblick einstürzen. The bridge might have collapsed at any moment. (Note mood and tense.)
Sie konnte nicht umhin, seinen Blick zu erwidern. She could not help returning his glance.

27. Mögen

(*a*) *Nun gut, er mag kommen.* All right then, let him come.
Sie mochte etwa so alt sein wie er [114]. (Cf. *konnte.*)

(*b*) . . . *die Bitte,* . . . *er möge ihm nicht nachstellen lassen,* . . .
[151]— . . . the request, that he should not have him followed . . . (use of *mögen* in the indirect speech subjunctive
after *bitten, die Bitte,* &c.).
Es möchte (wohl) besser sein, . . . It might (perhaps) be
better . . . (cautious statement, cf. *dürfte, könnte*).
Ich möchte wohl sagen, . . . I think I can say that . . . (cautious
statement).

28. Müssen

(*a*) *Gerade ihm mußte ich begegnen!* I had to go and meet him, of
all people!
Der Park . . . *mußte gleich in den Wald übergehen* [141]. The
park must have merged into the forest. (N.B. Imperfect,
since the context is a narrative in the imperfect.)
*Woher wußte sein Bruder, daß er krank war, fragte er sich.
Er mußte es von Herrn Schröder erfahren haben.* (N.B. The
context is a narrative in the imperfect. Cf. the preceding
example.)

29. Sollen

(*b*) *Ich sollte meinen,* . . . I should think (cautious statement).

30. Wollen

(*a*) . . . *5000 Lire, die er ihm* . . . *geliehen haben will* [74]. 5,000 lire
which he claimed to have lent him (i.e. but had not really
lent him).
Es will mir nicht in den Sinn! I can't get the hang of it (implying that what is to be learnt has an awkward will of its own).
Blumen wollen gepflegt sein. Flowers need to be cared for.
(N.B. Use of *sein*—not *werden*—in expressions of this
kind, implying 'need to be'.)

(*b*) *Ich wollte, ich wäre jetzt in Deutschland.* I wish I were in Germany now.

31. Note:

(i) *tun* and *gehen* are sometimes omitted after a modal verb,
e.g. *Niemand darf das ohne gräfliche Erlaubnis* [78]. No one
may do so without the count's authority. *Wohin wollen Sie?*
Where do you want to go?

(ii) The past participles *gemußt, gewollt,* &c., are rarely found. They imply *tun* or some other verb which has already been mentioned, e.g. *Er sagte mir, ich sollte mitkommen. Ich habe es nicht gewollt, ich habe es gemußt.*

(iii) Modal verbs are sometimes used as nouns, e.g. *Wollen und Können sind nicht dasselbe.* Wanting to do a thing and being able to do it are not the same. *Soll und Haben*—debit and credit.

32. Use of prepositions after certain verbs. Cf. also Topics 12 and 16, pp. 81–83 and 105–6.

'Accusative or Dative' prepositions govern the accusative except for those marked (D).

(D) *sich ängstigen vor/um*	be worried about (a situation)/(a person)
ankommen auf[1]	depend on (s.th. or s.o.)
(D) *arbeiten an*	work on (e.g. a book, an essay, a model)
sich ärgern über	be annoyed at (s.th. or s.o.)
aufhören mit[2]	stop, cease
aussehen nach[3]	have the look of
sich bedanken für (bei jm.)	thank (s.o.) for
sich begnügen mit	make do with, be satisfied with
beharren bei (or auf (D))	insist on, persist in
beitragen zu	contribute to
sich bemühen um	take an interest in, concern o.s. with, be responsible for
sich beschränken auf[4]	be restricted to, restrict o.s. to
sich besinnen auf	recollect
(D) *bestehen auf*	insist on
bleiben bei	keep to, stick to (opinion, &c.)
sich einigen auf[5]	agree on
sich erbarmen über	have pity on
feuern auf	fire at
sich hüten vor[6]	take care not to
kämpfen um	fight for, struggle for
nachsuchen um	apply for (a job, &c.)
(D) *sich rächen an*	take revenge on
rechnen auf	reckon, count on (s.th. or s.o.)
sich schämen wegen/vor (D)	be ashamed of (s.th.)/feel ashamed (in front of s.o.)
schelten auf	scold, rebuke
schießen auf	shoot, fire at

stehen zu	stand by (s.o.)
sich streiten um	argue about
taugen zu	be fit for
trinken auf	drink to (the health of, &c.)
werden zu[7]	become
sich wundern über	be surprised at
(D) *zunehmen an*	increase in (size, &c.)
(D) *zweifeln an*	doubt, have doubts in

[1] e.g. *Das kommt auf dich an. Es kommt darauf an, ob das Wetter schön bleibt.*
[2] *Wann hörst du endlich mit dieser Arbeit auf?* When are you going to stop this work?
[3] e.g. *Es sieht nach Regen aus.*   [4] *Der Artikel beschränkte sich auf eine Erörterung der wichtigsten Punkte.* The article was restricted to (restricted itself to) a discussion of the most important points. N.B. *beschränken auf*—to restrict, limit, s.th. or s.o. (else) to.   [5] e.g. *Man einigte sich auf folgenden Plan* [133].   [6] Cf. French 'se garder de': *Ich werde mich hüten, das zu tun.*   [7] The phrase implies a development into something new or different: *Er wurde zum Schrecken der ganzen Nachbarschaft.* He became the terror of the whole neighbourhood.

TENSE

33. The use of tenses in German and English is largely the same (but it is important to take care with indirect speech and question —see Topic 6, pp. 40–41). There are, however, some major differences from the English tense usages, especially in the case of the German perfect.

Present

34. (i) The *historic present* is often used in prose to stress the drama of a situation:

> *Eines Tages erhält Mr. Wilkins eine gerichtliche Vorladung ins Hotel geschickt.* [74]

35. (ii) In time expressions corresponding to the English use of 'for' with the perfect, where the action or state is continuing at the present time, the present tense is used:

> *Ich bin schon drei Tage* (or *seit drei Tagen*) *in London.*

36. (iii) Present with future sense: with first persons, usually to imply intention; with second and third persons, usually to predict:

> *In einer halben Stunde bin ich wieder da.* I'll be back in half an hour.
> *Morgen regnet es bestimmt.*—It'll rain tomorrow for sure.

Perfect

37. (i) In conversation, the perfect is used to denote single events in the past:

> *Hast du ihn heute gesehen?* Did you see (have you seen) him today? (Cf. **41** below.)

38. (ii) An important function of the perfect tense is to link past events with the present time from which the speaker or writer is viewing them:

> *Kolumbus hat Amerika entdeckt.* Columbus discovered America. (i.e. 'It was Columbus who discovered America'.)
>
> *Wer hat dieses Haus bauen lassen?* Who had this house built?

39. (iii) The perfect is also used to denote that the past event, state, &c., is 'a thing of the past', that it is irretrievably gone:

> *Das ist ein schönes Haus gewesen.* That was once a fine house.

40. (iv) The perfect is sometimes used instead of the future perfect:

> *Bis sieben Uhr ist das Schiff eingelaufen (wird . . . eingelaufen sein).* By seven the ship will have entered harbour.

Imperfect

41. The imperfect is used to describe events, actions, states, &c., in the past without reference to the present. It is therefore the *narrative tense* of both literary and spoken German (though the perfect is much used in S. Germany in conversational narrative), and denotes events, actions, states, &c., in their relationship to one another as they *were*. Thus it corresponds to English preterite (e.g. 'thought'), continuous past ('was thinking') or habitual past ('used to think').

42. In time expressions corresponding to the English use of 'for' with the pluperfect, where the action or state *was* continuing in the *past time* referred to, the imperfect is used (cf. **35**):

> *Ich war damals schon drei Tage* (or *seit drei Tagen*) *in London, als dein Brief gekommen ist.*

Future and future perfect

The future and future perfect are sometimes used to imply

43. (i) A hope or assumption:

> *Hoffentlich werden Sie meinen Standpunkt verstehen!*
> *Er wird doch nicht schlechten Leuten in die Hände gefallen sein?*
> [124]
> *Der Preis wird kaum mehr als 15 Mark betragen* (amount to).

44. (ii) A demand:

Du wirst deinen Aufsatz noch einmal schreiben ! You will (are to) write out your essay again.

Passive infinitive

The passive infinitive is used as in English, except that

45. (i) After the verb *sein* in sentences which imply a modal verb (cf. Topic 10, 2 (ii), p. 65), an active infinitive must be used:

Der Aufsatz ist in deutscher Sprache abzufassen. The essay is to be written in German. (Or: . . . *soll in deutscher Sprache abgefaßt werden.* But this has a less official ring.)
Das ist kaum zu verstehen. (Or: *Das kann man kaum verstehen.*)

46. (ii) *lassen* must be followed by an active infinitive.

Er läßt sich nichts sagen. He will not be told different, be corrected.
Man hat ihn verhaften lassen. They had him arrested.
Möchten Sie sich ein neues Haus bauen lassen? Would you like to have a new house built?

47. Subjunctive compared with indicative

The difference in mood between the indicative and the subjunctive appears in the subjunctive situations which occur in the grammar to Topics 5, 6, and 8 of Part I. In those situations the subjunctive is seen as used (*a*) in conditional statements; (*b*) in indirect speech; and in certain phrases expressing a wish; (*c*) after *als* (*ob*) (or *als wenn*), and (*d*) in modal verbs for cautious expression of an opinion or for stating, questioning, or negating what might be or might have been (or what ought to be or ought to have been) the case in a particular situation. Cf. also Grammar Section 25, 27, 29, and 30 for other uses of modal verbs in the subjunctive.

The subjunctive is seen in these instances to be the mood which expresses the idea that the action, state, &c., denoted by the verb is, in one sense or another, lacking in 'reality'. For example (letters in brackets relate to the instances quoted above):

(*a*) *Wenn er groß wäre.* If he were great (*in fact*, he is not or may not be great).
(*b*) *Sie sagte, er sei groß.* She said he was great (this is her opinion, which may or may not represent *fact*).

(c) . . ., *als wäre er groß*, . . .—. . . as though he were great (but this may not be, perhaps is not *in fact* the case).

(d) *Er könnte groß sein*. He could (might) be great (but the actual *fact* of greatness in him is not yet realized or not yet proved).

Er hätte groß sein sollen. He ought to have been great (but his potential greatness never became *fact*).

In modern German there is a growing tendency away from the subjunctive in certain usages (e.g. after *damit*. See 52); and in some situations where the subjunctive might appear to be required (e.g. after *hoffen*) the reality of the idea expressed by the verb is so strong in the mind of the speaker or writer that the indicative is used. N.B., however, that in the remark *Das wär's also !* or *Nun, das wäre das !* Well, that's that! the subjunctive *is* used even though the *reality* of what has been done is the very point the speaker is making.

The following additional usages of the subjunctive are important:

48. (i) After *denken, meinen, glauben*, &c., *in past tenses* where what follows is shown not to be, in fact, the case:

Zuerst dachte ich, sie sei verrückt . . . [14]
Er glaubte, daß der Mann betrunken sei, . . . [77]

49. (ii) After verbs expressing a request, often with *mögen* in the present or imperfect subjunctive (see also 27 (*b*)):

Sie verlangte, daß der Stiel . . . festgemacht werde. [56]
Sie bat, ich möchte den Stiel festmachen.

N.B. Care must be taken with the mood of the verb after *wollen*. In the present tense, the indicative is normal nowadays:

Ich will, daß er mitkommt. I want him to come with me (us).

In the imperfect, the subjunctive is still used, but it is often replaced by the imperfect subjunctive of *sollen* + infinitive:

Ich wollte, daß er mitkäme (or *mitkommen sollte*).

50. (iii) Often following a negative where the subordinate verbal idea is seen by the speaker or writer as unattainable, uncertain, improbable, incredible:

Ich habe nichts, was ich Ihnen bieten könnte, als . . . [107]
Ich konnte gar nicht begreifen, wie man . . . Bücher dieser Art anhäufen könne . . . [145]

51. To render the 'future in the past' *würde* + infinitive is generally used:

> *Ich war unsicher, ob ich die Antwort wissen würde.* (Compare the direct form: *Werde ich die Antwort wissen?*)

52. Choice written German may use the present subjunctive in a *damit*-clause, especially where the outcome remains in some doubt. But the indicative is increasingly found (even where the outcome is uncertain) in written German, and/or *können* or *sollen* or a conditional introduced, in order to avoid the subjunctive. The need to do this is even more strongly felt in spoken German:

> *Ich gebe ihm Geld, damit er sich Brot kaufen kann.*
> *Ich gab ihm Geld, damit er sich Brot kaufen konnte (kaufe).*
> *Sprich lauter, damit er dich besser hört (hören kann)!*
> *Die Einbrecher tragen Masken, damit sie niemand erkennt (erkennen kann, erkennen soll).*
> *Die Einbrecher trugen Masken, damit sie niemand erkennen konnte (erkennen sollte, erkennen würde, erkenne).*

53. Alternatives to the imperative

(i) Infinitive (often used in general instructions):

> *Bitte einsteigen und die Türen schließen!*
> *Aufstehen, Hans!*

(ii) Past participle (in some military orders):

> *Stillgestanden!* Attention!

NOUNS

GENDER

Gender by ending of noun (commonly found endings which may cause difficulty)

54. Masculine: *-ich, -ig, -ling.* (For weak masculine nouns of foreign origin, see Topic 11, 2 (iii), p. 72.):

> *der Teppich, der Rettich*—radish, *der Kranich*—crane (bird); *der Honig*—honey, *der Käfig*—cage, *der Essig*—vinegar; *der Schmetterling*—butterfly, *der Feigling*—coward, *der Frühling.*

55. Feminine: many words of foreign origin[1] (indicated by their ending, e.g. *-ade, -age, -äne, -anz, -enz, -ette, -ie, -ik, -ine, -ion, -isse, -tät, -itis, -ive, -sis* or *-se, -ur*):

> *die Marmelade*—jam, marmalade, *die Garage, die Hyäne, die Eleganz, die Intelligenz*—intelligentsia, intelligence, *die*

Etikette—etiquette, *die Harmonie, die Akustik, die Maschine, die Mission, die Kulisse*—wing (of stage), *die Universität, die Bronchitis, die Initiative, die Basis* or *Base, die Karikatur.*

56. Neuter: *-chen, -lein, -icht, -tel, -tum*[2] and words of foreign origin (indicated by the endings *-ett, -in,*[3] *-(i)um, -ma, -ment*):

das Mädchen, das Häuschen, das Fräulein, das Ringlein,[4] das Dickicht—thicket, das Röhricht—reeds, das Drittel, das Viertel, das Königtum—kingdom, das Eigentum—property; das Ballett—ballet, das Quartett, das Benzin, das Nikotin, das Album, das Datum, das Natrium—sodium, das Dogma, das Komma, das Experiment, das Abonnement[5]—subscription (to a newspaper, &c.).

[1] The feminine suffix *-in* (e.g. *Königin, Prinzessin, Russin*) is of German origin.
[2] N.B. **der** *Reichtum*—wealth, **der** *Irrtum*—error, mistake. [3] Long *-i-*.
[4] Most diminutives in standard German are formed with *-chen*. Where the diminutive is used in an affectionate sense, e.g. *Mariechen, Hündlein*, both suffixes are found, although it is true to say that *-chen* is more typical of northern, *-lein* of southern dialects. N.B. *das Ringlein*—the little ring (as distinct from *der kleine Ring*—the small ring). [5] Some words ending *-ment* are of Latin origin, e.g. *das Experiment*. These are pronounced as they are spelt, with the stress on the last syllable. Others are of French origin, e.g. *das Abonnement, das Appartement, das Bombardement*. The *last syllable* of such words is given the French pronunciation.

Gender by type of noun

57. Masculine

(a) Names of seasons, months, and days: *der Herbst, der Winter, der Januar, der Oktober, der Freitag, der Sonntag*, &c.

(b) Compass directions, winds, rain (snow, hail, &c.): *der Westen, der Süden, der Nordosten, der Passat*—trade-wind, *der Monsun, der Regen, der Schnee, der Hagel, der Reif*—hoarfrost.

(c) Names of most earth and rock types: *der Sand, der Lehm*—clay, *der Schiefer*—slate, *der Kies*—gravel, *der Granit.* But: **die** *Erde,* **die** *Kreide.*

(d) Names of most types of money: *der Dollar, der Rubel, der Schilling, der Franken.* But: **die** *Mark,* **die** *Lira,* **die** *Rupie,* and **das** *Pfund* (see also **151**).

58. Feminine

(a) Names of trees and of many varieties of flowers: *die Eiche, die Tanne, die Ulme, die Lärche, die Pappel; die Tulpe, die Narzisse, die Nelke*—carnation, *die Rose.*

(b) Numbers used as nouns (cf. 147): *die Null, die Eins, die Vier, die Siebzig.*

(c) Most names of ships: *die „Bremen"*, *die „Prinz Eugen"*, *die „United States"*.

59. Neuter

(a) Names of most metals and chemical elements: *das Silber, das Blei, das Gold, das Platin, das Nickel, das Kupfer*; *das Uran, das Kalzium, das Brom*. But: **der** *Stahl*, **die** *Bronze*, and **der** *Schwefel*—sulphur.

(b) Other parts of speech and letters of the alphabet used as nouns: *das Schöne*,[1] *das Gelesene*,[1] *das Hin und Her*—comings and goings, *das Für und Wider*—pros and cons, *das Lesen, das Schreiben, das Abc, das Z*, &c.

(c) Collective nouns in *Ge-*:[2] *das Getümmel*—din, *das Gesumme*—humming, *das Gebirge*.

[1] See Topic 14, p. 93.   [2] See 70.

N.B. Cf. 73 for details of the genders of countries, districts, mountains, cities, rivers, &c.

NOUNS OF THE SAME FORM BUT DIFFERENT GENDER
AND MEANING

60. Related nouns

das Band (⸚er)	ribbon	*der Band (⸚e)*	volume (book)
der Bauer (-n)	peasant	*das (and der) Bauer (-)*	bird-cage
der Erbe (-n)	heir	*das Erbe*[1]	inheritance
der Flur (-e)	corridor	*die Flur (-en)*	field
der Gehalt (-e)	content[2]	*das Gehalt (⸚er)*	salary
der Hut (⸚e)	hat	*die Hut*[3]	guard
der Junge (-n)	boy	*das Junge*[4]	young (animal)
der Kunde (-n)	customer	*die Kunde (-n)*[5]	news
der Schild (-e)	shield[6]	*das Schild (-er)*	notice (-board)
der See (-n)	lake	*die See*[7]	sea
das Steuer (-)	steering-wheel	*die Steuer (-n)*	tax
der Stift (-e)	pencil, apprentice (coll.)	*das Stift (-e and -er)*	religious foundation

der		das	
Verdienst (-e)	earnings	*Verdienst* (-e)[8]	merit
das Wehr (-e)	weir	*die Wehr* (-en)	defence
der Weise[9]	seer, wise man	*die Weise*[10]	manner, way

[1] plur. *die Erbschaften*. N.B. *Erbschaft* is the usual word for legacy.   [2] e.g. *der Gehalt* (or *Inhalt*) *eines Romans*—the content of a novel (*der Inhalt* also—contents, table of contents).   [3] *auf der Hut sein*—to be on one's guard.   [4] Adjectival noun. See Topic 11, note, pp. 72–73.   [5] Now normally replace by *Die Nachricht*.   [6] i.e. as in *Schilde und Speere*—shields and spears.   [7] No plural of *die See* is formed. N.B. The seven seas—*die sieben Meere*.   [8] *Das war sein Verdienst*—That was his achievement, that was due to him. *Goethes Verdienste um die deutsche Literatur*—Goethe's services, contribution to German literature.   [9] Adjectival noun.   [10] Plural rare.

61. Unrelated nouns

der *Alp* (-e)[1]	nightmare	die *Alp* (-en)	mountain pasture
das *Harz*	resin	der *Harz*	Harz Mountains
die *Heide* (-n)	moor	der *Heide* (-n)	heathen
der *Kiefer* (-)	jaw	die *Kiefer* (-n)	Scotch pine
die *Leiter* (-n)	ladder	der *Leiter* (-)	leader
die *Mark* (*Mark* and *Mark-stücke*)[2]	mark (coin)	das *Mark*	marrow (of bone)
die *Mark* (-en)[3]	border country		
der *Marsch* (⸚e)	march	die *Marsch* (-en)	fen, fenlands, marsh, marshes
die *Mast*	mast (fodder)	der *Mast* (-en)	mast (of ship)
das *Messer* (-)	knife	der *Messer* (-)	meter
der *Reis* (*Reissorten*)	rice	das *Reis* (-er)[4]	twig
der *Tau*	dew	das *Tau* (-e)	hawser, rope
die *Taube* (-n)	dove, pigeon	der *Taube*[5]	deaf man
das *Tor* (-e)	gateway	der *Tor* (-en)	fool

[1] Usually: *das Alpdrücken. Ich hatte Alpdrücken*—I had a nightmare. The plural *Alpe* is rare.   [2] Cf. *100 Mark*—100 marks; *100 Markstücke*—100 mark pieces.   [3] *Die Mark* usually refers to *die Mark Brandenburg* (the March of Brandenburg; cf. Welsh Marches).   [4] Found mainly in poetry.   [5] Adjectival noun (cf. *die Taube*—deaf woman).

62. Plural of foreign words (Fremdwörter)

N.B. Many *Fremdwörter* have more than one plural form, e.g. *Aromas* and *Aromen*. For the sake of clarity only one form is given in most instances in the list below.

(i) *der Bankier—Bankiers,*[1] *der Streik—Streiks, der Park—Parks, der Scheck—Schecks* (cheque).

(ii) *der Fonds—Fonds*[2] (fund).

(iii) *der Ballon—Ballons,*[3] *der Karton—Kartons,*[2] *der Balkon—Balkons*[2] (and *Balkone*), *das Karussell—Karussells* (roundabout), *der Leutnant—Leutnants.*

(iv) *das Drama—Dramen, das Dogma—Dogmen, das Thema—Themen* (subject—of a discussion, &c.). N.B. *Komma—Kommas, Aroma—Aromas, Lexikon—Lexika.*

(v) *das Museum—Museen, das Album—Alben, das Datum—Daten.* N.B. *das Mineral—Mineralien* (minerals in general) or *Minerale* (e.g. *Kohle und Salz*), *das Prinzip—Prinzipien* (principle), *das Reptil—Reptilien, das Konto—Konten* (account—at a bank, &c.), *das Risiko—Risiken* (risk).

(vi) *der Rhythmus—Rhythmen, das Epos—Epen* (epic). N.B. In the genitive these become: *des Rhythmus, des Epos.* Cf. also *des Kommunismus, des Konservatismus.*

(vii) *der Krokus—Krokusse, der Zirkus—Zirkusse, der Omnibus—Omnibusse.* N.B. In the genitive these become: *des Krokus, des Zirkus,* but *des Omnibusses.*

N.B. Groups (i)–(iii) above contain examples of common words of French or English origin; group (iv), words of Greek origin; groups (v)–(vii), words of Greek, Latin, and Italian origin.

Note the shift in stress as between the singular *der Akkumulátor, der Mótor,* and their plurals: *Akkumulatóren, Motóren.*

[1] French pronunciation.   [2] French pronunciation; but the *-s* is pronounced in the plural.   [3] French pronunciation, both singular and plural.

PROPER NAMES AND TITLES

The following difficulties should be noted:

63. Of the weak masculine nouns used as titles (e.g. *Herr, Präsident, Fürst*) only *Herr* is declined before the proper name; but in the comparatively rare instances where an article is used, the noun is declined.[1]

Hat er das Buch über Prinz Max beendet?
Er hat unter Fürst Bismarck gedient.
Fürst Bismarcks Memoiren;
Bundespräsident Scheels Rede;

but:

Sie half Herrn Schmidt.
Herrn Schmidts Auto steht draußen.

[1] *Er trat in den Dienst des Fürsten Esterházy.*

64. Proper names ending in -*s* (and -*ß*, -*x*, -*z*, -*tz*) may, in accordance with certain traditions, form a genitive with the addition of an article, or by the use of the apostrophe:

Der Wagen des Anton Schmitz or *Anton Schmitz' Wagen.*
Die Dramen des Euripides or *Euripides' Dramen.*[1, 2]
Marx' „Kapital".[1, 3]
Professor Heuss' Rede.[1, 3]
Die Taten des Moses.[4] *Die Prophezeiungen des Isaias.*[4]

[1] Where authorship is implied, *von* (i.e. English 'by') may always be used as an alternative: *Die Dramen von Euripides*; *„Das Kapital" von Marx*; *die Rede von Professor Heuss.*   [2] The article is frequently used in the genitive of the names of classical authors which end in -*s*. Cf. *des Sophokles, des Aristoteles.*   [3] The article may *not* be used in these instances.   [4] The article is used before Biblical names ending in -*s* when these occur in a scriptural context in the genitive case. N.B. *Jesus Christus* is declined in the genitive: *Jesu Christi.* Cf. sometimes also: *des heiligen Johannis; das Evangelium Matthäi (Lucä, Marci)*—The Gospel according to St. Matthew (Luke, Mark).

65. *der junge Goethe, der alte Georg*, &c., become in the genitive *des jungen Goethe, des alten Georg*, &c., i.e. the proper name remains uninflected. Cf. title and proper name in the genitive:

der Sieg Kaiser Heinrichs or ⎰ the victory of (the) Emperor
der Sieg des Kaisers Heinrich ⎱ Henry

Where an additional description occurs after the proper name, the genitive inflexion is used:

der Sieg Kaiser Heinrichs III. (des Dritten).[1]
der Sieg des Kaisers Heinrich III. (des Dritten).
der Tod Heinrichs des Löwen—the death of Henry the Lion.

[1] In the accusative, *Heinrich den Dritten*; in the dative, *Heinrich dem Dritten.*

66. There is a tendency to drop the genitive -*s* with months of the year:

Die ersten kalten Tage des Januar (or *des Januars*).
Die Ereignisse des 6. Juli, des 24. Dezembers.

N.B. *In den ersten Tagen des Monats Januar.* Here the genitive -*s* is always omitted, since the case has already been sufficiently indicated by the genitive article and the genitive ending of *Monats*.

67. Where it is felt to be correct to exclude the article from the inverted commas placed around a title—i.e. only with very well-known titles, such as those of famous plays or the names of newspapers—the inflexions of nouns and adjectives are affected:

Er spielt in Schillers „Räubern".[1]
Das steht in der „Frankfurter Allgemeinen Zeitung".

> [1] The title of the play is, of course, '*Die Räuber*'.

68. The plurals of surnames end in -*s*: *die Meyers, die Lehmanns, die Schmidts.* N.B. *Schulz—die Schulzens; Klotz—die Klotzens.*

69. Mixed declension nouns

Some mixed declension masculine nouns may be confused with weak masculine nouns. They are mainly of two types: the nominative singular of some ends in -*e*, of others in -*n*. *The genitive singular of all ends in -ns,* and in all other cases, singular and plural, the ending is -*en.* Thus:

	Sing.	Plur.
N.	*der Gedanke*	*die Gedanken*
A.	*den Gedanken*	*die Gedanken*
G.	*des Gedankens*	*der Gedanken*
D.	*dem Gedanken*	*den Gedanken*

The most important nouns of this class are:

der Buchstabe	letter (of the alphabet)	*der Glaube*	faith, belief
		der Haufen	pile, heap
der Felsen[1]	rock, cliff	*der Name*	name
der Frieden[2]	peace	*der Samen*	seed
der Funke	spark	*der Schaden*	damage, harm
der Gedanke	thought, idea	*der Schreck*[4]	shock
der Gefallen[3]	favour, kindness	*der Wille*	will, desire

> [1] In a figurative sense, *der Fels.*
> [2] *der Friede* is also frequently found.
> [3] e.g. *Würden Sie mir einen Gefallen tun?*
> [4] Or, *der Schrecken.*

N.B. *der Funken, der Glauben,* and *der Haufe* are sometimes used.

Note: *das Herz*: the one mixed declension neuter noun with gen. sing. *-ens,* dat. *-en* (acc. *das Herz,* gen. *des Herzens,* dat. *dem Herzen,* plur. *Herzen*).

die Erde, die Ehre show mixed declension in the sing. in two expressions only: *auf Erden* (in biblical and poetic language) and *in Ehren halten*—to hold in honour, revere.

70. Collective nouns

Collective nouns are frequently indicated by the prefix *Ge-*. They are, without exception, neuter. Those derived from verbs ending *-en* or *-n* usually have *-e* as the final letter: *rennen — das Gerenne* (a great deal of running hither and thither); and those derived from verbs ending *-ern* or *-eln* have *-er* and *-el* respectively: *poltern — das Gepolter* (din), *rasseln — das Gerassel* (rattling noises). Others are derived from nouns, and sometimes add umlaut.

Neuter collective nouns in *Ge-* may denote associations of *things,* e.g. *Gemäuer*—masonry, *Gebälk*—rafters, *Gebirge*—range of mountains. Or they may denote associations of *actions* or *sounds* (sometimes in a contemptuous sense[1]): *Gelaufe* (cf. *Gerenne*), *Gedränge*—crowding, crowd, *Geklopfe*—continual knocking; *Gebrüll*—roaring, *Gedröhn*—droning, *Gesumm*—humming, &c.

Collective meaning is also sometimes implied by the endings *-heit, -keit, -igkeit, -schaft, -tum*: *Christenheit*—Christendom, *Dreifaltigkeit*—Trinity, *Mannschaft*—team, *Judentum*—Judaism.

[1] e.g. *Getue*—fussing around, *Geklimper*—mere strumming (on an instrument).

GEOGRAPHICAL NAMES

71. Difficult names of European cities and their inhabitants

Antwerpen	Antwerp	*Florenz*	Florence
Athen	Athens	*Genf*	Geneva
Basel	Basle	*Gent*	Ghent
Belgrad	Belgrade	*Genua*	Genoa
Bern	Berne	*den Haag*	The Hague
Brügge	Bruges	*Kopenhagen*	Copenhagen
Brüssel	Brussels	*Lüttich*	Liège
Bukarest	Bucharest	*Mailand*	Milan
Dünkirchen	Dunkirk	*Moskau*	Moscow

Neapel	Naples	*Triest*	Trieste
Nizza	Nice	*Venedig*	Venice
Prag	Prague	*Warschau*	Warsaw
Rom	Rome	*Wien*	Vienna
Straßburg	Strasbourg	*Zürich*	Zurich

The names of inhabitants of cities are formed by the addition of *-er* to the names of the cities: *Genfer, Straßburger, Wiener*, &c. N.B. *Antwerper, Basler, Florentiner, Genueser* (adj. noun), *Haager, Kopenhagener, Mailänder, Neapler* and *Neapolitaner, Nizzaer* and *Nizzarde* (weak masc.), *Römer*.

N.B. *Halberstadt — Halberstädter*, &c.

72. Nouns of nationality

The German nouns of nationality sometimes cause difficulty. They are of three types:

(a) **Weak masculines** (fem. with *-in*):[1] *Ire, Schotte, Franzose (Französin), Pole, Tscheche, Russe, Chinese, Schwede, Däne, Finne, Jugoslawe, Ungar, Bulgare, Rumäne, Jude*, &c. N.B. *Asiate*—Asian.

(b) Those which end in *-er* (fem. in *-in*): *Waliser*—Welshman, *Engländer, Holländer, Belgier, Norweger, Spanier, Italiener, Österreicher, Schweizer, Albaner, Japaner, Inder, Araber, Neger*, &c. N.B. *Europäer, Afrikaner, Australier, Amerikaner*.

(c) *Deutscher* (adj. noun).[2]

[1] Cf. Topic 11, p. 72.   [2] Cf. Topic 11, p. 71.

73. Gender

Names of countries and districts are generally neuter. Names of countries or districts ending in *-ei, -ie*, or *-e* are feminine: *die Türkei, die Pikardie, die Ukraine, die Provence*, &c. (cf. Topic 4, 1 (i) (*d*), p. 27). Note also *die Schweiz, die Pfalz* (Palatinate), *die Krim* (Crimea), *die Riviera, die (Ant)arktis, die Sahara*.

Note the plural names: *die Vereinigten Staaten von Amerika* or *die USA, die Niederlande*.

Town names are neuter.

Names of mountains are generally masculine (*der Berg* is understood): *der Großglockner, der Montblanc, der Vesuv, der Olymp*.

Names of mountain ranges are mainly masculine: *der Taunus, der Harz, der Himalaja*; but: *die Eifel, die Sierra Nevada*.

Names of German rivers are mainly feminine, but some are masculine: *die Mosel, die Donau, die Ruhr, die Weser, die Lahn, die Elbe, die Oder,* &c.; but: *der Rhein, der Main, der Neckar, der Inn.*

Names of most foreign rivers are masculine, but those ending in *-a* or *-e* are generally feminine: *der Nil, der Amazonas, der Ganges, der Don*; but: *die Wolga, die Seine, die Themse.*

N.B. **die** *Weichsel* — Vistula.

ADJECTIVES

COMPARISON OF ADJECTIVES

74. Umlaut not occurring in comparison of adjectives

The commonest monosyllabic adjectives which do not take umlaut in the comparative and superlative are:

barsch—rough (voice), *blank*—shining, *brav,*[1] *falsch, flach, kahl*—bald, *klar, lahm, matt, platt*—flat, *rasch, sanft, schlank, wahr, zahm, zart*—delicate.

froh, hohl—hollow, *morsch*—rotten, *roh, stolz, toll*—crazy, *voll.*

bunt, dumpf—dull (sound), *plump*—clumsy, *rund, stumpf*—blunt.

> [1] e.g. *Braver Hund!*—Good dog! *Ein braver Junge*—a good boy.

75. weniger ... als ...

The negative of *kostbarer als* is *weniger kostbar als* (in very choice speech, *minder kostbar als*).

The negative superlative consisting of *am wenigsten* and an adjective is very rarely used. Instead, the superlative of an adjective which itself renders the negative idea is preferred:

the least heavy of the three weights—*das leichteste der drei Gewichte.*

the least high of the towers—*der niedrigste der Türme.*

76. Comparative in the sense of 'fairly ...'

The comparative adjective may imply 'fairly ...' (cf. note 11, p. 85):

ein jüngerer Mann—a fairly young man.

eine ältere Dame—an elderly lady.

die neuere Literatur—recent literature.

eine größere Menge—a fair quantity.

77. Use of mehr

mehr is not normally used to form the comparative as such. However, it may be used in the sense 'rather than' with the stronger stress on the adjective which immediately follows *mehr* (cf. 131):

Er ist mehr faul als unverständig. He is lazy rather than stupid.

78. Use of je . . . desto (um so) . . .

'The more . . . the more . . .' is in German: *je* . . . (subordinate clause) . . . *desto* (or *um so*) . . . (main clause):

Je kürzer die Tage, desto (um so) länger werden die Nächte.
Je mehr er arbeitet, um so (desto) müder wird er.
Similarly: *Mein Fehler war um so dümmer, da ich die Antwort ganz gut wußte.* My mistake was all the more stupid as I knew the answer quite well.

79. Use of aller-, weitaus, bei weitem, denkbar with superlative adjectives

'the best (longest, most beautiful, &c.) of all'—e.g. *das allerbeste Buch, die allerlängste Aufgabe, die allerschönste Route*, &c.
'by far the . . .'—e.g. *der weitaus beste Roman; bei weitem die schönsten Gedichte*, &c.
'. . . imaginable'—*die denkbar schlimmsten Folgen*—the worst consequences imaginable.

80.

Note also: 'greatest possible', 'best possible', 'very first' (chance encounter):

Wir haben den größtmöglichen Erfolg gehabt.
Ich werde die bestmögliche Gelegenheit ergreifen. I shall seize the best possible opportunity.
Ich habe den erstbesten Menschen angesprochen. I spoke to the very first person (I met).

N.B. The use of *möglichst* is restricted to such adverbial phrases as *möglichst bald* (*so bald wie möglich*), *möglichst schnell* (*so schnell wie möglich*), &c.

81. Use of allzu

A more stressed form of *zu* is *allzu*. The word is often compounded with the adjective when the latter is monosyllabic:

Wir wollen ohne allzulange Vorbereitungen abreisen.
Seine allzu langweiligen Bücher habe ich nicht gelesen.

82. Linking of so (. . . wie)

so is normally linked with *genau* and *eben* in such phrases as:

genauso groß wie ich—exactly the same height as I.

ebenso klein wie du—just as small as you.

N.B. *Das Buch ist doppelt so lang* (or *noch einmal so lang*) *wie das letzte.* The book is twice as long (as long again) as the last.

UNINFLECTED ADJECTIVE

83. The adjective is not inflected when it follows the noun to which it refers, whether or not it occurs with the verb *sein*:

Der König, klug und weise, befahl . . . The king, shrewd and wise, commanded . . .

84. It remains uninflected in certain stock expressions, e.g.

auf gut Glück—trusting to luck, at random;[1] *gut zwei Meilen*— a good two miles.

bayrisch Bier; *Kölnisch Wasser*; *Preußischblau*; *Alt-Wien*— Old Vienna; *Groß-Berlin*—Greater Berlin.

[1] e.g. *Wir sind auf gut Glück losgegangen.* We set off, trusting to luck.

85. Certain colour adjectives of foreign origin are not inflected: e.g. *lila*—lilac, *rosa*—pink, *creme*—cream:

ein lila Kleid (or *ein lilafarbenes Kleid*);
ein rosa Hut (or *ein rosafarbener Hut*).

FORMATION OF ADJECTIVES

86. Adjectives formed from the names of materials

(*a*) *-ern* with umlaut: *stählern* (*Stahl*), *hölzern*, *gläsern*, *tönern* (*der Ton*—clay);

(*b*) *-ern* without umlaut: *eisern*, *kupfern*, *bleiern*, *silbern*, *steinern*;

(*c*) *-en*: *golden*, *seiden* (*die Seide*—silk), *wollen*, *eichen*, *papieren*, *irden* (*Erde*).

87. Adjectives formed from the names of towns and districts

Adjectives may be formed from the names of towns and of some districts by the addition of *-er* (invariable ending):

der Kölner Dom; *im Kölner Dom*; *die Frankfurter Messe*; *bei der Frankfurter Messe*; *die Badener Hügellandschaft*—the hills of the district of Baden.

N.B. *Darmstädter Kirchen*; *Neustädter Fledermäuse* [134], &c. (from *Darmstadt, Neustadt*, &c.).

Adjectives are usually formed from the names of districts by means of the suffix -*isch*:

hessisch (*Hessen*); *bay[e]risch* (*Bayern*); *württembergisch* (*Württemberg*); *westfälisch* (*Westfalen*); *sächsisch* (*Sachsen*).

88. Compound adjectives

Where an adjective is felt to be very closely linked in meaning to another word (whether an adjective or another part of speech), a compound adjective is often formed:

(*a*) (Examples from Part I): *blaugefroren*; *mitschuldig*; *eisigkalt*; *meistzitiert*; *vielgelesen*; *nadelspitz*; *streichholzschachtelartig*;[1] *hellgelb*; *vielstöckig*; *schwindelerregend*; *dunkelgestreift*.

(*b*) Similes (cf. *so . . . wie . . .*) may often be expressed by a compound adjective: *totenblaß*—as pale as death; *kerzengerade*—as straight as a die (German: candle); *stocksteif*; *steinalt*; *mutterseelenallein*; *turmhoch*; *todmüde*; *todtraurig*; *mäuschenstill*; *spiegelblank*; *blitzschnell*; *bettelarm*, &c.

(*c*) Compound adjectives of colour:
hellrot, dunkelblau, tiefgrün, &c.
blaugrün, grauschwarz, &c.

N.B. bluish-grey—*bläulich-grau*; reddish-yellow—*rötlich-gelb*, &c.

[1] Note the significance of the suffixes -*artig* (of such-and-such a type); -*förmig*; and -*bar* (capable of); -*mäßig* (in such-and-such a manner, e.g. *regelmäßig*); -*gemäß* (in accordance with, e.g. *traditionsgemäß*).

89. Adjectives and past participles followed by a preposition

The use of prepositions after certain past participles is dealt with in Topic 16. The following list contains examples of adjectives and past participles which are followed by certain prepositions. 'Accusative or Dative' prepositions govern the accusative except for those marked (D).

(D) *arm an*	poor in
begierig nach	desirous of
beliebt bei	popular with
bereit zu	prepared for
besorgt um	worried about
bezeichnend für	characteristic of
eifersüchtig auf	jealous of

einverstanden mit	in agreement with
empfänglich für	sensitive to
erschöpft durch	exhausted by
fähig zu	capable of
freundlich zu	friendly towards
froh über	glad at
geeignet zu/für	suitable for
hart gegen	hard towards
(D) *interessiert an*	interested in
neidisch auf	envious of
(D) *reich an*	rich in
stolz auf	proud of
streng gegen	strict towards
(D) *überlegen an*	superior in
zornig auf/über	angry with/at

PRONOUNS

90. Personal pronouns in the genitive

The genitives of *ich, du, er/sie/es, wir, ihr, sie/Sie* are:
meiner, deiner, seiner/ihrer/seiner,[1] *unser, euer, ihrer/Ihrer.*

The genitives of the personal pronouns do not occur very frequently, but they are sometimes required, e.g. after prepositions governing the genitive, as genitive objects and in such expressions as 'five of us':

Statt meiner wird mein Bruder kommen.
Die Freunde hatten sich ihrer angenommen. Her friends had looked after her.
Wir waren unser fünf. There were five of us.
Es waren ihrer sechs. There were six of them.

[1] For all practical purposes the genitive demonstrative pronoun *dessen*, or, in some expressions, the old genitive *es* (now felt rather to be an accusative) take the place of the neuter *seiner*:
  Ich war mir dessen völlig bewußt. I was fully aware of it.
  Ich habe (or *bin*) *es satt.* I am tired of it.
  Er ist es nicht würdig. He is not worthy of it.

91. Reflexive pronouns

Reflexive pronouns should, as a general rule, be introduced into the sentence as soon as possible (cf. Topic 2, pp. 8–9) and before long object phrases and phrases relating to a verbal idea occurring at the end of the sentence:

*Kannst du **dich** noch an den traurigen alten Mann mit dem Hund erinnern?*

*Vater sagte, ich sollte **mir** an meinem älteren Bruder ein Beispiel nehmen.* Father said I ought to take an example from my elder brother.

92. Reciprocal pronouns

The reciprocal pronoun 'each other', 'one another' of the third person is *sich*, or where this is ambiguous, *einander* (invariable). *einander* is more commonly used than *uns* and *euch* as the reciprocal pronoun of the first and second persons plural respectively:

Sie liebten sich sehr.
Wir wollen einander helfen.
Warum müßt ihr einander kritisieren?

einander is joined to a preceding preposition:

Sie saßen nebeneinander.
Seid nett zueinander!
Habt ihr miteinander gesprochen?

Declension of indefinite pronouns

93. The following indefinite pronouns are not declined:

allerlei (allerhand), etwas, genug, mehr, nichts, ein paar, ein wenig.

jemand and *niemand* are sometimes declined in the accusative and dative (*jemanden, jemandem; niemanden, niemandem*). The genitive, which is not common, must be declined; *jemandes Haus; niemandes Freunde.*

jedermann (everyone) remains uninflected except for the genitive *jedermanns: Das ist nicht jedermanns Sache.* Not everyone is capable of doing it.

94. *viel* and *wenig* are sometimes used in the inflected forms *vieles* and *weniges*. They then decline throughout in the normal way. *viel* and *wenig* are also usually declined in the dative:

Viel kann ich nicht sagen.
Vieles hat mir gefallen.
Sie versteht so wenig.
Ihm gefällt so wenig.
Er ist mit wenigem (vielem) vertraut. He is familiar with few (many) things.

The choice between *viel* and *vieles*, *wenig* and *weniges* is sometimes a matter of usage or rhythm. The general distinction is that *viel* corresponds to the English 'much', *vieles* to 'many things', *wenig* to 'little', *weniges* to 'few things'.

USAGES OF VARIOUS INDEFINITE PRONOUNS

95. all-

> *alle zehn Jahre*—every ten years.
> *alles* in the sense of 'everybody': *Alles einsteigen!* All aboard!
> *Alles rennt und schreit durcheinander.* Everybody is running and shouting in confusion.

96. anders

> *jemand anders* (nom. and acc.), *jemandem anders* (dat.)[1]—someone else.
> *niemand anders*[2]—no one else.
>
> Similarly: *wer anders? was anders? wo anders?* (*woanders*—somewhere else.)

[1] The genitive 'of someone else' becomes *eines anderen* (*ein anderer* is an alternative to *jemand anders* in the sense 'someone different'). [2] *niemand* is treated like *jemand* throughout.

97. beide

(*a*) *wir beide*—we two, both of us; *ihr beide* (or *beiden*)—both of you. The word-order in such sentences as the following should be noted:

> *Wir waren beide krank.* We were both ill.
> *Wir beide waren krank, aber die anderen wurden verschont.* We two were ill but the others escaped.

(*b*) *beides* as neuter pronoun: *Heißt es „jemand" oder „jemanden" im Akkusativ? — Wir können beides sagen.*

98. einer, eins, &c.

(*a*) After the definite article:

> *Sie trug zwei Rosen in der Hand, die eine rot und die andere gelb.*
> *Von diesen Zigaretten kosten die einen zwei Mark, die anderen zwei Mark fünfzig.*

(*b*) *so einer*—such a person, someone like that:

> *Wer will so einem glauben?*

(*c*) *was für einer?*—see 111 (*a*).

(*d*) *manch einer* (or *mancher*) is used in a general sense:

> *Manch einer (mancher) hat so etwas gesagt.* Many a person has said that sort of thing.

(*e*) *unsereiner* (colloquial: people like us, our sort) declines in the accusative and dative; it is rarely used in the genitive:

> *Was kann unsereiner tun?*
> *Wer möchte unsereinem helfen?*

(*f*) *irgendeiner* (*irgend jemand*)—someone or other:

> *Irgendeiner muß es gesehen haben.*
> *Wir müssen irgend jemand fragen.*

N.B. *irgendeiner*, and *irgendwer*, *irgendwelcher*, *irgendwas*, *irgendwie*, *irgendwo*, &c., are compounded; *irgend jemand* and *irgend etwas* should be written as separate words.

99. einig-

(*a*) In its usual plural sense, *einige* may be followed by a number:

> *einige Tausend Besucher*—a few thousand visitors.
> *einige dreißig Antworten*—some thirty replies.

(*b*) *einig-* is also used in a singular or collective sense:

> *einige Zeit später*—some time later.
> *einiges davon*—a certain amount of it.

100. es

(*a*) *es* used as temporary subject:

> *Es zogen drei Burschen wohl über den Rhein* (frequently found in verse, as here).
> *Es kann keiner behaupten, ich hätte ihn nicht gewarnt.* No one can maintain that I did not warn him. (Frequently used for purposes of stress and/or style.)

(*b*) Care must be taken in translating 'it is I', &c.:

> It is I (me). *Ich bin es.*
> It is we (us). *Wir sind es.*

N.B. I am this man. *Dieser Mann bin ich.*

(*c*) *es* is used (or understood) as the subject of various impersonal expressions:

> *es regnet, es schneit, es hagelt, es donnert,* &c.
> *mir ist warm, mir ist kalt, mir ist angst,*[1] *mir ist bange,*[1] *mir graut davor,*[1] *mir ist wohl*—I feel well.

[1] *mir ist angst (bange) davor; mir ist angst und bange davor; mir graut davor*—I'm scared of it.

101. man

man has as its accusative *einen*, as its dative *einem*. The possessive 'one's' is *sein*.

102. welcher, welche, welches, &c.

welcher, welche, welches, &c., are used with the meaning 'any one', 'any':

Ich habe genug Käse. Willst du welchen haben?
Hier sind Blumen. Willst du welche mitnehmen?

Relative pronouns

103. Revision: the relative pronouns take the same form as the definite article except for the genitive, and the dative plural. These are:

	Masc.	*Fem.*	*Neut.*	*Plural*
Gen.	*dessen*	*deren*	*dessen*	*deren*
Dat.				*denen*

No article is used before a noun following *dessen* or *deren*:

Der Garten, dessen Mauer zwei Meter hoch ist, . . .
Er sprach mit den Schülern, deren Namen er gut kannte.

104. *dessen* and *deren* may be used in place of a possessive adjective to avoid any ambiguity:

(Der Sonnenschein) reicht bis zum Westfuß des Schwarzwalds.
   Da **dessen** *Berge viel steiler emporragen als die Westseite*
   der Vogesen, so ist hier die Lufthebung viel plötzlicher . . . [154]
   . . . As the mountains of the latter (i.e. its mountains) . . .

105. *welcher, welche, welches*, &c., are sometimes used in place of the usual relative pronouns. It is advisable for the English student to keep to the more normal *der, die, das*, &c., for *welcher*, &c., is restricted almost entirely to choice prose style and is apt to appear mannered or comic (or both) if inappropriately used.

106. The relative pronoun *was* is used:

 (*a*) after an indefinite word: *das, was* . . .; *alles, was* . . .;
    etwas, was . . .; *nichts, was* . . .; *viel, was* . . .; *das Beste,*
    was . . .; &c.;

 (*b*) referring to a whole idea: *Sie hat einen Ausflug vorge-*
    schlagen, was uns sehr gefallen hat;
       was must be used as the relative pronoun in the case

of clauses in apposition to *es*: *Es war nicht Mitleid, was ich wollte, sondern Hilfe.* It was not sympathy I wanted, but help.

(*c*) standing for *das, was* as subject or direct object of a sentence: *Was man heute nicht tun kann, läßt sich morgen machen.* What you can't do today you can (always) do tomorrow.

107. The following prepositions (and *only* these) may be combined with *wo(r)-* as an alternative to preposition + relative pronoun, referring to *things*, not persons:

an, auf, aus, bei, durch, für, gegen, hinter, in, mit, nach, neben, über, unter, um, von, vor, zu, zwischen; e.g.

Das Messer, womit ich schneide or . . ., *mit dem ich schneide* . . .
Das Bett, worauf ich schlafe or . . ., *auf dem ich schlafe* . . .
Das Glas, woraus du trankst or . . ., *aus dem du trankst* . . .

These relatives should not be confused with the corresponding pronominal adverbs *damit, dadurch, daraus,* &c. (with that, it, them; through that, it, them, &c.).

N.B. 'Into which' has the special form *worein*; 'in which' is *worin*. Cf. *darein* and *darin*.

In modern German *womit, worauf, woraus,* &c., are being replaced more and more by the preposition + relative pronoun.

Interrogative pronouns

108. *wer?* and *was?* are declined:

	For persons (sing. and plur.)		For things (sing. and plur.)	
Nom.	*wer?*	who?	*was?*	what?
Acc.	*wen?*	whom?	*was?*	what?
Gen.	*wessen?*	whose?	*wessen?*	of what?
Dat.	*wem?*	to whom? for whom?		

Strictly speaking, there is no dative *wem?*—to what?, and any question such as *Wem haben Sie das Geld gegeben?* can only be intended to mean 'To whom did you give the money?' If the answer must be '*Der Blindenanstalt*' ('To the Home for the Blind') the answer is not felt to be inappropriate to the question; the reply has personified the institution. Confusion does not normally arise, for questions whose English equivalent is 'To what . . .' are put in other ways:

To what do you attribute your success? *Wie erklären Sie sich Ihren Erfolg?* or *Welchen Gründen schreiben Sie Ihren Erfolg zu?*

Examples of the use of genitive interrogative pronouns:

Wessen Hut ist dies?

Wir wußten nicht, wessen hier gedacht wurde. We did not know what was being commemorated here (*gedenken* governs a genitive object).

109. *womit, woran, wobei*, &c., when used as interrogative pronouns, must always refer to *things*, never to persons (cf. *womit*, &c., as relative pronouns, 107).

Wodurch hast du mich erkannt? How (by what means) did you recognize me?

Worauf soll ich die Vase stellen? What shall I put the vase on?

Wozu all diese Vorbereitungen? What are all these preparations for?

For *persons*, the preposition followed by the pronoun must be used:

Durch wen hast du das erfahren? Through whom did you learn that?

Auf wen soll ich warten? For whom am I to wait?

110. Concord of interrogative pronoun and verb

Compare:

Wer **sind** *diese Jungen?* Who *are* these boys?

and

Wer **war** *heute zu Hause? — Hans, Christoph und Bernhard.*
Who *was* at home today?—Hans, Christoph, and Bernhard.

i.e. the German and English choice of number is identical in situations with *wer?*

111. Was für and Welch

(*a*) *was für?*—what kind of? is treated as a single indeclinable pronoun; the *für* has no effect on the case of the following noun:

Was für ein Mann ist er? In was für einem Haus wohnt er?
Was ist das für ein komischer Schlüssel?

(*b*) *was für, was für ein, welch* are used in exclamations:

Singular:

Was für ein schönes Haus! What a fine house!

or

Welch ein schönes Haus![1]

Plural:

Was für schöne Häuser!

Welch schöne Häuser!

Of these, *was für . . .!* is the more common.

---

[1] *Welch schönes Haus!* is a poetic usage.

Demonstrative pronouns

112. 'The one who', 'Those who'

The demonstrative pronoun followed by a relative pronoun is *der, die, das* or the plural *die* in the appropriate case (NB gen. plur. *derer*); or preferably *derjenige* (*denjenigen, desjenigen, demjenigen*), *diejenige* (&c.), *dasjenige* (&c.), or the plural *diejenigen* (&c.):

> *Die besten Ergebnisse haben diejenigen erzielt, die die andere Methode gewählt haben*—cf. p. 64.

> Similarly: . . . *wurden von denjenigen erzielt, die* . . .; . . . *hat derjenige erzielt, der* . . ., &c.

In general statements ('He who hesitates is lost', 'Those who work hardest do best', &c.) *wer* is used. The sense of the sentence is often reinforced by the inclusion of the demonstrative pronoun *der*:

> *Wer diese Erklärung nicht verstanden hat, soll es sofort sagen.* Anyone who has not understood this explanation is to say so at once.

> *Wer einmal in den Alpen war, der kann sie nie vergessen.*·

113. derselbe, der . . .; solche, die . . ., &c.

derselbe, der—the same one who, and *solche, die*—the kind who (which) are declined in the same way as *derjenige, der* and *alle, die* respectively:

> *Diejenigen, die den Einbruch verübt haben, sind dieselben, die den Portier erschlagen haben.* Those who committed the burglary are the ones who killed the doorman.

> *Was für Nägel sind das? — Das sind solche, die man in Beton schlagen kann.* What sort of nails are those?—The sort you can knock into concrete.

114. 'Former' and 'Latter'

The idea of 'the former' and 'the latter' is denoted by *dies-* and *jen-* with the appropriate ending for number, gender, and case:

> *Autofahrer und Fußgänger sind beide Verkehrsteilnehmer. Für diese gilt das gleiche wie für jene.* Motorists and pedestrians both use the roads. What applies to the latter applies to the former.

erster- and *letzter-* are also sometimes found, especially in the plural and in the singular neuter (e.g. *letztere, ersteres*). They are generally used without a definite article, except in the genitive.

115. selbst and selber

The demonstrative pronouns *selbst* and *selber* are invariable. *Selbst* is slightly preferable to *selber* in prose. They should be placed close to the noun or pronoun which they are intended to stress:

Ich habe es selbst geschrieben. I wrote it myself.
Ich selbst habe es geschrieben. I myself wrote it.

The difference in emphasis—such as it is—is the same in the two languages.

N.B. *selbst* is sometimes used adverbially before a noun with the sense of *sogar* (cf. 128). The following noun then carries the main stress of the phrase:

Seit langem war ich ohne Geld, selbst ohne Wohnung . . . [246]

ADVERBS

COMPARISON OF ADVERBS

116. Irregular comparison

Revision:

Positive	Comparative	Superlative
gut (wohl)	besser	am besten
gern(e)	lieber	am liebsten
sehr	mehr	am meisten
bald	eher	am ehesten

117. Superlative adverb ending -ens

bestens: *Ich möchte Ihnen bestens danken.* I should like to thank you most sincerely.
nächstens: *Er besucht uns nächstens.* He is visiting us in the near future.

Note also: *spätestens um sieben Uhr*; *frühestens am Dienstag*; *mindestens zwei Kilogramm*—at least two kilogrammes (referring to quantity); *wenigstens ich müßte das wissen!*—I at least (I at any rate) should know that! *Wir waren meistens zu Hause.*

DIFFICULT ADVERB USAGES

The following (118–32) are some of the adverbs which cause difficulty in translation and prose composition:

118. auch

(*a*) Position. *auch* should, as a general rule, be placed before what it refers to:

> *Auch Tante Tüttchen hatte nie anders gedacht,* . . . [248]
> *Ich habe telephoniert, und ich habe auch geschrieben.*
> *Sie wunderte sich, daß sie nicht auch mich gesehen hatte.* She was surprised that she had not seen me as well.

(*b*) *auch in the sense of* 'even' (cf. 128)

> *Auch jetzt ist es nicht zu spät.*
> *Auch die Armen haben ihre Rechte.*
> *Auch langsam fahren ist in dieser Stadt gefährlich.*

(*c*) Interrogative word + auch: *English*: . . . *ever*.

> *Was er auch sagen mag, ich werde ihm nicht glauben.*[1] Whatever he may say, I will not believe him.
> *Wohin er auch ging, sie war nicht zu sehen.*[1] Wherever he went she was not to be seen.
> Similarly: *wer . . . auch*; *wann . . . auch*; *wie . . . auch*, &c.

[1] In sentences introduced by a concessive clause, the normal main clause word-order is sometimes kept, even though the main clause does not begin the statement, for greater stress.

119. draußen, drinnen, &c.; außen, innen, &c.

draußen, drinnen, droben, &c., have always a demonstrative sense, although it is often only slightly felt:

> *Hier im Hause ist es schön warm; draußen schneit es.*—. . . outside (or: out there . . .).
> *Wo ist Ilse?* — *Dort drinnen.* Where is Ilse?—Inside (in there).

außen, innen, vorn(e), hinten, &c., denote position without demonstrative force:[1]

> *Der Schrank war sowohl innen wie auch außen gestrichen.* The cupboard was painted both inside and out.
> *Der Schüler ging nach vorne.* The pupil went to the front.
> *Er blieb hinten stehen.* He remained standing at the back.

[1] The demonstrative idea is sometimes given by the addition of *da* or *dort*: *da vorne*; *dort hinten*. The adverb *unten* does have a certain demonstrative sense in some contexts, e.g. *Bleib unten!*—Stay down there (down below, &c.).

120. eben, gerade, ausgerechnet

(a) *eben* and *gerade* are usually interchangeable in the meaning 'just':

> *Eben (gerade) dann kam er herein.* Just then he came in.
> *Wir waren gerade (eben) dabei, den Fernsehapparat einzuschalten.* We were just about to switch on the television.

(b) *gerade* and *ausgerechnet* are sometimes used in the sense '. . . of all (things, people, days, &c.)' . . . !:

> *Gerade (ausgerechnet) ihm mußte ich begegnen!* I had to go and bump into him, of all people!
> *Ausgerechnet (gerade) heute regnet es!* Today, of all days, it is raining!

121. eigentlich (see also Topic 9, p. 59)

eigentlich may be translated, according to context, by: really; actually; in actual fact; in its proper sense; originally, &c.:

> *Er hat eigentlich recht.* He is really (actually, in actual fact) right.
> *Dieses Wort ist eigentlich als Adverb zu verstehen.* This word is really (in its proper sense) to be understood as an adverb.

122. endlich and schließlich

(a) *schließlich*—finally, at the end, in the end; *endlich*—at last, after all this, in the end.

The difference between *schließlich* and *endlich* may be illustrated by the choice of word in the following context:

> Speaker, towards the end of a dull address: *Schließlich, meine Damen und Herren, . . .*
> Audience: *Endlich!*

(b) Both words can mean 'after all', 'when all's said and done', &c.:

> *Schließlich (or endlich) sollte sie wissen, daß . . .* After all, she should know . . .

123. erst, erst jetzt, eben erst

(a) 'only' in the sense 'not until' is rendered by *erst*:

> *Ich bin erst gestern angekommen.*
> *Erst am Freitag werden wir seine Antwort erhalten.*
> *Erst als sie hereinkam, erkannte er sie.*
> *Ich habe es eben erst (or erst jetzt) gesehen.* I have only just seen it.

(b) *erst* as a reinforcing adverb (cf. also **126** (b)):

> *Das brauche ich dir nicht erst zu sagen.* I don't need to tell you that, do I?
> *Dann ging es erst richtig los!* Then things really *did* get hot!

124. Position of nicht

The position of *nicht* sometimes causes difficulties. Compare the position of *nicht* in the following examples:

> *Ich tanze nicht.*
> *Ich tanze heute nicht.*
> *Ich habe heute nicht getanzt.*
> *Es wird heute nicht getanzt.*
> *Es wurde heute nach elf Uhr nicht mehr getanzt.*
>
> *Ich* { *werde* / *würde* / *will* } *nicht tanzen.*
> *will heute nicht tanzen.*
> *habe heute nicht tanzen wollen.*

Thus *nicht*, if it negates the *verb*, is placed near to the verb (in the case of verbs with a dependent part, before the participle or infinitive). An adverb may come between *nicht* and the verb. Where it is required to negate any other idea of the sentence, *nicht* is usually placed *before* that idea:

> *Nicht ich tanze, sondern meine Frau tanzt.* It is not I but my wife who dances.
> *Ich tanze nicht heute, sondern morgen.*
> *Es wird nicht im Saal, sondern auf der Terrasse getanzt.*

However, it is impossible to lay down a rule which will cover every instance. It is as well to observe the position of *nicht* wherever it seems unfamiliarly placed and to consider *why* it has that particular position in the sentence.

125. noch

The following more difficult senses in which *noch* occurs should be noted:

(a) *noch immer, immer noch; nur noch*:

> *Diese Gedichtsammlung ist alt, aber noch immer (immer noch) die beste.* This anthology of poems is an old one but still the best. (Strong stress.)
> *Wir haben nur noch zehn Tage Zeit.* We have only ten days left.
> *Das Kind begann nur noch lauter zu schreien.* The child only began to cry all the louder.

(b) *noch* + comparative (cf. also *nur noch*, (a) above):

Diese Aufgabe ist noch schwieriger, als ich gedacht hatte. This exercise is even more difficult than I had thought.

Heute wird die Sitzung noch länger dauern. The meeting will last even longer today.

(c) *noch* used to express an addition to what already exists (cf. (b)):

was noch? what else? *wer noch?* who else?

Das muß ich noch sagen: . . . There's something else I must say . . .

(d) *noch* used to express the idea that there is (was, will be, &c.) still time for something:

Bevor der Zug abfuhr, rief er mir noch Grüße zu. He called out goodbye to me again before the train started.

Similarly, to express 'not later than':

Noch heute werden wir die Antwort wissen.

126. schon

(a) *schon* used to express the idea that there is (was, will be, &c.) no delay (contrast with *erst*. See 123).

Wir müssen schon in zwei Tagen in London sein.

Kaum daß man am Urlaubsort angekommen ist, . . . da stürzt man sich schon . . . in die verheißene Gegend. [128]

(b) *schon* used to express the short length of time required, the easiness of the task:

Das werde ich dir schon erklären. I'll soon explain it to you.

Es wird schon gehen. I'll manage all right; it won't be too bad, &c.

(c) *schon* as a reinforcing particle:

Die Straße konnte von Personenwagen nicht befahren werden, von Lastwagen schon gar nicht (or *erst recht nicht*). The road was not usable by cars, let alone (i.e. 'and certainly not') by lorries.

127. 'much': viel or sehr?

viel is sometimes confused with *sehr*. *viel* expresses *quantity*; *sehr* expresses *the degree to which, the extent*. Thus:

Wir haben viel (zu viel) darüber gesprochen. We talked much (too much) about it.

Das ist eine vielgelesene Zeitung (i.e. it has *many* readers).

and

Das verwirrt mich zu sehr. That puzzles me too much.

Das schmerzt so sehr ! That hurts so much!

128. 'even': sogar,[1] nicht einmal; auch, auch nicht

sogar expresses that which is *even more* than what has been mentioned or implied; *nicht einmal* that which is *even less.* *auch* may be used instead of *sogar*, and *auch nicht* instead of *nicht einmal* (provided it does not lead to ambiguity: *auch nicht*, with a stress on *auch* means 'not . . . either', 'nor'):

> *Hast du Glück ! Du warst schon in Frankreich und Deutschland,*
> *sogar in Italien.*[2] *— Ich war nicht einmal*[3] *auf den Kanal-*
> *inseln.* You *are* lucky! You have already been to France and
> Germany, even to Italy.—I haven't even been to the
> Channel Islands.

[1] Cf. also *selbst*, 115.   [2] Or: *auch in Italien.*   [3] But not: *Ich war auch nicht auf den Kanalinseln*, which means: 'I have not been to the Channel Islands either.' The ambiguity does not arise in the extract from Kafka, p. 78: . . . *auch nicht der schwächste Lichtschein deutete das große Schloß an.*

129. sonst: otherwise, else, besides

> *Was hat er sonst gesagt ?*
> *Wen sollen wir sonst einladen ?*
> *Wir hatten sonst noch viele Fragen zu stellen.* We had many other
> questions to ask (i.e. in addition to those we had already
> asked).

130. wohl expressing probability

wohl is frequently used where English would use expressions such as 'I suppose', 'I should think', 'no doubt', 'must . . .', &c. (cf. also Topic 8, p. 55).

> *Das ist wohl möglich.* I suppose that is possible.
> *Er wird das Examen wohl bestanden haben.* He has no doubt
> passed the examination.

131. vielmehr, eher

vielmehr and *eher* correspond to English 'rather' in the sense of the sentence:

> *Das ist vielmehr (eher) Sache der Schule als des Staates.* That is
> a matter for the school rather than the state.

eher (or *mehr*: cf. 77) are used where an adjective follows:

Sie war eher mittelgroß als groß. She was of medium height rather than tall.

It is important not to confuse *vielmehr* and *viel mehr* (much more).

132. zwar (freilich, allerdings)

(*a*) *zwar* (and *freilich, allerdings*) are concessive adverbs. They may be translated by 'admittedly', 'it must be granted', 'indeed', &c.

(*b*) *zwar* . . ., *aber* . . . is a commonly found alternative to *obschon, obgleich, obwohl*:

> *Er ist zwar alt, aber noch sehr rüstig.* Although he is old he is still very agile.

> *Zwar sind die Preise nur um ein wenig gefallen, aber das ist schon etwas.* Although the prices have only dropped by a little, even that is something.

(*c*) *und zwar* corresponds to English 'namely', 'that is to say', 'to wit', &c.:

> *Wir werden noch zwei Gäste einladen, und zwar Herrn und Frau Meyer.*

CONJUNCTIONS

133. Provided a clear distinction is drawn between main and subordinate clauses, no great difficulties should arise in the use of the conjunctions. Note:

(*a*) Co-ordinating conjunctions sometimes link subordinate clauses:

> *Obschon es regnet* **und** *der Himmel bedeckt ist,* . . .

> *Wenn ich durch das Dorf ging* **oder** *im Gespräch mit einem Bekannten vor dem Wirtshaus stand,* . . .

(*b*) Double subordinations should, on principle, be avoided. Especially in spoken German, they lead to unnecessary complications of word-order. Thus:

> I think *that* *if* things had been different he would have been less fortunate

is better translated by:

> *Ich meine, wenn es anders gewesen wäre, so hätte er weniger Glück gehabt*

than by:

> *Ich meine, daß, wenn es anders gewesen wäre, er weniger Glück gehabt hätte.*

134. Co-ordinating conjunctions

Revision: The commonest co-ordinating conjunctions are:
und, aber, oder, denn, sondern; *allein* in the sense 'but' is comparatively rare.

Many co-ordinating conjunctions are in fact adverbs or adverbial phrases used with the force of conjunctions. The following more difficult conjunctions of this type should be known:

in addition, furthermore, moreover, &c.	*außerdem, überdies, ferner, zudem*
. . . now . . . now . . .[1]	*. . . bald . . . bald . . .*
. . . partly . . . partly . . .	*. . . teils . . . teils . . .*
. . . first . . . then . . .	*. . . erst . . . dann . . .*
. . . half . . . half . . .	*. . . halb . . . halb . . .*
otherwise	*sonst*
on the other hand[2]	*dagegen, hingegen*
rather[3]	*vielmehr*
the more, all the more	*desto, um so*[4]
consequently, as a result, hence, thus, so, &c.	*infolgedessen, daher, also, deshalb, deswegen, darum*
yet, nevertheless	*doch, dennoch*
for this purpose	*dazu*

[1] e.g. *Sie hatte in jedem Zimmer zu tun; bald war sie in der Küche, bald im Wohnzimmer, bald in den Schlafzimmern.*   [2] *Ich fuhr schon am Montag; dagegen konnte Lotte erst am Dienstag fahren.*   [3] e.g. *Ich halte es für falsch, all das Geld auszugeben; vielmehr sollten wir einen Teil davon behalten.*   [4] Cf. 78.

Subordinating conjunctions

135. The following list contains subordinating conjunctions which are often not well known:

whereas, whilst[1]	*während*
as soon as	*sobald*[2]
as often as	*sooft*
as long as	*solange*
in so far as	*sofern*
as far as	*soviel, soweit*[3]
except that	*nur daß*[4]
without	*ohne daß*[5]
hardly	*kaum daß*
instead of	*statt daß, anstatt daß*[6]

especially as	*zumal*
in the event of, if	*falls*[7]
even if	*wenngleich, wenn . . . auch*[8]

[1] In German, 'whereas' (*während*) must occur in the latter part of the sentence, e.g. *Ich trinke gern Tee, während Fritz Kaffee vorzieht.*   [2] The conjunctions *sobald, sooft, solange,* &c., are written as *one* word. The adverb phrases *so bald, so oft, so lange,* &c., are written as two words, e.g. *schreibe so bald wie möglich; ich habe es so oft gesehen,* &c.   [3] e.g. *soviel (soweit) ich weiß*—as far as I know.   [4] e.g. *Ich habe weiter keine Beschwerden, nur daß ich nicht lange stehen kann.*—I have nothing else wrong with me (lit. no other complaints, troubles) except that I cannot stand for long.   [5] e.g. *Ohne daß ich auch nur ein Wort gesagt hätte, reichte er mir die Hand.* Without my having said a word, he held out his hand to me. (See 50 for the use of the subjunctive here; and see 136 (*b*)).   [6] *statt (anstatt)* are usually followed by an infinitive construction. But see 136 (*b*).   [7] The rules for the use of indicative or subjunctive with *falls* are the same as those for *wenn*.
[8] Cf. 118 (*b*) and 128; e.g. *(Diese Feindseligkeit) hat ihn immer tief geschmerzt, wenn er diesem Gefühl auch nur selten Ausdruck verliehen hat.* [107]

136. Note also:

(*a*) *dadurch, daß* is sometimes used like *indem* to express the *means by which* (see also (*b*) below):

> *Dadurch, daß ich ihm bei seiner Arbeit half, konnte er ein besseres Zeugnis bekommen.* Through my helping him with his work, he was able to get a better report.

(*b*) *dadurch, daß . . ., als daß* ('than that', or 'for' after a negative or *zu* + adjective), *ohne daß, statt (anstatt) daß* **must** be used instead of *zu* + infinitive where the subject of the main clause is different from that of the subordinate clause:

> *Er wollte nichts anderes, als daß wir bei ihm bleiben sollten.*
> *Er war zu krank, als daß der Arzt ihn hätte retten können.*

See also (*a*) above, and 135 (5).

PREPOSITIONS

137. Less common prepositions governing the dative

ab—as from: *ab April*[1]
dank—thanks to: *Dank dieser Erbschaft kann er sich ein Haus kaufen.*
gemäß—in accordance with—*Der Verordnung gemäß*[2] *habe ich auf dem Parkplatz geparkt.*
nebst[3]—together with.
samt[3]—together with, attended by.

[1] N.B. *ab erstem April; ab zwölftem Januar.*   [2] Note the position. *Gemäß der Verordnung* is also possible, though less good style.   [3] Rarely found.

138. Less common prepositions governing the accusative

gen[1]—*gen Himmel*—towards heaven, skyward.
per[2]—*per Auto fahren*—to go by car.

[1] Obsolete. Cf. note 5 and its context, p. 130. [2] *per* is sometimes used to denote 'by means of', but is usually better replaced by another preposition.

139. Less common prepositions governing the genitive

By far the largest number of prepositions govern the genitive. Many belong to the sphere of official jargon (e.g. *aufgrund*—on the basis of, *betreffs*—with reference to, *zwecks*—with a view to) and are better avoided. The following list contains examples of a number of prepositions governing the genitive which should be known:

ausschließlich—excluding—*ausschließlich der Versandkosten*— excluding the postage.
einschließlich—including.
halber—for the sake of: *der Sicherheit halber*[1]
infolge[2]—as a result of: *infolge des Krieges*
kraft—by virtue of: *kraft meines Amtes erkläre ich* . . .
längs—alongside, along: *längs der Landstraße*
laut[3]—according to: . . . *eine Vorladung, laut welcher* . . . [74]
mittels[4]—by means of: *mittels eines Seils*—by means of a rope
oberhalb—(situated) above: *oberhalb des Wasserfalls*
unterhalb—(situated) below: *unterhalb des Dorfes*
unweit—not far from: *unweit des Bahnhofs*
zufolge[5]—in accordance with: *zufolge seines Wunsches*
zugunsten[5]—in favour of: *eine Entscheidung zugunsten dieser Partei*

[1] Note the position. [2] *infolge* can only refer to happenings, never to persons or things. [3] Followed by an uninflected noun in such phrases as: *laut Vertrag*—in accordance with contract; *laut Gesetz*—according to the law. [4] *durch* should be used instead of *mittels* except where the emphasis is to be placed on the *means used* to achieve a result. [5] *zufolge* and *zugunsten* often follow the noun. In this case they govern the dative: *seinem Wunsche zufolge*; *dieser Partei zugunsten*. This position is preferred where the phrase containing the preposition begins the sentence.

140. Use of prepositions in pairs

Prepositions are sometimes used in pairs grouped around the word to which they refer:

Er kam langsam **auf** *mich* **zu**. He came slowly towards me.
Gegen *das Meer* **hin** *wird die Landschaft öder*. Towards the sea the country-side becomes more barren.

Gegen *die Stadt* **zu** *geht die Straße bergauf.* Towards the town
the road goes uphill.

Vom *Fenster* **aus** *konnte ich gerade auf den Fluß sehen.* From
the window I could see directly on to the river.[1]

Es ist gut zehn Kilometer **von** *dort* **her.** It is a good ten kilometres from there (i.e. away, from there to here).

[1] *von . . . aus* is used to mean 'from' in the sense 'from the vantage point of'.

141. Repetition of the preposition

The preposition must be repeated in German:

(*a*) Where a reply is made to a question involving a preposition, e.g.

In welchem Lande wurde er geboren? — **In** *Rußland.*
Für wen hat sie gearbeitet? — **Für** *meinen Vater.*

(*b*) With phrases in apposition to another phrase involving a
preposition:

Er liebte sie in seiner Art, **in** *der Art eines tüchtigen und verständigen Mannes, der . . .* [95]

*Und man kann sagen, daß seine Größe in seiner fast promethei-
schen Einsamkeit liegt,* **in** *seiner Unfähigkeit, die ganzen
Ausmaße seines Charakters . . . anzupassen.* [107]

142. Use of bei

Of all the German prepositions, *bei* covers the widest range of
meanings. The following examples are taken from Part I :

Bei der Erkundung in etlichen Häusern . . . [42]
*Bei dem Gerumpel in seiner Nähe aber habe das Kind nur noch
lauter zu schreien begonnen.* [42]
Vorsicht beim Gebrauch der indirekten Rede! [45]
Bei diesem Gewackel sei kein Arbeiten. [56]
. . . ob der Klub bei solchen Schulden noch bestehen kann, . . . [61]
*Nun, wie wäre es vielleicht mit einer weiteren Anleihe bei der
Bank?* [61]
Bei der Gerichtsverhandlung erklärt der Bettler . . . [74]
*Es war ihm nämlich beim Vorbeischreiten gewesen, . . . als sei der
Fahrer auf das Steuer niedergesunken.* [77]

Any unfamiliar usage of *bei* should be carefully noted as it is
met. It is clear from the above examples that no one English
preposition will cover every usage of *bei*.

143. Use of von

The following uses of *von* should be noted:

(*a*) *von* in the sense 'from amongst':
Welches von diesen Büchern willst du haben?

(*b*) *von* used with compass directions:
östlich von Chicago [57]; *im Norden von England* (or: *im Norden Englands*).

(*c*) *von* in adjectival phrases:
ein Mann von Mut;
In ruhigen Zeiten ist das Tal von lieblicher Schönheit. [134]

(*d*) *von* used to show the relationship between two nouns:
Das Werk eines Verfassers von Kriminalromanen—the work of a writer of detective stories (but: *die Verfasser großer Kriminalromane*, where the genitive ending of the adjective clearly shows the relationship between the two nouns).

N.B. *von* must be used before a double genitive where the first genitive noun is not preceded by an article or adjective which would show the genitive inflexion:
die Geschichte von Deutschlands politischer Entwicklung—the history of Germany's political development (but: *die Geschichte* **der** *politischen Entwicklung Deutschlands*).

NUMBER AND QUANTITY

144. Forms of zwei, drei, vier, &c.

(*a*) *zu zweit, zu dritt, zu sechst*, &c., are used to mean 'the two of them', 'in a group of three', &c.
Sie gingen zu dritt die Landstraße entlang. The three of them walked along the road.

(*b*) *zu zweien, zu dreien*, &c., are used to mean 'two (&c.) at a time':
Die Mädchen gingen zu zweien über die Straße. The girls crossed the street two at a time (in pairs).

N.B. Cf. Topic 1, pp. 3–4, for the genitive forms *zweier, dreier*.

45. Forms of zwanzig, dreißig, &c.

(*a*) The invariable adjectives *zwanziger, dreißiger*, &c., are used with *Jahre* to refer to a decade of a century:
die dreißiger Jahre—the thirties (e.g. 1930's).

(*b*) The nouns *die Dreißiger, Vierziger,* &c., are variable; these, and the feminine singulars *die Dreißig, die Vierzig,* &c., refer to a person's age:

> *Er stand in den Dreißigern.* He was in his thirties.
> *Sie war etwa Mitte Zwanzig.* She was roughly in the middle twenties.

146. Dutzend, hundert, tausend, Million

Hundert and *tausend* may, as in English, be used as nouns:

> *Hunderte (Tausende) haben den Film gesehen.*
> *Mehrere Hunderte (Tausende) haben den Film gesehen.*
> *Hunderte (Tausende) und aber Hunderte (Tausende)*—hundreds (thousands) and hundreds (thousands).
> *Sie kamen zu Hunderten und Tausenden.* They came in hundreds and thousands.

If the nouns *Dutzende, Hunderte, Tausende,* or *Millionen* are followed by an adjective and noun, the adjective shows the genitive case, or *von* is introduced:

> *Dutzende*⎫
> *Hunderte*⎪ *klein er Fische* (or *von kleinen Fischen*) *schwammen*
> *Tausende*⎬   *im Wasser.*
> *Millionen*⎭

If no other adjective is present to show the case, *Dutzend, Hundert,* and *Tausend* take an adjectival inflexion, but with *Millionen, von* must be used:

> *Das Erdbeben hat den Tod Dutzend er (Hundert er, Tausend er) kleiner und großer Fische verursacht.* The earthquake caused the death of dozens (hundreds, thousands) of fish, both large and small.

but:

> *Das Erdbeben hat den Tod von Millionen kleiner und großer Fische verursacht.*

N.B. The decimal point is represented in German by the comma

7·42—*7,42* (*sieben Komma zweiundvierzig*).

The number of thousands (beginning with 10,000) must be followed by a small space:

> 10,000—*10 000*; 15,209—*15 209* (written: *zehntausend*; *fünfzehntausendzweihundertneun*).

Similarly with numbers involving millions (but here the space is always left between the thousands and hundreds):

10,005,567—*10 005 567* (written: *zehn Millionen fünftausend-fünfhundertsiebenundsechzig*).

147. Gender of numerals

Dutzend, Hundert, and *Tausend* are *neuter*.
Million, Milliarde (a thousand million) are *feminine*.
Other cardinal numbers are *feminine* (the gender is taken from the implied '*die Zahl . . .*'): *die Null, die Eins, die Zwei, die Zwanzig,* &c. (cf. 58 (*b*)).

148. Fractions

Fractions (except 'half'—*halb* used as an adjective, or *die Hälfte*) end in -*tel* (from *Teil*) and are *neuter*:

ein Drittel; *zwei Drittel*; *drei Viertel*, &c. See also 152 (*b*).

The adjective *halb* is declined:

die halbe Erde—half the earth; *in der halben Welt*—in half the world; *eines halben Apfels*, &c.;

but: one and a half—*anderthalb* or *eineinhalb*; *zweieinhalb, dreieinhalb*, &c., are *not* declined:

anderthalb Pfund; *fünfeinhalb Kilometer*; *bis zu siebeneinhalb Meilen*, &c.

'Three-quarters' is treated as one unit:

Dreiviertel der Besucher waren Deutsche.
in einer Dreiviertelstunde or *in (einer) dreiviertel Stunde* (but: *in einer Viertelstunde*).

149. 'each'

(*a*) 'Each', 'at a time', is *je* (note the position):

Sie gingen je dreimal hin. Each of them went three times.
Wir haben je zwei Äpfel. We have two apples each.
Je zwei von ihnen sangen das Lied. Two of them at a time sang the song.

(*b*) 'Each' referring to things in a purchasing context, is *das Stück* or *pro Stück*:

Die Postkarten kosten zwanzig Pfennig das (or *pro*) *Stück.*
das Stück may denote any unit, e.g. packet, bar, tablet, &c.:
Was kostet das Stück? What do they cost a packet (a bar, a tablet, &c.)? *Geben Sie mir bitte zwei Stück* (see 151(*b*)).

150. Adjectives with the suffix -lei

The following, like *allerlei*, are invariable:

einerlei—of one kind: *Hemden von einerlei (gleicher)*[1] *Farbe.*
das ist mir einerlei—it's all the same to me.
zweierlei, dreierlei, &c.: *Wir haben dreierlei Sorten probiert.*

Many other adjectives may be formed with *-lei*, e.g.

hunderterlei—hundreds of kinds of; *tausenderlei*; and *keinerlei, mancherlei, vielerlei*, &c.

> [1] The adjective *gleich* should be preferred to *einerlei*.

151. Plural of measures of quantity and currency units

(a) Those ending in *-e* are expressed in the plural:
   drei Flaschen Wein; *vier Tonnen Kohle*; *acht Tassen Kaffee*;

(b) those ending in a consonant are expressed in the singular:
   acht Pfund Fleisch; *zwei Faß Bier* (barrels); *zehn Zoll* (inches);
   vier Fuß; *zwanzig Mark*; *dreißig Pfennig*; *zwei (englische)
   Pfund (£2)*; *fünfzehn Dollar*; N.B. *zehn Yard* or *Yards*.

(c) The plural of foreign currency units is sometimes given a
   German form, sometimes left in its foreign form: *1000 Lire*,
   but *1000 Peseten*. If in doubt, check in the dictionary.

152. Inflexion of expressions of quantity in genitive and dative

(a) *Genitive:*

$$\text{der Preis} \begin{cases} \textit{eines Glases Bier} \\ \textit{eines Pfundes Fleisch} \\ \textit{einer Tonne Kohle} \end{cases} \text{or} \begin{cases} \textit{eines Glas Biers} \\ \textit{eines Pfund Fleisches} \end{cases}$$

(b) *Dative:*

mit drei Liter or *Litern*—with three litres;
von vier Fünftel or *Fünfteln des Gewichts*—of four-fifths of the
   weight;

but where the measure of quantity is qualified by a preceding
article or adjective it takes the normal dative inflexion:

mit den drei Litern Benzin;
von den vier Fünfteln des Gewichts;

and where there is no preceding qualification, but the measure of quantity is followed by another noun, the dative inflexion is generally not used:

mit drei Liter Benzin;
von vier Fünftel (sometimes, *Fünfteln*, as above) *des Gewichts.*

153. The adjective in measures of quantity

The inflexions of adjectives (and the use of *mit*) in the following instances should be noted.

N.B. The genitive of the adjective and following noun is rare nowadays in, for example, 'a glass of clear water', except where the phrase occurs after a preposition governing the dative (cf. (*b*) below). If the container itself needs to be expressed in the genitive (cf. (*c*) below), *mit* must be introduced before the following adjective:

(*a*) *ein Glas klares Wasser* (subject or direct object of the sentence);

(*b*) *mit einem Glas klaren Wassers* (following a preposition governing the dative);

(*c*) *eines Glases mit klarem Wasser* (container—*Glas*—in the genitive).

154. voll and voller: 'full of'

voll and the invariable *voller* used in the sense 'full of' do not normally require *von*. The choice of *voll* or *voller* is largely a question of usage or feeling in the particular context. *voll*, however, is *always correct*.

ein Haus voll (voller) Gäste;
ein Eimer voll Wasser.

Where *voll*, *voller* are followed by an adjective, the adjective and its noun must usually be expressed in the genitive:

ein Haus voll (voller) junger Gäste; [1]
ein Eimer voll kalten Wassers. [2]

Where it is required to stress the idea that the container is 'filled right up' *voll* is used:

ein Korb voll Eier;
ein Glas voll Wein.

---

[1] *voller junger Gäste* is less acceptable because of the doubling of the -*er* ending.
[2] The strong genitive ending (-*s*) with nouns following *voll* is often avoided, however, and the accusative used instead: *ein Eimer voll kaltes Wasser.*

PART III

PROSE PASSAGES AND POEMS FOR
TRANSLATION

The Objects of Travel

Im achtzehnten Jahrhundert gab es zwei Reisen, von denen der
Weltmann mindestens eine gemacht haben mußte: die „Kleine
Tour" und die „Große Tour" durch Europa. Die kleine Tour
berührte Wien und Paris, die große Tour dazu auch noch Rom
und London. Europa wurde als Ganzes gesehen, und die Reise
sollte einem den anschaulichen Begriff dieses Ganzen vermitteln.
Doch mit der Französischen Revolution und der Romantik
wendete sich der Sinn des Reisens in das genaue Gegenteil, denn
nun reiste man „ins Blaue", in die Exotik, zu den einsamen
Wasserfällen ... kurz, man reiste, um aus dem geordneten Ganzen
irgendwohin auszubrechen. In der großen Tour wollte man sein
Gefühl der Gemeinsamkeit bestärken, in der romantischen Reise
dagegen sein Gefühl der Einsamkeit, daß man etwas Besonderes
war. Ob klassisch, ob romantisch — immer reiste man also in
der eigenen Seele umher: in Landstrichen, die von der Phantasie
sorgfältig bearbeitet worden waren. Reisen war ein Versuch, die
Welt in des Menschen Brust mit der großen Welt da draußen
irgendwie in Einklang zu bringen. In jeder Reise reist man
zu etwas hin und von etwas weg; jede Reise ist zugleich eine
Eroberung und eine Flucht. Die klassische Reise betont die Eroberung, die romantische die Flucht. Das sind die beiden ewigen
Typen des Reisens, die es immer geben wird.

SIGISMUND VON RADECKI: *Vom Reisen und vom Zuhause*

Redstarts

Vom Fenster aus kann ich sehen, wie drüben auf dem Dachgiebel
ein schwarzer Vogel hüpft. Jetzt knickst er, macht einen Bück-
ling, und der rote Schwanz zittert. Der kleine Vogelleib drückt
sich nach unten und schnellt in die Ausgangsstellung zurück.

Nun springt der Hausrotschwanz über zwei, drei Dachziegel, schnurrt empor, fliegt um den Schornstein, rüttelt in der Luft und hascht eine Spinne vom Stein. Mit einem eleganten Schwung landet er wieder auf dem First. Es ist das rußschwarze Männchen. Das bräunlichgraue Weibchen holt gerade auf der anderen Seite des Giebels eine Fliege aus der Luft. Es hat eine Pause beim Brüten gemacht. Seit zehn Tagen sitzt es auf seinem Nest in einem Loch unter dem Dachgesims. In drei Tagen werden die Jungen aus den Eiern schlüpfen. Es mögen fünf oder sechs sein. Dann werden die beiden Vogeleltern noch viel mehr Käferchen, Motten und Asseln fangen müssen als jetzt. Denn die Jungen müssen von früh bis spät gefüttert werden, damit sie in zwei Wochen so groß wie die Alten werden und ausfliegen können.

Die Hausrotschwänzchen sind Stadt- und Dorfbewohner. Sie waren es nicht immer. Ursprünglich waren sie Gebirgsvögel. Aber die Steinbauten, die der Mensch errichtet, sind ihnen ebenso lieb wie die natürlichen Felswände. Seit etwa hundertsechzig Jahren singen die Hausrotschwänze ihr Lied in den Städten. Schon in der Frühe des Morgens schallen die gepreßten Töne vom First, mehr ein Geräusper als eine Musik. Erst am Schluß folgen ein paar flinke, helle Pfiffe. Zuweilen bringt es ein Hausrotschwanz im Pfeifen auch weiter, so daß sich das Lied ganz hübsch und weniger zischend anhört. Es ist ein Laut, wie wenn der Sturmwind um die Gipfel fetzt.

RICHARD GERLACH: 'Rotschwänzchen' (*Rheinischer Merkur*)

Over the Atlantic

Während das Flugzeug langsam Höhe gewinnt und die Besatzung vorne in der Kanzel sich erfrischt, sitzt der Navigator über seiner Karte, trägt auf Formularen Werte ein, dreht an einem Rechenschieber, prüft nach, ob seine Geräte in Ordnung sind und ob die Navigationshilfen auf dem Festland gut empfangen werden können. Man könnte sich vorstellen, daß dieser junge Mann nachts etwas Besseres zu tun wüßte als auf einer großen Karte Linien zu zeichnen, auf einen Zettel für Laien unverständliche Zahlen aufzuschreiben und dann zu behaupten, da und da müsse jetzt das Flugzeug stehen. Es ließe sich denken, daß er wissenschaftlicher Assistent bei einem Professor sein könnte, aber dazu hat er wohl keine Lust. Ob er Gedichte schreibt, war in dieser Flugnacht nicht zu erfahren. Hier hatte er keine Zeit dazu. Denn er hatte dem Kapitän zu melden, wann 20 Grad West überflogen

werden. Ihm ist es anvertraut, ständig den Standort des Flug-
zeuges und den Kurs, der eingehalten werden muß, zu berechnen.
Eine komplizierte Apparatur sorgt zwar dafür, daß das Flugzeug
seinen Kurs genau hält — der Pilot braucht die Steuer nicht
selbst zu betätigen —, aber welcher Kurs zu fliegen ist, das kann
hier über dem Atlantik nur von der Besatzung entschieden
werden. Es gibt keine geheimnisvollen Geräte, die das Flugzeug
automatisch auf gerader Linie über den Atlantik führen können.
Es gibt keine Radarstation, bei der man ständig den Standort
erfragen könnte; es gibt kein Instrument, das den Standort
automatisch anzeigt. Nur wenn das Flugzeug in den Radar-
bereich eines Wetterschiffes kommt, kann von diesem der Standort kontrolliert werden.   WILHELM SEUSS: 'Nachtflug über den Atlantik'
(*Frankfurter Allgemeine Zeitung*)

A Failure

Es war in anderen Zeiten, und ich verschweige den Namen, den
ich trug. Er ist nicht wert, daß er sich in der Überlieferung
erhält.
  Ich war unglücklich, zugrunde gerichtet an Leib und Seele
durch eigene Schuld. Die Eltern hatten an meiner Erziehung
nicht gespart. Ich hatte hohe Schulen absolviert, auch hatte es
an Mitteln für meine Reisen und Studien nicht gefehlt. Doch
war ich gescheitert, heruntergekommen durch Verschwendung,
Laster und Hang zum Müßiggang. Seit langem war ich ohne
Geld, selbst ohne Wohnung, und meine Bekannten, nachdem sie
müde geworden, mir zu helfen, mieden mich. Auch suchte ich
sie nicht mehr auf, denn ein Gefühl des Hasses gegen die Menschen und die Gesellschaft zerfraß mich ganz und gar. Ich
fühlte mich nur an den Zufluchtsorten der Ausgestoßenen und
der Verworfenen wohl. Der Mittel beraubt, den teuren und
auserwählten Lastern noch zu frönen, mußte ich mich mit
Ausschweifungen begnügen, die billig und häßlich sind — dem
rohen Trunke, der Gesellschaft von Dirnen, wie sie in den
Elendsvierteln hausen, und vor allem dem Glücksspiel in den
Spelunken der großen Stadt.   ERNST JÜNGER: 'Ortners Erzählung'
(from *Heliopolis*)

An Argument with the Sentry[1]

„Es geht nicht", sagte der Posten mürrisch.
„Warum?" fragte ich.
„Weil's verboten ist."
„Warum ist's verboten?"

„Weil's verboten ist, Mensch, es ist für Patienten verboten, 'rauszugehen."

„Ich", sagte ich stolz, „ich bin doch verwundet."

Der Posten blickte mich verächtlich an: „Du bist wohl 's erste Mal verwundet, sonst wüßtest du, daß Verwundete auch Patienten sind, na geh schon jetzt."

Aber ich konnte es nicht einsehen.

„Versteh mich doch", sagte ich, „ich will ja nur Kuchen kaufen von dem Mädchen da."

Ich zeigte nach draußen, wo ein hübsches kleines Russenmädchen im Schneegestöber stand und Kuchen feilhielt.

„Mach, daß du 'reinkommst!"

Der Schnee fiel leise in die riesigen Pfützen auf dem schwarzen Schulhof, das Mädchen stand da, geduldig, und rief leise immer wieder: „Chuchen² . . . Chuchen . . ."

„Mensch", sagte ich zu dem Posten, „mir läuft's Wasser im Munde zusammen, dann laß doch das Kind eben 'reinkommen."

„Es ist verboten, Zivilisten 'reinzulassen."

„Mensch", sagte ich, „das Kind ist doch ein Kind."

Er blickte mich wieder verächtlich an. „Kinder sind wohl keine Zivilisten, was?"

Es war zum Verzweifeln, die leere, dunkle Straße war von Schneestaub eingehüllt, und das Kind stand ganz allein da und rief immer wieder: „Chuchen . . ." obwohl niemand vorbeikam.

Ich wollte einfach 'rausgehen, aber der Posten packte mich schnell am Ärmel und wurde wütend: „Mensch", schrie er, „hau jetzt ab, sonst hol' ich den Feldwebel."

„Du bist ein Rindvieh", sagte ich zornig.

„Ja", sagte der Posten befriedigt, „wenn man noch 'ne Dienstauffassung hat, ist man bei euch ein Rindvieh."

HEINRICH BÖLL: Auch Kinder sind Zivilisten

¹ The setting of the story is a German military hospital on the Russian front in the last war.   ² *Chuĉhen*—i.e. 'khakes', to represent the Russian guttural sound.

On an Italian Beach

Das Meer ist warm, aber es geht schon ein frischer Wind, man sucht die Sonne, wenn man geschwommen ist. Auch der Sand, wenn man sich eingraben möchte, erinnert an Herbst; er bleibt an der Haut, kühl und feucht, und die Luft ist so, daß man plötzlich, wenn man mit geschlossenen Augen liegt, an unsere braunen und roten Wälder denkt. Bereits sind sie dabei, die

bunten Kabinen abzubrechen, und die Barken sind auf den Sand
gezogen. Jeder Tag kann der letzte sein. Nur zwei fremde
Mädchen sind noch da. Ich weiß nicht einmal, welche Sprache
sie reden. So mächtig lärmt das Meer, wenn es seine Wogen mit
rollendem Donner auf den Strand wirft. Stundenlang schaue ich
auf ihr zischelndes Verkräuseln,[1] jedesmal spiegelt der Sand,
blinkend vor Nässe, die langsam wie ein Löschblatt vermattet,
und wieder bleiben die leeren Muscheln zurück, meistens andere,
sie sickern in den Sand, es bilden sich die kleinen Grübchen, bis
die nächste Woge kommt, sich aufbäumt und höhlt, so daß die
Sonne sie durchleuchtet, und mit gischtender Krone zusammen-
bricht, stampfend, klatschend, kichernd. Und draußen liegt noch
ein ganzes Meer voll solcher Wogen, die unter der Sonne tanzen.
Einmal kriecht ein schwarzer Frachter über den Horizont; seinen
Rauch sieht man einen halben Morgen lang.

MAX FRISCH: *Tagebuch*

[1] (*. . . schaue ich auf*) *ihr zischelndes Verkräuseln*—(watch them) unfurl, hissing
and dwindling. Cf. *sich kräuseln*—to curl.

The Comfort of a Home

Auch Tante Tüttchen hatte nie anders gedacht, als daß dieses
Haus Grundlage und Gesetz ihres Lebens sei. Es hatte ihr ganzes
Dasein vom Tage ihrer Geburt an umhegt und getragen. Es war
das Dauernde und Bestehende, während Menschen fortgehen
konnten oder starben. Jener junge Hauslehrer zum Beispiel war
fortgegangen, die Schwester hatte geheiratet, und die Eltern
waren gestorben. Das Haus aber war stehengeblieben, und man
hatte mit allem Kummer ins stille Giebelzimmer zurückkehren
dürfen. Man konnte die breite Kalksteintreppe unter dem
Säulengiebel immer wieder hinaufsteigen, so schwer das Herz
vielleicht auch war, man konnte in Mutters Boudoir flüchten oder
sich im Giebelzimmer aufs Bett werfen und die Tränen weinen,
die vor den Menschen verborgen bleiben mußten. — Man konnte
am Flügel im Saal der Freude freien Lauf lassen, wenn der Flieder
unter den Fenstern so überschön duftete, und man konnte über
die Kalksteinstufen auch wieder hinausgehen, wenn man des
bergenden Daches nicht mehr bedurfte. Das alles konnte man,
— der bewegliche, flüchtige Mensch, der man war. Das Haus
stand indessen und wartete, und umfing und entließ und war da,
wenn man zurückkehrte.

ELSE HUECK-DEHIO: *Tante Tüttchen*

The Discovery of Atomic Fission

Vielfach stellt man sich die Atomphysik als eine Wissenschaft vor, die jahrzehntelang fieberhaft nach dem Schlüssel zur technischen Verwertung der Energie in den Atomen gesucht hätte, bis sie ihn endlich in der Uranspaltung fand. Nichts kann falscher sein. Die Uranspaltung war eine ungesuchte, unerwartete, rein wissenschaftliche Entdeckung. Ich glaube auch, daß nur Menschen, denen es nicht um die Anwendung ging, den Weg zur Atomenergie finden konnten. Ganz neue Zusammenhänge entdeckt nicht das Auge, das auf ein Werkstück[1] gebeugt ist, sondern das Auge, das in Muße den Horizont absucht.

Hahn und Straßmann[2] veröffentlichten ihre Entdeckung im Januar 1939. Veröffentlichung gilt in der Wissenschaft als Pflicht; sie bedeutet, daß man seine Ansichten der Kontrolle der Kollegen unterwirft. *Nach* der Veröffentlichung wurde mehreren Forschern auf der Welt gleichzeitig die technische Anwendbarkeit klar. Mit einem Schlag wußten im März 1939 vielleicht 200 Wissenschaftler in allen großen Ländern, daß nun wahrscheinlich Atombomben möglich sein würden, aber auch von Atomkraft getriebene Maschinen. Was sollten sie tun?

Im engen Kreis wurde bei uns in Deutschland dasselbe diskutiert, wie in Amerika: Ob Geheimhaltung die Menschheit noch vor diesen Bomben schützen könne. Tatsächlich war es schon zu spät. Vielleicht wäre es nicht zu spät gewesen, wenn eine weltweite und ausnahmslose Verständigung der Physiker zustande gekommen wäre. Zu einem Schritt von solcher politischer Tragweite waren wir nicht vorbereitet.

C. F. VON WEIZSÄCKER: 'Die Verantwortung der Wissenschaft im Atomzeitalter' (Zwei Vorträge. Kleine Vandenhoeck-Reihe, Band 42)

[1] a job on the workbench.   [2] Hahn and Straßmann: German chemists, famous for their work in nuclear chemistry.

Evening in the Mountains

Sie hatten die unregelmäßig bebaute, der Eisenbahn gleichlaufende Straße ein Stück in der Richtung der Talachse verfolgt, hatten dann nach links hin das schmale Geleise gekreuzt, einen Wasserlauf überquert und trotteten nun auf sanft ansteigendem Fahrweg bewaldeten Hängen entgegen, dorthin, wo auf niedrig vorspringendem Wiesenplateau, die Front südwestlich gewandt, ein langgestrecktes Gebäude mit Kuppelturm, das vor lauter

Balkonlogen von weitem löcherig und porös wirkte wie ein Schwamm, soeben die ersten Lichter aufsteckte. Es dämmerte rasch. Ein leichtes Abendrot, das eine Weile den gleichmäßig bedeckten Himmel belebt hatte, war schon verblichen, und jener farblose, entseelte und traurige Übergangszustand herrschte in der Natur, der dem vollen Einbruch der Nacht unmittelbar vorangeht. Das besiedelte Tal, lang hingestreckt und etwas gewunden, beleuchtete sich nun überall, auf dem Grunde sowohl wie da und dort an den beiderseitigen Lehnen — an der rechten zumal, die auslud, und an der Baulichkeiten terrassenförmig aufstiegen. Links liefen Pfade die Wiesenhänge hinan und verloren sich in der stumpfen Schwärze der Nadelwälder. Die entfernteren Bergkulissen, hinten am Ausgang, gegen den das Tal sich verjüngte, zeigten ein nüchternes Schieferblau. Da ein Wind sich aufgemacht hatte, wurde die Abendkühle empfindlich.

THOMAS MANN: *Der Zauberberg*

A Boy in a Monastery School

Zwei Menschen im Kloster gab es, zu denen Goldmund sein Herz hingezogen fühlte, die ihm gefielen, die seine Gedanken beschäftigten, für die er Bewunderung, Liebe und Ehrfurcht fühlte: den Abt Daniel und den Lehrgehilfen Narziß. Den Abt war er geneigt für einen Heiligen zu halten, seine Einfalt und Güte, sein klarer, sorglicher Blick, seine Art, das Befehlen und Regieren demütig als einen Dienst zu vollziehen, seine guten, stillen Gebärden, das alles zog ihn gewaltig an. Am liebsten wäre er der persönliche Diener dieses Frommen geworden, wäre immer gehorchend und dienend um ihn gewesen, hätte all seinen knabenhaften Drang nach Devotion und Hingabe ihm als beständiges Opfer dargebracht und ein reines, edles, heiligmäßiges Leben von ihm gelernt. Denn Goldmund war gesinnt, nicht nur die Klosterschule zu absolvieren, sondern womöglich ganz und für immer im Kloster zu bleiben und sein Leben Gott zu weihen; so war es sein Wille, so war es seines Vaters Wunsch und Gebot, und so war es wohl von Gott selbst bestimmt und gefordert. Niemand schien es dem schönen, strahlenden Knaben anzusehen, und doch lag eine Bürde auf ihm, eine Bürde der Herkunft, eine geheime Bestimmung zu Sühne und Opfer. Auch der Abt sah es nicht, obwohl Goldmunds Vater einige Andeutungen gemacht und deutlich den Wunsch geäußert hatte, sein Sohn möge für immer hier im Kloster bleiben. Irgendein geheimer Makel schien an der Geburt Goldmunds zu haften, irgend etwas

Verschwiegenes schien Sühne zu fordern. Aber der Vater hatte dem Abt nur wenig gefallen, er hatte seinen Worten und seinem ganzen etwas wichtigtuerischen Wesen höfliche Kühle entgegengestellt und seinen Andeutungen keine große Bedeutung eingeräumt.

HERMANN HESSE: *Narziß und Goldmund*

Germany's Role in European Politics after 1945

Es schien nach der totalen Niederlage ausgeschlossen, daß Deutschland im nächsten Menschenalter überhaupt eine politische Rolle spielen werde. Die Alliierten rechneten damit, daß Deutschland für ein halbes Jahrhundert bloßes Verwaltungsgebiet der Sieger bleiben werde. Wie die Dinge 1945 lagen, hätte das bedeutet, daß Deutschland über kurz oder lang bolschewisiert und eine Kolonie der Sowjets geworden wäre.

Der russische Diktator war klüger und realistischer als Hitler. Aber auch Stalin überspannte den Bogen. Der Versuch, Griechenland durch einen Bürgerkrieg zu bolschewisieren, die tatsächliche Bolschewisierung Chinas, die Umwandlung der volksdemokratischen Tschecho-Slowakei in einen rein kommunistischen Staat, die Sprengung des interalliierten Kontrollrates in Deutschland, die Blockade Berlins, endlich aber im Jahre 1950 der Überfall auf den nichtkommunistischen Teil von Korea veränderten in kürzester Zeit die weltpolitische Lage. Amerika entschloß sich, den Vormarsch des Kommunismus aufzuhalten. Die Truman-Doktrin bedeutete eine Wende, auf die früher oder später eine Änderung der westlichen Politik gegenüber Deutschland folgen mußte. Hatte man zunächst gemeint, die Weltgeschichte werde fortan ohne Deutschland gemacht werden, so bemühte man sich nun, Deutschland wieder aufzubauen und es zu einem wirtschaftlichen und politischen Faktor in der westlichen Politik, zu einem militärischen in der westlichen Verteidigung zu machen.

EMIL FRANZEL: *Von Bismarck zu Adenauer*

A Concert in the Park

Das Konzert im Volksgarten begann um fünf Uhr nachmittags. Es war Frühling, die Amseln flöteten noch in den Sträuchern und auf den Beeten. Die Militärkapelle saß hinter dem eisernen, an den Spitzen vergoldeten Gitter, das die Terrasse des Restaurants von der Allee des Gartens trennte und also die zahlenden und

sitzenden Gäste von den unbemittelten Zuhörern. Unter ihnen
befanden sich viele junge Mädchen. Sie waren der Musik hingegeben. Aber die Musik bedeutete an jenen Abenden mehr als
Musik, nämlich: eine Stimme der Natur und des Frühlings. Die
Blätter überwölbten die schmetternde Wehmut der Trompeten
— und ein Wind, der kam und ging, schien für kurze Weilen
die ganze Kapelle samt allen Geräuschen auf der Terrasse in
entlegene Gebiete zu entführen, aus denen sie mehr geahnt
als vernommen wurden. Gleichzeitig hörte man die langsam
knirschenden Schritte der Fußgänger in der Allee. Aus ihrem
gemächlichen Tempo klang das Behagen wider, das die Musik
den Ohren bescherte. Wenn die Instrumente laut wurden, die
Trommeln zu wirbeln begannen oder gar die Pauken zu dröhnen,
so war es, als rauschten auch die Bäume stärker und als hätten
die heftigen Arme des Herrn Kapellmeisters nicht nur den
Musikern zu gebieten, sondern auch den Blättern. Wenn aber
plötzlich ein Flötensolo den Sturm unterbrach, so klang es in
diesem Garten nicht wie die Stimme eines Instruments, sondern
wie eine Pause, die singt. Dann fielen auch die Vögel wieder
ein — als hätte der Komponist an dieser Stelle Amseln vorgesehen. Der Duft der Kastanien war so stark, daß er selbst die
süßesten Melodien überwehte und daß er dem Gesicht ent-
gegenschlug wie ein Bruder des Windes . . .

JOSEPH ROTH: *Panoptikum*

The Insects' Compass

Wenn wir nachts in einer fremden Gegend angekommen sind
und am Morgen zum erstenmal ausgehen, schauen wir uns gut
um, damit wir wieder heimfinden. Wir suchen uns das Bild des
Hauses einzuprägen, in dem wir Unterkunft gefunden haben,
vielleicht auch eine Baumkrone in seiner Nachbarschaft, einen
Kirchturm oder andere Wegmarken. Bienen machen es ebenso,
wenn sie ihre Wohnung zum erstenmal verlassen. Sie merken
sich zu ihrer Orientierung das Aussehen des Bienenstocks und
auffällige Landmarken in seiner Umgebung.

Bei längerem Marsch in einer unbekannten Landschaft be-
nützen wir den Kompaß, um die gerade Richtung einzuhalten.
Insekten auch! Sie gebrauchen den Kompaß der alten Seefahrer
und Naturvölker: sie steuern nach der Sonne. Daß es bei Ameisen
so etwas gibt, weiß man schon seit fast 50 Jahren. Wenn eine
Ameise ihr Nest verläßt, um einen Erkundungsspaziergang zu
machen, so kann sie sich in einem unübersichtlichen oder an

Wegmarken armen Gelände die geradlinige Fortbewegung sichern, indem sie auf die Stellung der Sonne achtet und den gleichen Winkel zu ihr beibehält. Ein eklatanter Beweis für diese Tatsache wurde durch folgendes Experiment geliefert: man schirmte den wandernden Ameisen die Sonne ab und zeigte sie ihnen von der entgegengesetzten Seite im Spiegel. Da machten sie sofort kehrt und setzten ihren Weg in spiegelbildlich falscher Richtung[1] fort. Läßt man sie ungestört, so stellen sie sich, sobald sie weit genug gelaufen sind, von sich aus[2] auf den spiegelbildlichen Sonnenstand um[3] und finden so zum Nest zurück. Für Bienen ist das gleiche Verhalten nachgewiesen.

PROF. DR. KARL RITTER VON FRISCH: 'Die Bienen und ihr Himmelskompaß' (*Rheinischer Merkur*)

[1] in the wrong direction as given by the mirror image.   [2] *von sich aus*—of their own accord.   [3] *sich auf den spiegelbildlichen Sonnenstand umstellen*—to change to the mirror-image bearing of the sun.

Plans for an Autobiographical Story

Meyer hat seine Jugendzeit nicht autobiographisch geschildert, obwohl es ihm des öftern — auch von seiner Schwester — nahegelegt wurde. In seinem Alter allerdings hat er während eines Aufenthaltes auf Schloß Steinegg (1891) den Entschluß gefaßt, einmal etwas „Modernes" zu gestalten und hiezu[1] Erinnerungen an seine Kindheit zu benutzen. „Mich gelüstet, einmal eine einfache Geschichte aus unserer Jugendzeit zu schreiben", äußerte er sich zu seiner Schwester. „Der Held wird der Sprößling eines unserer zur Reformationszeit ins alte Zürich übergesiedelten Geschlechter.[2] Er ist der Sohn eines ruhigen und ehrenwerten Hauses. Da beschreibe ich meine eigene Knabenzeit. Meine Stube im grünen Seidenhof;[3] weißt du noch? Die Erinnerungen aus der Knabenzeit, meine damaligen stillen Kämpfe und Erlebnisse wären mein eigentlicher Gegenstand. Bei der Verarbeitung dieses Stoffes möchte ich das Novellistische[4] auf das Einfachste, Unentbehrlichste beschränken — ein paar leichte Züge." Die Erzählung sollte ein Gewissensproblem behandeln. Über Anfänge hinaus, die aber nicht die geplanten Schilderungen aus der Kinderzeit bringen, ist sie nicht gediehen.

HELENE V. LERBER: *Conrad Ferdinand Meyer*

[1] *hiezu = hierzu.*   [2] patrician families.   [3] Do not translate. Name of part of a house which was formerly owned by silk merchants.   [4] 'the *Novelle* elements' (i.e. extreme concentration on certain unusual events affecting the main character).

In Prison

Die Tür ging hinter mir zu. Das hat man wohl öfter, daß eine Tür hinter einem zugemacht wird — auch daß sie abgeschlossen wird, kann man sich vorstellen. Haustüren zum Beispiel werden abgeschlossen, und man ist dann entweder drinnen oder draußen. Auch Haustüren haben etwas so Endgültiges, Abschließendes, Auslieferndes. Und nun ist die Tür hinter mir zugeschoben, ja, geschoben, denn es ist eine unwahrscheinlich dicke Tür, die man nicht zuschlagen kann. Eine häßliche Tür mit der Nummer 432. Das ist das Besondere an dieser Tür, daß sie eine Nummer hat und mit Eisenblech beschlagen ist — das macht sie so stolz und unnahbar; denn sie läßt sich auf nichts ein, und die inbrünstigen Gebete rühren sie nicht.

Und nun hat man mich mit dem Wesen allein gelassen, nein, nicht nur allein gelassen, zusammen eingesperrt hat man mich mit diesem Wesen, vor dem ich am meisten Angst habe: Mit mir selbst.

Weißt du, wie das ist, wenn du dir selbst überlassen wirst, wenn du mit dir allein gelassen bist, dir selbst ausgeliefert bist? Ich kann nicht sagen, daß es unbedingt furchtbar ist, aber es ist eines der tollsten Abenteuer, die wir auf dieser Welt haben können: Sich selbst zu begegnen. So begegnen wie hier in der Zelle 432: nackt, hilflos, konzentriert auf nichts als auf sich selbst, ohne Attribut und Ablenkung und ohne die Möglichkeit einer Tat. Und das ist das Entwürdigendste: Ganz ohne die Möglichkeit zu einer Tat zu sein. Keine Flasche zum Trinken oder zum Zerschmettern zu haben, kein Handtuch zum Aufhängen, kein Messer zum Ausbrechen oder zum Aderndurchschneiden, keine Feder zum Schreiben — nichts zu haben — als sich selbst.

WOLFGANG BORCHERT: *Die Hundeblume*

The Start of a Motor Tour in Greece

Wir hatten alles hervorragend geplant, Mykenä,[1] die Stadt des Agamemnon, Sparta mit dem phantastischen Klosterhügel Mistra und Epidauros gehörten unter anderem zu unsern geplanten Reisezielen. Straßen gab es dick und weniger dick auf der Karte eingezeichnet, die all dies auf einfache Weise verbanden, und ein Auto stand vor einer Athener Garage . . . und damit begannen unsere Reiseabenteuer. Der Garagenbesitzer war so entzückt von den Vorzügen seines Vehikels, das zudem vorher ein höherer Beamter unserer Gesandtschaft mit Erfolg benutzt hatte, daß dieses Entzücken selbst auf meine kritischen Augen ansteckend wirkte und wir uns voll Zuversicht in den Wagen setzten. Gott sei Dank merkten wir noch vor Verlassen des verkehrsreichen Athen, daß der Kofferraum zwar verschließbar, aber nicht aufschließbar war. Daß die Handbremse sich offenbar ihrer höheren Zwecke nicht bewußt war, wurde uns erst später klar, ebenso die Tatsache, daß der Kühler von unheilbarem Durst befallen war. Da es der Durst eines Abstinenten war, hatten wir in diesem Land, da Wasser eine Kostbarkeit und eine wohlschmeckende Quelle eine Goldgrube sind, einige Mühe, ihn zu stillen. So war es ein wahres Wunder, daß wir dennoch nach einigen Stunden in Korinth ankamen. Schon hatten wir gemerkt, daß allzuhäufiges Schalten oder gar Anhalten nicht gerade das war, was unser schwarzer und solid aussehender Fiat liebte; so hielten wir nur einmal, als wir soeben den Kanal von Korinth überquert hatten.

BETTINA HÜRLIMANN: 'Kreuz und quer durch den Peloponnes'
(from *Atlantis*)

¹ Mycenae.

Scott's Last Days

Drei müde, geschwächte Menschen schleppen sich durch die endlose eisig-eiserne Wüste, müde schon, hoffnungslos, nur der dumpfe Instinkt der Selbsterhaltung spannt noch die Sehnen zu wankendem Gang. Immer furchtbarer wird das Wetter, bei jedem Depot höhnt sie neue Enttäuschung, immer wieder zu wenig Öl, zu wenig Wärme. Am 21. März sind sie nur mehr zwanzig Kilometer von einem Depot entfernt, aber der Wind weht mit so mörderischer Kraft, daß sie ihr Zelt nicht verlassen dürfen. Jeden Abend hoffen sie auf den nächsten Morgen, um das Ziel zu erreichen, indes schwindet der Proviant und die letzte Hoffnung mit ihm. Der Brennstoff ist ihnen ausgegangen, und das Thermometer zeigt 40 Grad unter Null. Jede Hoffnung erlischt: sie haben jetzt nur mehr die Wahl zwischen Tod durch Hunger oder Frost. Acht Tage kämpfen diese drei Menschen in einem kleinen Zelt inmitten der weißen Urwelt gegen das unabwendbare Ende. Am 29. März wissen sie, daß kein Wunder mehr sie retten kann. So beschließen sie, keinen Schritt dem Verhängnis entgegenzugehen und den Tod stolz wie alles andere Unglück zu erdulden. Sie kriechen in ihre Schlafsäcke, und von ihren letzten Leiden ist nie ein Seufzer in die Welt gedrungen.

In diesen Augenblicken, einsam gegenüber dem unsichtbaren und doch atemnahen Tod, während außen der Orkan an die dünnen Zeltwände wie ein Rasender anrennt, besinnt sich Kapitän Scott aller Gemeinsamkeit, der er verbunden ist. Allein im eisigsten Schweigen, das noch nie die Stimme eines Menschen durchatmet, wird ihm die Brüderschaft zu seiner Nation, zur ganzen Menschheit heroisch bewußt. Eine innere Fata Morgana des Geistes beschwört in diese weiße Wüste die Bilder all jener, die ihm durch Liebe, Treue und Freundschaft jemals verbunden waren, und er richtet das Wort an sie. Mit erstarrenden Fingern schreibt Kapitän Scott, schreibt Briefe aus der Stunde seines Todes an alle Lebendigen, die er liebt.

STEFAN ZWEIG: 'Der Kampf um den Südpol'
(*Sternstunden der Menschheit*)

The Double[1]

Es geschieht in mehreren Städten, daß Schauspieler telephonisch von einem Herrn aufgerufen werden, der angibt, ich zu sein, und sie dringendst ersucht, den armen Mann Soundso mit Geld zu unterstützen. Sagen die Schauspieler „Ja" — und sie sagen meistens ja, denn sie sind gute Leute und wollen einem Kritiker nicht gern etwas abschlagen — so kommt der arme Mann ins Haus und kassiert ein. Zuweilen besetzt er die Rolle seines Protektors auch anders, wählt für das telephonische Gespräch andere Namen als den meinen, aber für mich hat er, das ist statistisch nachzuweisen, besondere Vorliebe. Sie geht manchmal so weit, daß er sich mit mir völlig identifiziert. Er tritt dann — dies geschah zum Beispiel in M, wo die Menschen kulturell so zurück sind, daß sie mein Gesicht nicht kennen — als ich auf und pumpt die Leute geradewegs an. Gelegentlich verlangt er auch unter meinem Namen von Theaterkanzleien Freibilletts. Ich glaube nicht, daß er diese, erhält er sie, dann zum Besuch der Vorstellungen benützt. Er hat selbst genug Komödie im Leibe, um die, die andere vormachen, entbehren zu können. Er verkauft lieber die Billetts. Vielleicht tut der Mann hier und da auch etwas Gutes für mich. Macht mir etwa durch Liebenswürdigkeit, die er entwickelt, einen Ruf als Charmeur. Oder bringt mich durch seinen Humor in den Verdacht, welchen zu haben . . .

ALFRED POLGAR: *Doppelgänger, du bleicher Geselle*

---

[1] N.B. The author was a theatre critic and essayist.

Spectators at the Races

. . . Ich sah in ein paar Gesichter hinein. Sie waren verzerrt wie von einem inneren Krampf, die Augen starr und funkelnd, die Lippen verbissen, das Kinn gierig vorgestoßen, die Nüstern pferdhaft gebläht. Spaßig und grauenhaft war mir's, nüchtern diese unbeherrschten Trunkenen zu betrachten. Neben mir stand auf einem Sessel ein Mann, elegant gekleidet, mit einem sonst wohl guten Gesicht, jetzt aber tobte er, von einem unsichtbaren Dämon beteufelt, er fuchtelte mit dem Stock in die leere Luft hinein, als peitschte er etwas vorwärts, sein ganzer Körper machte — unsagbar lächerlich für einen Zuschauer — die Bewegung des Raschreitens leidenschaftlich mit. Wie auf Steigbügeln wippte er mit den Fersen unablässig auf und nieder über dem Sessel, die rechte Hand jagte den Stock immer wieder als Gerte ins Leere, die linke knüllte krampfig einen weißen Zettel. Und immer mehr dieser weißen Zettel flatterten herum, wie Schaumspritzer gischteten sie über dieser graudurchstürmten Flut, die lärmend schwoll. Jetzt mußten an der Kurve ein paar Pferde ganz knapp beieinander sein, denn mit einem Male ballte sich das Gedröhn in zwei, drei, vier einzelne Namen, die immer wieder einzelne Gruppen wie Schlachtrufe schrien und tobten, und diese Schreie schienen wie ein Ventil für ihre delirierende Besessenheit.

STEFAN ZWEIG: *Phantastische Nacht*

Extract from President Heuss's Speech at Buckingham Palace, 20 October 1958

„Majestät! Sie haben der Begrüßung, die Sie an mich richteten, eine menschliche Wärme geliehen, die mich rührt und bewegt. Indem ich Ihnen für die Worte der Anerkennung danke, die Sie gefunden haben, so möchte ich sie doch, stellvertretend für zahllose andere, auf alle jene Frauen und Männer bezogen wissen, die nach dem Ende des unheilvollen tragischen Krieges in meinem Vaterland die Hand anlegten, dem deutschen Volke eine Lebenszukunft zu sichern.

Dies ihr Mühen wäre vergeblich gewesen, hätten sich nicht aus den Leidenschaften, die immer das politisch-militärische Machtringen begleiten, die Einsichten erhoben, daß nach einem Krieg, mit anderen Methoden, auch ein Frieden gewonnen werden müsse.

Sie haben, Majestät, davon gesprochen, welchen starken Anteil die Regierung des Vereinigten Königreichs von Großbritannien und Nordirland an dieser Entwicklung genommen hat, nicht die Regierung allein, sondern trotz mancherlei bitterer Erfahrungen auch weite Schichten der Bevölkerung. Ich denke dabei nicht lediglich an die materiellen Hilfen, auf die unser Volk für einen Neubeginn angewiesen war, sondern auch an Stütze und Rat beim Werden einer neuen Staatlichkeit, einer neuen Ordnung des Volkslebens, bei der nicht mehr Brutalität und Willkür, sondern ein freier, sich selbst verantwortender Bürgersinn die zuverlässigen Grundlagen des Gemeinwesens bilden."

A Colourful Scene

In der ersten Hauptstraße, die er betrat, war er in einen Strom von Fußgängern geraten, von dem er sich sorglos mitziehen ließ, wobei er ganz vergaß, daß er eigentlich zur Residenz gewollt hatte. Es mußte der unsagbar heitere Frühlingstag sein, der die Leute in solchen Scharen ins Freie lockte. Nicht nur behäbige Bürgersfamilien mit fröhlichen Kindern aller Altersschichten waren auf den Beinen, auch kleine Trupps blitzender Offiziere, Gruppen junger Frauenzimmer in blumenbunten Kleidern, ehrwürdig aussehende Herren mit Meerrohren,[1] vertieft in zweifellos staatsbewegende Gespräche, gewaltige Fregatten seidenraschelnder Matronen mit Sonnenschirmchen und Pompadours[2] ausgerüstet, zogen dahin, und dies alles war gar nichts gegen die ununterbrochene Folge prächtiger Karossen und Reiter, die sich auf der Mittelbahn der breiten Allee, in die die Straße übergegangen war, vorwärts bewegte. Mit fast noch größerem Erstaunen als auf die von Brokat und Silberspitzen schimmernden Damen, die in den Wagen lehnten, und auf ihre eleganten Begleiter starrte Tobias auf die den federbuschgeschmückten Gespannen vorauskeuchenden Läufer, auf die von blitzenden Tressen und Knöpfen überladenen Kutscher und Lakaien, unter denen er mehr als einen turbangekrönten Mohren entdeckte. Die Lust des Schauens, die er empfand, war derart, daß er allmählich in einen leichten, aber durchdringenden Rausch zu geraten vermeinte, mit der ganzen Entrücktheit und Selbstvergessenheit, die die Anzeichen dieses Zustandes sind.

INA SEIDEL: *Lennacker*

---

[1] *Meerrohr*: an older word for *cane*. Nowadays, *Rohrstock*; here, *Spazierstock*.
[2] *Pompadour*: nowadays, *Strickbeutel*.

The Swiss Character

Was nun die Nüchternheit betrifft, die dem Schweizer oft vorgeworfen wird, so ist diese allerdings vorhanden; aber man ist im Irrtum, wenn man glaubt, deswegen könne die Schweiz keine Künstler hervorbringen. Die Trockenheit des Schweizers ist die des kindlich oder bäuerlich verschlossenen Menschen, in dessen Innern die Phantasie oft um so kräftiger glüht, weil sie nicht beständig nach außen verschwendet wird. Besonders aber sollte man endlich wissen, was die Romantiker unter vielen Schmerzen an sich selbst erfuhren, daß künstlerisches Empfinden, Reizbarkeit und die Sehnsucht nach dem Schönen keineswegs den schaffenden Künstler machen, daß vielmehr, wie E. T. A. Hoffmann sagte, dem künstlerischen Feuer eine gute Dosis Phlegma beigemischt sein müsse, damit es nicht den Menschen verzehre, anstatt ihm in seiner heiligen Werkstatt zu dienen. Indem das Phlegma gegen den Einfluß fremder und eigener Reize festmacht, verleiht es dem, der es im rechten Maße besitzt, eine gewisse Überlegenheit, die sich beim Schweizer bescheidentlich als Humor äußert und ihn seine Eigenart unbefangen genießen läßt.

RICARDA HUCH: Gottfried Keller

Hamlet

Ein unnachweisbares Verbrechen ist geschehen. Der König von Dänemark ist ermordet von seinem Bruder, der darauf selbst den Thron bestieg und die Gattin des Ermordeten heiratete. Ein Gespenst hat es Hamlet, dem Sohn des ermordeten Königs, ihm allein, ohne Zeugen, mitgeteilt. Niemand außer dem Verbrecher selbst, dem König, weiß von dem Verbrechen. Wie die Ordnung in Dänemark jetzt ist, würde niemand den Mord, teilte man ihn mit, glauben. Das Gespenst ist, weil Gespenst, für Hamlet kein absolut gültiger Zeuge. Das Allerwesentlichste hat keinen Nachweis für sich und ist doch fast wie gewußt von Hamlet. Hamlets Leben hat durch diese Bindung die einzige Aufgabe, das Unnachweisbare nachzuweisen und, ist es nachgewiesen, zu handeln.

Das ganze Drama ist das Wahrheitssuchen Hamlets. Die Wahrheit aber ist nicht allein die Antwort auf die isolierte Frage nach dem Tatbestand des Verbrechens, sondern mehr: der gesamte Weltzustand ist derart, daß dies geschehen konnte, daß es verborgen bleiben konnte, daß es jetzt sich der Offenbarmachung entzieht. Im Augenblick als die Aufgabe für Hamlet klar ist, weiß er auch:

> Die Zeit ist aus den Fugen: Schmach und Gram,
> Daß ich zur Welt, sie einzurichten, kam! (I, 5)

Wem geschah, was Hamlet geschah — wer weiß, was niemand weiß, und es doch nicht gewiß weiß —, dem zeigt sich alle Welt neu und anders. Er bewahrt bei sich, was er nicht mitteilen kann. Jeder Mensch, jede Situation, jede Ordnung erweist sich durch Widerstand, dadurch, daß sie Mittel werden zum Verdecken der Wahrheit, als selber unwahr. Alles ist brüchig. Es versagen, je auf ihre Weise, auch die wohlmeinendsten Besten (Ophelia, Laertes). „Ehrlich sein heißt, wie es in dieser Welt hergeht, ein Auserwählter unter Zehntausenden sein" (II, 2).

KARL JASPERS: Über das Tragische

Lectures

Was die Physik angeht, so wurde sie damals noch in der Universität[1] gelehrt. In dieser sah ich die Hochburg des unbedingten Geistes, und hier hatten wir Mediziner eigentlich nichts zu suchen; aber gerade dieses Ausgeschlossensein konnte mich manchmal reizen, an dem alten Physiker Lommel respektvoll vorüber zu Lipps, dem Philosophen, oder zu Iwan von Müller, dem Lehrer der alten Sprachen, zu gehen. Schließlich aber wurde mir der tägliche Umweg überhaupt lästig, und ich fand mich damit ab, mir mein Wissen nur noch in jenen äußeren empirischen Bezirken zu erwerben, die den künftigen Ärzten vorbehalten waren. Die Physikstunde zu schwänzen, machte mir übrigens auch aus anderen Gründen keine Gewissenspein. Lommel hatte das Licht erforscht, wunderbare Entdeckungen waren ihm dabei gelungen, er bereitete Wilhelm Röntgen, dem Strahlenfinder, den Weg. Nun aber kränkelte er und sprach mit so schwacher Stimme, daß mir die Hälfte seiner Ausführungen verlorenging. Außerdem hatte ein Vetter Hugos, während er selbst noch auf der höheren Schulbank saß,[2] einen so feinen Leitfaden jener Wissenschaft geschrieben, daß es schlechterdings unmöglich war, in der Prüfung durchzufallen, wenn man sich die kurzen Fragen und Antworten des dünnen Büchleins einprägte. „Physik, leicht gemacht", hätte man diesen Katechismus nennen können; die Studenten nahmen auch den Vorteil wahr, die

Auflagen jagten sich und verstärkten sehr das Taschengeld des jungen Mannes, der den Text immer wieder den neuen Theorien anpaßte. HANS CAROSSA: *Das Jahr der schönen Täuschungen*

[1] i.e. in the university building, not in a separate science block. [2] i.e. while he was still at the *Gymnasium* (*höhere Schule*).

The Heidelberg Romantics

Aber die eigentliche Stadt der Romantik, wo sie ihr wildestes Fest feierte, dessen Raketen und Funkensprühen weithin sichtbar wurde, war Heidelberg, das altehrwürdige, malerische, von Hügeln und Wäldern umringte, mit der herrlichen Schloßruine, von der man auf den reizenden Schlangenlauf des Neckars herabsieht. Clemens Brentano hatte hier das Nest für Weib und Kind gebaut und lockte den Freund Arnim nach; zu ihnen gesellte sich Görres, jung, wagemutig, zuversichtlich, überströmend von Ideen, mit einer schönen, sanften Frau und lieblichen Kindern. Die schöne, gute Sophie Mereau, harmonisch wie Karoline Schlegel, aber in kleineren Maßen, und die ruhige, beharrliche Frau Görres, die, wie Clemens sagte, zehn Bücher zugleich lesen konnte, sorgten für gemütliche Häuslichkeit. Daß sie sämtlich nur beschränkte Geldmittel zur Verfügung hatten, erhöhte den Reiz des jungen, hoffnungsvollen Lebens. Der vielseitige Görres las als Privatdozent an der Universität über Mythologie und Physiologie und fesselte die jungen Zuhörer unwiderstehlich durch seine Persönlichkeit und seine Rede. Eichendorff, der damals, von Halle kommend, in Heidelberg studierte und sich hier völlig der Romantik hingab, fand, daß Arnim und Brentano sich zu Görres verhielten wie Schüler zu ihrem Meister. Eichendorff war so eingefangen von Görres' genialem Wesen, daß er lange Zeit in seinem Stile sprach; aber noch viele andere Schüler behielten das dankbare Gefühl, von ihm geweckt, angeregt und auf immer bereichert worden zu sein.

RICARDA HUCH: *Die Romantik* (abridged extract)

Latin and Greek

Latein und Griechisch. Immer hörte ich sie in einem Atemzuge nennen, und doch, wie durchaus ungeschwisterlich erschienen sie mir! Die Sprache der Römer: vertraute Buchstaben, vertrauter Tonfall, im Anklang an bekanntes welsches Sprachgut vertraute Worte. Und makellose Klarheit: sauber aufgerichtete

Lettern, scharfgefügte Sätze, Buchstaben, Worte und Sätze aufrecht gereiht wie ein Heer in Frontstellung. Und sicher errichtet die Satzgefüge, wie Gebäude, an denen jeder Balken trägt, jeder Stein stützt, und wie Gebäude über konzentrischem Grundriß in sich bestehend und umschlossen. Buchstaben, Sätze und Satzgefüge von berückender Selbstherrlichkeit, überwältigend im Einklang des Gleichschrittes.

Aber nun das Griechische: unvertraute Lettern, unvertraute Laute, Wortbild und Satzmusik verwirrend fremd. Nichts von der senkrechten Sicherheit und strammen Sachlichkeit der lateinischen Schrift: sanft geneigt die zierlichen Zeichen, wie Ähren im Windhauch, und flimmernd gereiht wie ziehende Wellen und fein bewimpelt wie die Segel über den Wellen und wie Segel, Windhauch und Welle lebendig hinströmend, unaufhaltsam weitereilend. Auch die Sätze ohne harte Trennung, sanft sich umschlingend, einer seine Musik an den anderen weitergebend, strömend von herzbedrängender Fülle und gänzlich hingegeben dem eigenen Sein, durchaus lebend von einer Welt, die einem anderen Raume anzugehören schien, dahin keine Erfahrung langte, selig in sich, unbekümmert um das Draußen. Und draußen stand ich; würde ich jemals den Weg finden in dieses lebendige, dieses geheimnisvoll verwirrende Jenseits?

MARIA WASER: *Der heilige Weg*

The Eighteenth Century

Das achtzehnte Jahrhundert ist die letzte große Kulturepoche Europas gewesen. Sie hat in den bildenden Künsten, vor allem in der Baukunst, Geringeres geleistet als frühere große Zeiten; desto größer ist ihre literarische Bedeutung, und in ihrer internationalen, ganz Europa umfassenden Geistigkeit hat sie eine Macht und Weite erreicht, an deren Glanz und Andenken wir als ärmere Enkel noch immer zehren.

Eine edle, großzügige Form von Humanismus, eine unbedingte Ehrfurcht vor der menschlichen Natur und ein idealer Glaube an die Größe und Zukunft menschlicher Kultur spricht aus allen Zeugnissen jener Zeit, auch aus denen der Satiriker und Spötter. Der Mensch ist an die Stelle der Götter gerückt, die Würde des Menschentums ist die Krone der Welt und das Fundament jedes Glaubens geworden. Diese neue Religion, deren revolutionäre Anfänge in England und Frankreich liegen, deren tiefster Prophet Kant und deren letzte Blüte Weimar gewesen

ist, dieser ideale Humanismus ist die Grundlage einer unsäglich
reichen Kultur gewesen, die uns Enkel schon mit dem Zauber-
glanz des Unbegreiflichen blendet und gegen deren mahnende
Übermacht wir uns nicht selten durch Spott zu wehren suchen,
indem wir die dekorative Außenseite jenes Geistes als hohl und
spielerisch zu erkennen meinen. Wir lächeln über die beschnit-
tenen Gartenhecken, über die geschweiften chinesischen Dächer
und schnörkelhaft launigen Porzellanfiguren jenes Jahrhunderts,
obwohl weder unsere Gärten noch Häuser seither irgend besser
oder schöner geworden sind, und wir reden gerne immer nur
von der Perücke jener steifen Zeit, die durch die Pariser Revolution, durch die Räuber und den Werther besiegt und in ihrer
hohlen Lächerlichkeit aufgedeckt worden sei.

HERMANN HESSE: Dank an Goethe

Martin Luther

Es ist die Eigenart bedeutender Menschen, unlösbar in ihrer
Zeit zu stehen, die sich in ihnen erfüllt, und ihr doch nicht ganz
anzugehören. Für Luther gilt das in besonderem Maße. Er ist
zugleich mittelalterlicher und moderner als die anderen Großen
seiner Jahrhunderthälfte, als etwa Erasmus, Paracelsus, Thomas
Münzer und Therese von Avila, woraus sich auch die in der
Forschung oft verhandelte Frage erklärt, ob er denn eigentlich
schon in die Neuzeit und nicht vielmehr noch ins Mittelalter
gehörte. Er sieht Dämonen, und seine Theologie ist ohne seinen
Glauben an die Realität des Satans nicht zu denken, theoretischer
Atheismus ist ihm Ruchlosigkeit wie nur je einem mittelalterlichen Menschen, und von der Renaissancelust am Diesseitigen
ist er so gänzlich unberührt, daß Nietzsche ihn als den großen
Verhinderer des Sieges der Renaissance beklagen konnte. Zugleich aber ist er in einem unbegreiflichen Maße frei von den
Rücksichten und Unentbehrlichkeiten, die auch den Menschen
seines Jahrhunderts banden: vom Glauben an die Unerschütter-
lichkeit der tragenden Institutionen des Kaisertums und der
kirchlichen Hierarchie, von aristotelischem Formalismus wie von
astrologischer Zeichendeutung, vom ängstlichen Eifer, das Wan-
kende zu stützen, wie vom utopischen Eifer, eine neue Welt zu
stiften. Er sieht die Zeitlichkeit und Zeitbedingtheit der ge-
schichtlichen Mächte und Gestalten, ohne die nach Meinung der
Zeitgenossen die Welt nicht bestehen kann, und kann deshalb
seinen um die Einheit von Reich und Kirche mit gutem Grunde

höchst besorgten Freund Melanchthon während des Augsburger Reichstages von der Coburg aus überlegen trösten: „Was fürchten wir nun die überwundene Welt gleich als wäre sie der Überwinder?" HELMUT GOLLWITZER: 'Begegnung mit Luther' (in *Luther*, an anthology of his writings compiled by Karl Gerhard Steck)

John Galsworthy

Ich werde die Bekanntschaft mit Galsworthy immer als einen menschlichen Gewinn ersten Ranges betrachten. Rein gesellschaftlich gesehen, als soziale Figur, stellt er, der typische Engländer aus gutem Hause, mit seinem hohen Wuchs, seiner ehrenhaften Gesundheit, der rosigen Gesichtsfarbe, die den Schnee des Hauptes Lügen straft, der Ritterlichkeit, Mäßigkeit, der liebenswürdigen Sittlichkeit seines Wesens, etwas dar wie eine Blüte westeuropäischer Zivilisation, und das Wort Gentleman, das so reich ist an physischen und moralischen Sinnbezügen, wäre erschöpfend, wenn es geistiger wäre. Sehr bald im Verkehr mit diesem Manne wird man dessen gewahr, was man weiß, nämlich daß man es zwar mit einem klassischen Gentleman zu tun hat, darüber hinaus aber — und man muß wohl sagen: eigentlich — mit einem Geistesmenschen, einem Wissenden und Empfindlichen, in dem Leiden und Formtrieb jene geheimnisvolle Mischung eingegangen sind, die die Quelle der Literatur ist, einem Schriftsteller mit einem Wort, dessen wohltuende menschliche Erscheinung — oder soll man sagen: Maske — die des Gentlemans ist.

THOMAS MANN: 'John Galsworthy zum sechzigsten Geburtstag'

Problems of Theatre Design

Das europäische Theater hat seinen Ursprung bei den Griechen. Abgesehen von den immer noch bestehenden geistigen Beziehungen, sind schon allein der äußeren Anlage nach unsere Theater- und auch die Kinogebäude ohne den antiken Theaterbau überhaupt nicht zu denken. Die großen und kleinen Zuschauerräume in ihrem Verhältnis zur Bühne oder zur Kinoleinwand, das heißt die möglichst gute Sicht und gute Akustik auf jedem Platz, der möglichst vollkommene Kontakt des Zuschauers mit dem Bühnengeschehen, sind Probleme, die in der Antike vor allem bei den Griechen bewundernswert gelöst waren und uns heute wieder besonders beschäftigen.

Das aus der Barockzeit überkommene Rang- und Logensystem

mit hufeisenförmigem Grundriß der Zuschauerräume und den vielen hinsichtlich Akustik und Sicht so schlechten Plätzen bedeutet vielerorts im Theaterleben immer noch eine wesentliche Schwierigkeit. Für eine Vorstellung, die man ärgerlicherweise nur halb oder von unbequemem Sitz aus lediglich mit Hals- und Körperverrenkungen sehen und hören kann, gibt man nicht gerne Geld aus. Die an sich selbstverständliche Forderung nach gutem Hören und guter Sicht ist beim Kino und Fernsehen heute im allgemeinen besser gelöst als beim Theater.

Nach dem letzten Weltkrieg richteten viele Städte Europas neben den Bemühungen zur Wiedererlangung normaler Lebensverhältnisse schon bald in erfreulicher Aufgeschlossenheit auch für die kulturellen Belange ihre Aufmerksamkeit auf die Restaurierung oder den Neubau ihrer Theater, zumal in Deutschland und in Österreich, während z. B. heute in der Schweiz fast alle wichtigen Theatergebäude einer Erneuerung bedürfen, abgesehen von den kürzlich errichteten Theatern u. a. in Lausanne, Baden oder Schaffhausen.

K. G. KACHLER: 'Heutige und antike Theaterprobleme'
(from *Atlantis*)

Thomas Mann

Thomas Mann wurde im Jahre 1875 in Lübeck als zweiter Sohn des angesehenen Kaufmanns und Senators Johann Heinrich Mann geboren. Das Datum und die Umstände seiner Geburt sind bezeichnend. Die Triumphe des Naturalismus in Deutschland fielen in Thomas Manns aufnahmefähigste Jugendjahre, aber als der junge Schriftsteller selbst zu veröffentlichen begann, hatten sich die Schwächen der naturalistischen Theorie und Praxis schon herausgestellt; so haben nur früheste, nach erster Veröffentlichung nicht wieder nachgedruckte Erzählungen an den Exzessen der Richtung teil, während ihre dauernden Errungenschaften, vor allem die Erkenntnis der Bedeutung von Milieu und Hintergrund, schon Manns erstem Roman, *Buddenbrooks*, zugute kamen und ein wesentlicher Zug seiner Erzählkunst blieben. Als nicht weniger grundlegend für Thomas Manns Eigenart erwiesen sich der bürgerliche, auf Tradition und Ordnung gerichtete Geist des Hauses, in dem er aufwuchs, und das patriarchalische Verhältnis des Vaters zu seinen Angestellten; von hier schon erklären sich Thomas Manns fast pedantische Ordnungsliebe und sein großes Verantwortungsgefühl, hier sind die Wurzeln seines später durch die Lektüre Nietzsches und Schopenhauers vertieften, erst nach extremer Steigerung gegen

Ausgang des ersten Weltkrieges überwundenen Konservatismus zu suchen. War Heinrich Mann geneigt, gegen sein Erbe zu rebellieren, so war es des jüngeren Bruders erster Instinkt, es zu übernehmen und zu verteidigen.

HANS EICHNER: *Thomas Mann*

Wilhelm Furtwängler

Die Musik unserer Zeit geht den Weg aus der Tradition in die Ratlosigkeit. Alle Werte sind ins Schwanken geraten, nur die Sensation scheint oberstes Ziel aller zu sein. Ruhiges Lernen und Ausreifen gibt es für den Musiker nicht mehr, so wenig wie Bildung und Selbstbewußtsein unter den Hörern. Kompositionen, Virtuosen, Aufführungsstile, Überzeugungen — alles das wechselt schneller als die Hutmode. Als allerneueste Modeströmung scheint sogar schon hie und da die Ansicht durchzubrechen, daß es so nicht mehr weitergehe. Vielleicht könnte heute selbst ein Mann mit Furtwänglers Lauterkeit so wenig dem allgemeinen Abgleiten Einhalt bieten, wie er gegen die braune[1] Kunstzerstörungswut etwas ausrichtete. Aber man erinnert sich, wie damals seine Standhaftigkeit allen Verzweifelnden neue Hoffnung gab und wie sein Beispiel schließlich wirksamer war als aller entfesselte Wahnsinn der Gewalthaber und ihn kraft seiner Richtigkeit überdauert hat. Er war zum Maß geworden, nach dem sich alle Musik bewußt oder unbewußt ausrichtete, ein Maß, das uns heute fehlt; das, wenn wir es noch hätten, Umwege und Auswüchse ersparen würde. Wir haben erlebt, daß der lautere Sinn für das Wohlabgemessene stärker ist als andere Triebkräfte in der Musik; wir haben den Magier, der das vollbracht hatte, mit uns wandeln sehen und haben ihn geliebt.

PAUL HINDEMITH: 'Wilhelm Furtwängler'
(*Rheinischer Merkur*)

[1] i.e. Nazi.

Bangnis

Noch eben waren die Birnen schwer,
Jetzt sieht man kaum mehr den Baum —
Das Dunkel kommt so plötzlich her
Und raubt sich den täglichen Raum
Und macht die Ebene wach und weit
Und macht die Wälder bang,
Und wer noch wandert um diese Zeit,
Dem werden die Straßen lang —

Und die auf den dunklen Treppen gehn,
Machen sich furchtsam Licht,
Und wer allein ist, dem kann es geschehn,
Daß er laut mit sich selber spricht —
Und Kinder fangen an zu schrein
Und rufen zur Mutter hin.
Das Dunkel aber spricht allein
Zu allen sein: Ich bin.   ALBRECHT GOES

Die Nacht

Ringsum ruhet die Stadt; still wird die erleuchtete Gasse,
    Und mit Fackeln geschmückt rauschen die Wagen hinweg.
Satt gehn heim von Freuden des Tags zu ruhen die Menschen,
    Und Gewinn und Verlust wäget ein sinniges Haupt
Wohl zufrieden zu Haus; leer steht von Trauben und Blumen,
    Und von Werken der Hand ruht der geschäftige Markt.
Aber das Saitenspiel tönt fern aus Gärten — vielleicht, daß
    Dort ein Liebendes spielt oder ein einsamer Mann
Ferner Freunde gedenkt und der Jugendzeit — und die Brunnen,
    Immerquillend und frisch, rauschen an duftendem Beet.
Still in dämmriger Luft ertönen geläutete Glocken,
    Und der Stunden gedenk rufet ein Wächter die Zahl.
Jetzt auch kommet ein Wehn und regt die Gipfel des Hains auf,
    Sieh! und das Schattenbild unserer Erde, der Mond
Kommet geheim nun auch; die Schwärmerische, die Nacht kommt,
    Voll mit Sternen, und wohl wenig bekümmert um uns
Glänzt die Erstaunende dort, die Fremdlingin unter den Menschen
    Über Gebirgeshöhn traurig und prächtig herauf.
                                    FRIEDRICH HÖLDERLIN

Die zwei Parallelen

Es gingen zwei Parallelen
ins Endlose hinaus,
zwei kerzengerade Seelen
und aus solidem Haus.

Sie wollten sich nicht schneiden
bis an ihr seliges Grab:
Das war nun einmal der beiden
geheimer Stolz und Stab.

Doch als sie zehn Lichtjahre
gewandert neben sich hin,
da wards dem einsamen Paare
nicht irdisch mehr zu Sinn.

Warn sie noch Parallelen?
Sie wußtens selber nicht, —
sie flossen nur wie zwei Seelen
zusammen durch ewiges Licht.

Das ewige Licht durchdrang sie,
da wurden sie eins in ihm;
die Ewigkeit verschlang sie,
als wie zwei Seraphim.

CHRISTIAN MORGENSTERN

Auf den alten Stationen

Auf den kleinen alten Stationen,
Die mein eigner Zug schon längst verlassen,
Ahn ich das Gedränge von Personen,
Die am Bahntrakt auf die Abfahrt passen.

Und ich möchte fast mich überheben
Über sie, die warten am Geleise,
Daß ich schon so weit auf meiner Reise
Vorgedrungen bin im Rüttel-Leben,

Daß ich kenne Brücken und Tunnelle,
Meer- und See- und Fels- und Stadtkulissen,
Daß mir gellen Aug und Ohr von Wissen,
Jenen unbekannt an ihrer Stelle,

Daß sie werden noch im Zeit-Zug sitzen,
Stumpf am Fenster schauen Funkenspiele
Und der tragischen Signale Blitzen,
Wenn ich ausgestiegen längst am Ziele.

FRANZ WERFEL

Totenspruch auf einen Vogel

O winziges Geschick! O Feder, die ich fand
salzweiß, doch blutbefleckt, im Parkweg auf dem Sand!
Bleib, Wandrer, stehen. Nein, — geh weiter, doch gemach,
denk nur sekundenlang dem kleinen Vogel nach.
O federleichter Tod! O furchtbares Gewicht,
die Schale dieser Welt belastend zum Gericht.
Ein Großes ist nicht groß, ein Kleines ist nicht klein.
Es kann kein Erdenmaß vor Gottes Antlitz sein.
Ich hob die Feder auf, ihr Schaft war sanft gespitzt,
ich hab den Totenspruch mit ihm in Sand geritzt.
In Sand, der vogelschnell von jedem Tritt zergeht,
den jeder Atemzug des stillsten Tags verweht.
Gefiele Gott dem Herrn ein Ewiges auf Erden,
so ließ er diesen Sand gewiß zu Marmor werden.
Er aber will, es sei vor ihm und uns ein Nu:
Sand, Schrift und Marmorstein, der Vogel, ich und du.

WERNER BERGENGRUEN

Unruhige Nacht[1]

Unheimlich wetterleuchtet die Front.
Aus Träumen auffahrend bellen Geschütze
weit in die Nacht hinaus,
schlagen mit feurigen Tatzen sinnlos um sich
und fallen wieder in Schlaf.
Fratzen im Schein weißer Leuchtkugelsonnen
starren Steine, Menschen und Säcke voll Sand.
Maschinengewehre, seltsamen Wahnsinns voll,
hacken eintönigen Takt in das Dunkel.
Unzufrieden murmelt nervöses Feuer der Infantrie
aus der Ferne, murrt und verhüllt sich.
An zehntausend Leichen hocken schlaflose Heere,
werden aufgescheucht von irren Befehlen
und sinken wieder in Wald und Sümpfe.

Schlachttag hängt in den Schollen.
Totgeglaubte schreien auf und verenden.
Mensch und Gefilde lechzen nach Nacht.

Aber die Erde, allunerschüttert,
wendet sich,
unbegreiflich Gestirn,
neuer Sonne entgegen.   RUDOLF G. BINDING

[1] One of the author's poems from the First World War.

Das Karussell
Jardin du Luxembourg

Mit einem Dach und seinem Schatten dreht
sich eine kleine Weile der Bestand
von bunten Pferden, alle aus dem Land,
das lange zögert, eh es untergeht.
Zwar manche sind an Wagen angespannt,
doch alle haben Mut in ihren Mienen;
ein böser roter Löwe geht mit ihnen
und dann und wann ein weißer Elefant.

Sogar ein Hirsch ist da ganz wie im Wald,
nur daß er einen Sattel trägt und drüber
ein kleines blaues Mädchen aufgeschnallt.

Und auf dem Löwen reitet weiß ein Junge
und hält sich mit der kleinen heißen Hand,
dieweil der Löwe Zähne zeigt und Zunge.

Und dann und wann ein weißer Elefant.

Und auf den Pferden kommen sie vorüber,
auch Mädchen, helle, diesem Pferdesprunge
fast schon entwachsen; mitten in dem Schwunge
schauen sie auf, irgendwohin, herüber —

Und dann und wann ein weißer Elefant.

Und das geht hin und eilt sich, daß es endet,
und kreist und dreht sich nur und hat kein Ziel.
Ein Rot, ein Grün, ein Grau vorbeigesendet,
ein kleines kaum begonnenes Profil.
Und manchesmal ein Lächeln, hergewendet,
ein seliges, das blendet und verschwendet
an[1] dieses atemlose blinde Spiel.

RAINER MARIA RILKE: *Ausgewählte Gedichte*, 1. Teil.
Insel-Bücherei, Band 400

[1] *verschwendet an* . . .—'yields lavishly to . . .'.

Rückblick

Bei jeder Wendung deiner Lebensbahn,
Auch wenn sie glückverheißend sich erweitert,
Und du verlierst, um Größres zu gewinnen —
Betroffen stehst du plötzlich still, den Blick

Gedankenvoll auf das Vergangne heftend;
Die Wehmut lehnt an deine Schulter sich
Und wiederholt in deine Seele dir,
Wie lieblich alles war, und daß es nun
Damit vorbei auf immer sei! — Auf immer.
Ja, liebes Kind, und dir sei unverhohlen:
Was vor dir liegt von künft'gem Jugendglück,
Die Spanne mißt es einer Mädchenhand.
Doch also ward des Lebens Ordnung uns
Gesetzt von Gott; den schreckt sie nimmermehr,
Der einmal recht in seinem Geist gefaßt,
Was unser Dasein soll. Du freue dich
Gehabter Freude; andre Freuden folgen,
Den Ernst begleitend; dieser aber sei
Der Kern und sei die Mitte deines Glücks!

EDUARD MÖRIKE

PASSAGES FOR PROSE COMPOSITION

Departure of the Thief

Mr. Wesson walked on to the platform. It wasn't worth while putting his attaché case in the left-luggage room[1]—the left-luggage room appeared to be closed anyhow—as the intrusion of Nelly Bly into his affairs had taken up[2] so much time that he had now barely twenty minutes or so to wait. There was no one else on the platform and Mr. Wesson strolled up and down feeling more at ease[3] than he had done for some days.[4] The Van Buren papers were safely hidden between his pyjamas and his shirts, he had a useful selection of passports, no one at the 'Pelican' would notice his disappearance until the following day, and then no one would know where he had gone . . . that, he remembered, was not quite accurate.[5] He had told the red-headed chamber-maid that he was going to America. A foolish thing to do, but he had felt some compunction at having to tie her up, and the admission that he was going so far away as America had been in the nature of an explanation. Mr. Wesson belonged to a courteous nation, a nation reverent of its womanhood, and he realized that any man owes an explanation to a girl whom he ties to a bedroom chair under the threat of splashing her with vitriol. Perhaps on this occasion he should have suppressed his better feelings, though. But it did not matter. In less than twenty minutes he would be on the train, and by Monday morning he would have disappeared entirely; while, in the unremarkable[6] grey suit which Mr. Wesson was wearing, Mr. Edward P. Huther of Indianapolis would be booking an Atlantic passage in Glasgow.

ERIC LINKLATER: *Poet's Pub*

[1] to put . . . in the left-luggage room—*in die Gepäckaufbewahrung geben.* [2] *in Anspruch nehmen.* [3] to feel at ease—*sich wohl fühlen.* [4] 'on the previous days'. [5] *stimmte nicht ganz.* [6] *unauffällig.*

A Soldier calls on a Nurse

The next afternoon I went to call on Miss Barkley again. She was not in the garden and I went to the side door of the villa where the ambulances drove up.[1] Inside I saw the head nurse,[2] who said Miss Barkley was on duty—'there's a war on, you know.'
I said I knew.

'You're the American in the Italian army?' she asked.

'Yes, ma'am.'

'How did you happen to do that? Why didn't you join up[3] with us?'

'I don't know,' I said. 'Could I join now?'

'I'm afraid not now. Tell me. Why did you join up with the Italians?'

'I was in Italy,' I said, 'and I spoke Italian.'

'Oh,' she said. 'I'm learning it. It's a beautiful language.'

'Somebody said you should be able to learn it in two weeks.'

'Oh, I'll not learn it in two weeks. I've studied it for months now. You may come and see her after seven o'clock if you wish. She'll be off[4] then. But don't bring a lot of Italians.'

'Not even for the beautiful language?'

'No. Nor for the beautiful uniforms.'

'Good evening,' I said.

'A rivederci,[5] Tenente.'

'A rivederla.'[5] I saluted and went out. It was impossible to salute foreigners as an Italian, without embarrassment. The Italian salute never seemed made for export.[6]

ERNEST HEMINGWAY: A Farewell to Arms

[1] *vorfahren.*   [2] *die Oberschwester.*   [3] *eintreten bei.*   [4] *dienstfrei haben.*
[5] *a rivederci, a rivederla*—forms for *auf Wiedersehen.* Do not translate.   [6] *war wohl niemals für den Export gedacht* (or *bestimmt*).

An Autumn Scene

It was pretty late in the autumn of the year,[1] when the declining sun, struggling through the mist which had obscured it all day, looked brightly down upon a little Wiltshire village, within an easy journey of[2] the fair old town of Salisbury.

Like a sudden flash[3] of memory or spirit kindling up the mind of an old man, it shed a glory upon the scene, in which its departed youth and freshness seemed to live again.[4] The wet grass sparkled in the light; the scanty patches of verdure in the hedges —where a few green twigs yet stood together bravely, resisting[5] to the last the tyranny of nipping winds and early frosts—took heart[6] and brightened up; the stream which had been dull and sullen all day long, broke out into a cheerful smile; the birds began to chirp and twitter on the naked boughs as though the hopeful creatures half believed that winter had gone by and spring had come already. The vane upon the tapering spire of the old church glistened from its lofty station in sympathy with[7] the general gladness; and from the ivy-shaded windows such gleams of light shone back upon the glowing sky, that it seemed as if the quiet buildings were the hoarding-place[8] of twenty summers and all their ruddiness and warmth were stored within.

CHARLES DICKENS: *Martin Chuzzlewit*

[1] Omit 'of the year'. [2] *eine kurze Reise von . . . entfernt.* [3] *das Aufleuchten.* [4] *wieder aufleben.* [5] Gram. 13. [6] *sich ein Herz nehmen.* [7] *in Sympathie mit.* [8] *der Sammelplatz.*

The English Character

. . . The English nature is not at all easy to understand. It has a great air of simplicity,[1] it advertises itself as simple,[2] but the more we consider it, the greater the problems we shall encounter. People talk of the mysterious East, but the West also is mysterious. It has depths that do not reveal themselves at the first gaze.[3] We know what the sea looks like from a distance: it is of one colour, and level, and obviously cannot contain such creatures as fish. But if we look into the sea over the edge of a boat, we see a dozen colours, and depth below[4] depth, and fish swimming in them. That sea is the English character—apparently imperturbable and even. The depths and the colours are the English romanticism and the English sensitiveness—we do not expect to find such things, but they exist. And—to continue my metaphor[5] —the fish are the English emotions, which are always trying to get up to the surface, but don't quite know how. For the most part we see them moving far below, distorted and obscure. Now and then they succeed and we exclaim, 'Why, the Englishman has emotions! He actually can feel!' And occasionally we see that beautiful creature the flying fish, which rises out of the water altogether into the air and the sunlight. English literature is a flying fish. It is a sample of the life that goes on day after day beneath the surface; it is a proof that beauty and emotion exist in the salt, inhospitable sea.

E. M. FORSTER: 'Notes on the English Character' (from *Abinger Harvest*)

[1] 'it is to all outward appearances (*dem äußeren Anschein nach*) simple'. [2] *bezeichnet sich selbst als einfach.* [3] *auf den ersten Blick.* [4] *auf.* [5] Gram. 22.

An Active[1] Old Lady

Of course, Ann had to visit her grandmother early in the holidays,[2] for old Mrs. Ingleside had an almost Chinese respect for[3] ancestor-worship and even demanded from her son a daily letter, which, however[4] difficult for ordinary creatures, is no great hardship for a Government official. Mr. Ingleside preferred writing to visiting; but he occasionally came down by the five o'clock train from Victoria, and was home again by midnight, having an increasing distaste for sleeping in other people's houses.[5]

Although an old lady of seventy-seven, Mrs. Ingleside was so active and keen that her companion went to bed thoroughly tired out almost every night: what with[6] walking, driving, shopping, discussing, and reading aloud. Mrs. Ingleside possessed a landau[7] in which, open or closed, she drove out each afternoon; and it was on these drives that her conversation was at its brightest. Why it is that the landau has no power to tire some people, and is so deadly a foe to others, I cannot explain; but so it is. Mrs. Ingleside descended from it at tea-time invigorated in mind and body;[8] her guests staggered to their bedrooms in a stupor of fatigue,[9] of which, however, she was unconscious.

E. V. Lucas: *Mr. Ingleside* (adapted)

[1] *munter.*   [2] Cf. Gram. 126 (*a*).   [3] *eine fast chinesisch anmutende Achtung vor.*   [4] *wie . . . auch immer . . .* Cf. Gram. 118 (*c*).   [5] *in anderer Leute Häusern.* Cf. *aus aller Herren Ländern*—from all over the world.   [6] 'after all the . . .'   [7] *der Landauer.*   [8] *an Leib und Seele.*   [9] 'in a state of complete exhaustion'.

A Faint

The journey next day, short though it was, and the first visit to his lawyer's, tired him. It was hot, too, and after dressing for dinner he lay down on the sofa in his bedroom to rest a little. He must have had[1] a sort of fainting fit,[2] for he came to himself very queer,[3] and with some difficulty rose and rang the bell. Why! It was past seven! And there he was, and she would be waiting.[4] But suddenly the dizziness came on again, and he was obliged to relapse on the sofa. He heard the maid's voice say:

'Did you ring, sir?'

'Yes, come here;' he could not see her clearly, for[5] the cloud[6] in front of his eyes. 'I'm not well, I want some sal volatile.'

'Yes, sir.' Her voice sounded frightened.

Old Jolyon made an effort.

'Don't go. Take this message to my niece—a lady waiting in the hall—a lady in grey. Say Mr. Forsyte is not well—the heat. He is very sorry. If he is not down directly, she is not to wait dinner.'

When she was gone, he thought feebly, 'Why did I say a lady

in grey?—she may be in[7] anything. Sal volatile!' He did not go off again, yet was not conscious of how Irene came to be[8] standing beside him, holding smelling salts to his nose and pushing a pillow up behind his head.[9] He heard her say anxiously: 'Dear Uncle Jolyon, what is it?', was dimly conscious of the soft pressure of her lips on his hand; then drew in a long breath of smelling salts, suddenly discovered strength in them, and sneezed.

JOHN GALSWORTHY: The Man of Property

---

[1] Gram. 28 (*a*).   [2] *eine Art Ohnmacht*.   [3] Expand: 'when he came to himself again (*wieder zu sich kommen*) he was feeling very queer' (Gram. 100 (*c*)). [4] 'she must (tense?) be waiting already'.   [5] *wegen*.   [6] *der Schleier*.   [7] 'be wearing'.   [8] *wie es dazu gekommen war, daß . . .*   [9] *hinter seinen Kopf schob* (or *hinter seinem Kopf zurechtschob*). Note the cases used after *hinter* in these expressions.

Return to School

After this Dick had parted from his elder sister Barbara and his younger brother Roly, and had arrived at the mat outside the dining-room door, where he still lingered shivering in the cold foggy hall.

Somehow he could not bring himself[1] to take[2] the next step at once; he knew pretty well what his father's feelings would be, and a parting is a very unpleasant ceremony to one who feels that the regret is all on his own side.

But it was no use putting it off any longer; he resolved at last to go in and get it over,[3] and opened the door accordingly. How warm and comfortable the room looked—more comfortable than it had ever seemed to him before, even on the first day of the holidays!

And his father would be sitting there in a quarter of an hour's time, just as he was now, while he himself would be lumbering along to the station through the dismal raw fog!

How unspeakably delightful it must be, thought Dick enviously, to be grown up and never worried by the thought of school and lesson-books; to be able to look forward to returning to the same comfortable house, and living the same easy life, day after day, week after week, with no fear of a swiftly advancing Black Monday.[4]

F. ANSTEY: Vice Versa (abridged extract)

---

[1] *es über sich bringen*.   [2] *tun*.   [3] *es hinter sich bringen*.   [4] There is no equivalent in German. Translate: 'first day of school after the holidays'.

The First Fall of Snow

The first fall of snow is not only an event but it is a magical event. You go to bed in one kind of world[1] and wake up to find yourself in another quite different, and if this is not enchantment, then where is it to be found? The very[2] stealth, the eerie quietness, of the thing[3] makes it more magical. If all the snow fell at once in one shattering crash,[4] awakening us in the middle of the night, the event would be robbed of its wonder.[5] But it flutters down,[6] soundlessly, hour after hour while we are asleep. Outside the closed curtains of the bedrooms, a vast transformation scene is taking place, just as if a myriad elves and brownies were at work,[7] and we turn and yawn and stretch and know nothing about it. And then, what an extraordinary change it is! It is as if the house you are in had been dropped down in another continent. Even the inside, which has not been touched, seems different, every room appearing smaller and cosier, just as if some power were trying to turn it into a woodcutter's hut or a snug log cabin. Outside, where the garden was yesterday, there is now a white and glistening level, and the village beyond is no longer your own familiar cluster of roofs but a village in an old German fairy-tale. You would not be surprised to learn that all the people there, the spectacled post-mistress, the cobbler, the retired school-master, and the rest, had suffered a change too,[8] and had become queer elvish beings, purveyors of invisible caps and magic shoes. You yourselves do not feel quite the same people you were yester-day. How could you when so much has been changed?[9]

J. B. PRIESTLEY: 'First Snow' (from *Apes and Angels*)

[1] 'in one world'.　　[2] *Schon . . .*　　[3] Omit 'of the thing'.　　[4] 'with one single, ear-splitting crash' (*der Krach*).　　[5] to rob s.o. (or s.th.) of s.th.—*jn. (or etwas) einer Sache berauben.*　　[6] *herabrieseln.*　　[7] *am Werk.*　　[8] *eine Verwandlung erfahren.*　　[9] *sich verwandeln.*

The Wrong Pilot

Half an hour later, when weariness and the drone of the engine had lulled him nearly off to sleep, Mallinson disturbed him again. 'I say,[1] Conway, I thought Fenner was piloting[2] us?'

'Well, isn't he?'[3]

'The chap turned his head just now and I'll swear[4] it wasn't him.'[5]

'It's hard to tell, through that glass panel.'

'I'd know Fenner's face anywhere.'[6]

'Well, then, it must be someone else. I don't see that it matters.'

'But Fenner told me definitely that he was taking this machine.'

'They must have changed their minds and given him one of the others.'

'Well, who is this man then?'

'My dear boy, how should I know?[7] You don't suppose[8] I've memorized the face of every flight-lieutenant[9] in the Air Force, do you?'

'I know a good many of them, anyway, but I don't recognize this fellow.'

'Then he must belong to the minority whom you don't know.' Conway smiled and added: 'When we arrive in Peshawur very soon you can make his acquaintance and ask him all about himself.'

'At this rate[10] we shan't get to Peshawur at all. The man's right off his course.[11] And I'm not surprised[12] either—flying so damned high he can't see where he is.'

JAMES HILTON: *Lost Horizon*

---

[1] *'Hör doch mal!'*.   [2] to pilot a machine—*eine Maschine führen* or *am Steuer (der Maschine) sitzen*.   [3] *'Wie, führt er sie nicht?'* or *'Wie, sitzt er nicht dran?'* (Cf. (2)).   [4] 'I could swear'.   [5] Gram. 100 (*b*).   [6] 'everywhere'.   [7] '. . . *woher* (or *wie*) *soll ich das wissen?'*   [8] Use *doch wohl nicht* to render the somewhat irritated tone.   [9] *der Leutnant*.   [10] *'Wenn es so weitergeht'*.   [11] to get off course—*vom Kurs abkommen*.   [12] 'no wonder'.

A Day-dream[1]

There are mornings even now when I arrive in my study like a demi-god who has been given a planet to play with. Outside my high windows the sunlight falls lovingly on all green[2] and growing things.[2] The paper on my desk looks as if it could be conjured[3] almost without effort into a masterpiece. The keyboard of the typewriter glitters invitingly. The old tin box of paper fasteners, which somehow has survived all moves and changes, looks like some battered[4] faithful sergeant who has been at my side in a hundred battles and sieges. The work, when we get down to it,[5] will be wonderful. And brighter than the gilt along the bookshelves are the illusions of the moment . . . critics are kind and wise . . . readers and audiences are enchanted. . . . Income tax is sixpence in the pound[6] . . . the United Nations[7] consists of united nations . . . and high and shining in the regard of all good folk

everywhere is that sagacious, witty, tender, profound writer . . .
who, now waking from his day-dream,[8] sits down, a fat grumpy
fellow, to slog away[9] till lunchtime.

J. B. PRIESTLEY: from *Delight*

[1] *der Wachtraum.*   [2] Neuter adjectival nouns.   [3] *verzaubern in.*   [4] *kampf-erprobt.*   [5] *sich daran machen.*   [6] *beträgt sechs Pence pro Pfund.*   [7] *die Vereinten Nationen.*   [8] Use *aus seinem Traum erwachen.*   [9] *sich durchquälen* (sep. vb.).

After the Match

The football match at Carisbrook was over. Dusk was already
falling, and during the last part of the game the flight of the ball
and even the movements of the players had been hard to follow
in the failing light. Now, looking across the field, I could see the
crowd dimly massing around the gates. Here and there a small
yellow flame flickered[1] where a smoker was lighting up,[2] and
the whole crowd moved under a thin blue haze of tobacco-smoke.
After all the cheering the place seemed very quiet, and from the
street outside came the noise of cars starting up[3] and whining off[4]
in low gear,[5] and a tram screeching round the corner under the
railway bridge. Overhead the sky was clear with a promise of
frost.[6] A few small boys ran with shrill cries under the goalposts;
the rest of the field lay empty in the grey light, and the smell of
mud came through the damp air. I shivered and glanced down
at my steaming jersey.

'Well, you'd better go and get changed,' said Betty. 'I don't
want you to catch cold. You'll be playing Southern[7] next Saturday now, won't you?'

'Yes,' I said. 'They were bound to win today. Beating Kai-
korai puts us level with them.'[8]

'Will you be too tired for the dance?'

'My old knee feels a bit sore but I'll ring you after tea. I must
go and get changed now. So long.'

A. P. GASKELL: *The Big Game*

[1] *aufflackern.*   [2] 'was lighting his pipe or cigarette'.   [3] *starten.*   [4] *auf-heulend davonfahren.*   [5] *im ersten* (or *kleinen*) *Gang.*   [6] 'a clear sky which promised to bring frost'.   [7] *FC Süd.*   [8] *bringt uns in Gleichstand mit ihnen.*

Haydn

His first appointment at the age of twenty-three was at a gentleman's country-house near Melk, where he had at his disposal a
few strings[1] and a couple each[2] of oboes and horns. Here at

Weinzirl he produced his first quartet and his first symphony, both containing minuets in addition to movements adapted from Emanuel Bach's model of the sonata.[3] In 1761 he took service with Prince Esterházy[4] and remained in that noble household till 1790. During those thirty years he had ample opportunity for experiment. He was much liked not only by his employer but by the musicians on the establishment.[5] For most of the time the prince resided at his new palace in Hungary which was remote from the world of Vienna. The result was that Haydn did an enormous amount of uninterrupted work. He explained the situation thus: 'As a conductor of an orchestra I could make experiments, observe what produced an effect and what weakened it, and was thus in a position to improve, alter, make additions or omissions and be as bold as I pleased; I was cut off from the world, there was no one to confuse and torment me, and I was forced to become original.'

FRANK HOWES: *Full Orchestra*

---

[1] *das Streichinstrument.*   [2] Gram. 149 (*a*).   [3] model of the sonata—*der Sonatentypus.*   [4] *Fürst Esterházy.* See Gram. 63, note 1.   [5] *der Hofmusiker.*

Frederick the Great and the Seven Years War[1]

It is said that the modern German mind has a horror of[2] a 'war on two fronts';[3] but in the Seven Years War, on which he was now launched,[4] Frederick the Great had to fight on *four* fronts at the same time. That, perhaps, is one reason why he is called 'the Great'. In the west he held up and eventually repelled a French invasion of Germany, thereby becoming to the Germans of later generations a kind of national hero; though it is doubtful if he would have recognized this picture of himself, for there was nothing particularly[5] 'national' about him, and he always spoke French in preference to German, which to him was a barbarous and uncouth tongue. On the east he was threatened by the Russians, in the north by the Swedes; while to the south the Austrians tried to combine with[6] the Saxons to drive him out of Silesia. Maria Theresa[7] had done her work well[8] in planning his overthrow and the reduction of his territory to[9] the limits of the original Brandenburg. But the execution of the plan was not so successful, and despite enormous losses and defeats, which on two separate occasions forced him to abandon his capital to the Russians and would have crushed a lesser man, the king in the end disappointed all the hopes of his enemies; and when the peace came to be made,[10] he remained in possession of every part of his kingdom, including Silesia.

J. S. DAVIES: From Charlemagne to Hitler

[1] der Siebenjährige Krieg.   [2] einen Schrecken haben vor.   [3] der Zwei-frontenkrieg.   [4] auf den er sich nunmehr eingelassen hatte.   [5] sonderlich.
[6] sich vereinigen mit or zusammengehen mit.   [7] In German: Maria Theresia.
[8] hatte klug gehandelt.   [9] auf (acc.).   [10] als es zum Friedensvertrag kam.

An Inquiry

It was now nearly half-past four, and Wimsey felt that he had a good chance of finding Mr. Goodrich at home. He was directed to his house—the big place up the first turning off the Wilver-combe Road—and found the good gentleman and his family gathered about a table well spread with bread and cakes and honey and Devonshire cream.[1]

Mr. Goodrich, a stout and hearty squire of the old school,[2] was delighted to give any assistance in his power. Mr. Martin had turned up at the house at about seven o'clock on the Tuesday evening and had asked permission to camp[3] at the bottom of Hinks's Lane.[4] Why Hinks's Lane, by the way? Well, there used to be a cottage there that belonged to an old fellow called Hinks— a regular character[5]—used to read the Bible through regularly every year, and it was to be hoped it did him good, for a grace-less[6] old scamp he was and always had been. But that was donkey's years ago,[7] and the cottage had fallen into disrepair. Nobody ever went down there now, except campers.[8] Mr. Martin had not asked for information about camping-grounds; he had asked straight out for permission to camp in Hinks's Lane, calling it by that name. Mr. Goodrich had never set eyes on Mr. Martin before, and he (Mr. Goodrich) knew pretty well everything that went on in the village.

DOROTHY L. SAYERS: Have his Carcase

[1] die Devonshire-Sahne.   [2] alter Schule.   [3] sein Zelt aufschlagen.   [4] Do not translate.   [5] ein sonderbarer Kauz.   [6] gottlos.   [7] das war Ewigkeiten her (slang).   [8] diejenigen, die zelten wollten.

The Morning of the Election[1]

On the morning of the election, I woke while it was still dark. There were knocks at the great gate, the rattle of the door open-ing, the clink of keys, voices in the court; it was six o'clock, and the servants were coming in to work. Although I had been late to bed, telling Roy the final news, I could not get to sleep again. The court quietened, and the first light of the winter dawn crept round the edges of the blind. As the grey morning twilight became visible in the dark room, I lay awake as I had done in other troubles and heard the chimes ring out over the town with indifferent cheerfulness. I was full of worry, though there was nothing left to worry about.

The light increased; there were footsteps, not only servants', passing through the court; I recognized Chrystal's quick and athletic tread.[2] Why was he in college so early? It was a solace when Bidwell tip-toed in. After his morning greeting, he said:

'So the great old day has arrived at last, sir.'

'Yes,' I said.

He stood beside the bed with his deferential, roguish smile.

'I know it's wrong of us to talk among ourselves, sir, but we've had a good many words about who is to be the next Master.'[3]

'Have you?'

'They're two very nice gentlemen,' said Bidwell. 'A very popular gentleman Dr. Jago is. I shouldn't say there was a servant in the college who had[4] ever heard a word against him.' He was watching me with sharp eyes out of his composed, deliberately bland[5] and guileless face.

'Of course,' he said when I did not reply, 'Dr. Crawford is a very popular gentleman too.'

C. P. SNOW: *The Masters*

---

[1] The novel *The Masters* concerns a bitter struggle between the Fellows of a Cambridge college arising from the election of a new Master.   [2] *(der) federnde Gang.*   [3] Do not translate.   [4] Gram. 50.   [5] *unschuldig.*

Mr. Badger's Kitchen

The floor was well-worn red brick, and on the wide hearth burnt a fire of logs, between two attractive chimney-corners tucked away in the wall, well out of any suspicion of draught.[1] A couple of high-backed settles, facing each other on either side of the fire, gave[2] further sitting accommodation[3] for the sociably disposed.[4] In the middle of the room stood a long table of plain boards placed on trestles, with benches down each side. At one end of it, where an arm-chair stood pushed back, were spread the remains of the Badger's plain but ample supper. Rows of spotless plates winked from the shelves of the dresser at the far end of the room, and from the rafters overhead hung hams, bundles of dried herbs,

nets of[5] onions, and baskets of eggs. It seemed a place where
heroes could fitly[6] feast after victory, where weary harvesters
could line up in scores along the table and keep their Harvest
Home[7] with mirth and song, or where two or three friends of
simple tastes[8] could sit about as they pleased and eat and smoke
and talk in comfort and contentment. The ruddy brick floor
smiled up at the smoky ceiling; the oaken settles, shiny with long
wear, exchanged cheerful glances with each other; plates on the
dresser grinned at pots on the shelf, and the merry firelight
flickered and played over everything without distinction.[9]

KENNETH GRAHAME: *The Wind in the Willows*

[1] *vor jedem Zugwind sicher geschützt.*   [2] 'offered'.   [3] *Sitzgelegenheit.*
[4] *die, die Gesellschaft suchten.*   [5] *voll.* Gram. 154.   [6] *gebührend.*   [7] *das
Erntefest halten.*   [8] Singular. Gram. 143 (c).   [9] *ohne Unterschied.*

London Dawn

Where he went he hardly knew. He had a dim memory of wandering through a labyrinth of sordid houses, of being lost in a giant
web of sombre streets, and it was bright dawn[1] when he found
himself at last in Piccadilly Circus. As he strolled home towards
Belgrave Square, he met the great waggons on their way to
Covent Garden. The white-smocked carters, with their pleasant
sunburnt faces and coarse curly hair, strode sturdily on, cracking
their whips, and calling out now and then to each other; on the
back of a huge grey horse, the leader of a jangling team, sat a
chubby boy, with a bunch of primroses in his battered[2] hat, keeping tight hold of[3] the mane with his little hands, and laughing;
and the great piles of vegetables looked like masses of jade against
the morning sky, like masses of green jade against the pink petals
of some marvellous rose. Lord Arthur felt curiously affected,
he could not tell why. There was something in the dawn's
delicate loveliness that seemed to him inexpressibly pathetic, and
he thought of all the days that break in beauty and that set in
storm. These rustics, too, with their rough, good-humoured
voices, and their nonchalant ways, what a strange London they
saw! A London free from[4] the sin of night and the smoke of day,
a pallid, ghost-like city, a desolate town of tombs!

OSCAR WILDE: *Lord Arthur Savile's Crime*

[1] *es war schon heller Tag.*   [2] *verbeult.*   [3] to keep tight hold of s.th.—*sich
an* (dat.) *etwas festhalten.*   [4] *frei von.*

(284)

Erasmus

From Erasmus's letters and portraits we can form a clear picture of what we should have found, if we had knocked on that door in August 1521. We should no doubt have been admitted readily,[1] for Erasmus was no recluse. Probably we should have found him sitting at his table, a man of just over fifty,[2] wearing perhaps even in summer one of the fur-lined gowns of the portraits,[3] with his fair curly hair, now turning grey, escaping from under[4] his square cap; we should recognize the calm eyes looking out from a thin face already lined, the firm straight mouth betraying both sensitivity and humour, and on the long delicate fingers touching the books piled before him, the gleam of rings. The room might resemble the study in which he was sketched in 1530, comfortably furnished according to the ideas of the time; chairs with elaborately carved arms, a table standing on solid end-pieces[5] adorned with grotesque animal heads, the walls hung with[6] tapestries in an arabesque design,[7] the windows framed with pilasters with carved capitals. A cupboard standing open would reveal[8] shelves of books in clasped bindings.[9] On the table, inkpots, hourglass, bookrests and a slender vase of flowers; opposite to the humanist a young secretary or servant pupil,[10] writing.[11]

MARGARET MANN-PHILLIPS: *Erasmus and the Northern Renaissance*

[1] to admit s.o. readily—*jn. bereitwillig hereinbitten.*   [2] Gram. 145 (*b*).
[3] . . . *Roben, wie wir sie aus den Bildnissen (Porträts) kennen.*   [4] *hervorquellen unter* (dat.).   [5] *Füße.*   [6] *behangen mit.*   [7] *von schnörkelhaftem Muster.*
[8] *erkennen lassen.*   [9] *mit verschlossenem Einband.*   [10] *ein ihm zu Diensten stehender Schüler.*   [11] *beim Schreiben.*

A Childhood Home

'I remember, I remember. . . .'[1] It is a pointless and futile occupation, difficult none the less not to indulge in.[2] I remember. Our house at Oxford was dark, spiky and tall. Ruskin himself, it was said, had planned it. The front windows looked out on to the Banbury Road. On rainy days, when I was a child, I used to spend whole mornings staring down[3] into the thoroughfare.[4] Every[5] twenty minutes a tram-car drawn by two old horses, trotting in their sleep, passed with an undulating motion more slowly than a man could walk. The little garden at the back once seemed enormous and romantic, the rocking-horse in the nursery a beast like an elephant. The house is sold now and I am glad

of it. They are dangerous, these things and places inhabited by
memory. It is as though, by a process of metempsychosis,[6] the
soul of dead events goes out and lodges itself in[7] a house, a flower,
a landscape, in a group of trees seen from the train against the
sky-line, an old snapshot, a broken penknife, a book, a perfume.
In these memory-charged[8] places, among these things haunted by
the ghosts of dead days, one is tempted to brood too lovingly
over the past, to live it again, more elaborately,[9] more consciously,
more beautifully and harmoniously, almost as though it were an
imagined life in the future. Surrounded by these ghosts one can
neglect the present in which one bodily lives. I am glad the place
is sold; it was dangerous.

ALDOUS HUXLEY: *Those Barren Leaves*

---

[1] 'I remember, I remember'—'*Ich weiß es noch ganz genau*'.   [2] Cf. 'Tolstoy', note 14, p. 168.   [3] spend . . . staring down . . .—. . . *damit verbringen, . . .
hinunterzustarren*.   [4] *die Hauptverkehrsstraße*.   [5] *alle*.   [6] *der See-
lenwanderungsprozeß*.   [7] *einziehen in*.   [8] *erinnerungsschwer*.   [9] *vollkommener*.

A Mutual Friend

I was staying the other day in the house of an old friend, a public
man,[1] who is a deeply interesting character, energetic, able,
vigorous, with very definite limitations. The only male guest
in the house, it so happened, was also an old friend of mine, a
serious man. One night, when we were all three in the smoking-
room, our host rose, and excused himself, saying that he had some
letters to write. When he was gone, I said to my serious friend:
'What an interesting fellow[2] our host is! He is almost more
interesting because of the qualities that he does not possess, than
because of the qualities that he does possess.' My companion,
who is remarkable for his power of blunt statement,[3] looked at me
gravely, and said: 'If you propose to discuss our host, you must
find someone else to conduct the argument;[4] he is my friend,
whom I esteem and love, and I am not in a position to criticize
him.' I laughed, and said: 'Well, he is my friend, too, and *I*
esteem and love him; and that is the very reason why I should
like to discuss him. Nothing that either you or I could say would
make me love him less; but I wish to understand him. I have a
very clear impression of him, and I have no doubt that you have
a very clear impression too; yet we should probably differ about
him in many points, and I should like to see what light you could

throw upon his character.' My companion said: 'No; it is inconsistent with my idea of loyalty to criticize my friends. Besides, you know I am an old-fashioned person, and I disapprove of criticizing people altogether.'

A. C. BENSON: *From a College Window*

[1] *eine bekannte Persönlichkeit.* [2] *Mensch.* [3] *seine Art, die Dinge geradeheraus zu sagen.* [4] *als Gesprächspartner.*

An Invitation from a King

Wagner was now fifty-one years of age. Through his whole career he had never known what it was to have a single penny free of encumbrance;[1] his income, such as it was,[2] had been always outnumbered by his debts.[3] His moments of success—*Rienzi* at Dresden, *Lohengrin* at Weimar—had been brilliant but had led to nothing substantial; there was no material basis on which to rest,[4] there was no outlook for the future. He had won the love of his friends and the applause of his public at a cost of[5] determined and almost universal hostility on the part of the critics; in the book of their judgement he was a branded heretic, beyond reconciliation or forgiveness.[6] Had he confessed defeat[7] in 1864 the whole history of operatic music would need to be rewritten; and he was within an ace of doing so.[8]

On May 2nd, 1864, Wagner was hiding from his creditors at an hotel in Stuttgart when there came an unexpected and unwelcome knock at the door. The scene which ensued was like that in Gogol's *Revisor*;[9] the visitor brought not a writ but an invitation. 'Come,' said the new King of Bavaria, 'come here and finish your work.' The first shock of surprise was astounding; Wagner half-suspected a trap or a deception; but the envoy was no less a personage than Herr Kabinett-Sekretär von Pfistermeister; the summons was immediate and brooked no delay.[10] On the afternoon of May 3rd he left Stuttgart and next day had his first audience with the King.

SIR W. H. HADOW: *Richard Wagner* (abridged extract)

[1] *einen einzigen Pfennig schuldenfrei zu haben.* [2] 'his small (*geringes*) income'. [3] Active voice, with 'debts' as subject. Use *überwiegen* (insep.). [4] *sich stützen auf* (acc.). Gram. 50. Use imperf. indic. or pluperf. subjunct. [5] *auf Kosten.* [6] 'beyond all reconciliation or forgiveness'. [7] to confess defeat—*sich geschlagen geben.* [8] *er hätte es um ein Haar getan.* [9] '*Revisor*'. [10] *ließ keinen Aufschub zu.*

A Dilemma

When Mrs. Bold came to the end of the walk[1] and faced the lawn, she began to bethink herself what she ought to do. Was she to wait there till Mr. Slope caught her, or was she to go in among the crowd with tears in her eyes and passion in her face? She might in truth have stood there long enough without any reasonable fear of further immediate persecution from[2] Mr. Slope; but we are all inclined to magnify the bugbears which frighten us. In her present state of dread she did not know of what atrocity he might venture to be guilty.[3] Had anyone told her a week ago that he would have put his arm round her waist at this party of Miss Thorne's, she would have been utterly incredulous. Had she been informed that he would be seen on the following Sunday morning walking down the High Street in a scarlet coat and top-boots, she would not have thought such a phenomenon more improbable.

But this improbable iniquity he had committed; and now there was nothing she could not believe of him.[4] In the first place, it was quite manifest that he was tipsy; in the next place it was to be taken as proved that all his religion[5] was sheer hypocrisy; and finally the man was utterly shameless. She therefore stood watching for[6] the sound of his footfall, not without some fear that he might creep out at her suddenly from among the bushes.

ANTHONY TROLLOPE: *Barchester Towers*

---

[1] *die Allee.*   [2] *von seiten* (+ gen.). *sich* (dat.) *etwas zuschulden kommen lassen.* acc. object).   [5] i.e. 'all his religiosity'.   [3] to venture to be guilty of s.th.—   [4] *zutrauen* (with dat. of person and   [6] *horchen nach.*

An Unexpected Confirmation

'For instance,' said Mr. Fotheringay, greatly encouraged.[1] 'Here would be a miracle. That lamp, in the natural course of nature,[2] couldn't burn like that upsy-down,[3] could it, Beamish?'

'*You* say it couldn't,' said Beamish.

'And you?' said Fotheringay. 'You don't mean to say[4]—eh?'

'No,' said Beamish reluctantly. 'No, it couldn't.'

'Very well,' said Mr. Fotheringay. 'Then here comes some-one, as it might be me, along here, and stands as it might be here, and says to that lamp, as I might do, collecting all my will[5]—"Turn upsy-down without breaking, and go on burning steady,"[6] and—Hullo!'[7]

It was enough to make anyone say 'Hullo!' The impossible, the incredible, was visible to them all. The lamp hung inverted in the air, burning quietly with its flame pointing down. It was as solid, as indisputable as ever a lamp was, the prosaic common lamp[8] of the Long Dragon bar.

Mr. Fotheringay stood with the extended forefinger and the knitted brows of one anticipating a catastrophic smash. The cyclist, who was sitting next the lamp, ducked and jumped across the bar. Everybody jumped, more or less. Miss Maybridge turned and screamed. For nearly three seconds the lamp remained still. A faint cry of mental distress[9] came from[10] Mr. Fotheringay, 'I can't keep it up,' he said, 'any longer.' He staggered back, and the inverted lamp suddenly flared, fell against the corner of the bar, bounced aside, smashed upon the floor, and went out.

H. G. WELLS: *The Man Who Could Work Miracles*

[1] Mr. Fotheringay is arguing that miracles are impossible. Mr. Beamish, who challenges every assertion of Mr. Fotheringay's on principle, has made 'the unexpected concession of a qualified assent to his definition of a miracle'.   [2] Preserve the illogical repetition of the idea of 'nature'.   [3] *mit dem Kopf nach unten.*   [4] See Topic 9 (iii), p. 60.   [5] *die Willenskraft.*   [6] '. . . *brenne ruhig weiter !*'   [7] '*Was ist denn das ! ?*'   [8] prosaic common lamp—*die ganz gewöhnliche Deckenlampe.*   [9] *ein unterdrückter Schrei geistig-seelischer Not.*   [10] *entfahren.* See Topic 15, p. 99.

The Dying Queen

In the middle of March 1603 it was clear to everyone that Queen Elizabeth was dying; her doctors were unable to diagnose the illness; she had little fever, but was constantly thirsty, restless and morose; she refused to take medicine, refused to eat, refused to go to bed. She sat on the floor, propped up with cushions, sleepless and silent, her eyes constantly open, fixed on the ground, oblivious to the coming and going of her counsellors and attendants. She had done nothing to recognize[1] her successor; she had made no provision[2] for the disposal[3] of her personal property, of the vast, heterogeneous accumulation[4] of a lifetime, in which[5] presents had come to her daily from all parts of the world; closets[6] and cupboards stacked high with jewellery, coin, bric-à-brac; the wardrobe of 2,000 outmoded dresses. There was always company in the little withdrawing room waiting for her to speak, but she sighed and sipped and kept her silence. She had round her neck a piece of gold engraved with characters; it had been

left to her lately by a wise woman who had died in Wales at the
age of 120. Sir John Stanhope had assured her that as long as
she wore this talisman she could not die. There was no need yet
for doctors or lawyers or statesmen or clergy.

EVELYN WAUGH: *Edmund Campion* (abridged extract)

[1] (In this context) *bestimmen.*   [2] *Anordnungen treffen.*   [3] 'how . . . was to
be disposed of' (*verteilen*).   [4] *die buntgemischte Ansammlung.*   [5] 'which consisted of . . .'   [6] *Truhen* (sing. *die Truhe*).

Letters to the Great

Roy was very modest about his first novel. It was short, neatly
written, and, as is everything he has produced since, in perfect
taste. He sent it with a pleasant letter to all the leading writers
of the day, and in this he told each one how greatly he admired
his[1] works, how much he had learned from his study of them, and
how ardently he aspired[2] to follow, albeit at a humble distance,[3]
the trail his correspondent had blazed.[4] He laid his book at the
feet[5] of a great artist as the tribute of a young man entering upon
the profession of letters[6] to one whom he would always look up to
as his master. Deprecatingly, fully conscious of his audacity in
asking so busy a man to waste his time on a neophyte's puny[7]
effort, he begged for criticism and guidance. Few of the replies
were perfunctory. The authors he wrote to, flattered by his
praise, answered at length. They commended his book; many
of them asked him to luncheon. They could not fail to be charmed
by his frankness and warmed by his enthusiasm.[8] He asked for
their advice with a humility that was touching and promised to
act upon it[9] with a sincerity that was impressive. Here, they felt,
was someone worth taking a little trouble over.[10]

W. SOMERSET MAUGHAM: *Cakes and Ale*

[1] Gram. 104.   [2] 'and that it was his most ardent wish (*sein sehnlichster
Wunsch*) . . .'   [3] *auf bescheidene Entfernung.*   [4] to blaze a trail—*eine Bahn
brechen.* [5] *zu Füßen.* [6] *die literarische Laufbahn.* [7] *gering.* [8] Recast
the sentence in the active voice with *müssen.*   [9] to act upon advice—*einem Rat
folgen* or the rather stronger *einen Rat befolgen.*   [10] *für den es sich lohnte, ein
wenig Mühe auf sich zu nehmen.*

The Russians

There are two ideas prevalent about the Russians. The first
envisages a miserable, starved, slave people, yearning for freedom
and constantly plotting to overthrow the government. The

second sees them as happy enthusiasts working furiously for the glory of the Socialist Fatherland.

Both these outlooks are completely untrue. The Russians have never known freedom, so they can scarcely be expected to yearn for it. They may not be well off, but they do not starve: they grumble a great deal, but they do not plot against the régime—most of them have known no other, and their complaints are directed against faults in its working rather than in the system itself. They are not particularly happy or enthusiastic: one seldom encounters a spontaneous smile. They are about the least politically minded people in Europe—despite the advantages of membership, only 3½ per cent. of them take the trouble to belong to the ruling party. They talk freely about homes, families, work, wages and football, as we do: most of them never mention politics, and know less about such matters than we do in Britain. You could live in Russia for some time without realizing that it *was* a Socialist fatherland. Men work and are paid: they do not pretend to work for love or a slogan. One Communist ruler once said to me sadly: 'We have come to the conclusion that most people work for money.' If we look at the Russians not as supermen or slaves but as very ordinary people, we are much more likely to understand them.

BERNARD NEWMAN: *Visa to Russia*

Bremen

Bremen is a great seaport even though it is sixty-five kilometres from the sea. The settlement which was founded in the ninth century was at the last crossing ford over the river Weser, and in its early days it had to fight hard to maintain the freedom of both banks of the Weser in order to retain its own access to the sea. Towards the end of the sixteenth century its life-line, the Weser, failed; the waterway silted up and only relatively small craft could use it. It was this fact which, together with political difficulties with Oldenburg, led it to found its own port and daughter-city, Bremerhaven, on the open sea, and on Hanoverian territory, in 1827. That port is still part of the same political unit as the mother-city. And meanwhile the river has been dredged so that ocean-going liners and the largest cargo steamers can get up to Bremen itself. The rebuilt docks with their elaborate installations for unloading grain vessels are worth a visit. Also Bremen seems to me to have solved one modern problem, that of the unsightly gasometer. To furnish a landmark to aircraft,

rather than from any aesthetic motive, it has made its gasometer
a chequer work of huge red and white squares, which is a consider-
able improvement upon the black monsters which disfigure other
cities.

MONK GIBBON: *Western Germany*

Theseus and the Minotaur

Theseus readily agreed to do as she said. As well as the ball of
wool she had brought him a sword, and, hiding this underneath
his cloak, he went forward into the labyrinth. The girls and the
other young men waited for him inside the gates, while he picked
his way along passages which turned and twisted and linked up
with other passages, winding in and out, turning abruptly, or
sweeping in long or short curves. As he went he unwound the
ball of wool and listened carefully for any noise that might tell
him of the whereabouts of the strange monster with whom he was
to fight. For long he wandered in complete silence and then, as
he approached a part of the labyrinth where the walls turned at
right angles, he heard the noise of heavy breathing, a noise that
might have been made by an animal or might almost have been
made by a man. He put down the ball of wool, gripped his sword
in his hand, and advanced cautiously to the corner. Looking
round it he saw a monstrous shape. Standing, with his head
lowered, was the figure of a giant, but, on the massive neck and
shoulders was not a human head but the swinging dewlaps, blunt
muzzle and huge horns of a bull. For a moment Theseus and
the Minotaur gazed at each other. . . .

REX WARNER: *Men and Gods*

Rio de Janeiro

The time I spent in Rio lengthened out to six months, but on the
whole it was a delightful experience in spite of my anxieties.
From the Embassy roof there was a perfect view in all directions,
and when it comes to views Rio is incomparable. Below, the
wonderful Beira Mar avenue passed under the ridge and entered
the suburb of Copacabana, beyond which it extended through
suburb after suburb along twelve miles of exquisite coastline.
In the evenings we often motored along this highway to return
after dark, when one of the most wonderful city lighting systems

in the world suddenly flashed out into full glory, throwing a carpet of shimmering reflections over the still waters of the bay. How drab and gloomy our worn-out English cities appear after such beauty as this! One could not be bored here. There was the unceasing activity of the harbour—the arrival and departure of liners, the fussing bay steamers racing like giant water-beetles to and from the state capital of Niteroi—the thronged avenues and gaily dressed people—the great sandy beaches which even the thousands of bathers could not crowd. If anything was required to complete the picture it was yachts. There was none, but some day they will come, for it is a wealthy place. I see it as the capital of civilization in embryo.

COL. P. H. FAWCETT: *Exploration Fawcett*

Germany

In 1918, after the First World War, Germany became a republic, with substantial territorial losses. In 1933, Adolf Hitler, as the leader of the strongest political party, became *Reich* Chancellor. In a short time he succeeded in eliminating the constitutional organs of the *Reich* and in turning the republic into a formless despotism. The politics practised by the National Socialists unleashed in 1939 the Second World War, which ended in 1945 with the total military defeat of Germany. The territory of the *Reich* was partitioned into four zones of occupation, and supreme governmental power was assumed by the occupying powers. The eastern provinces of the *Reich* were cut off and, after the expulsion of the greater part of the German inhabitants, were placed under Polish and Soviet administration. Berlin was placed under the joint administration of the four occupying powers and in 1948 was divided into a Western Sector (West Berlin) and a Soviet Sector (East Berlin). In the three western zones of occupation the way was opened to the German people from 1948 for the establishment of a State conforming with the national will. In the Soviet Zone, however, profound political, economic and social changes were carried through with the aim of incorporating this German territory in the Soviet *bloc*.

PROFESSOR HELMUT ARNTZ: *Germany in a Nutshell*
(published by the Press and Information Office of the
Federal German Republic)

In the Rocky Mountains

I boarded the west-bound train at Calgary and soon was passing through the foothills of the Rockies. The line followed the turbulent Bow River, whose valley was one of the loveliest I had ever seen. Tributaries dashed through the pine woods to join the main stream. The valley contracted, then widened to reveal glimpses of lofty summits ahead, which lured the eye with their glistening snow-slopes.

The line swung across the river and later skirted a lake cupped in the hills. The valley grew steeper, the mountains drew in on both sides of the track. They closed in behind and loomed up in front of us like an impenetrable wall, so steep indeed that I wondered how the line would find a passage through its precipitous face. But, still keeping company with the Bow, we approached it, and twisting and turning entered The Gap, whose gaunt almost perpendicular sides shot up boldly to heights so dizzy that they made our huge locomotive with its long line of coaches look as puny as a toy train. Then suddenly we emerged from this giant portal to find ourselves in the Rockies. Around us rugged peaks rose above mountain shoulders of bare rock. Particularly striking was the serrated edge of Fairholm Range, away to northward, whose high promontories stood guardian over snow-filled valleys.

J. H. STEMBRIDGE: *A Portrait of Canada*

National Pride

'The natives of England,' wrote an Italian ambassador to London about four and a half centuries ago, 'whenever they see a handsome foreigner, they say that he looks like an Englishman, and that it is a great pity he should not be an Englishman.' In England this remark has been quoted to prove the lamentable decline of Roman susceptibilities, since a thousand years earlier the observant Gregory the Great, looking for the first time on a shipment of Britons, had made the shrewder remark: 'Not Angles but angels.' This old reassurance drifted into my mind the other night when I heard over the radio an American senator, speaking from those cavernous lungs which the Almighty reserved for American senators, trumpet: 'I am an American—who is there in the whole wide world that does not envy the name?' Being in a defensive mood, I was reminded in turn of a Chinese general I met here in an army camp during the war. He had just been

given a heart-warming account of the economic potential of
China. He made a grateful little bow, and as the American
general's arm went round his shoulder he remarked: 'Automobiles
and cola drinks very good for Americans. But please, we should
like remain Chinese.'

ALISTAIR COOKE: 'What's the Matter with America?'
(from *Letters from America*)

The Work of the Philosopher

The philosopher does not discover new facts. His concern is our
everyday view with its common landmarks, duty, obedience, law,
desire. He does not set out, as the scientist does, grasping his
compass, towards lands no man has trod, nor return thence
bearing strange treasures and stranger tales. He is rather to be
pictured ascending the tower of some great cathedral such as
St. Stephen's, Vienna. As he goes up the spiral stairway, the
common and particular details of life, the men and tram-cars,
shrink to invisibility and the big landmarks shake themselves
clear. Little windows open at his elbow with widening views.
There is conscience; over there is duty; there is conscience again
looking quite different from this new level; now he is high enough
to see law and liberty from one window. And ever there haunts
him the vision of the summit, where there is a little room with
windows all round, where he may recover his breath and see the
view as a whole, and the Schottenkirche and the Palace of Justice
in their true relative proportions, and where that gargoyle (deter-
minism, was it?) which loomed in on him so menacingly at one
stage in his ascent shall have shrunk to the speck that it is.

J. D. MABBOTT: *The State and the Citizen*

A Pacifist's Attitude to the First World War

I spent the evening of August 4th walking round the streets,
especially in the neighbourhood of Trafalgar Square, noticing
cheering crowds, and making myself sensitive to the emotions of
passers-by. During this and the following days I discovered to
my amazement that average men and women were delighted at
the prospect of war. I had fondly imagined, what most Pacifists
contended, that wars were forced upon a reluctant population by
despotic and Machiavellian governments.

I was tortured by patriotism. The successes of the Germans before the Battle of the Marne were horrible to me. I desired the defeat of Germany as ardently as any retired colonel. Love of England is very nearly the strongest emotion I possess, and in appearing to set it aside at such a moment, I was making a very difficult renunciation. Nevertheless, I never had a moment's doubt as to what I must do. I have at times been paralysed by scepticism, at times I have been cynical, at other times indifferent, but when the war came I felt as if I heard the voice of God. I knew that it was my business to protest, however futile protest might be. My whole nature was involved. As a lover of truth, the national propaganda of all the belligerent nations sickened me. As a lover of civilization, the return to barbarism appalled me. As a man of thwarted parental feeling, the massacre of the young wrung my heart. I hardly supposed that much good would come of opposing the war, but I felt that for the honour of human nature those who were not swept off their feet should show that they stood firm.

BERTRAND RUSSELL: *Portraits from Memory and Other Essays*

An Unhappy Marriage

Had Elizabeth's opinion been all drawn from her own family, she could not have formed a very pleasing picture of conjugal felicity or domestic comfort. Her father, captivated by youth and beauty, and that appearance of good humour which youth and beauty generally give, had married a woman whose weak understanding and illiberal mind had very early in their marriage put an end to all real affection for her. Respect, esteem, and confidence had vanished for ever; and all his views of domestic happiness were overthrown. But Mr. Bennet was not of a disposition to seek comfort for the disappointment which his own imprudence had brought on, in any of those pleasures which too often console the unfortunate for their folly or their vice. He was fond of the country and of books; and from these tastes had arisen his principal enjoyments. To his wife he was very little otherwise indebted, than as her ignorance and folly had contributed to his amusement. This is not the sort of happiness which a man would in general wish to owe to his wife; but where other powers of entertainment are wanting, the true philosopher will derive benefit from such as are given.

JANE AUSTEN: *Pride and Prejudice*

Night in Camp

Night is a dead monotonous period under a roof; but in the open world it passes lightly, with its stars and dews and perfumes, and the hours are marked by changes in the face of Nature. What seems a kind of temporal death to people choked between walls and curtains, is only a light and living slumber to the man who sleeps afield. All night long he can hear Nature breathing deeply and freely; even as she takes her rest, she turns and smiles; and there is one stirring hour unknown to those who dwell in houses, when a wakeful influence goes abroad over the sleeping hemisphere, and all the outdoor world are on their feet. It is then that the cock first crows, not this time to announce the dawn, but like a cheerful watchman speeding the course of night. Cattle awake on the meadows; sheep break their fast on dewy hillsides, and change to a new lair among the ferns; and houseless men, who have lain down with the fowls, open their dim eyes and behold the beauty of the night.

R. L. STEVENSON: *Travels with a Donkey in the Cevennes*

The Political Consequences of the Thirty Years War in Germany

Within Germany itself, the political consequences of the Thirty Years War were almost entirely bad. Modelling themselves on Louis XIV, the post-Westphalian princes either stultified or abolished outright the local diets by means of which their fathers' tyranny had to some extent been mitigated. Autocracy became the tradition of the country.

Meanwhile, Austrian power had been finally and for ever excluded from western and northern Germany. The states which still nominally formed part of the Empire were in fact independent of the Hapsburgs—independent enough to be, as Richelieu and Father Joseph had intended them to be, under the influence of the Bourbons. So far as France was concerned, this was an admirable arrangement; but it was an arrangement that could persist only on two conditions: first, that French monarchy should remain stable, neither unduly declining nor unduly expanding its power, and second, that the Germans themselves should not be reunited, either voluntarily or under compulsion. By the beginning of the nineteenth century both these conditions had ceased to be fulfilled. The French monarchy had declined and collapsed, to be replaced by an aggressive military dictatorship that scared all Europe into opposition; and the Prussian monarchy had arisen and was in a position to create a new unified German state. By breaking the power of Austria, Richelieu and Father Joseph had made sure that, when Germany came to be united, it should not be united as a federated, non-national and not wholly German empire, but as a highly centralized, purely Teutonic nation.

ALDOUS HUXLEY: Grey Eminence

The Life and Soul of the Party?

Mr. Smeeth could not do any conjuring, but if he had been given unlimited powers, he knew one trick that he would have liked to perform that instant, a trick that involved the immediate disappearance of Mr. Fred Mitty. It was Saturday night, the little party was in full swing, and they were all in the front room, all, that is, except the Mitty girl and Edna, who had gone out together for an hour or so, probably round to the pictures. In addition to the Mitty pair, there were Dalby and Mrs. Dalby (whose sister told fortunes with cards). Mr. Smeeth had seen the room when it had had more people in it, but he had never known it when it had seemed so full. He had always thought of Dalby, who lived at 11 Chaucer Rd., was a bandy-legged insurance agent, and fancied himself as a wag and a great hand at parties, as a noisy chap, but compared with Fred Mitty he was quiet and decent and merely another Smeeth. It had not taken Mr. Smeeth ten minutes to discover that he disliked Mitty intensely, and everything that Mitty had done and said since (and for the last half-hour or so he had insisted on calling Mr. Smeeth 'Pa') had only increased that dislike, which did not stop short at Fred, but extended to Mrs. Mitty and the girl, Dot. He had never known three people he disliked more.

J. B. PRIESTLEY: Angel Pavement

History

History is read by different people for various reasons; it has many uses and values. To me, its chief but not its only value is poetic. Its poetic value depends on its being a true record of actual happenings in the past. For the mystery of time past continually enthralls me. Here, long before us, dwelt folk as real as we are today, now utterly vanished, as we in our turn shall vanish. History can miraculously restore them to our vision and understanding, can tell us a little of what were their hopes and fears, their words and works. The curtain of cloud that hides the scenes of the past is broken here and there, and we have magic glimpses into that lost world, which is as actual as our own, though placed on another step of the moving staircase of time. Forward we cannot see at all; backward we can see fitfully and in part. In that strange relation of past and present, poetry is always inherent, even in the most prosaic details, in Greek potsherds and Roman stones, in Manor rolls and Parliamentary reports, all hallowed in our imagination by the mere passage of the years.

And apart from this consecration by time which envelops all the past, so many of the things which history reveals belong by their own nature to the stuff of poetry, the passions and aspirations of men and even of nations, their dramatic failures and successes, the action of chance the disposer, the wonderful creativeness of man, the brief life of his best creations and hopes and systems, above all his indomitable spirit, always beaten down and rising again in some new, utterly unpredictable form. As a great poem, as an epic without beginning or end, I read History and never tire.

G. M. TREVELYAN: 'Stray Thoughts on History'
(*An Autobiography and Other Essays*)

Greek Drama and Modern Science

The effect of Greek dramatic literature was many-sided so far as concerns the various ways in which it indirectly affected medieval thought. The pilgrim fathers of the scientific imagination as it exists today are the great tragedians of ancient Athens, Aeschylus, Sophocles, Euripides. Their vision of fate, remorseless and indifferent, urging a tragic incident to its inevitable issue, is the vision possessed by science. Fate in Greek Tragedy becomes the order of nature in modern thought. The absorbing interest in the particular heroic incidents, as an example and a verification of the workings of fate, reappears in our epoch as concentration of interest on the crucial experiments. It was my good fortune to be present at the meeting of the Royal Society in London when the Astronomer Royal for England announced that the photographic plates of the famous eclipse, as measured by his colleagues in Greenwich Observatory, had verified the prediction of Einstein that rays of light are bent as they pass in the neighbourhood of the sun. The whole atmosphere of tense interest was exactly that of the Greek drama: we were the chorus commenting on the decree of destiny as disclosed in the development of a supreme incident. There was dramatic quality in the very staging—the traditional ceremonial, and in the background the picture of Newton to remind us that the greatest of scientific generalizations was now, after more than two centuries, to receive its first modification. Nor was the personal interest wanting: a great adventure in thought had at length come safe to shore.

ALFRED NORTH WHITEHEAD: *Science and the Modern World*

PROSE EXTRACTS AND POEMS FOR COMMENTARY

Children on Holiday

Ist einer unter uns, dem in seiner Kindheit „das weit hinaus
erglänzende Meer" schöner erschien als die bunten, seltsam
geformten Muscheln am Strand? Die grandiosen Linien der
Landschaft interessanter als ein Flugzeug, das über den weiten
5 Himmel zog, oder ein Ameisenhaufen mit seinem kribbelnden
Gewimmel? Was für Bilder tauchen in der Erinnerung auf, wenn
wir an glückliche Ferientage zurückdenken? Die kleine Hütte
aus Zweigen und Moos, die wir im Walde bauten; die erhitzten,
lachenden Gesichter der Spielgefährten; die grüngoldene Ei-
10 dechse, die durchs Heidekraut huschte; der Hase, der in wildem
Schreck vor unsern Füßen aufsprang aus seinem Lager im sonnenwarmen Sand; der sprudelnde Bach, in dem wir uns kühlten.
Kinder haben wenig Sinn für landschaftliche Reize. Um so
inniger und tiefer ist ihre Freude an allem Nahen, Lebendigen.
15 Was aber ersehnen die Eltern für ihren Urlaub? Weite Fahrten
in die lockende Ferne! Werden die Ferienpläne nur nach den
Wünschen der Erwachsenen bestimmt, dann haben die Kinder
wohl Freude an dem bunten Vielerlei, werden aber bald lustlos
und abgespannt, weil sie in das Chaos der unablässig auf sie
20 eindringenden Bilder keine Ordnung bringen können. Die Er-
lebnisfähigkeit eines Kindes richtet sich eben auf andere Bereiche.
So entsteht eine sehr bedenkliche Reaktion; sie gewöhnen sich
an die oberflächliche Art mancher Erwachsener, berühmte Aussichtspunkte, Kirchen, Museen und Schlösser zu „erledigen",
25 ohne das Geschaute wirklich zu erleben. Wer schon so früh, noch
unfähig zum wahren Genießen, von unverständigen Eltern durch
vieler Herren Länder geschleppt wird, der stumpft ab. Ihm ist für
spätere Zeiten der Zugang zu den erlesenen Schönheiten verwehrt.
Nach den Ferien übertrumpfen sich die schwatzenden Kinder:
30 „Wir waren in den Dolomiten!" — „Wir in der Schweiz!" —
„Wir haben eine Reise durch ganz Italien gemacht!" Monika
hält sich befangen im Hintergrund, bis sie auf Fragen bekennen
muß: „Wir waren nur in der Lüneburger Heide." Lebhaft
beteuert sie: „Aber herrlich war es, bestimmt ganz prima!" und
35 schweigt dann entmutigt vor dem überlegenen Lächeln der
anderen. Und doch hat sie den besseren Teil erlebt. Wie be-
glückend kann das Beisammensein der Familie in einem kleinen

Erholungsort sein! Jetzt haben die im Alltagsleben oft so
gehetzten Eltern wirklich einmal Zeit für ihre Kinder: sie wandern mit ihnen, spielen Federball oder helfen fröhlich beim 40
Burgenbau. Dann wieder überlassen sie die Kinder ihrem Spiel,
machen Spaziergänge oder ruhen lesend im Liegestuhl. Abends
geht's gemeinsam auf Schleichwegen durch den Wald, um Rehe
zu belauschen. — Das ist Ferienglück für die Kinder! Nach den
langen Monaten in der engen Wohnung, in Schulräumen, im 45
gefährlichen Großstadtgewühl nun das Spiel in Licht, Luft und
Freiheit.   MAGDALENE ZIMMERMANN: 'Glück der Kinder' (adapted)
                                                 (*Rheinischer Merkur*)

(i) Analyse the construction of the passage as a piece of essay-
writing.

(ii) What is the writer's main argument in this passage? How
convincingly, in your opinion, does she argue her point?

(iii) Translate the last paragraph of the passage.

(iv) Translate carefully the following phrases, explaining their
significance in their context; and comment on any aspects of
syntax or word-formation occurring in them which you regard as
specially important for a student of German:

„das weit hinaus erglänzende Meer" (lines 1–2); ein Ameisenhaufen mit seinem kribbelnden Gewimmel (lines 5–6); der
Hase, der in wildem Schreck vor unsern Füßen aufsprang aus
seinem Lager im sonnenwarmen Sand (lines 10–12); Um so
inniger und tiefer ist ihre Freude an allem Nahen, Lebendigen
(lines 13–14); Ihm ist für spätere Zeiten der Zugang zu den
erlesenen Schönheiten verwehrt (lines 27–28).

A Party of Travellers visit a Hermit in an old Mine-working

Der Einsiedler zeigte ihnen seine Bücher. Es waren alte Historien
und Gedichte. Heinrich blätterte in den großen schöngemalten
Schriften; die kurzen Zeilen der Verse, die Überschriften,
einzelne Stellen und die saubern Bilder, die hie und da, wie
verkörperte Worte, zum Vorschein kamen, um die Einbil- 5
dungskraft des Lesers zu unterstützen, reizten mächtig seine
Neugierde. Der Einsiedler bemerkte seine innere Lust und
erklärte ihm die sonderbaren Vorstellungen. Die mannigfaltigsten
Lebensszenen waren abgebildet. Kämpfe, Leichenbegängnisse,
Hochzeitfeierlichkeiten, Schiffbrüche, Höhlen und Paläste; Kö- 10
nige, Helden, Priester, alte und junge Leute, Menschen in
fremden Trachten und seltsame Tiere kamen in verschiedenen
Abwechselungen und Verbindungen vor. Heinrich konnte sich

nicht satt sehen und hätte nichts mehr gewünscht, als bei dem
15 Einsiedler, der ihn unwiderstehlich anzog, zu bleiben und von
ihm über diese Bücher unterrichtet zu werden. Der Alte fragte
unterdes, ob es noch mehr Höhlen gäbe, und der Einsiedler sagte
ihm, daß noch einige sehr große in der Nähe lägen, wohin er ihn
begleiten wollte. Der Alte war dazu bereit, und der Einsiedler,
20 der die Freude merkte, die Heinrich an seinen Büchern hatte,
veranlaßte ihn, zurückzubleiben und sich während dieser Zeit
weiter unter denselben umzusehen. Heinrich blieb mit Freuden
bei den Büchern und dankte ihm innig für seine Erlaubnis. Er
blätterte mit unendlicher Lust umher. Endlich fiel ihm ein Buch
25 in die Hände, das in einer fremden Sprache geschrieben war, die
ihm einige Ähnlichkeit mit der lateinischen und italienischen zu
haben schien. Er hätte sehnlichst gewünscht, die Sprache zu
kennen, denn das Buch gefiel ihm vorzüglich, ohne daß er eine
Silbe davon verstand. Es hatte keinen Titel, doch fand er noch
30 beim Suchen einige Bilder. Sie dünkten ihm ganz wunderbar
bekannt, und wie er recht zusah, entdeckte er seine eigene
Gestalt ziemlich kenntlich unter den Figuren. Er erschrak und
glaubte zu träumen, aber beim wiederholten Ansehn konnte er
nicht mehr an der vollkommenen Ähnlichkeit zweifeln. Er traute
35 kaum seinen Sinnen, als er bald auf einem Bilde die Höhle, den
Einsiedler und den Alten neben sich entdeckte.

(i) Translate from the beginning of the passage to 'wohin er
ihn begleiten wollte' (line 19).

(ii) With detailed reference to the narrative technique, the
subject-matter, and the style (especially the use of adjectives and
adverbs) assign the passage to the period of German literature in
which you think it was written.

(iii) Does the passage appeal to you or not? Explain the
reasons for your view.

The following passage is taken from the war diary of a young
historian, Dr. Felix Hartlaub. It is concerned with experiences
in his own unit.

Am Kaiser-Wilhelm-Kanal
September 1939

Bauern und Soldaten

Der uralte Gegensatz. Jetzt, Kriegsanfang, noch vielfach ver-
schleiert. — Das schweigende Bauernhaus, der halbbeladene
Wagen davor. Die Soldaten kommen mit Lastwagen, springen

ab, werfen Gerät herunter. Ein Gatter fällt um, ein Zaun wird durchschnitten. Die Wagen schaukeln über den Wiesenboden, 5 sinken ein, die Räder fassen nicht mehr; im Nu sind tiefe Furchen in die Wiese gewühlt. Gesträuch wird hineingeworfen, Stroh aus der Miete vor dem Bauernhaus gezerrt, die Wassergräben verschüttet. Der Bauer ist plötzlich da, läuft hierhin, dorthin, möchte verstecken, ableiten, hilft, mit dem Blick auf die Zer- 10 störung, den Wagen anschieben, stimmt verlegen in kamerad-schaftliche Zurufe ein, muß einen Spaten, Bretter hergeben, sieht seine Utensilien mit rätselhafter Geschwindigkeit sich aus dem Hofe lösen. Dabei sind es Städter, er hat es schon gesehen, sie machen alles falsch. Die Kühe sind bereits durch den nieder- 15 gelegten Zaun auf die Straße entwichen; langsam setzen sich einige Soldaten in Trab, um sie zurückzutreiben, zünden sich dabei eine Zigarette an. Die Frauen beobachten an dem kleinen Küchenfenster. Ein Soldat ist bereits in der Küche und möchte Milch, der andere sich die Stiefel abbürsten. Einer verhandelt 20 bereits über den Ankauf eines Huhns, das er nach Hause schicken möchte, der vierte möchte sich ein Rad pumpen, um zum Bäcker zu fahren. Die Hände in den Taschen, den Kopf im Mantel-kragen, sich mit Bedeutung den Dreck von den Stiefeln tretend, kommen sie einer nach dem anderen durch die niedere Tür in 25 die Küche, mit den Nagelschuhen über die Fliesen. Die Frauen bringen das Gewünschte mit der Miene zurückweichender Ver-neinung, lachen steif und leer zu den Scherzen der Soldaten. Der Bauer steht dabei, will Einwendungen machen, gibt statt dessen Ratschläge, Auskünfte. Die Soldaten sind alles harmlose 30 Berliner Jungens, Angestellte, Akademiker. Aber sie haben in den paar Wochen Krieg gelernt, einen Bauernhof zu taxieren, die Kühe, die Hühner, die Obstbäume mit einem Blick zu erfassen, sich im Schutze der Uniform alles nur irgend Mögliche zusammenzufechten, als stünden die sieben mageren Jahre bevor. 35 Alles nur irgend Eßbare essen, alles ausnutzen, mitnehmen, be-halten.   (Abridged extract)

(i) What attitude does the farmer adopt towards the soldiers?

(ii) Translate the following phrases and comment on any par-ticular significance they have in their context:

(*a*) Der uralte Gegensatz (line 1).

(*b*) Dabei sind es Städter . . . machen alles falsch (lines 14–15).

(*c*) . . . sich mit Bedeutung den Dreck von den Stiefeln tre-tend (line 24).

(*d*) mit der Miene zurückweichender Verneinung (lines 27–28).

(e) Aber sie haben in den paar Wochen Krieg gelernt, einen
Bauernhof zu taxieren (lines 31–32).

(iii) What literary merits has this account, in your opinion?
Answer with detailed reference to the text, commenting on what-
ever aspects of vocabulary usage and narrative technique seem to
you to be especially effective.

Goethe's Influence

Goethes große Eigentümlichkeit wirkte auf seine Umgebung auf
eine dreifache Art. Schwache, kleinliche und dabei, wie immer,
eitle Naturen, die ihn auf keine Weise zu fassen fähig waren,
denen nur sein Ruhm und der sichtbare Ausdruck von Großheit,
5 der ihm so eigen war, imponierte, — suchten, so wohlfeil sie nur
immer konnten, von diesen letzten Äußerlichkeiten etwas an sich
zu bringen —

　　„und wie er sich räuspert und wie er spuckt,
　　　das haben sie ihm glücklich abgeguckt";

10 die Jünglinge, die seine Jugend mitlebten, taten, als kämen sie
ohne Umweg aus Jaxthausen, Wahlheim oder Auerbachs Keller.
Es war ihnen ganz genial zumute, und sie gedachten vorderhand,
ehe sie die Welt mit ihren Schöpfungen erbeben machen wollten,
sich's recht wohl sein zu lassen.
15　　Der Rausch ging vorüber, die Jugend alterte — aber die Narr-
heit blieb oder vielmehr wuchs; denn der Jugend vergibt man
sie, dem Alter nicht. Goethe kam, mit Steinen und Antiken
beladen, aus Italien, sprach wenig und war vornehmer geworden.
Nun setzten jene die Brille auf die Nase, gaben sich das Ansehen,
20 Kunstkenner zu sein, und ließen dann und wann ein gnädiges
Orakel zu uns armen Sterblichen herniederschallen. Sie taten,
als sei ihnen ebenso ruhig zumute wie ihrem Meister, als steckte
hinter ihren vieldeutigen Reden ebensoviel Sinn als hinter den
seinen. Dies war das abscheuliche Unheil der Goethe-Tuerei,
25 aus dem wir, leider! noch nicht völlig erlöst sind. — Eine zweite
Art der Einwirkung, jener völlig entgegengesetzt, erlitten kräftige,
originelle Naturen, die entweder eine innere Diskrepanz mit
Goethes Wesen in sich fühlten oder, von vornherein jeder
Übermacht feind, je mehr seine Würde sich entfaltete, desto
30 mehr sich gegen sie waffneten. — Die dritte Art seines Einflusses,
den er zumal in nächster Nähe geübt zu haben scheint, war die
erfreulichste. Sie glich der Wirkung, welche dieselbe Eine Sonne
auf die mannigfachen Produkte der irdischen Vegetation ausübt:

jedes dieser Gewächse gedeiht nach dem Maßstabe, der ihm
eingeboren ist. Und so kam durch Goethes Anregung, aber   35
ohne seinen Zwang, mancher treffliche Geist zum Bewußtsein
seiner selbst und der Sphäre, in welcher er für sich etwas dar-
stellen konnte, was, in demselben Kreise, keinem anderen
möglich war. Unterdrückung eigener Kräfte aus Verzweiflung
am Gelingen, im Anblick eines übergewaltigen Geistes, wirkte   40
Goethe gar nicht; denn sein ganzes Sein, Dichten und Lehren
war anregend, aufmunternd, fördernd, belebend.

                                                    (Abridged extract)

(i) Describe briefly the three types of influence which, according to the author, Goethe's personality exerted on his contemporaries.

(ii) *Either*: Explain as far as you can the allusions to Goethe's
works and the references to periods of Goethe's life which occur
in the passage;

Or: Explain the significance of any three of the following:

(*a*) Schwache, kleinliche und dabei, wie immer, eitle Na-
    turen . . . etwas an sich zu bringen (lines 2–7).
(*b*) Goethe kam . . . war vornehmer geworden (lines 17–18).
(*c*) Dies war das scheußliche Unheil der Goethe-Tuerei
    (line 24).
(*d*) eine innere Diskrepanz mit Goethes Wesen (lines 27–28).
(*e*) Und so kam durch Goethes Anregung, . . . keinem anderen
    möglich war (lines 35–39).

(iii) By what means does the author sketch the personality of
Goethe and ridicule his imitators?

Developments in Scientific Thought

Man bezeichnet die Welt der Gegenstände im Gegensatz zur
Sinnenwelt auch als die reale Welt. Doch muß man mit dem
Wort „real" vorsichtig sein. Man darf es hier nur in einem vor-
läufigen Sinn verstehen. Denn mit diesem Wort verbindet sich
die Vorstellung von etwas absolut Beständigem, Unveränder-   5
lichem, Konstantem, und es wäre zuviel behauptet, wenn man die
Gegenstände des kindlichen Weltbildes als unveränderlich hin-
stellen würde. Das Spielzeug ist nicht unveränderlich, es kann
zerbrechen oder auch verbrennen, die Lampenglocke kann in

10 Scherben gehen, und dann ist es mit ihrer Realität in dem genannten Sinne vorbei.
Das klingt selbstverständlich und trivial. Aber es ist wohl zu
beachten, daß beim wissenschaftlichen Weltbild, wo die Verhältnisse ganz ähnlich liegen, dieser Tatbestand keineswegs als
.5 selbstverständlich empfunden wurde. Wie nämlich für das Kind
in seinen ersten Lebensjahren das Spielzeug, so waren für die
Wissenschaft durch Jahrzehnte und Jahrhunderte hindurch die
Atome das eigentlich Reale in den Vorgängen der Natur. Sie
waren es, die beim Zerbrechen oder Verbrennen eines Gegen-
20 standes unverändert die nämlichen blieben und daher das Bleibende in allem Wechsel der Erscheinungen darstellten. Bis sich
zur allgemeinen Überraschung eines Tages herausstellte, daß
auch die Atome sich verändern können. Wir wollen daher, wenn
wir im folgenden[1] von der realen Welt reden, dieses Wort
25 zunächst immer in einem bedingten, naiven Sinn verstehen,
welcher der Eigenart des jeweiligen Weltbildes angepaßt ist, und
wir wollen uns dabei stets gegenwärtig halten, daß mit einer
Veränderung des Weltbildes zugleich auch eine Veränderung
dessen, was man das Reale nennt, verbunden sein kann.
30   Jedes Weltbild ist charakterisiert durch die realen Elemente,
aus denen es sich zusammensetzt. Aus der realen Welt des prak-
tischen Lebens hat sich die reale Welt der exakten Wissenschaft,
das wissenschaftliche Weltbild, entwickelt. Aber auch dieses ist
nicht endgültig, sondern es verändert sich immerwährend durch
35 fortgesetzte Forschungsarbeit, von Stufe zu Stufe.
Eine solche Stufe bildet dasjenige wissenschaftliche Weltbild,
welches wir heute das klassische zu nennen pflegen. Seine realen
Elemente und daher charakteristischen Merkmale waren die
chemischen Atome. Gegenwärtig ist die wissenschaftliche For-
40 schung, befruchtet durch die Relativitätstheorie und die Quantentheorie, im Begriff, eine höhere Stufe der Entwicklung zu
erklimmen und sich ein neues Weltbild zu schaffen. Die realen
Elemente dieses Weltbildes sind nicht mehr die chemischen
Atome, sondern es sind die Wellen der Elektronen und Pro-
45 tonen . . . Vom heutigen Standpunkt aus müssen wir also den
Realismus des klassischen Weltbildes als einen naiven bezeichnen.
Aber niemand kann wissen, ob man nicht einmal in Zukunft von
unserem gegenwärtigen modernen Weltbild das nämliche sagen
wird.

---

[1] The passage is taken from the book *Vorträge und Erinnerungen*, by Max Planck,
the eminent physicist.

(i) Translate the second paragraph of the passage.

(ii) Explain the significance of the following words and phrases as they are used in their context:

Sinnenwelt (line 2); die Vorstellung von etwas absolut Beständigem, Unveränderlichem, Konstantem (lines 5–6); dann ist es mit ihrer Realität in dem genannten Sinne vorbei (lines 10–11); Weltbild (line 13); befruchtet durch die Relativitätstheorie und die Quantentheorie (lines 40–41).

(iii) *Either*: Write a critical appreciation of the passage as an introduction to recent developments in scientific ideas for the intelligent layman, commenting on the means the author uses to make his meaning plain and tracing the steps by which the argument is developed;

Or: Write a précis of the passage *in German* in about 100 words.

The German Language

Jede Sprache hat ihre Eigenarten. Der Schweizer Dichter Heinrich Federer hat das Wesen der deutschen Sprache einmal durch einen schönen Vergleich veranschaulicht: „Französisch ist ein edler Park, Italienisch ein großer, heller, bunter Wald. Aber Deutsch ist beinahe wie ein Urwald, so dicht und geheimnisvoll, 5 so ohne großen Durchgang und doch tausendpfadig. Im Park kann man sich nicht verirren, in der italienischen Waldhelle nicht so leicht und gefährlich; aber im Deutschen kann einer in vier, fünf Minuten im Dickicht verschwinden."

In der Tat: die deutsche Sprache bietet dem einzelnen eine 10 grenzenlose Fülle von Ausdrucksmöglichkeiten; sie führt ihn in das blühende Leben hinein und läßt den Armen dort glücklich und — schuldig werden. Ihre Begriffe haben nicht den scharfen Umriß der französischen, weil die bildliche Bedeutung ihrer Wurzel mitschwingt; sie sind weniger konventionell, weil sie 15 nicht aus der Schule einer unermüdlichen Geselligkeit kommen; sie sind keine bloßen abstrakten Rechenpfennige, sondern jedermann kann selbst die Münzen prägen, die er ausgibt. Französisch schreibt gut, wer so schreibt wie die anderen; nur die unauffällige Schönheit ist gestattet. Deutsch kann man nur 20 gestaltend, nur individuell schreiben. Darum widerstrebt das Deutsche der Vollkommenheit; in einer so wunderlichen Sprache wie der deutschen, sagt Goethe, bleibt immer etwas zu wünschen übrig. Sie ist nie abgeschlossen, sondern stets im Aufbruch. Sie ist nicht so prächtig wie die italienische, nicht so klar wie die 25

französische und nicht so handlich wie die englische. Aber das
Raunende und Dämmernde, der Traum und die Ahnung,

> die große Kunst des Hintergrundes
> und das Geheimnis zweifelhafter Lichter,

30 sie gewinnen im Deutschen Gestalt. Die Ruhe und das Behagen
des wohlumfriedeten Hauses gewährt uns das Deutsche nur
selten, stets reißt es die Fenster auf und gibt den Blick frei auf
die Unendlichkeit, und der Zugwind eines ewigen Werdens läßt
Papiere und Gedanken durcheinanderflattern. Kurzum, das
35 Deutsche ist die Sprache der Deutschen, die Gott mit dem Hang
zum Grenzenlosen gesegnet und geschlagen hat, für die der Weg
mehr bedeutet als das Ziel und der Kampf mehr als die Vollendung.

> (Reproduced by permission of the Verlag Bibliographisches Institut AG,
> Mannheim, quoted from *Der Große Duden*, vol. ii, *Stilwörterbuch der
> deutschen Sprache*, edited by Paul Grebe and Gerhart Streitberg, preface
> by Ludwig Reiners)

(i) State briefly the main points which the author makes in this
passage.

(ii) Explain the significance of the following:

Ihre Begriffe . . . mitschwingt (lines 13–15); in einer so wunderlichen Sprache . . . etwas zu wünschen übrig (lines 22–24); Sie
ist nie abgeschlossen, sondern stets im Aufbruch (line 24).

(iii) *Either*: What light does this passage throw upon the work,
in prose or poetry, of any German author or authors you have
read?

Or: Translate lines 26–38 (from Aber das Raunende . . . to . . .
die Vollendung). Explain what you understand by: das Deutsche
ist die Sprache der Deutschen, die Gott mit dem Hang zum
Grenzenlosen gesegnet und geschlagen hat.

Alter Arbeiter

> Wenn er durch den kühlen Morgen geht,
> schief die Kappe auf ergrautem Kopf,
> in zerfurchter Hand den Henkeltopf,
> und dann wartend am Fabriktor steht:
> 5   späht er wohl noch eine kurze Weile
> forschend in die graue Straßenflucht,
> sieht Gestalten sinnlos und in Eile
> fortgerissen von versteckter Wucht,

hört das Donnern naher Hochbahnzüge,
das dem Tag Triumph und Wehe brüllt,   10
und die e i n e, ungeheure Lüge
seines Lebens ist ihm jäh enthüllt.

Schmerzlich fühlt er sich von seinen Taten,
spürt er sich von seinem Werk getrennt,
als von einem Kinde, das mißraten   15
auch den eigenen Vater nicht mehr kennt.
Und es wächst in ihm bezwungner Groll,
peitscht das Blut erregter durch die Adern,
daß er fluchen muß den grauen Quadern,
die er heut wie je betreten soll.   20

Bis sein Auge, zornverdunkelt, fällt
auf die Brücke, drüber Züge gleiten.
Da umleuchtet Glanz sein Weiterschreiten,
und er sieht sein dunkles Los erhellt.

Hat er diese Brücke doch gebaut,   25
diese eine mit noch tausend andern,
drüber Millionen Füße wandern
sichren Weg, dem jeder Schritt vertraut.

Um den alten Werkmann klingt ihr Tritt,
Lobgesänge kommender Geschlechter,   30
die ihn preisen als bestellten Wächter,
der mit dunklen Mächten tapfer stritt.

Und noch einmal ist er ganz durchbebt
von den ungezählten Hammerschlägen,
die er tat, die Brückenform zu prägen,   35
selig wissend, daß er groß gelebt.   KARL BRÖGER

Answer the following questions with close reference to the text:

(i) At what period do you think this poem was written?

(ii) By what means does the author create atmosphere in
lines 1–20?

(iii) What do you understand by 'die e i n e, ungeheure Lüge
seines Lebens' (lines 11–12) and 'sein dunkles Los' (line 24)?

(iv) Contrast the ideas expressed in the first half of the poem
(lines 1–20) with those expressed in the second half (lines 21–36),
discussing the author's choice of vocabulary (especially verbs
and adjectives) throughout.

(v) Translate lines 25–36 of the poem.

Der Mai

Im Galarock des heiteren Verschwenders,
ein Blumenzepter in der schmalen Hand,
fährt nun der Mai, der Mozart des Kalenders,
aus seiner Kutsche grüßend, über Land.

5   Es überblüht sich, er braucht nur zu winken.
Er winkt! Und rollt durch einen Farbenhain.
Blaumeisen flattern ihm voraus und Finken.
Und Pfauenaugen flügeln hinterdrein.

Die Apfelbäume hinterm Zaun erröten.
10   Die Birken machen einen grünen Knicks.
Die Drosseln spielen, auf ganz kleinen Flöten,
das Scherzo aus der Symphonie des Glücks.

Die Kutsche rollt durch atmende Pastelle.
Wir ziehn den Hut. Die Kutsche rollt vorbei.
15   Die Zeit versinkt in einer Fliederwelle.
Oh, gäb es doch ein Jahr aus lauter Mai!

Melancholie und Freude sind wohl Schwestern.
Und aus den Zweigen fällt verblühter Schnee.
Mit jedem Pulsschlag wird aus Heute Gestern.
20   Auch Glück kann weh tun. Auch der Mai tut weh.

Er nickt uns zu und ruft: „Ich komm ja wieder!"
Aus Himmelblau wird langsam Abendgold.
Er grüßt die Hügel, und er winkt dem Flieder.
Er lächelt. Lächelt. Und die Kutsche rollt.

ERICH KÄSTNER: *Die dreizehn Monate*

(i) Explain the following, commenting on any special significance they may have in their context:

fährt nun der Mai, der Mozart des Kalenders,/aus seiner
Kutsche grüßend, über Land. (lines 3–4); es überblüht sich
(line 5); Oh, gäb es doch ein Jahr aus lauter Mai! (line 16);
mit jedem Pulsschlag wird aus Heute Gestern. (line 19).

(ii) Write a critical appreciation of the poem, paying careful
attention to imagery and versification. How far does the poem
seem to you to express a mood of 'Melancholie und Freude'?

Ich

In dem Geschwätz und Gewühl,
  vor dem plätschernden Brunnen am Markte,
stand ich lachend und jung
  in der Freundinnen Schar.
Kannte Krug und Gesicht,   5
  kannte Giebel und Stuben,
kannte, was feilschend und laut
  um die Buden sich drängt.
Lästerte, neckte und pries,
  lauschte und horchte geduldig,   10
gab mit flinkem Mund
  Rede und Witzwort zurück.

Aber fern von der Stadt
  im Schoß der waldigen Düne,
lag meine Seele still,   15
  wie das Tier im Dickicht sich birgt.
Hörte das sanfte Sausen
  der knarrenden Kiefernstämme,
hörte in regloser Luft
  durchsichtiger Flügel Geklirr.   20
Bis vom Strande her
  in die ängstlich harrende Stille,
unruhvoll und bedrängt
  wie mein Herz, die Brandung gepocht.
Zitternd erharrten wir da   25
  bis sich der Sturm erhoben,
bis der dräuende Gott
  mich und die Wogen erlöst.

Und ich sang in den Wind,
  in das Wirbeln rauchender Dünen,   30
in das dröhnende Brausen
  sang mein tönender Mund.
Sang meiner einsamen Heimat
  Götter und rote Burgen,
sang ihr mütterlich Herz,   35
  sang ihr grüngrünes Kleid.
Sang, was groß und gekrönt
  durch meine Träume gewandert,
blutüberströmtes Haupt,
  gallegetränktes Herz.   40

Sang meiner seltsamen Schwestern
mondlichtgezeichnete Stirnen,
sterblichen Leibes wie ich,
jenseitiger Weisheit kund.

45   Sang ich, mir selber kaum deutbar,
was Schatten und Erde mich lehrten,
sang ich Liebe und Tod —
sang ich das eigne Geschick.   AGNES MIEGEL

(i) Translate lines 1–12 of the poem.

(ii) In what part of Germany is the poem set? Answer with reference to the internal evidence of the poem.

(iii) Discuss the means the author uses to create atmosphere and contrast, with special reference to the use of sound contrasts in the words of individual lines.

(iv) Write a short note on the versification of the poem.

(v) What does the author say of her own destiny as a poet?

Unendlichkeit

Wer weiß der Vögel Flug,
Und wer den Weg des Windes?
Wer folgt dem Wolkenzug,
Dem Lächeln eines Kindes,

Dem Licht im Weizenfeld,
Dem Fall der Regentropfen,
Dem Herbstlied aller Welt:
Früchte, die niederklopfen?

Du würdest arm und alt,
Eh daß du könntst durchdringen
Die ewige Gewalt
In den geringen Dingen.   ALBRECHT GOES

Parabase

Freudig war, vor vielen Jahren
Eifrig so der Geist bestrebt,
Zu erforschen, zu erfahren,
Wie Natur im Schaffen lebt.

Und es ist das ewig Eine,
Das sich vielfach offenbart:
Klein das Große, groß das Kleine,
Alles nach der eignen Art;
Immer wechselnd, fest sich haltend,
Nah und fern und fern und nah,
So gestaltend, umgestaltend —
Zum Erstaunen bin ich da.

J. W. v. GOETHE

(i) State briefly the central thought expressed in each of the above poems.

(ii) Translate the following phrases and explain the significance they have in their context:

(*a*) Früchte, die niederklopfen.
(*b*) Die ewige Gewalt/In den geringen Dingen.
(*c*) das ewig Eine.
(*d*) Zum Erstaunen bin ich da.

(iii) Compare and contrast the thought-content, style, and versification of the two poems.

Johann Kepler

Gestern als ich vom nächtlichen Lager den Stern mir im Osten
    Lang betrachtete, den dort mit dem rötlichen Licht,
Und des Mannes gedachte, der seine Bahnen zu messen,
    Von dem Gotte gereizt, himmlischer Pflicht sich ergab,
Durch beharrlichen Fleiß der Armut grimmigen Stachel
    Zu versöhnen umsonst und zu verachten bemüht:
Mir entbrannte mein Herz von Wehmut bitter. Ach! dacht ich,
    Wußten die Himmlischen dir, Meister, kein besseres Los?
Wie ein Dichter den Helden sich wählt, wie Homer, von Achilles'
    Göttlichem Adel gerührt, schön im Gesang ihn erhob,
Also wandtest du ganz nach jenem Gestirne die Kräfte,
    Sein gewaltiger Gang war dir ein ewiges Lied.
Doch so bewegt sich kein Gott von seinem goldenen Sitze,
    Holdem Gesange geneigt, den zu erretten, herab,
Dem die höhere Macht die dunkeln Tage bestimmt hat,
    Und euch Sterne berührt nimmer ein Menschengeschick:
Ihr geht über dem Haupte des Weisen oder des Toren
    Euren seligen Weg ewig gelassen dahin!

EDUARD MÖRIKE

(i) What do we learn from the poem of the life and character of Kepler?

(ii) How would you describe the metre of this poem? Compare or contrast the subject-matter of the poem with that of any other German poem you know which employs the same or approximately the same metre.

(iii) How does the poet's use of vocabulary, word-order, and imagery serve to create atmosphere?

(iv) *Either*: Translate the poem;

Or: Write an exposition *in German* of the thought-content of the poem.

Elegie von Abschied und Wiederkehr
geschrieben in Amerika, Herbst 1939

Ich weiß, ich werde alles wiedersehen,
Und es wird alles ganz verwandelt sein.
Ich werde durch erloschne Städte gehn,
Darin kein Stein mehr auf dem andern Stein —
Und selbst wo noch die alten Steine stehen,
Sind es nicht mehr die altvertrauten Gassen —
Ich weiß, ich werde alles wiedersehen
Und nichts mehr finden, was ich einst verlassen.

Der breite Strom wird noch zum Abend gleiten.
Auch wird der Wind noch durch die Weiden gehn,
Die unberührt in sinkenden Gezeiten
Die stumme Totenwacht am Ufer stehn.
Ein Schatten wird an unsrer Seite schreiten
Und tiefste Nacht um unsre Schläfen wehn —
Dann mag erschauernd in den Morgen reiten,
Wer lebend schon sein eignes Grab gesehn.

Ich weiß, ich werde zögernd wiederkehren,
Wenn kein Verlangen mehr die Schritte treibt.
Entseelt ist unsres Herzens Heimbegehren,
Und was wir brennend suchten, liegt entleibt.
Leid wird zu Flammen, die sich selbst verzehren,
Und nur ein kühler Flug von Asche bleibt —
Bis die Erinnrung über dunklen Meeren
Ihr ewig Zeichen in den Himmel schreibt.

CARL ZUCKMAYER

Eitelkeit der Welt

Du siehst, wohin du siehst, nur Eitelkeit auf Erden.
Was dieser heute baut, reißt jener morgen ein;
Wo jetzund Städte stehn, wird eine Wiese sein,
Auf der ein Schäferkind wird spielen mit den Herden.

Was jetzund prächtig blüht, soll bald zertreten werden;   5
Was jetzt so pocht und trotzt, ist morgen Asch' und Bein;
Nichts ist, das ewig sei, kein Erz, kein Marmorstein.
Jetzt lacht das Glück uns an, bald donnern die Beschwerden.

Der hohen Taten Ruhm muß wie ein Traum vergehn.
Soll denn das Spiel der Zeit, der leichte Mensch, bestehn?   10
Ach, was ist alles dies, was wir für köstlich achten,

Als schlechte Nichtigkeit, als Schatten, Staub und Wind,
Als eine Wiesenblum', die man nicht wieder findt!
Noch will, was ewig ist, kein einzig Mensch betrachten.

ANDREAS GRYPHIUS (1616–64)

(i) Explain what you understand to be the significance of the lines:

Und es wird alles ganz verwandelt sein (Zuckmayer, line 2).

Dann mag erschauernd . . . sein eignes Grab gesehn (Zuckmayer, lines 15–16).

Und was wir brennend suchten, liegt entleibt (Zuckmayer, line 20).

Nichts ist, das ewig sei, kein Erz, kein Marmorstein (Gryphius, line 7).

Soll denn das Spiel der Zeit, der leichte Mensch, bestehn? (Gryphius, line 10).

Noch will, was ewig ist, kein einzig Mensch betrachten (Gryphius, line 14).

(ii) In what respects may both these poems be regarded as prophetic? What similarities and what differences do you observe in the thought and mood of the poems?

(iii) Write a detailed analysis of *one* of the two poems, considering some or all of the following: versification; the effectiveness of the poem as a representation of a mood and/or as a commentary on a particular period of history; the imagery of the poem.

GENERAL GRAMMAR INDEX

A number in roman type (e.g. 17) refers to the *page*. A number in italic type (e.g. *17*) refers to the *article number* in the Grammar Section.

STRONG AND ANOMALOUS VERBS

The term 'Strong and Anomalous Verbs', as used in the *Oxford–Harrap Standard German–English Dictionary*, has been adopted as the most suitable general description of the verbs given in this list, which is organized in what it is hoped will be found the most practical way. The following points should be noted:

(i) With few exceptions, only the simple forms of verbs are given. Verbs with prefixes, whether separable or inseparable, whether reflexive or not, follow the pattern of the simple verb, e.g. *aufnehmen, abnehmen, entnehmen, vernehmen, sich ausnehmen, sich benehmen*, except that inseparable verbs drop the *ge-* of the past participle: (*hat*) *vernommen*, (*hat*) *sich benommen*, &c.

(ii) The layout is alphabetical for speed of reference; but this should not be allowed to obscure the underlying recurrent patterns, which a student can and should find for himself: *binden, finden, winden*, &c.; *beißen, gleiten, leiden, reißen, reiten*, &c.; *brennen, kennen, rennen*, &c.

(iii) The list will not do the work of a dictionary. Although some footnotes are given to clarify points of meaning and usage, the student needs to learn how to check exact meanings and usages of verbs (especially whether transitive or intransitive in German).

(iv) Only the forms which are more likely to give difficulty or which are essential as a reminder to the pattern of the personal forms are given. Thus it is essential that the student should know the system of vowel changes that applies to each verb and those closely akin to it (see (ii) above); he must be particularly careful about the vowel changes from -*e*- to -*i*- or -*ie*- and from -*a*- to -*ä*- in the 2nd and 3rd person singular of the present tense (column 2 in the list), e.g. *ich gebe* but *du gibst, er gibt, ich stehle* but *du stiehlst, er stiehlt, ich backe* but *du bäckst, er bäckt*; and he must carefully note the correspondence between the 2nd and 3rd persons of verbs that show the *e/i* or *e/ie* change and their familiar imperative forms: *gibst/gibt* and *gib!, hilfst/hilft* and *hilf!, empfiehlst/empfiehlt* and *empfiehl!*, &c., but *bäckst/bäckt* and *back(e)!, schläfst/schläft* and *schlaf(e)!, fährst/fährt* and *fahr(e)!*, &c.

The other personal forms of the imperative are regularly constructed on the model: *geben Sie! bringen Sie!* (polite form, singular and plural); *gebt! bringt!* (familiar form, plural). Note that *gib! empfiehl! iß!*, &c. do not have a final -*e* (*siehe* does only in the sense of the archaic 'lo!' and the meaning 'see, refer to', e.g. *siehe unten*—see below). The familiar imperative (singular) is normally spoken and written without a final -*e* nowadays: *komm! geh! laß!*, &c.

Alternative forms are shown where they occur. The (*es*) of 2nd person singulars, present tense (*du bläs(es)t, du gieß(es)t*, &c.) is generally omitted.

(v) The imperfect subjunctive is not shown in the list. This is because (*a*) it is easily formed from the imperfect indicative (see Topic 5, p. 34), and (*b*) because its usage in *speech* is very restricted (see Topic 5, p. 35 and Topic 6, pp. 40–41) except for very common verbs (*haben, sein, werden, lassen, gehen, kommen, wissen, tun*, &c., and the modal auxiliaries). Where two forms of the imperfect subjunctive exist (*verstände/verstünde, befähle/beföhle*, &c., see p. 34), the standard form may always be used if required. It is, of course, vitally important to be able to recognize the imperfect subjunctive and its meaning in the written word, and to gain experience of the kind of situations in which it can and should be used.

(vi) Except where the auxiliary *ist* is shown before the past participle, the verb conjugates in perfect tenses with *haben*. The broad principle is that the auxiliary *sein* is used for intransitive verbs of movement and verbs denoting a change of state, whether strong or weak, e.g. *laufen, steigen, fallen, hüpfen*, &c., and *sprießen, schwellen, werden, verschwinden, verdunsten*—evaporate, &c., but *haben* is used for *transitive* verbs of movement, whether strong or weak, e.g. *bringen, schließen, treiben, rücken*—move.

(vii) The modal past participles *gedurft, gekonnt, gesollt*, &c., are shown below the more usual *dürfen, können, sollen*, &c. They are used only where there is an implied 'to do it', i.e. in such statements as *Ich habe es nicht gewollt, ich habe es gemußt.*

STRONG AND ANOMALOUS VERBS

Infin.	2nd and 3rd pers. sing. Present	1st and 3rd pers. sing. Impf.	Past Part.	Imper. (fam.)	English Infin.
backen	bäckst bäckt	buk[1] backte	gebacken	back(e)!	bake, fry
befehlen	befiehlst befiehlt	befahl	befohlen	befiehl!	order, command
beginnen	beginnst beginnt	begann	begonnen	beginn(e)!	begin, start
beißen	beiß(es)t beißt	biß	gebissen	beiß(e)!	bite
bergen	birgst birgt	barg	geborgen	birg!	rescue
bersten	birst birst	barst	ist geborsten	birst!	burst
betrügen	betrügst betrügt	betrog	betrogen	betrüg(e)!	deceive, trick
biegen	biegst biegt	bog	gebogen	bieg(e)!	bend
bieten	bietest bietet	bot	geboten	biet(e)!	offer
binden	bindest bindet	band	gebunden	bind(e)!	tie, bind
bitten	bittest bittet	bat	gebeten	bitte! bitt!	ask, request

[1] *buk* is the more regional or country form, *backte* the more urban.

Infin.	2nd and 3rd pers. sing. Present	1st and 3rd pers. sing. Impf.	Past Part.	Imper. (fam.)	English Infin.
blasen	bläs(es)t bläst	blies	geblasen	blas(e)!	blow, play (a wind instrument)
bleiben¹	bleibst bleibt	blieb	ist geblieben¹	bleib(e)!	stay, remain
braten	brätst brät	briet	gebraten	brat(e)!	roast
brechen	brichst bricht	brach	gebrochen	brich!	break
brennen	brennst brennt	brannte	gebrannt	brenn(e)!	burn
bringen	bringst bringt	brachte	gebracht	bring(e)!	bring
denken	denkst denkt	dachte	gedacht	denk(e)!	think
dreschen	drischst drischt	drosch	gedroschen	drisch!	thresh
dringen	dringst dringt	drang	gedrungen	dring(e)!	penetrate, thrust
dürfen	darfst darf	durfte	{ dürfen gedurft	—	be allowed
empfehlen	empfiehlst empfiehlt	empfahl	empfohlen	empfiehl!	recommend
erbleichen	erbleichst erbleicht	erblich	ist erblichen	erbleich(e)!	go pale
erlöschen	erlisch(e)st erlischt	erlosch	ist erloschen	erlisch!	go out (of a light)

Infinitive	Present	Preterite	Past participle	Imperative	Meaning
erschrecken[2]	erschrickst erschrickt	erschrak	ist erschrocken	erschrick!	be frightened
essen	ißt ißt	aß	gegessen	iß!	eat
fahren	fährst fährt	fuhr	ist gefahren	fahr(e)!	travel, go (by vehicle)
fallen	fällst fällt	fiel	ist gefallen	fall(e)!	fall
fangen	fängst fängt	fing	gefangen	fang(e)!	catch
fechten	fichst ficht	focht	gefochten	ficht!	fence, skirmish
finden	findest findet	fand	gefunden	find(e)!	find
flechten	flichtst flicht	flocht	geflochten	flicht!	twine, braid
fliegen	fliegst fliegt	flog	ist geflogen	flieg(e)!	fly
fliehen	fliehst flieht	floh	ist geflohen	flieh(e)!	escape, flee
fließen	fließ(es)t fließt	floß	ist geflossen	fließ(e)!	flow
fressen	frißt, frissest frißt	fraß	gefressen	friß!	eat (of animals)
frieren[3]	frierst friert	fror	gefroren[3]	frier(e)!	freeze

[1] Note the auxiliary verb.

[2] Intrans. vb. 'To frighten' is the *weak vb. erschrecken.*

[3] *frieren* is conjugated with both *sein* and *haben* according to sense. Compare: *Gestern ist das Wasser im Teich gefroren*—Yesterday the water in the pond froze; and *Gestern hat es stark gefroren*—There was a heavy frost yesterday.

Infin.	2nd and 3rd pers. sing. Present	1st and 3rd pers. sing. Impf.	Past Part.	Imper. (fam.)	English Infin.
gären	gärst gärt	gor	ist gegoren	gär(e)!	ferment
gebären	gebierst gebiert	gebar	geboren	gebier!	give birth, bear (offspring)
geben	gibst gibt	gab	gegeben	gib!	give
gedeihen	gedeihst gedeiht	gedieh	ist gediehen	gedeih(e)!	prosper, thrive
gehen	gehst geht	ging	ist gegangen	geh(e)!	go, walk
gelingen[1]	—	gelang	ist gelungen	geling(e)!	succeed, be successful
gelten	gilst giltst gilt	galt	gegolten	gilt!	be reckoned as, be valid
genesen	genes(es)t genest	genas	ist genesen	genes(e)!	get well
genießen	genieß(es)t genießt	genoß	genossen	genieß(e)!	enjoy
geschehen	—	geschah	ist geschehen	—	happen
gewinnen	gewinnst gewinnt	gewann	gewonnen	gewinn(e)!	win
gießen	gieß(es)t gießt	goß	gegossen	gieß(e)!	pour
gleichen[2]	gleichst gleicht	glich	geglichen	gleich(e)!	resemble, be like

Infinitive	Present	Preterite	Past participle	Imperative	Meaning
gleiten	gleitest / gleitet	glitt	ist geglitten	gleit(e)!	slide, slip
glimmen	glimmst / glimmt	glomm	geglommen	glimm(e)!	glow
graben	gräbst / gräbt	grub	gegraben	grab(e)!	dig
greifen	greifst / greift	griff	gegriffen	greif(e)!	grasp, seize
haben	hast / hat	hatte	gehabt	hab(e)!	have
halten	hältst / hält	hielt	gehalten	halt(e)!	hold, stop
hängen² (hangen)	hängst / hängt	hing	gehangen	häng(e)!	hang
hauen	haust / haut	hieb	gehauen	hau(e)!	hack, chop, hit
heben	hebst / hebt	hob	gehoben	heb(e)!	lift, raise
heißen	heiß(es)t / heißt	hieß	geheißen	heiß(e)!⁴	be named
helfen⁵	hilfst / hilft	half	geholfen	hilf!	help
kennen	kennst / kennt	kannte	gekannt	kenn(e)!	be acquainted with, know

[1] 3rd pers. impersonal usages only. Very commonly with impers. *es* as subject: *es gelingt mir.* ....

[2] With dat. object: *Er gleicht dir genau*—He's just like you.

[3] See Gram. 12, note 2. Compare the weak (trans.) verb *hängen* and the strong (intrans.) verb *hängen*: *Er hängte das Bild an die Wand* and *Das Bild hing an der Wand*; similarly, *Er hat das Bild an die Wand gehängt* and *Das Bild hat an der Wand gehangen.*

[4] The imperative is unlikely except in the older usage of *heißen* = command, order.

[5] *helfen* governs a dat. object.

Infin.	2nd and 3rd pers. sing. Present	1st and 3rd pers. sing. Impf.	Past Part.	Imper. (fam.)	English Infin.
klimmen	klimmst klimmt	klomm	ist geklommen	klimm(e)!	clamber, climb
klingen	klingst klingt	klang	geklungen	kling(e)!	sound
kneifen	kneifst kneift	kniff	gekniffen	kneif(e)!	pinch
kommen	kommst kommt	kam	ist gekommen	komm(e)!	come
können	kannst kann	konnte	können / gekonnt	—	be able
kriechen	kriechst kriecht	kroch	ist gekrochen	kriech(e)!	creep, crawl
laden	{ lädst / ladest { lädt / ladet	lud	geladen	lad(e)!	load, invite[1]
lassen[2]	{ läßt / lässest { laßt	ließ	{ gelassen[2] { lassen[2]	{ laß! { lasse!	leave, let
laufen	läufst läuft	lief	ist gelaufen	lauf(e)!	run
leiden	leidest leidet	litt	gelitten	leid(e)!	suffer, endure
leihen	leihst leiht	lieh	geliehen	leih(e)!	lend

Infinitive	Present	Past	Past participle	Imperative	Meaning
lesen	liest / liest	las	gelesen	lies!	read
liegen	liegst / liegt	lag	gelegen	lieg(e)!	lie, be lying
lügen	lügst / lügt	log	gelogen	lüg(e)!	lie, tell a lie
melken	milkst / milkt	molk	gemolken	milk!	milk
messen	mißt / missest	maß	gemessen	miß!	measure
mißlingen [3]	— / mißlingt	mißlang	ist mißlungen	—	fail, not succeed
mögen	magst / mag	mochte	gemocht	—	like
müssen	mußt / muß	mußte	gemußt	—	have to
nehmen	nimmst / nimmt	nahm	genommen	nimm!	take
nennen	nennst / nennt	nannte	genannt	nenn(e)!	name
pfeifen	pfeifst / pfeift	pfiff	gepfiffen	pfeif(e)!	whistle
preisen	preis(es)t / preist	pries	gepriesen	preis(e)!	praise, esteem
quellen	quillst / quillt	quoll	ist gequollen	quill!	stream, pour

[1] 'invite' is more commonly *einladen*.

[2] Where *lassen* is used to mean 'have, get (s.th. done)' the past part. is *lassen*. See Topic 18, pp. 119-20.

[3] 3rd person (impersonal) usages only. Very commonly with impers. *es* as subject: *es mißlingt mir immer . . . .* Compare with *gelingen*.

Infin.	2nd and 3rd pers. sing. Present	1st and 3rd pers. sing. Impf.	Past Part.	Imper. (fam.)	English Infin.
raten[1]	rätst rät	riet	geraten	rat(e)!	advise[1], guess
reiben	reibst reibt	rieb	gerieben	reib(e)!	rub
reißen	reiß(es)t reißt	riß	gerissen	reiß(e)!	snatch, tear
reiten[2]	reitest reitet	ritt	ist geritten[2]	reit(e)!	ride
rennen	rennst rennt	rannte	ist gerannt	renn(e)!	race, run
riechen	riechst riecht	roch	gerochen	riech(e)!	smell
ringen	ringst ringt	rang	gerungen	ring(e)!	wrestle, struggle
rinnen	rinnst rinnt	rann	ist geronnen	rinn(e)!	trickle
rufen	rufst ruft	rief	gerufen	ruf(e)!	call, shout, cry
saufen	säufst säuft	soff	gesoffen	sauf(e)!	drink heavily, booze
saugen	saugst saugt	sog	gesogen	saug(e)!	suck
schaffen[3]	schaffst schafft	schuf	geschaffen	schaff(e)!	create
schallen	schallst schallt	scholl schallte	geschallt geschollen	schall(e)!	resound

scheiden[4]	scheidest scheidet	schied	ist geschieden	scheid(e)!	depart
scheinen	scheinst scheint	schien	geschienen	schein(e)	seem, shine
schelten	schiltst schilt	schalt	gescholten	schilt!	scold, rebuke
schieben	schiebst schiebt	schob	geschoben	schieb(e)!	push
schießen	schieß(es)t schießt	schoß	geschossen	schieß(e)!	shoot, fire
schinden	schindest schindet	schund	geschunden	schind(e)!	flay, exploit
schlafen	schläfst schläft	schlief	geschlafen	schlaf(e)!	sleep
schlagen	schlägst schlägt	schlug	geschlagen	schlag(e)!	beat, hit
schleichen	schleichst schleicht	schlich	ist geschlichen	schleich(e)!	creep
schleifen	schleifst schleift	schliff	geschliffen	schleif(e)!	trail (on floor), sharpen (knife, &c.)
schließen	schließ(es)t schließt	schloß	geschlossen	schließ(e)!	shut, close
schlingen	schlingst schlingt	schlang	geschlungen	schling(e)!	tie, wind (around)

[1] In the sense of 'advise', *raten* governs a dat. object of the person: *Was rätst du mir?*

[2] *reiten* can of course be used as a transitive verb, in which case it is conjugated with *haben*: *Hast du dieses Pferd geritten?*

[3] *schaffen* as a weak verb has a variety of meanings, including, 'to work (hard)', 'to shift', 'to get through (work)'. Forms of *schaffen* with a prefix (*verschaffen, beschaffen, anschaffen, abschaffen*, and many more) are always weak.

[4] *scheiden* alone is little used nowadays, but note that it has various forms with prefixes: *ausscheiden*—to drop out (of race, activity, &c.), *verscheiden*—to expire, pass away, &c.

Infin.	2nd and 3rd pers. sing. Present	1st and 3rd pers. sing. Impf.	Past Part.	Imper. (fam.)	English Infin.
schmeißen	schmeiß(es)t schmeißt	schmiß	geschmissen	schmeiß(e)!	chuck, fling
schmelzen	schmilz(es)t schmilzt	schmolz	ist geschmolzen	schmilz!	melt
schnauben[1]	schnaubst schnaubt	schnob	geschnoben	schnaub(e)!	pant, snort
schneiden	schneidest schneidet	schnitt	geschnitten	schneid(e)!	cut
schrecken	(See erschrecken[2])				frighten
schreiben	schreibst schreibt	schrieb	geschrieben	schreib(e)!	write
schreien	schreist schreit	schrie	geschrie(e)n	schrei(e)!	scream, shout
schreiten	schreitest schreitet	schritt	ist geschritten	schreit(e)!	stride
schweigen	schweigst schweigt	schwieg	geschwiegen	schweig(e)!	be silent, say nothing
schwellen[3]	schwillst schwillt	schwoll	ist geschwollen	schwill!	swell (up)
schwimmen	schwimmst schwimmt	schwamm	ist geschwommen	schwimm(e)!	swim, float
schwinden	(See verschwinden)				dwindle
schwingen	schwingst schwingt	schwang	geschwungen	schwing(e)!	swing, oscillate
schwören	schwörst schwört	schwor schwur	geschworen	schwör(e)!	swear, vow

Infinitive	Present	Imperfect	Perfect	Imperative	Meaning
sehen	siehst / sieht	sah	gesehen	sieh(e)!	see
sein[4]	bist / ist	war	ist gewesen	sei!	be
senden[5]	sendest / sendet	sandte / sendete	gesandt / gesendet	send(e)!	send, broadcast
sieden	siedest / siedet	sott / siedete	ist { gesotten / gesiedet	sied(e)!	boil, seethe
singen	singst / singt	sang	gesungen	sing(e)!	sing
sinken	sinkst / sinkt	sank	ist gesunken	sink(e)!	sink
sinnen	sinnst / sinnt	sann	gesonnen	sinn(e)!	ponder
sitzen	sitz(es)t / sitzt	saß	gesessen	sitz(e)!	sit, be sitting
sollen	sollst / soll	sollte	sollen / gesollt	—	have to
spalten	spaltest / spaltet	spaltete[6]	gespalten[6]	spalt(e)!	split
speien[7]	speist / speit	spie	gespie(e)n	spei(e)!	spit

[1] Used mainly of horses, but can also refer to a 'snort', e.g. of disgust. Mainly weak nowadays.

[2] Trans. compounds are weak: *erschrecken, abschrecken, aufschrecken*, &c. *Schrecken* as a trans. verb is not common; it is also weak in this sense.

[3] Transitively, weak (i.e. to swell s.th.); conjugated with *haben*.

[4] Full present tense: *ich bin, du bist, er/sie/es ist, wir sind, ihr seid, sie/Sie sind*.

[5] The forms *sandte, gesandt* are the more common; but *senden* = 'broadcast' is always weak.

[6] Note the imperfect and past participle forms.

[7] Archaic. *Spucken* (weak) is the usual word nowadays.

Infin.	2nd and 3rd pers. Present	1st and 3rd pers. Impf.	Past Part.	Imper. (fam.)	English Infin.
spinnen	spinnst / spinnt	spann	gesponnen	spinn(e)!	spin
sprechen	sprichst / spricht	sprach	gesprochen	sprich!	speak
sprießen	sprieß(es)t / sprießt	sproß	ist gesprossen	sprieß(e)!	sprout
springen	springst / springt	sprang	ist gesprungen	spring(e)!	jump, spring
stechen	stichst / sticht	stach	gestochen	stich!	stab, prick, sting
stehen	stehst / steht	stand	gestanden	steh(e)!	stand
stehlen	stiehlst / stiehlt	stahl	gestohlen	stiehl!	steal
steigen	steigst / steigt	stieg	ist gestiegen	steig(e)!	rise
sterben	stirbst / stirbt	starb	ist gestorben	stirb!	die
stinken	stinkst / stinkt	stank	gestunken	stink(e)!	stink, smell bad
stoßen	stöß(es)t / stößt	stieß	gestoßen	stoß(e)!	push, shove
streichen	streichst / streicht	strich	gestrichen	streich(e)!	cross out, paint (house &c.)
streiten	streitest / streitet	stritt	gestritten	streit(e)!	argue

Infinitive	Present	Imperative	Past	Past participle	Meaning
tragen	trägst / trägt	trag(e)!	trug	getragen	carry
treffen	triffst / trifft	triff!	traf	getroffen	meet, hit (target, &c.)
treiben	treibst / treibt	treib(e)!	trieb	getrieben	drive (cattle, &c.), go in for (hobby, &c.)
treten[1]	trittst / tritt	tritt!	trat	ist getreten	tread, walk, kick
triefen	triefst / trieft	trief(e)!	troff	getroffen	drip
trinken	trinkst / trinkt	trink(e)!	trank	getrunken	drink
trügen[2]	(See *betrügen*)				be deceptive
tun	tust / tut	tu(e)!	tat	getan	do, put
verderben[3]	verdirbst / verdirbt	verdirb!	verdarb	verdorben	ruin, spoil, corrupt
verdrießen	verdrieß(es)t / verdrießt	verdrieß(e)!	verdroß	verdrossen	annoy, vex
vergessen	vergißt / vergißt	vergiß!	vergaß	vergessen	forget
verlieren	verlierst / verliert	verlier(e)!	verlor	verloren	lose
vermeiden	vermeidest / vermeidet	vermeid(e)!	vermied	vermieden	avoid
verschwinden	verschwindest / verschwindet	verschwind(e)!	verschwand	ist verschwunden	disappear

[1] In the sense 'to kick', conjugated with *haben*.
[2] *trügen* refers to impressions, not to persons: *Der Schein trügt*—appearances are deceptive.
[3] In the intrans. sense 'to corrupt, go bad', conjugated with *sein*.

Infin.	2nd and 3rd pers. sing. Present	1st and 3rd pers. sing. Impf.	Past Part.	Imper. (fam.)	English Infin.
wachsen	wächs(es)t / wächst	wuchs	ist gewachsen	wachs(e)!	grow
wägen[1]	wägst / wägt	wog	gewogen	wäg(e)!	weigh
waschen	wäsch(e)st / wäscht	wusch	gewaschen	wasch(e)!	wash
weben	webst / webt	wob	gewoben	web(e)!	weave
weichen	weichst / weicht	wich	ist gewichen	weich(e)!	give way, yield
weisen	weis(es)t / weist	wies	gewiesen	weis(e)!	point
wenden	wendest / wendet	wandte / wendete	{ gewandt / gewendet	wend(e)!	turn
werben	wirbst / wirbt	warb	geworben	wirb!	woo, make publicity for
werden[2]	wirst / wird	wurde	ist geworden	werd(e)!	become
werfen	wirfst / wirft	warf	geworfen	wirf!	throw
wiegen	wiegst / wiegt	wog	gewogen	wieg(e)	weigh, rock
winden[3]	windest / windet	wand	gewunden	wind(e)!	wind
wissen[4]	weißt / weiß	wußte	gewußt	wiss(e)!	know (facts, details, &c.)

wollen	willst will	wollte	{ wollen { gewollt	wolle!	want
ziehen	ziehst zieht	zog	gezogen	zieh(e)!	pull
zwingen	zwingst zwingt	zwang	gezwungen	zwing(e)!	force, compel

[1] Transitive verb: *Er wog den Stein in der Hand.* Compare with the intrans. verb *wiegen* = to weigh (so much).

[2] The passive past participle is *worden*: *Er ist gesehen worden.* Contrast with e.g. *Er ist groß geworden*—he has grown (become) big. Note also that the familiar imperative is *werde!*

[3] And *sich winden*—to twine, entwine itself, writhe.

[4] 1st pers. sing. present: *ich weiß.*